Corporeal Words: Mikhail Bakhtin's Theology of Discourse

Corporeal Words: Mikhail Bakhtin's Theology of Discourse

Alexandar Mihailovic

NORTHWESTERN UNIVERSITY PRESS / EVANSTON, ILLINOIS

Northwestern University Press
Evanston, Illinois 60208-4210

Printed in the United States of America

ISBN 0-8101-1459-3

Library of Congress Cataloging-in-Publication Data

Mihailovic, Alexandar.
Corporeal words : Mikhail Bakhtin's theology of discourse / Alexandar Mihailovic.
p. cm.—(Studies in Russian literature and theory)
Includes bibliographical references and index.
ISBN 0-8101-1459-3 (cloth : alk. paper)
1. Bakhtin, M. M. (Mikhaĭlovich), 1895–1975. 2. Russian literature—History and criticism—Theory, etc. 3. Discourse analysis, Literary. 4. Criticism—Soviet Union. 5. Literature—Philosophy. 6. Theology—Terminology. I. Title. II. Series.
P85.B22M54 1997
801'.95'092—dc21 97-13576
CIP

The paper used in this publication meets the minimum requirements of the American National Standard for Information Sciences—Permanence of Paper for Printed Library Materials, ANSI Z39.48-1984.

In memory of my grandparents

Contents

Acknowledgments ix

Introduction: Mikhail Bakhtin and Russian Orthodoxy 1

Chapter One: Bakhtin's Conception of Discourse (*Slovo*) 17

Chapter Two: Answerability and Ethics: Toward a Philosophy of Activism 51

Chapter Three: The Russian Intelligentsia: Bakhtin's Ideological Critique 87

Chapter Four: "Without Confusion or Separation": Bakhtin and the Chalcedonian Ideal of the Divided Union 125

Chapter Five: Carnival and Embodiment in *Rabelais and His World* 149

Chapter Six: The Word Made and Unmade: Rabelais, Bakhtin, and Stalin 183

Chapter Seven: The Ethics of Authorship in Bakhtin's Last Writings 213

Notes 235

Works Cited 259

Index 273

Acknowledgments

I thank the following people for the assistance they showed me during my research and writing of this book. Several made perspicacious comments on earlier versions of this study, most notably Vladimir Alexandrov, Victor Erlich, Michael Holquist, Robert L. Jackson, and Gary Saul Morson. My participation in the discussion group on Russian philosophy with Richard Gustafson, Ellen Chances, and Amy Mandelker proved invaluable in giving preliminary form to some of the ideas expressed here, and I still fondly remember our unconstrained and productive Saturday talks in Manhattan six years ago. I owe a special debt to Amy Mandelker for her careful and engaged reading of the entire manuscript. Caryl Emerson's close readings, advice, and unflagging encouragement have been instrumental in shaping many parts of this book, and I deeply appreciate her confidence in the viability of this project.

Many colleagues and friends in Russia were helpful in their responses to my work and in assisting me during my archival research. I am most grateful to Bakhtin's former students and friends in Moscow for sharing their insights and recollections, among them Viacheslav Ivanov, Sergei Bocharov, and Vadim Kozhinov. Vitaly Makhlin has been both a friend and a valued colleague during our lively Moscow conversations about the critic. I also thank Nikolai Nikolaev for a particularly stimulating discussion in Saint Petersburg about Bakhtin's activities during the twenties in Leningrad. Assisting me in more official but no less valued ways were Fred Choate, Dmitri Urnov, Valentina Rubtsova of the Muzyka publishing house and Sergei Avaizian at the Institute of World Literature in Moscow. Natalia Rogova of the Manuscript Division at the National State Library in Saint Petersburg helped me greatly to conduct my research, as did Natalia Volkova, the director of the Russian State Archives of Literature and Art in Moscow. Research for this book was supported by a grant from the International Research and Exchanges Board, with funds provided by the U.S. Department of State (Title VIII) and the National Endowment for the Humanities. None of these organizations is responsible for the views expressed in this study. Nor, should I add, are any of the people thanked here.

My colleagues at Hofstra University's Department of Comparative Literature have been most supportive of my work on this project, and I thank in particular Neil Donahue and our department chairperson Helene Waysek. At the university administration level, Dean Robert Vogt of the Hofstra College of Liberal Arts and Sciences has been equally helpful. My editor at Northwestern University Press, Susan Harris, has been the model of professionalism and courtesy. Last but certainly not least, I thank my wife Helga Druxes for her patient vetting of drafts, steadfast support, and infectious enthusiasm.

Introduction

Mikhail Bakhtin and Russian Orthodoxy

> This was Emerson's incontestable virtue to every one who appreciated him, that he recognized no God outside of himself and his interlocutor, and recognized him there only as the *liaison* between the two, taking care that all their intercourse should be holy with a holiness undreamed of before by man or angel.
>
> —Henry James Sr.

ALTHOUGH MANY scholars have speculated about the influence of Eastern Orthodox religious thought on Mikhail Bakhtin's life and work, few have been moved to examine it in detail. Like a cat circling a bowl of hot milk, critics interested in Bakhtin's theories have considered the possibility without ever really approaching it. In both Russia and the West, Bakhtin has become a revered figure, an almost mythic sage whose gnomic utterances have been pored over with a talmudic zeal. The idea that he was grounded on something as mundane as the traditional religiosity of his generation inspires a certain apprehension, as if the exploration of the topic would diminish his stature as a critic and divest him of his legendary status. In what sense was Bakhtin "Orthodox"? The idea of Orthodoxy in its strictly denominational sense is perhaps less troubling than its lower-case version as a set of official and generally acknowledged set of rules or expectations. In his tremendously influential study on Rabelais, Bakhtin extols the lower bodily stratum's joyous irreverence toward the official discourse of church and state. From this perspective, it is difficult to see Bakhtin as the adherent of any orthodoxy, much less a confessional one. In the Russian context, the stigma of officialdom is further compounded by the lack of separation between church and state since the time of Peter the Great, a situation only nominally changed in the postrevolutionary era given the Soviet government's tight leash on the church. And yet, as people have intuited, there is much in Bakhtin's criticism that does indeed lend itself to theological paradigms: his conceptions of dialogue and polyphony seemingly resonant with trinitarian unity within diversity and the notion of embodied social discourse highly suggestive of an incarnational model. Clearly, these paradigms need to be distinguished from their official redactions as institutional dogma, a distinction that the

Swedenborgian Henry James Sr. vividly understood. The peregrination of these ideas in Bakhtin's criticism is a story whose conclusion is as unexpected as it is unorthodox.

In the West, the posthumous popularity of Bakhtin began in earnest during the eighties and continues to grow apace. The ideological revanchisms of the Reagan era and the collapse of East bloc communism were partly responsible for transforming the Russian critic into something of a touchstone for cultural criticism in the United States, Europe, and the Third World. Discussions of Bakhtin's work have become ideologically charged; as a result, the suggestion that he was influenced by theological categories and was perhaps even an adherent of the Russian Orthodox Church—a view initially articulated by Julia Kristeva and Tzvetan Todorov but more substantively discussed by Michael Holquist and Katerina Clark in their 1984 biography of the critic[1]—has been met with considerable hostility. One such commentator chastises Holquist and Clark for "effectively identif[ying] Bakhtin's known affiliation to the Russian Orthodox Church as the secret of all his writing, the ultimate signified of its diverse signifiers," the Russian critic becoming "in their hands a topic in the 'history of ideas'; a shamefaced theologian who adopts the opportunistic guise of a Philosopher of Freedom."[2] For theorists such as Raymond Williams, Wlad Godzich, and Stanley Aronowitz, and literary critics such as Robert Young, Allon White, and Ken Hirschkop, Bakhtin was precisely the kind of nontraditional Marxist needed to rescue leftist scholarship in the humanities and the social sciences from its ideological and historical impasse;[3] to assert therefore that his link to Orthodoxy in its Russian form was also a significant influence on his thought is perceived as a political attack upon all of contemporary literary and cultural theory in its Althusserian mode.

Interestingly, when these critics have bothered to address at all the issue of Bakhtin's palpable nonsupport of the system of state socialism under which he lived, they inadvertently adopt an image reminiscent of early church history, portraying him as an underground supporter of true Marxism in opposition to the pharisaical one of the Soviet Union.[4] This conceit curiously echoes Russian nativist idealizations of Bakhtin as something of a modern Orthodox thinker, Nestorian scribe, or even a national saint.[5] Recent memoirs about the critic's final years in Moscow testify to this informal campaign of canonization, no doubt spurred on by nostalgia brought on by the perceived trivialization of intellectual life in the wake of the Soviet collapse. The critic Georgy Gachev recently wrote of visits to the ailing writer as acts of pious devotion or even a pilgrimage, Bakhtin himself becoming something of "a living church."[6] But even during the sixties when Bakhtin was still alive many members of the Russian intelligentsia saw in him something of a spiritual mentor. "[Your books] have entered into my life, have turned it upside down; in the most fundamental of ways they have activated and confirmed me to myself," enthused the Moscow stage director Yuri Zavadski in an unpublished letter, "your existence is especially dear and important to me since I am possessed by the idea of unheard-of complexity and answerability [*otvetstvennost'*]."[7] Perhaps the nadir in sentimentality was reached in a 1989 poem dedicated to Bakhtin that has the critic sitting at "his desk like Noah on his ark," where he "guffaws with Rabelais until midnight, and sobs with Dostoevsky til the morning" and "dreams of one thing only: that in every word there should be more good." A voice says to the poet, "There are no prophets in our fatherland," to which he replies "But how one yearns for a prophet!"[8] Some of the hagiographic glosses on Bakhtin from Russia coalesce into a halo where the religious and the nationalistic are virtually inseparable; in the Marxist scholarship on Bakhtin, the urge for a similar codification and enshrinement of Bakhtin's work as sacred texts is no less strong.

Even more curiously, the tendency to see religion and Marxism as mutually exclusive is shared by both Western Marxists and Bakhtin's Russian, non-Marxist enthusiasts. In an interview conducted for this book, Viacheslav Ivanov, a linguist and acquaintance of Bakhtin, claimed that Bakhtin was indeed religious, parenthetically remarking, "You know, of course, that Bakhtin was always categorically opposed to Marxism."[9] Sergei Bocharov has concurred in this view, quoting a conversation in which Bakhtin stated to him, "I am not a Marxist [and] was never interested in Marxism in the slightest,"[10] noting in the same piece Bakhtin's interest in the intersection between christology and philosophy.[11] In a recent published interview, Vadim Kozhinov—another critic who, along with Bocharov and Gachev, was responsible for "rediscovering" Bakhtin—describes Bakhtin as being an Orthodox Christian who was critical of Soviet irreligion yet uncanonical in some of his own philosophical views, a tendency common in many Russian thinkers who draw on certain theological conceits.[12] Among Russian critics of late, there has been overall a tendency to see Bakhtin as an essentially Russian figure, the whole issue of his religion being subsumed under the rubric of national identity. In an important memoiristic article, Kozhinov argues for the highly marked Russian religiosity of Bakhtin's life and work.[13] As seen by Kozhinov—a figure controversial for his outspoken political views—Bakhtin's distinctively Russian piety has the virtue of being doubly anticommunist, in being nationalist as well as religious. Any substantive rebuttal to this provocative and debatable position is, unfortunately, not forthcoming from the majority of Bakhtin's Marxist supporters in the West for two very simple reasons: few of them know Russian and those who do (such as Hirschkop, Wlad Godzich, and David Shepherd) consider the possible theological references in his work to be unworthy of examination. The language impediment and the indifference of many of these commentators to Russian cultural realia are considerable obstacles to engaging with the issue of Bakhtin's relation to the traditions—and the often complex and highly varied political manifestations—of Russian spirituality.

It is not my intention to question the overall validity of the Marxist view of Bakhtin's work. Nonetheless, to the extent that many in the West have made claims on Bakhtin as an exclusively Marxist critic and therefore uninterested in theology (a field that, in its Eastern European form, some of them perceive as being anathema to any progressive politics) one is justified in taking them to task. Some of these commentators drown any specific criticisms of Slavist scholarship in contemptuous remarks about the entire field as a bastion of methodological and political conservativism; others, such as Ken Hirschkop in his argument for the importance of Bakhtin's essay "Discourse in the Novel," build convincing cases for the persistence of certain Marxist categories and terms in his work, subjecting both to meticulous readings and identifying sources whenever possible.[14] Applied to theological paradigms, I believe that the same textological approach is at least as productive in coming to terms with Bakhtin's theories of carnival and dialogue, it not more so. Explicit references to the *loci classici* of Marxism-Leninism are exceedingly rare in Bakhtin's work, a curious feature in the work of a putatively Marxist critic living in a society that officially extolled Marx's theories. The counterargument that Bakhtin was compelled to muffle his Marxism because it was too conceptually bold and iconoclastic for the tastes of the Stalinist establishment is nothing more than wishful thinking: there is absolutely no evidence in the Dostoevsky and Rabelais studies or even in Voloshinov's and Medvedev's more politically oriented books (believed by some to have been written by Bakhtin himself) that he was anything like a sympathizer of Bukharinism or a closet Trotskyite. In other words, he did not express either openly or covertly any of the arguments common to the oppositional Russian left of the time. The 1973 Duvakin interviews do demonstrate, on the other hand, that Bakhtin was outspokenly anti-Leninist. All this is not to say that there are no Marxist features or ramifications in his work or that Marxism did not exert an influence on him; in addition to some of the points raised by Hirschkop, there is no question, for example, that in his 1941 essay "Epic and the Novel," Bakhtin's conception of the evolution of the novel is indebted to certain Marxist aspects of dialectics. The real issue is whether Bakhtin defined himself as a Marxist any more than he did as a religious philosopher in the Russian nativist vein. On both counts, there is no indication that he ever did so.

Leaving aside these idle questions concerning the critic's possible self-categorization, on the basis of textual evidence there are at least two compelling reasons for regarding Bakhtin's relation to theology as being central to his work (which is not to say that it represents the ultimate signifier or key to understanding his ideas). The first is the sheer density, paradigmatic clarity, and deliberate orchestration of Bakhtin's theologically inspired terms and conceptual categories, demonstrated by this study. Theological categories and terms recalling christology in general and Trinitarianism in particular emerge in almost every essay in Bakhtin's long and varied career. Bakhtin's adaptation of the Johannine logology with its incarnational model and paradigm of unity within diversity is his most highly marked use of such conceptions and is particularly evident in his conceptions of novelistic discourse and polyphony. From *Rabelais and His World* to *Problems of Dostoevsky's Poetics*, a noticeable shift occurs in Bakhtin's use of these images. The theological metaphors in Bakhtin's work subsequently operate more as structural paradigms than as philosophical or hortatory precepts.

The other reason for taking seriously the theological subtext of Bakhtin's work is that it has become a given in Russian interpretations of him, a fact much more significant than meets the eye and not at all a posteriori. For those scholars who have most carefully excavated the original Russian texts over the past five years, theological categories and terms have indelibly imprinted themselves upon the landscape of critical discourse about Bakhtin's work. Since in many instances these close readings take Bakhtin's distinctive terms as points of departure for reconstructing some of his more abstruse ideas, they in effect form a conceptual continuum with his work that cannot be so easily dismissed as examples of willful misprision. In some cases, such as in the work of the Derrida translator Mikhail Ryklin, these interpretations are written very much under the influence of Bakhtin himself, echoing his mode of argumentation and even syntactical structure. In the spirit of these critics, one hastens to add here that Bakhtin's use of theological terms was far from being uninflected and unmediated, containing as it did hidden commentaries on such politically sensitive issues as the self-valorization and sanctification of the Stalinist state. Among recent interpretations in this vein, perhaps the most daring and potentially controversial is K. G. Isupov's 1995 article "The Death of the 'Other,'" published in the Russian collection *Bakhtinology*.[15] Isupov asserts the absolute integrality of specifically Russian Orthodox conceptions of the subject to Bakhtin's theory of dialogue, as I have done in the present study. Isupov takes as a point of departure the assumption that Bakhtin's dialogue is fundamentally an expression of love as eros. The actual dynamics or operation of this eros are, however, disturbingly problematic from the perspective of the Other interacting with the subject. As Isupov explicates Bakhtin's conception of dialogue, erotic love requires the death of the Other in order for consummation to take place; therefore eros and thanatos are in fact twin and indissolubly linked impulses. According to Isupov, the sense in which every event of reciprocated love is really a manifestation of a *Liebestod* is central to many Orthodox conceptions of martyrdom and divinity that foreground *kenosis*, or the emptying out of the self, a process that after all paradoxically posits the complete purging of consciousness as a prerequisite for salvation. Isupov takes as a given Bakhtin's indebtedness to Russian Orthodox theological categories, juxtaposing the critic's statements about dialogue with numerous textual examples from the works of modern Russian religious philosophers and writers such as Solovyov, Bulgakov, Lossky, Shestov, and Prishvin; where he differs from those (such as Kozhinov) who also emphasize the importance of Russian religiosity in Bakhtin's work is in his evaluation of the *significance* of this influence upon the critic's thought.

This evaluation becomes evident in one of Isupov's most audacious moves, as he explicitly links Eastern Orthodoxy's annihilation of the other with political authoritarianism in general and Stalinism in particular, implicitly suggesting that the purges were possible precisely because of the particular kind of spirituality that operated on the level of the Russian collective unconscious.[16] Isupov's argument is ingenious and is bound to raise the hackles of many Russians. The conceptual sources of his article are eclectic and largely unacknowledged, in all likelihood including Freud, Wilhelm Reich (particularly his study of Nazism, *The Mass Psychology of Fascism*), Foucault, the poststructuralists Iurii Lotman and Boris Uspensky's attack on the notion of a "Russian" carnival, and Mikhail Ryklin's 1990 article about Bakhtin, "Bodies of Terror" (published in English in 1993). Certainly Isupov seems to do for Bakhtin's relation to theology what Ryklin does for *Rabelais and His World* and the Stalin era: demystifying and even perhaps debunking the critic for his unwitting complicity in the reproduction and reinforcement of authoritarian power structures. Where Isupov diverges from Western Marxists is in his assumption that one must acknowledge the structural importance of theological categories in Bakhtin's theory of dialogue in order to uncover its full ideological significance; for Isupov, the examination of the influence of Orthodox thought on Bakhtin is precisely what opens up the critic's work to an understanding of its political content. In other words, Isupov does not regard the influence of Orthodoxy on Bakhtin as one reinforcing a politically reactionary quietism and lack of interest in social issues; on the contrary, for him the presence of these thought structures are precisely what activate the texts in those ways.

However, it must be said that to the extent that Isupov views any breach of the individual identity as a threat to its very existence, his orientation is very much that of a Western critic. This fact becomes clearer if we compare his article with analyses of Bakhtin by Western critics who insist on the necessity of the extinction of the individual as a category in polyphony, dialogue, and carnival. The difference between them is only that commentators such as Aronowitz, Hirschkop, and David Shepherd welcome this development whereas Isupov regards it critically. In both instances the reaching out from one subject to another (and indeed any penetrating of the membrane of individual autonomy) is perceived as being potentially fatal to the self. Identity is thus framed in absolute terms, as constituting that which does not—or perhaps should not—undergo change. As a result, the category of the self is rendered a straw man, a fragile totem deliberately positioned to be torn apart by the slightest stirring of the world around it. What apparently does not occur to any of these critics is that a more fluid version of the self is possible, one that preserves its unitary nature while responding to and interacting with the social vicissitudes around it. The idea that identity and self are nothing more than rigid templates of social constructedness or expressions of ethnicity does not interest Bakhtin.[17] As he put it in a recently published second group of notes toward a reworking of the Dostoevsky book, "the dialogic relations among living voices cannot be rendered in rational terms, they should not be reduced to a naked opposition of *pro* and *contra*. All spiritual, cognicized and contemplated relations are dialogic."[18]

The christological terminology of interrelation and coexistence that Bakhtin brings to bear on the conception of dialogue in particular addresses this issue of the contingent autonomy of the individual. Bakhtin's thoughts on this matter can best be gauged by a particularly revealing moment in *Problems of Dostoevsky's Poetics* (discussed in Chapter 4): his description of Dostoevsky's world as a church that makes possible a profound pluralism of separate and unmerged souls but without the agency of a disembodied unifying spirit. The statement can be read as a shrewdly critical commentary on the facile communitarianism of much Russian political and religious thought from Solovyov to the Leninist statism of the Soviet Union. For Bakhtin, the image of the church represents above all a forum shared by its communicants, one shaped by contestation leavened by the recognition of the need for coexistence and the mutual influence it brings to bear on those involved in it. Bakhtin envisions communication as a tense equilibrium between the anarchic demands of identity and the imperatives of communal life. Plurality is as miraculous as it is fragile; its internal coherence is poised between the two poles of disruptive individualism and a stifling authoritarian spirit. In view of the current upheavals in Russian political life, Bakhtin's emphasis on the fragility of democratic life is nothing short of prophetic.

The reverberations of diction with christological overtones are audible in virtually every piece Bakhtin wrote. At first glance, their significance is difficult to evaluate. The topoi of enfleshment, *perichoresis,* or interpenetration, the Chalcedonian ideal of bisected unity, and the crypto-Johannine logos very often converge at crucial points of his argument; they are not metaphors or figures of speech drained of their philosophical content but leitmotifs brought into mutual relation in a way that underscores their theological provenance. This contextualization of christological allusions (enfleshment in the Rabelais book, for example, occurring as a result of a Chalcedonian interlocking of language levels) transforms them into much more than merely illustrative tropes but still less than actual expressions of faith. Exactly how "orthodox" an adherent of the Eastern rite Bakhtin was cannot be ascertained by these evocative references in themselves or even at the textual sites of their interaction.

And yet, as Vladimir Nabokov once put it in regard to Lermontov's prose, "it is an agglomeration of otherwise insignificant words that come to life. . . . [I]t is the compound effect that counts and this total effect can be traced down . . . to the beautiful timing of all the parts and particles."[19] What these references amount to is a philosophical narrative on the concepts of dialogue and carnival, central to Bakhtin's work over his entire career. In these concepts Bakhtin redefines the concept of sacrifice as constituting not a willed abrogation of personality (*lichnost'*) but a temporary relinquishing of the essentially Enlightenment ideal of individual autonomy. Reshaping as it does identity along the way, dialogue is inevitably dynamic but painful; as Bakhtin makes especially clear in *Problems of Dostoevsky's Poetics,* the Dostoevskian hero's suffering is never far from dialogic interaction. This pain and the subsequent embodiment of consciousness that displace it constitute a kind of redemption, a journey whose direction or path would have been unclear had Bakhtin not put soteriological markers along the way, drawing a vivid parallel between the story of the Christ figure and the travails of the participant in dialogue.

This kind of suffering and often unwitting selflessness is entirely different, however, from the self-annihilation and debasement of others—really flip sides of the same coin—often demanded by many political movements. The particular kind of transformation that dialogue sets into motion entails what seems at first to be an exchange of qualities innate to the subject rather than the semiotic bric-a-brac extrinsic to it. In Bakhtin, there is little room for postmodernism, with its outworn signs that obliterate the subject. Bakhtin characterizes the latter impedimenta as reified literary genres and as other, nonliterary and monologic forms of speech. These ossified texts or modes of textual production in fact bear the brunt of his criticism, contrary to the contentions of his Marxist commentators that a critique of capitalist economy underlies his work.[20] True carnival consists of a simultaneity of praise and blame; its debased ideological counterpart is the mere concatenation of those two rhetorical modes. In the latter instance, the shift from praise to blame is as precipitous as it is pernicious, inevitable when they are separated (as during the Stalin era) into their rigidly engenred forms. The danger (or, depending on one's politics, the virtue) of carnival is not that it foments revolution, but quite the opposite: it is far more likely to become a bulwark of authoritarianism by dissolving into its constituent elements, praise and blame subsequently unpacking themselves with frightening linearity instead of being folded into each other in the manner of interdwelling hypostases. During much of Bakhtin's life, the most prominent example of a linear conception of time was dialectical materialism. *Rabelais and His World* represents a throroughgoing if concealed critique of this view of history. In the immediate aftermath of the Second World War, Bakhtin wrote in notes for a reworking of his dissertation into a book that "[t]ime here is not a line, but a complex form of the body's return."[21] The theological concepts of Chalcedonian doctrine and *perichoresis* represent a cluster of images utterly counter to conceptions of textual and ideological linearity. It is thus that christological schemata become central to Bakhtin's criticisms of the major self-images of his society and age.

Bearing this in mind, one quickly realizes that the term *exchange*—with its connotation of sequential temporality—is entirely misleading and inappropriate when used in regard to Bakhtin's carnival: *interchange* is more accurate, the process involving not the substitution of one essence by another but a constant operation of mutual influence. As we shall see, this dynamic is achieved only fleetingly in carnival. Carnival and dialogue are not synonymous; the latter in fact represents a multiplicity of conceivable perspectives whereas it is the former that is, paradoxically, completely constricted by binary distinctions. The ideal interchange advanced by Bakhtin is, in fact, precarious in carnival: to paraphrase Michael André Bernstein in one of the first skeptical treatments of Bakhtinian carnival, such a hierarchical intershuffling of values can all too easily turn bitter and violent on the marketplace square.[22] In a particularly revealing moment during the 1973 interviews, Bakhtin calls Kerensky (the leader of the Provisional Government in 1918) a mediocrity and a demagogue, at Duvakin's prompting adding that yes, there was something carnivalistic about him ([k]oe-chto u nego bylo karnaval'noe), although it was not deliberate and certainly not in his nature.[23] Carnival is ethically ambivalent. Dialogue is not: it denotes the full efflorescence and ethical intersubjectivity of the refracted word. Bakhtin's allusions to theological thematics throw into sharper relief the exact relation between these two concepts, ones for which his work is most celebrated.

In this book I discuss the elaborately wrought subtextual imagery, wordplay, and palpable orality of Bakhtin's work, much of which is brought to bear in effecting conceptual shifts in theological discourse. Bakhtin's indebtedness to Eastern Orthodox thought goes far beyond the proliferation in his criticism of terms denoting embodiment and transubstantiation that was first noted by Clark and Holquist in their pathbreaking biography.[24] In many ways his style recalls the intricate aesthetic of "word-weaving" (*pletenie sloves*) developed by the fifteenth-century Russian hagiographer Epiphanius the Wise. In his early essay "Toward a Philosophy of the Act" Bakhtin almost playfully develops the paradoxical idea of unity as both a union and a single, isolated oneness ("the emotional-volitional tone seeks to express the truth of a given moment, and that relates to the ultimate, unitary, and once-occurent unity [*edinomu i edinstvennomu edinstvu*]"), echoing Epiphanius's description of Saint Stefan of Perm's single-handed assimilation of monotheistic holy literature while living "alone and isolated [*v'edinen'i i uedinen'i*]," alone asking for help from the One God (*edin, uedinen'i, edin u edinogo Boga pomoshchi prosia*).[25] In this regard Caryl Emerson's remark about the curiously stilted and convoluted orality of Bakhtin's Russian style—his tendency toward an oracular and sermonistic mode (*skazanie*) instead of a essaistic linearity—is well taken.[26] As both she and Gary Saul Morson point out, however, "[w]hether or not Bakhtin was religious, it is quite possible to be religious without making all of one's writing a concealed theology."[27] Like many writers of his generation, Bakhtin deliberately employed various christological metaphors, often in a distinctly self-conscious way; unlike other writers such as Solovyov, however, his awareness of what such images meant in theology and piety was more profound; such knowledge could only intensify the sense of the gap between the ideal and the painful real of the time in which he lived. In the Rabelais book and in both the 1929 and 1963 editions of the Dostoevsky study he uses the christological metaphor of enfleshment as something of a rhetorical marker, signaling the importance of certain contexts that normally would not call for such imagery.

The analysis of theological echoes in Bakhtin's terminology and literary theory will take a roughly chronological approach since his adaptation of theological terms and concepts takes a highly discernible developmental path over the course of his career. The outline of the chapters is as follows. Bakhtin's conception of discourse (*slovo*) is a thread that runs through his work over virtually the entire span of his career. His 1929 book *The Problems of Dostoevsky's Art* represents an important stepping-stone in his elaboration on the metaphor of space in the conception of discourse. There Bakhtin describes the operation of the authorial word in terms of one zone or area of consciousness influencing another, a characterization that is (as he might put it) a simultaneous and Janus-faced look at the past (the patristic notion of hypostatic interpenetration or *perichoresis*) and at the future (Bakhtin's own concept of polyphony). "Discourse in the Novel" (1934–35) and "Forms of Time and the Chronotope in the Novel" (1937–38; 1973) represent the most protracted and sophisticated treatment of discourse until *Problems of Dostoevsky's Poetics* in the early sixties. The incarnational metaphor is particularly strong in the latter work, which has clear links to "Toward a Philosophy of the Act" written many years earlier: in both texts Bakhtin discusses the way in which dialogic interaction among people and classes represents the only true and substantial life of a language. According to Bakhtin, such moments of social engagement are the only moments when language can be truly said to take on life, substance and (metaphorically) flesh. In the scheme of these two essays—which, I shall argue, represent something of a single theoretical edifice and should be read and interpreted together—the unit of reified space in time known as the chronotope becomes the embodiment of discourse.

But it is already in the early twenties, in "Toward a Philosophy of the Act" and "Author and Hero in Aesthetic Activity," that the incarnational and eucharistic model clearly emerges in Bakhtin's criticism, albeit via a series of filters. Some of these mediating influences are significantly tinctured with theological concerns (as in the writings of "God-Seekers" such as Solovyov), and others have a more literary coloring. What is particularly revealing even in the miasma of these rough unfinished works is Bakhtin's systematic use of theological terms in tentative coordination with the concept of a metalinguistic word or *slovo*. From there it is a very short step indeed to the contemplation of the powerful confluence of theology, philosophy, and social criticism that dominated much of Russian belles-lettres from the turn of the century up to the Civil War of 1918–20. The influence on Bakhtin of the "God-Seekers" in general and the contributors to the 1909 collection *Vekhi* (Landmarks) becomes evident once the terminology of Bakhtin's two earliest extant essays ("Art and Answerability" and "Toward a Philosophy of the Act") are examined. In these early works Bakhtin attempts to restore the category of personality (*lichnost'*) to contemporary debates about ethics. Although the term *slovo* does not figure prominently at this point of Bakhtin's career, certain aspects of the concept of the individual consciousness or *lichnost'* anticipate it. The ideal of "not merged yet not separate" first outlined in the ecumenical council at Chalcedon in 451 emerges as particularly important to Bakhtin, providing a template for his conceptions of consciousness, dialogue, and carnival.

Chapters 5 and 6 represent an extended analysis of Bakhtin's Rabelais book (originally submitted as a dissertation in 1940) from two different yet ultimately complementary perspectives. The first of these chapters simply reconstructs Bakhtin's conception of carnival in *Rabelais and His World* in its relation to the concepts of embodiment (*voploshchenie*) and participation (*prichastnost'*) that had also figured so prominently in his previous work. Carnival represents a loophole in an otherwise dour existence, an avenue leading to transgredience and transcendence. This element of carnival is particularly resonant in the Soviet context. Bakhtin's conception of carnival is closely connected with that of discourse (*slovo*), a link at first easy to miss given the generally low profile of the latter term in the book. An examination of Bakhtin's terminology in his analysis of Rabelais reveals, however, that at this point of his career discourse is in fact defined in terms of carnival.

Chapter 6 takes the structuralist conclusions of Chapter 5 into the realm of contemporaneity and comes up with unexpectedly disturbing conclusions.

The communion with the grotesque body that forms the basis of Bakhtin's carnival loses its sanguine aspect and takes on a sanguinary one when viewed in the light of the calamitous political events during which it was conceived. As interpreted by the Russian scholar Mikhail Ryklin, the gorging of the collective body in Bakhtin's book is a metaphor of an almost Hegelian character, representing a dialectical dynamic among the traumas of collectivization, forced rural famine and purges during the thirties, and the fortification of the Stalinist state. But Ryklin's interpretation is limited in not placing this metaphor in the context of the christological echoes in Bakhtin's terminology, which (beside shedding an entirely new light on his possible attitude toward theology and even religion itself) represents the key to understanding his references to Stalinism. A closer look at the Rabelais study reveals that carnival represents a very particular kind of social embodiment or communion, one Bakhtin modeled after the Chalcedonian paradigm of Christ's life as a bisected unity of the human and the divine. For Bakhtin, true carnival is animated by a keen awareness of the multiform ways in which high and low culture interact within a particular body politic, a consciousness that prevents it from descending into the genocidal saturnalia that Ryklin describes. From the perspective of conventional religious belief, Bakhtin's boldly eclectic appropriation of these doctrinal points of reference for his cultural theory could be viewed as presumptuous, if not borderline blasphemous.

In Chapter 7 several of Bakhtin's last writings are examined in the context of theological terms and categories. After the critical stance adopted by Bakhtin during the preceding thirty years toward theological conceptions of language, late works such as "Toward a Reworking of the Dostoevsky Book," the second edition of the Dostoevsky book, and "From Notes Made 1970–71" reveal a surprising return to christological terminology far more sophisticated than that of his essays of the twenties. Here the paradox of polyphony is portrayed in terms that are patently those of Trinitarian coinherence. At this final stage one gets the sense that the paradox and ambivalence of Bakhtin's gravitation toward theological discourse reaches something of an apogee.

"I am more philosopher [than philologist], and remain so up to the present day. I am a thinker; I am a philosopher."[28] Bakhtin's admission late in his life from the recently published interviews conducted by the Mayakovsky scholar Viktor Duvakin is hardly a revelation. The "God-seeking" Russian philosophers were, in all likelihood, the most convenient conduit through which Bakhtin was able to draw elements of incarnational theology into his critical vocabulary; he was especially sympathetic to their attempt to liberate theology from its institutional framework and into philosophy. Significantly, religious philosophers such as Solovyov highlighted the tense equilibrium and perpetually unresolved dialectic between words and the Word rather than an ascendancy of one over the other or a resolution between the two, thus rendering a more metaphysical interpretation of Trinitarian doctrine than that of contemporary specialists in theology. In his otherwise highly favorable 1923 review of Moscow University Professor L. M. Lopatin's theses on the Eastern Orthodox Church, the religious philosopher Pavel Florensky states that the decisions of modern-day professional theologians are in fact completely unauthoritative and nugatory in matters of doctrine and faith.[29] The fact that he himself was a priest did not prevent Florensky from making the distinction between dogma and the actual responsibilities and implications of belief. Bakhtin's application of the Johannine incarnational model to his theory of discourse is ultimately too syncretic and idiosyncratic to serve as evidence for his putative personal religiosity.

But Bakhtin's basic attitude toward the christological metaphor was a searching and, one suspects, somewhat painful one. With the effective co-opting in 1943 of much of the Russian Orthodox Church for politically cynical reasons by Stalin,[30] a believer like Bakhtin must have experienced a sense of betrayal and felt the need to retreat from institutional forms of piety. In this context, his use of the christological metaphor against Stalinism emerges as extremely shrewd, an employment of the same rhetorical armament that the Soviet leader himself tried to appropriate in an effort to buoy the religious and nationalist feelings of Russians during a war that followed the social devastation wrought by the purges. With such developments in political ideology and compromises in belief made during the thirties and forties, one can only imagine Bakhtin's disgust. It is no wonder that he refused absolution on his deathbed, even from the dissident priest Dmitri Dudko.[31]

In an undated essay that seems to have been written during the Russian Civil War, Florensky comments on the worldly religiosity in Russia in a way that strikes a deep chord with Bakhtin's possibly ambivalent relation to Russian institutional Orthodoxy. Undoubtedly bearing in mind the enduring notion of Moscow as the "Third Rome" or last bastion of true Christianity, Florensky asserts that religiosity in Russia is tainted by a sense of spiritual arrogance, a self-perception that it represents the belief of the elect. "The Russian people have lost their patrimony thinking that this was a gift they received at birth, an innate quality that, as such, would never wither and die." In words that have all too real continued relevance, Florensky goes on to say that "[t]he present-day situation in Russia is not an incidental illness or a chance absence of resources but a profound trauma of being, experienced over several generations." In his most damning statement, he contends that the Russian people have become accustomed to seeing in themselves the sole repository of universal piety, a grandiose self-perception that they can no longer distinguish from piety in its devotional form and whose fundamental self-contradiction continues to escape their notice. As a result, they do not perceive as catastrophic the destruction of personal piety in their land, since religious principles had already, for all intents and purposes, been pushed out by ethnic and statist ones in matters of belief.[32] The similarities of both tone and content are unmistakable here to Piotr Chaadaev's famous statement from a century before in *Les Lettres philosophiques* (1837) that Russians are like illegitimate children without partimony or a real sense of history: "We grow, but we do not mature. . . . We are like children who have never been made to think for themselves."[33] For all his own piety, Florensky felt compelled to sound what can only be called an ethical critique of religious nationalism in Russian culture.

In the final analysis, the only record that really matters is the one on which Bakhtin's reputation rests: the texts themselves. That Bakhtin and other members of his circle were observant Christians is evident from letters (many still unpublished) kept in the Yudina collection at the Russian State Library Archives in Moscow. Maria Veniaminovna Yudina was a renowned pianist who remained close to Bakhtin and his wife for almost fifty years; Holquist and Clark (and, more recently, the Yudina scholar A. M. Kuznetsov) have brilliantly documented the Bakhtins' friendship with her, which must have been difficult at times because of her eccentricity and ease at taking offense.[34] In one letter dated 27 July 1965, she upbraids the ailing critic and his wife for not coming to see her after her fourth day in Moscow, adding the prickly words, "May both of you be protected under God's blessing, in spite of the fact that you are betraying an old friend," painfully adding at the end, "Forgive me."[35] Many of her letters to them and theirs to her begin or end with either Easter blessings or some other kind of religious benediction, a formerly common epistolary practice that had begun to disappear as early as the twenties.[36] The recurrence of such statements suggests that religious practice of some sort did play a role in their lives; what it consisted of precisely is impossible to say on the basis of these fugitive scribblings. Nonetheless, this and the fact of Bakhtin's arrest on grounds of participation in the religious organization Voskresenie should be borne in mind when addressing the matter of theological markers in his work.[37] The biographical reconstruction around Bakhtin's work provides at best the oblique illumination of a footlight, sharply bringing out certain details to the virtual occlusion of others.

It is in light of Florensky's critique of ideological religiosity as false consciousness that one can speak of Bakhtin's thought as an expression of belief. Everything in this study points to dialogue as a moral category; its saturation with soteriological properties inevitably gives way to a syllogistic drift, morality itself becoming christological in its frame of reference. In a newly published memoir, the late Vladimir Turbin—yet another Russian Bakhtin disciple—frankly describes a tense moment between him and the convalescing critic. Making an anti-Semitic remark, Turbin got more than he bargained for from Bakhtin: "The Jews have argued with God, made peace with Him, accepted and rejected His Grace. . . . And we Russians, what have we done? Thrown [the Slavic pagan idol] Perun into the river?"[38] Like Florensky, Bakhtin viewed the ethnic component in Russian religiosity with some mistrust. For him theology ultimately emerged as a function of discourse, becoming real and taking on flesh only when it came among people; the value of religion as authority or phalange of beliefs was of secondary significance. In his criticism confessional affiliation was completely subordinated to the principle of dialogue, which in a very real sense represented to him the essence of piety. Bakhtin's close friend Yudina, a Russian Jew who was deeply involved in the Orthodox church but who never renounced her Judaism, believed in the same principle; in her unpublished notes on Orthodox doctrine she wrote, "[f]or me prayer means personal relations."[39] Bakhtin's intense and protracted mining of the Trinitarian paradigm for the foundations of his literary theory is highly evocative, especially against the backdrop of a literary and political establishment hostile to the idea of any form of theology as an ethical framework. To say that Bakhtin's relation to theology and faith lies within the shadowy realm of Florensky's devout yet noninstitutional and politically skeptical sensibility somehow does not go far enough. Bakhtin's use of christological terms and categories as markers of conceptual parts in his work speaks of a profound intellectual commitment; to the extent that he always considered himself first and foremost a philosopher, their role takes on much greater significance than it would in the work of conventional literary philology. In a national tradition where philosophy, theology, and nationalism have never been far apart, the neochristological manifestations in his work come to occupy keystone positions in his ethical conception of life. Bakhtin's theology of discourse was certainly not one of simple and unmediated belief. Like Florensky and Yudina, for all his piety he was acutely cognizant of the dilemmas of devotion in Russia.

To follow theologically inspired utterances made by Bakhtin over many years is to realize the extent to which he was not a politically oriented critic, philosopher, or ethicist in any clear-cut or traditionalist sense, his self-categorization notwithstanding. The motifs of the Johannine word, the Chalcedonian paradox of a fused yet divided consciousness, and the notion of interpenetration of the human and divine serve a purpose that in the final analysis is structural and heuristic rather than doctrinal or philosophical. But the structural is never secondary or aleatory for Bakhtin. We cannot dismiss his interest in theology as simply terminological because the interaction among christological motifs saturates his critical lexicon of dialogue, carnival, and polyphony and is in fact crucial in defining the interrelatedness of those latter concepts. The internal unity of Bakhtin's terminology is reinforced by these motifs that, from the panoptic view of more than forty years of his writing, coalesce into a clearly defined subtext. In a certain sense, theology in Bakhtin becomes thoroughly humanized and aestheticized, the christological metaphor emerging as a rhetorical and theoretical model rather than a devotional paradigm, a structure in whose interstices he could arrange his ideas about the antihierarchical drift of language and culture. By subsuming christology thoroughly into the workings of his theory, Bakhtin makes it an integral part of a larger context, one that is unfinished and therefore narrative. From his 1919 "Art and Answerability" to his writings of the sixties and seventies, Bakhtin engages in what can only be called a novelization of christology. To the extent that the novel for Bakhtin is defined precisely by "the diversity of voices and heteroglossia [that] enter [it] and organize themselves within it into a structured [*stroinuiu*] artistic system," structure is never simply a convenient grid or multichambered ossified shell fulfilling a mechanical function, as perceived by some Formalists and structuralists: it represents meaning itself, rendered dialogically.[40] As Bakhtin put it in the 1929 *The Problems of Dostoevsky's Art*, in the novel "the real connections begin where the ordinary plot ends, having fulfilled its service function."[41] As a demonstration of novelistic discourse itself, the theological subtext in Bakhtin's criticism is clearly crucial to the real connections of his work. To paraphrase Henry James Sr., the connection between self and Other is the only God of Bakhtin's creative universe. By fully entering into that constellation of ideas, Bakhtin's own dialogue with the philosophical legacy of Orthodoxy becomes instrumental in shaping the spirit of dialogism that almost all scholars agree is the enduring idea of his work.

Chapter One

Bakhtin's Conception of Discourse (*Slovo*)

> But we have forgotten, that none but the word is illumed among earthly travails; and in the Gospel According to John, that the Word is God.
> —Nikolai Gumilev (1916)

IN A SERIES of sketchy yet revealing notes he wrote from 1970 to 1971, Bakhtin explicitly connects both theoretical and applied linguistics to the Johannine philosophy of the word: "Metaphysics and the philosophy of the word. Ancient teachings about logos. John [Ioann]. Language, speech, speech communication, utterance [*vyskazyvanie*]. The specific nature of speech communication."[1] In a suggestive article tracing Bakhtin's roots in turn-of-the-century Russian religious thought, Natalia Bonetskaia notes the systemic consistency and unity of Bakhtin's ideas throughout his work, particularly in regard to the theological and philosophical ramifications of language.[2] Nonetheless, his exact attitude toward the Johannine logos is difficult to glean from the fragment above. Clark and Holquist pointedly link Bakhtin's conception of the word with enfleshment or embodiment (*voploshchenie*)—the word becoming real and substantial when people engage in dialogic interaction—without specifically discussing his possible indebtedness to the logos of John 1:1 and 1:14: "In the beginning was the Word [Greek, *logos*; Russian, *slovo*], and the Word was with God, and the Word was God. . . . And the Word was made flesh [Russian, *plotiiu*], and dwelt among us."[3] The philological ramifications of the logos doctrine have a history older than the Gospel's. Nowhere are these lines of filiation more evident than in Bakhtin's conception of *slovo*, a term embracing language, discourse, or even the isolated utterance. It is from this rough aggregate of meanings—migraine-provoking for any translator—that Bakhtin shapes one of the cornerstones of his conception of polyphony, fully formed in *Problems of Dostoevsky's Poetics.* Far from being self-contradictory, Bakhtin's conception of discourse (*slovo*) displays a significant measure of consistency over the many years of his writing, and resists the attempts at periodization to which some of his other terms are more susceptible.

The Johannine paradigm of the enfleshed word—which, as many commentators have noted, is the evangelist's refutation of the Gnostic belief in the inherent evil of matter[4]—is singularly felicitous for the Russian critic's theory of language as both social or supraindividual and subjective in its shaping and transformation by the participants in dialogue. Like the Johannine divine Word, Bakhtin's *slovo* denotes communality of those interacting with it and not any particular word or utterance; at the same time, in its capacity as a reified and embodied phenomenon, the Bakhtinian use of the term can also, in some instances, represent the individual utterance. In light of this metaphor, the participants in Bakhtinian dialogue begin to emerge as communicants in a eucharistic sense as well as in a strictly linguistic one. In the midst of the ideological standoff that holds together the various forces of the novel, Bakhtin's *slovo* emerges as an organic and assimilative rather than a closed and hierarchical structure, as a matrix whose correspondences of call and reply, pressure and counterpressure maintain the architectonic equilibrium and viability of the whole. Nonetheless, certain features of Bakhtin's application of the Johannine model vitiate the assumption that it represents an expression of belief; in this respect, it possesses the same highly ambivalent ideational significance as do other theological allusions in Bakhtin's work. Bakhtin tinkers considerably with the conception of the logos, transforming it into a metacritical trope whose problematically shifted relation to its doctrinal source becomes a conceptual touchstone for the integrative contestation of dialogue within the novel.

THE HERMENEUTICS OF THE DIVINE WORD

Like most biblical allusions in a literary context, the apparent Johannine subtext of Bakhtin's Word is complex in its ramifications because of its inscribed history of exegetical commentary. What follows is a highly foreshortened and selective historical view of the connotations of the Johannine and the pre-Christian logos as they pertain to Bakhtin's theory. In rereading Bakhtin's work from this perspective, we need to come to terms not only with some of the exegetical and doctrinal progeny of the so-called Johannine prologue, but also with its distant ancestors. The older Hellenic and Judaic views of logos that together form a part of the fascinating syncreticism of the Johannine prologue are themselves highly resonant with Bakhtin's conception of discourse.

To an even greater extent than the Johannine Word and Bakhtin's discursive word, the pre-Christian logos as a philosophical term was anything but a single and simple spoken word. In the fragments that have survived of Greek Stoicism (c. 300–200 B.C.E.), the term variously denotes reason, the rational order, or even the controlling deity of the universe himself. As one commentator puts it, in Stoicism "[i]t is the universal *logos* which is at work both in the connexion between cause and effect and between premises and conclusions."[5] The Stoics' conception of logos as the ordering principle in the world had been borrowed and modified from Heraclitus (c. 535–475 B.C.E.), in whose fragments titled "On Nature" (*Peri phuseos*) it represents the unifying principle of order and reason in an otherwise chaotic universe.[6] At the turn of the century in Russia, Prince Sergei Trubetskoi wrote a book-length study and several articles on the logos doctrine, tracing its various peregrinations from antiquity to Judaism and Christianity. At one point he states that Heraclitus's logos roughly means "true reasoning" (*istinnoe rassuzhdenie*).[7] Although the emphasis on rationality as the underlying principle of the universe finds little resonance in Bakhtin's work, the idea of the existence of some sort of base for various concrete phenomena does play out a certain role in his analysis of culture. Significantly, in "Discourse in the Novel" the novelistic word represents just such a base; in the Rabelais book, the grotesque body becomes the guiding principle of cultural evolution. The logocentric essence of the grotesque body becomes evident if one bears in mind Heraclitus's understanding of logos. According to Heraclitus's scheme, opposed to the ordering influence of logos is the force of time, which he characterizes as "a child playing at draughts, a child's kingdom" (fragment 79).[8] In his book on Rabelais, Bakhtin quotes Heraclitus's famous statement in arguing that Rabelaisian time is irreverently (and sometimes cruelly) capricious, often destructive of every individual body within its reach. The grotesque body therefore emerges as a saving constant in Rabelais's world, perpetually ravaged by the wanton unpredictability of time. In this instance, the logological subtext in Bakhtin's Rabelais book becomes clearer when bearing in mind the full philosophical content of his reference. Because Bakhtin relies on Heraclitus's aphorism in no fewer than four prominent places in his book, it is safe to say that his allusion is hardly idle and peripheral and probably begs from the reader a fuller orientation toward its source.[9]

Departing from the apparent rationalist and homogeneous tendency underlying Heraclitus's logos, the Stoics asserted the multiplicity of the universe in the form of various logoi (words) unfolding within the unitary logos. According to the Stoics, *logos spermatikos* (seminal logos) engenders a diversified reality; at the same time, that reality indelibly carries the birthmarks of a common origin, in whose limited volume reside all the seeds of all subsequent existence. This incipient diversification of universal meaning thus remains controlled and determined from the beginning: "[God], in looking at the birth of the world, holds within himself all the seminal *logoi,* according to which each thing is produced, as required by necessity" (*Stoicum veterum fragmenta* 2.1027).[10] Throughout his career Bakhtin grappled with the idea of diversity within unity, a struggle that ultimately produced his conception of the multifacetedness of novelistic discourse (with its tension between the categories of *slovo* [word] versus *slová* [words]) and the related idea of polyphony. In Stoicism the individual words or logoi were said to pass through two stages after their generation from *logos spermatikos*. First, the individual thought takes shape in the mind but remains unuttered (*nevyskazannoe*): at this stage the word is referred to as *logos endiathetos* or inner language. Second, the thought becomes uttered, which (according to the early Christian exegetes adapting Stoicism) is transformed into the Word of God. This second stage leading to transfiguration is referred to as the *logos prophorikos* or uttered (*vyskazannoe*) word.

There is no doubt that Bakhtin was well acquainted with the works of the Stoics. In the 1973 Duvakin interviews he indicates that he knew Sergei Trubetskoi's widely used 1910 textbook *A Course in the History of Ancient Philosophy* and mentions taking the elective of Ancient Greek during his gymnasium years and describes studying Greek philosophy at the University of Odessa under a well-known specialist in Aristotle.[11] In a 1919 postcard from Nevel (showing a young Bakhtin together with his friend Lev Pumpiansky and three others), the critic writes of discussing Greek philosophy with his friends, in particular the work of the Cynics and Socratics.[12] The dynamic of the gestation and generation of the word does play a key role in almost all of Bakhtin's writing, particularly in his study of Rabelais, where the fleshing-out of the metaphor itself is taken to such a level of development that the process is characterized in organic, and sometimes even carnal, terms. According to Bakhtin, the transformation of the merely conceived or intellected word to the one that is uttered and revealed is central to Dostoevsky's writing; it is in this shift toward the concretization of the thought that one sees the "profound dialogism of the word" (*glubinnyi dialogizm slova*).[13]

The shifting connotations of the Greek logos that went into the famous "beginning" (in both senses) of the Johannine Gospel and the subsequent glosses of it by commentators operating within the highly divergent worlds of Latin and Greek learning are too intricate to delve into here; in fact, few of these permutations are directly relevant to the cipher that many of Bakhtin's terms represent. Nevertheless, one doctrinal bellwether is crucial in the present context. The elaboration and fuller integration of these pre-Christian concepts into Johannine logology was attempted during the Seven Ecumenical Councils, which date from 325 to 787 and form the backbone of christology as espoused in the theological tradition of the Eastern church. Bakhtin's treatment of the individual consciousness recalls the paradox of the ever-continuous yet reified being of the Trinity's hypostases, first set forth in the Nicean council in 325. As one religious historian has put it, in its groundbreaking role as the first systematic effort to define the nature of the Trinity, the ecumenical council at Nicea was both "the first in eminence and significance for all [the subsequent councils] that followed."[14] It was at this council that the utter oneness or consubstantiability (Greek, *homoousia;* Latin, *consubstantio;* Russian, *edinosushchie*) of Christ the Son with God was declared; it lent further and more sophisticated development to the Stoicist concept of *logos spermatikos* by applying it more explicitly to the Johannine verses, suggesting the generation and growth of both divine being and language. The first Nicean council set out to demonstrate the "incarnate economy of the Trinity," the internal structure of what might be called the "co-being" of the Father, Son, and Holy Ghost. These three members of the Trinity are traditionally referred to either as hypostases (Greek, *upostas;* Russian, *ipostas*) or as persons (Greek, *prosopon;* Latin, *persona;* Russian, *litso*).

But it is arguably the Fourth Ecumenical Council at Chalcedon in 451 that played a special role in systematizing and refining the tenets of incarnational christology that had been filtered through Stoicist logology.[15] The concept of *homoousia* (Russian, *edinosushchie*) or consubstantiality forms the basis for the doctrinal innovations of the fourth council. The stem *ousia* means essence, nature, or being (Latin, *substantia, natura;* Russian, *estestvo*). The council at Chalcedon was notable in affirming not only the consubtstantiality of Father and Son, but also the two natures (Russian, *estestvá*) of Christ as human and divine. The consubstantiality of these natures was defined as a close mutual influence and even interdependence. The classic statement of the fourth council was that the two natures of Christ exist "without confusion [*neslitno*], without change, without separation [*nerazdel'no*]."[16] As elucidated in one nineteenth-century Russian commentary, Chalcedonian doctrine dictates that the human and divine natures of Christ coexist in one hypostasis, not in two individuals who are riven and separate from each other (*rassekaemogo ili razdeliaemogo*); they are united in the one and the same person of the only-born son, the Word of God (*Boga Slova*).[17] In Russian and Orthodox homiletics the characterization of the Trinity as consubstantial (*edinosushchnaia*) is very common; somewhat less frequent and conventional is the explicit association of Chalcedonian lexemes such as "undivided" with the entire Trinity when in fact they really describe the two natures of Christ.[18] In his study of the noncanonical songs of Russian religious folk poetry, Georgy Fedotov adduces several examples of Chalcedonian terms used to describe the internal coherence of the Trinity, such as the "one Trinity undivisible [*nerazdelimoi*]" or "undivided [*nerzadel'yia*]."[19] In the nineteenth century, even a progressive and eclectic cleric and sermon writer such as the Archimandrite Fiodor (who influenced virtually every contemporary Russian writer interested in Orthodoxy, among them Gogol, Dostoevsky, Berdiaev, and arguably even Solovyov) scrupulously distinguishes between the Trinity and the Chalcedonian idea of the divided union of Christ's person.[20] As we shall see in Chapter 4 where this topic is treated in greater depth, Bakhtin often bent the Chalcedonian formula to his own particular uses by alluding to it in contexts where the immediate configuration of ideas would not entirely fit with it.

All the same, this is not to say that there are no affinities or doctrinal parallels between Chalcedonian dogma and the internal unity of the Trinity. As already shown, the idea of consubstantiality was central to both. By more than half a century, the Greek patristic concept of *perichoresis* or interpenetration (Latin, *circumincessio, permeatio;* Russian, *vzaimoproniknovenie, vzaimoproniknovennost'*) used to describe the coinherence of the Trinity's hypostases in some ways anticipated the Chalcedonian notion of separation tempered by unity. Although the Latin equivalent was used by Augustine in his treatise on the Trinity, *perichoresis* has traditionally played a greater role in Orthodox christology than in Western Christianity. The term was originally adapted by the Church Fathers from the Stoicist legacy and was taken to mean the passing through, coextension, or interpenetration of physical bodies at all points of each other.[21] As developed by the theologians Gregory of Nazianzus (often referred to in the Orthodox tradition as Gregory the Theologian, ?329–?390) and John of Damascus (?675–749), the term constituted an important conception in elaborating upon and clarifying the doctrines of the consubstantiality of the Father and Son in their unimpeded interaction yet fundamental separateness.[22] Many commentators understand the concept of *perichoresis* as emblematic of the overall emphasis on the interdwelling of the three parts of the Trinity that is distinctive of Orthodoxy as a theological belief-system. The modern-day Orthodox theologian Kallistos Ware elaborates on the axiological implications of this doctrine in a way that effectively illuminates Bakhtin's references to it. "There is," Ware explains, "in God something analogous to 'society' " in the sense that "He is not a single person, loving himself alone, not a self-contained monad or 'The One.' " God is rather a "triunity: three equal persons, each one dwelling in the other two by virtue of an unceasing movement of mutual love," and "[t]he final end of the spiritual Way is that we humans should become a part of this Trinitarian coinherence or *perichoresis,* being wholly taken up into the circle of love that exists within God."[23] The Russian translation of this concept (*vzaimoproniknovenie*) occurs in many instances throughout Bakhtin's writing as a term and a idea, sometimes through related words such as *pronikat'* (to penetrate, permeate) and *[vzaimo]proniknovennost'* ([inter]penetrability). Particularly significant from the Bakhtinian perspective is the assertion here of the miraculous paradox of one human generation being spatially coterminous and temporally coincident with another, to the point where they are unified within a single person or hypostasis. The divine Word is unitary, but has within it a multiplicity of interlocking essences.[24] At Chalcedon, simultaneity and interrelation were asserted, the shuffling and intermixing of human and divine essences going against the grain of their presumed hierarchical ordering and reaching an apogee of paradox. This increasingly complex and ramified vision retained, however, an insistence on the interdependence and therefore unity of Christ's person, divinization still predominant over humanization. As John Henry Newman put it, the doctrine was simply "chang[ing] in order to remain the same."[25]

Bakhtin's reliance on these ramifications of logos—both in its philosophical antecedents of Stoicism as well as its subsequent doctrinal elaboration of certain aspects of Stoicist categories—are apparent in "Discourse in the Novel." In that essay Bakhtin identifies the "concrete" word (*konkretnoe slovo*) with the utterance (*vyskazyvanie*) and states that "no living [*zhivoe*] word relates to its object in a *singular* way," for "between the word and its object, between the word and the speaking subject, there exist an elastic environment of other, alien words about the same object." The object-directed word subsequently becomes "dialogically agitated" in the "tension-filled environment of alien words," and "weaves in and out of complex interrelationships [*vzaimootnosheniia*], merges [*slivaetsia*] with some, recoils from others, intersects [*peresekaetsia*] with yet a third group, and all this may crucially shape discourse [*slovo*]."[26] The Stoicist distinction between the unitary source and the plurality of manifested speech or utterance is powerfully evident in Bakhtin, especially in light of Trubetskoi's influential summations of it. But Bakhtin also perpetrates a telling inversion upon the traditional dichotomy of inner versus outer speech: for him, it is the multiplicitous manifestations of spoken speech that generate the single entity of discourse. By turning this theogony on its head, Bakhtin puts himself in the position of a philosophical sectarian or perhaps even heretic in relation to the Johannine and Stoicist traditions of the embodied word. A trichotomy of categories emerges from Bakhtin's description of polyphony that is in some ways reminiscent of the Stoicist conception of the three stages of the birth of the word: object, concrete word, and discourse. In a comment one Russian theologian made in 1901 that was undoubtedly inspired at least in part by studies in logology such as Trubetskoi's, the pre-Christian tripartite division of the word according to the Stoics was one of the most important conceptual sources of the Trinity.[27] Bakhtin uses the same structural scheme of the Stoicist logos in describing the genesis of the word from concrete object to discourse, transferring it to an aggressively secularizing context.

Other images and terms in this statement from "Discourse in the Novel" are even more resonant in their Christological echoes. Bakhtin's use of *vzaimootnosheniia* (interrelationships) to describe the networking of the concrete word is homologous to the interpenetration or *perichoresis* (*vzaimoproniknovenie*) of logos with other segments of the Trinity. Furthermore, his comment that the word merges (*slivaetsia*) with some while recoiling from others recalls both lexically and conceptually the conditional fusion of the twin natures of Christ the Word defined at council of Chalcedon. Finally, the word's intersection with a third group of alien words is distinctly reminiscent both of the triunity of God and the divine economy in which each hypostasis of the Trinity is said to interdwell with the others. But the Stoicist two-stage conception of the birth of logos, the coinherence of the Trinity, and the twin natures of Christ reverberate throughout Bakhtin's description of the exteriorization of the word in an almost jarringly obvious manner. A Russian reader of Bakhtin's generation would immediately pick up these references and find them disturbing because the critic aestheticizes the classical theological notions that he relies so heavily upon, reducing them to terminological markers or motifs. Moreover, in completely erasing the boundaries of the partially distinct notions of triunity, the Stoicist trichotomy, and the Chalcedonian divided union, Bakhtin is, in essence, playing non-canonical variations on christological themes, recombining them in ways that are anything but traditional.

TWENTIETH-CENTURY RUSSIAN MANIFESTATIONS OF THE JOHANNINE WORD

At this point a bird's-eye view is needed of the territory of logos or the metalinguistic and transcendent word: it has perhaps become a bit overgrown with the thicket of terms and concepts cultivated over the last several pages. Neither literary criticism nor certainly literature itself should be forgotten in this journey through the hypostatic Word. It was perhaps the contemporary literary manifestations or adaptations of the Johannine word that were particularly significant in piquing Bakhtin's interest in the biblical passage. As Nils Åke Nilsson notes, the use of *slovo* in the metonymic sense of discourse and poetic language was common in literary debates after 1910, beginning with Symbolists and continuing with the Acmeists and Futurists.[28] However, the stage had certainly been set even earlier than that. Andrei Bely's 1908 essay "Symbolism"—written six years before Bakhtin's arrival in Saint Petersburg—incisively maps out the locus for many of the subsequent metapoetic disquisitions. "The word of consciousness [*soznaniia*] must have flesh, and flesh must have the gift of speech," asserts Bely.[29] Steven Cassedy emphasizes the importance of Bely's analogy between the aesthetic philosophy of Symbolism and Johannine logology and comes to the conclusion that for Bely the symbol constitutes the word made flesh.[30] In his essay of the following year "The Magic of Words" Bely develops the theological implications of his statements from "Symbolism" to an even further extent. As one commentator notes, Bely there eclectically draws not just on Christian gnosis, but also on the occult, neo-Kantianism, anthroposophy, and other philosophic motifs.[31]

Bely was not, however, the only writer of the time who used the image of the Johannine word in such an explicit manner. In his 1909 essay "Horomedon," the poet Maksimilian Voloshin refers explicitly not only to both the Heraclitean and the Johannine subtext of logos, but also quite possibly to its Stoicist interpretation as logos as *spermatikos,* the seed and progenitor of the entire visible universe. Voloshin portrays John the Evangelist as a Michelangelesque sculptor, bringing life into inert material with his famous statement "In the beginning was the Word . . . and the Word became flesh!"[32] Significantly, Voloshin leaves out the Johannine identification of the Word as God: for him, the artists themselves are creators, competing with God and perhaps even transcending in glory and accomplishment the divine creation of the universe. With a less explicit reference to any of these loci classici, the manifestos of the Futurist group Hylaea by literary theorists such as Kruchonykh and Livshits (with their apodictic and homilistic style and insistence on the self-sufficient word [*samovitoe slovo*] and the word as such [*slovo kak takovoe*]) manifest at the very least strong reminiscences of the Johannine word.[33] Kruchonykh's conception of transrational language (*zaumnyi iazyk*) is especially saturated with the logos subtext. In his manifesto-like essay "The New Ways of the Word" he asserts the need to create a new language that is free and universal. Kruchonykh envisions this new word as being "broader than its meaning"; together with "its component sounds," it is the carrier of both the idea and the transrational, the latter constituted by "irrational parts, mystical and aesthetic."[34]

Bakhtin's own response to these contemporary theoretical trends is difficult to reconstruct since his remarks about modern Russian literature are restricted to his Vitebsk lectures transcribed by the Mirkina sisters and to laconic references here and there in the writings that come under his own name. In one of his lectures from the early twenties, however, Bakhtin recognizes an affinity between Bely's and Dostoevsky's novels, noting that both writers portray characters who are possessed by a yearning for transcendence and communion (*toksa po voploshcheniiu*) with the earth (*pochva; zemlia*).[35] Bakhtin was undoubtedly aware of the philosophical and literary implications of the metaphor of transubstantiation or the word made flesh in the writings of his literary contemporaries immediately before the Revolution. In a certain sense, Trotsky's memorable accusation of the Formalists as Johannites worshiping the Word above all else can be applied to many members of the Russian intelligentsia of Bakhtin's and Bely's generations. They articulated their yearning for embodiment in a manner of mystical schismatics adrift in an indifferent or hostile world.

Perhaps the most vivid expression of the two-tiered conception of the word as both language in general and utterance in particular occurs in Nikolai Gumilev's poem "The Word" published in his 1921 collection "Pillar of Fire." As Nilsson points out, Gumilev's five-stanza meditation on the multiple facets of the spoken and written word is in many ways emblematic of contemporary literary and linguisitic polemics of that time.[36] Gumilev's poem is both a manifesto-like statement of Acmeist principles and a synthesis of Henri Bergson and Vladimir Solovyov. The syncreticism in the thought of the latter two thinkers was especially congenial to Russian literary exegetes of the Johannine Word, who cast the notion of the interconnectedness of the physical universe in the mold of the interdwelling of the hypostases of the Trinity, an action referred to in the statements of the ecumenical councils and the writings of the church fathers as *perichoresis*. In asserting the importance of crossing phenomenological barriers within the Word, Gumilev also posits something very much like the Chalcedonian ideal of hypostatic interpenetration of one aspect or side of the word with another. The last stanza throws a particularly revealing light on the internal composition of the Word as it was often outlined by both Gumilev and contemporaries: "We have placed as a limit [*predelom*] to the Word the impoverished limits of nature [*skudnye predely estestva*], and, like bees in an abandoned beehive, dead words [*slova*] putrify."[37] Gumilev's *slovo* represents both essence or singularity as well as the multiplicity of moribund words. This tension between the two meanings of the term are also amplified by the Formalist critic Victor Shklovsky in his 1914 pamphlet "The Resurrection of the Word [*Voskreshenie slova*]": "The most ancient poetic creation of man was the creation of the word [*tvorchestvo slova*]. Now words [*slova*] are dead, and language is like a graveyard, but an image was once alive in the newly-born word."[38] Working against the demotic hubbub of Futurism and the hieratic backdrop of the theological tradition, Gumilev and Shklovsky modify this semantic constellation by recasting the hypostatic word into a category that, while clearly more inclusive than the individual utterance or prosaic word, is also evidently more mediated and contextual than the scriptural, upper-case Word.

Gumilev and Shklovsky were not, however, the only Russians at that time whose conception of discourse hinged on the occurrence of a revivifying or transformational event. Osip Mandelshtam, in his essay "The Word and Culture," makes a statement about the enemies of the live Word in terms that are strikingly reminiscent of Gumilev: "I experience an almost physical sensation of the unclean goatish spirit that comes from the enemies of the word."[39] In "On the Nature of the Word" (first published separately in 1922) Mandelshtam stresses the transubstantive and incarnational aspect of language. Like Gumilev, Mandelshtam was an Acmeist whose literary production in the teens and early twenties was dominated by the urge to define the movement; both poets for a brief period were preoccupied by what may be termed an aesthetic of the manifesto. However, unlike Gumilev (and as noted by Victor Terras), Mandelshtam's conception of *slovo* distinctly evinces an ambience of religiosity.[40] Using the last two stanzas of Gumilev's poem as an epigraph, Mandelshtam asserts that the Russian language is a Hellenic language in the sense that its culture of Eastern Orthodoxy provides one of the few living links to Greek antiquity. Russian takes on special relevance and vitality through its participation in a kind of cultural apostolic succession, transubstantiating itself into flesh that resonates and speaks.[41] The idea of the poet as a masonic artisan, one who inherits the past's rich cultural-linguistic legacy while also infusing new life into it, was central to the work of Acmeists such as Gumilev, Mandelshtam, Anna Akhmatova, and Sergei Gorodetsky. As different as Acmeism and Futurism were, the Acmeist offshoot known as Adamism complemented Kruchonykh's view of the word as such or the word as thing, seeking, in Sergei Gorodetsky's words, "to see things that Adam saw at the time of creation." This asethetic imperative is in fact the obverse of Bakhtin's, who in "Discourse in the Novel" makes a statement that may very well be polemically oriented toward Adamism: "Only the mythical Adam, who approached a virginal and as yet verbally unqualified world with the first word, could really have escaped from start to finish [the] dialogic inter-orientation [*vzaimoorientatsiia*] with the alien word that occurs in the object."[42] Bakhtin emphasizes not so much the fact or artifact of the embodied word as Mandelshtam and Gorodetsky do, but the process of interpenetrative and perichoresical mutual relation between words. Acmeism sees embodiment as a linear succession whereas Bakhtin believes it to be a lateral or cross-sectional dynamic of mutual interrelation.

The vertiginous shuttling back and forth between the various senses of the term *slovo* with all its theological nuances and incarnational ramifications, was a practice rooted in the teens and twenties among Russian poets and critics, a time when Bakhtin formed many of his most important theoretical principles, one that left an indelible mark on his critical terrain.[43] From the vantage point of the movements described so far, two variants of the Trinitarian paradigm emerge. The first is the church-sanctioned and promulgated exposition of the doctrine of the Word in its Stoic background, scriptural setting and patristic elaboration; the second, the metaphoric and at times metapoetic transformation of the same doctrine at the hands of poets such as Gumilev, Mandelshtam, and scholars of language and literary art such as Shklovsky, Potebnia, and Vygotsky. An examination of Bakhtin's most-cited essay suggests that both the classic doctrinal as well as modernist appropriations of the Christological logos served as precedents for his conception of discourse.

"DISCOURSE IN THE NOVEL": THE WORD DIVIDED

In Moscow on 8 August 1936 the scholar Matvey Isaevich Kagan wrote to his wife that Bakhtin was finally recovering from a bout of his chronic osteomyelitis. Noting that he was beginning to look better, Kagan mentions in the letter that Bakhtin had just lent him a manuscript copy of an essay titled "On Discourse in the Novel." As a specialist in philosophy who (like Boris Pasternak) had studied in Marburg under the neo-Kantian Hermann Cohen, Kagan was piqued by the apparent similarity of Bakhtin's piece to one that he himself had written on Turgenev. He nevertheless concludes the letter with the chagrined observation that his friend's work is, on the whole, more thorough and significant than his own.[44] Kagan's response to the piece is understandable; the essay, written between 1934 and 1935 and presented as a paper at the Institute of World Literature in 1940, is unquestionably one of most systematic and least fragmentary of Bakhtin's works.

Of all the assumptions underlying "Discourse in the Novel," the one delineated with the greatest clarity is that discourse represents a single matrix with interstices for various kinds or levels of language. In the first chapter of the essay (titled "Modern Stylistics and the Novel"), Bakhtin outlines previous attempts at analyzing and classifying novelistic language and sets forth the primary terms in his own critical vocabulary. As straightforward as this section is, the net of scholarly reference Bakhtin casts over it highlights certain aspects of his argument about the artistic preeminence of the novel as a genre. One reference that at first does not seem particularly important is to Gustav Shpet's 1927 book *The Internal Form of the Word.* Bakhtin takes to task Shpet's view of the novel as a primarily rhetorical genre, vastly inferior to the poetry. According to Shpet, poetry represents the highest form of both literary and linguistic expression, the fullest realization of the word, whereas the novel never transcends its sources, rooted in the rhetorical genres. Bakhtin turns Shpet's dichotomy on its head, assigning a logocentric position to the novel and a peripheral one of jerry-built formalism to poetry.[45] Nonetheless, in spite of Bakhtin's polemic, there are a number of telling parallels between his position and that of Shpet. The following statement from *The Internal Form of the Word* may in fact represent a source for Bakhtin's conception of discourse:

> Language as such, in its aggregate, has its internal laws, forms of forms, in the internal *logical* forms explained above; in this respect it is the archetype [*proobraz*] of every cultural and social phenomenon, which must have its homologous internal forms. Art is [just such a] cultural and social phenomenon, which incidentally, as the means of *expression* [*sredstvo vyrazheniia*] can also serve the goal of communication. [The role of art] in this sense is analogous to the word, and we can speak about its internal forms as being genuinely logical.[46]

In his book Shpet works very much within the Stoicist distinction between the inner or unspoken word (*logos endiathetos*) and the spoken and exteriorized one (*logos prophorikos*); it is a dichotomy that is very strong in Bakhtin's essay as well but without specific reference to the trappings of the logos doctrine that enjoyed so much vogue among Russian religious philosophy of Shpet's time. Like Bakhtin, Shpet does not privilege the inner form of the word—its content—over the outer form; he writes that expression and meaning (*vyrazhenie i smysl*) in fact represent not only a single indivisible structural whole (*nerazryvnoe strukturnoe edinstvo*), but also a sui generis being or existence (*bytie*) of the socio-cultural type.[47] Interestingly, in a footnote to this statement Shpet cites the concept of the "God-man" (*bogochelovek*) as one example of the inextricable pairing of expression and meaning, a clear acknowledgment of Solovyov. As will soon become apparent, the idea of the maximalization of communication as an apotheosis of humanity plays a key role in Bakhtin's essay as well.

Among Bakhtin's introductory remarks to "Discourse in the Novel" is the following summary of the concept of heteroglossia (*raznorechie; raznogolositsa*) as it is realized in the genre of the novel. Bakhtin's discussion of these terms is similar to Shpet's in the sense that both writers insist on the mediating potential that the word has for bringing people together. In the following discussion the affinities between Shpet's and Bakhtin's idealistic conceptions of language become especially distinct:

> The novel can be defined as a diversity of social speech types (sometimes even diversity of languages) and a diversity of individual voices, artistically organized. The internal stratification of any single national language into social dialects, characteristic group behavior, professional jargons, generic languages, languages of generations and age groups, tendentious languages, languages of the authorities, of various circles and of passing fashions, languages that serve the specific sociopolitical purposes of the day, even of the hour (each day has its own slogan, its own vocabulary, its own emphases)—this internal stratification present in every language at any given moment of its historical existence is the indispensable prerequisite for the novel as a genre. The novel orchestrates all its themes, the totality of the world of objects and ideas depicted and expressed in it, by means of the social diversity of speech types [*raznorechie*] and by the differing individual voices that flourish under such conditions. Authorial speech, the speeches of narrators, inserted genres, the speech of characters are merely those fundamental compositional unities with whose help heteroglossia [*raznorechie*] can enter the novel; each of them permits a multiplicity of social voices and a wide variety of their links and interrelationships (always more or less dialogized). These distinctive links and interrelationships between utterances and languages, this movement of the theme through different languages and speech types, its dispersion into the rivulets and droplets of social heteroglossia, its dialogization—this is the basic distinguishing feature of the stylistics of the novel.[48]

Like Shpet's word, the category of the novel in Bakhtin's essay has an internal essence that, when realized or externalized, facilitates communication among people. Shpet refers to this interaction simply as *soobshchenie* (communication) and has very little to say about it; for Bakhtin, it is paramount, the novel representing the single medium from which such linguistic diversity can effloresce. Bakhtin devotes considerably more space than Shpet to the nature and various types of this human interrelation; he also stresses the confrontational aspect of linguistic interchange. The various conflicts of discourse in Bakhtin are contained or prevented from boiling over by the genre of the novel. Bakhtin emphasizes both the dissonance and the harmony of novelistic heteroglossia; immediately after this paragraph he goes on to say traditional studies of style are ineffective in analyzing the juxtaposition (*sochetanie*) of languages and styles into a higher unity (*vysshee edinstvo*) and that they have no approach to the distinctive social dialogue of languages (*k svoeobraznomu sotsial'nomu dialogu iazykov*) that one finds in the novel.[49]

Shpet's insistence on the social significance of the word is unusual for Russian treatments of the logos doctrine, which customarily describe it in such highly theoretical terms that any question of empirical manifestation is left untreated.[50] Both Bakhtin and Shpet believe that language possesses an internal structure that is shaped by social circumstances; Bakhtin, however, is more explicit and detailed about this, highlighting the novel's internal stratification (*vnutrenniaia razsloennost'*). In Shpet's conception of the word and Bakhtin's of the novel, one can see a convergence of ideas on language as social structure that is made all the more curious by Bakhtin's attack on Shpet's treatment of the novel. By criticizing one very minor and parenthetical remark in Shpet's *Internal Structure of Word,* Bakhtin almost goes out of his way to indicate his acquaintance with the book, the terminology of which is distinctly echoed in his own work.

But in spite of this indebtedness to Shpet, the term *slovo* itself remains elusive, and the influence that the diverse novelistic voices in particular bring to bear upon discourse is still unclear. As characterized in the third chapter "Heteroglossia in the Novel," the category of heteroglossia, while apparently related to the polyphony described in *Problems of Dostoevsky's Poetics,* differs from it in certain crucial respects:

> Heteroglossia, once incorporated into the novel (whatever the forms for its incorporation), is *another's speech in another's language,* serving to express authorial intentions but in a refracted way [*sluzhashchaia prelomlennomy vyrazheniiu*]. Such speech constitutes a special type of *double-voiced discourse.* It [i.e., discourse (*slovo*)] serves two speakers at the same time and expresses simultaneously two different intentions: the direct intention of the character who is speaking, and the refracted [*prelomlennuiu*] intention of the author. In such discourse there are two voices, two meanings and two expressions. And all the while these two voices are dialogically interrelated, they—as it were—know about each other (just as two exchanges in a dialogue know of each other and are structured in mutual knowledge of each other [*stroiatsia v*

> *etom vzaimnom znanii o sebe*]); it is as if they actually hold a conversation with each other. Double-voiced discourse is always internally dialogized [*vnutrenne dialogizovano*].[51]

Heteroglossia is the unmediated cacophonous din that precedes novelistic discourse; it represents the stubborn social reality that is subsumed yet never truly assimilated into the author's voice. As Anne Shukman has noted, the essential distinction for Bakhtin is not the artificial and contrived Formalist dichotomy of literature on one hand and the social or historical reality on the other but between personality (*lichnost'*) and thing (*vesch'*).[52] Heteroglossia provides the source material and existential trial proofs for the novel; it is the rehearsal for polyphony's dissonant yet exactingly complex harmony and makes itself heard through the Eolian Harp–like figure of the author. The interaction between the author and the Other (or others) constitutes an animistic moment, an instant during which an intersubjective exchange seems genuinely to take place and the insentient body of discourse awakens from its monological slumber. In the history of Bakhtin's writing, polyphony is in fact antecedent to heteroglossia, which was not developed until many years after the first appearance of the former term in *Problems of Dostoevsky's Art* (1929). Bakhtin developed the concept of heteroglossia in "Discourse in the Novel" in order to emphasize that not all many-voiced discourses constitutes polyphony, the achievement of which is very hard-won indeed. From this essay onward, the transformational shift from heteroglossia to polyphony emerges as an enduring theoretical concern in Bakhtin's writings.

This image of the dialogization of novelistic language as a life-infusing, almost Promethean aesthetic event is evident or implicit at various points throughout "Discourse in the Novel." As seen above, discourse is characterized as a level of signification that is shot through with a multitude of voices. At the end of chapter 2 of the essay, Bakhtin drafts a brief for language not as an inert medium "in" which the author speaks but rather as a conduit *through* which he communicates with others, "a language that has somehow more or less materialized [lit., embodied or enfleshed (*oplotnennyi*)], become objectivized, that he merely ventriloquates [lit., that is moved away from his lips (*otodvinutyi ot ego ust*)]."[53] Once the utterance leaves the speaker's lips, it takes on an embodied or enfleshed life of its own.

In the same passage Bakhtin proceeds to emphasize that his understanding of the term *slovo* is highly concrete in both of its meanings. The hypostasized word (discourse) is not, in fact, more "abstract" than the isolated utterance or voice:

> The prose writer makes use of words that are already populated with the social intentions of others and compels them to serve his own new intentions, to serve a second master [*sluzhit' vtoromu gospodinu*]. Therefore the intentions of the

> prose writer are refracted [*prelomliaiutsia*], and refracted *at different angles,* depending on the degree to which the refracted, heterglot languages he deals with are socioideologically alien, already embodied [*oplotnennosti*] and already objectivized.[54]

The abundance here of both generally physical and specifically corporeal metaphors is arresting. Language becomes "materialized" and "objectified" into a ventriloquist's prop as the nonauthorial tongues and voices are "fleshed-out" (or reified) while criss-crossing each other or being refracted through a prism. Moreover, an even more focused and specifically concrete image is wrought in Bakhtin's description of this process of consolidation and solidification: that of political struggle. Each word becomes a domain comprised of various inclinations and points of view; the author's ideological dominion is shaken as his unmediated and monological voice is subsumed into novelistic discourse; in effect, the participation of the nonauthorial voices leads to the disenfranchisement of the author. Elsewhere in "Discourse in the Novel" Bakhtin describes the authoritative word (*avtoritarnoe slovo*) as a nightmare version of an utterly inflexible and impermeable authorial one, the ultimate nonreciprocal voice: it "demands that we acknowledge it . . . quite independent of any power it might have to persuade us internally" and "we encounter it with its authority already fused [*soedinennym*] to it." Authoritative discourse is utterly authoritarian: while it "may organize around itself great masses of other kinds of discourses (which interpret it, praise it, apply it in various ways)," it "does not merge [*ne slivaetsia*] with these (by means of, say, gradual transitions)" but "remains sharply demarcated, compact and inert," entering into our verbal consciousness as a compact and indivisible mass." "One cannot divide it up [*razdeliat'*]," says Bakhtin, "agree with one part, accept but not completely another part, reject utterly a third part."[55] Bakhtin's conception of discourse is as materialist as that of the isolated utterance, the latter represented by the single, highly specific, and concrete voice and the former by the redistribution of semiotic property following the overthrow of the author's ideological tyranny in the novel. All of this is framed in the Chalcedonian terminology of the divided union of Christ's natures, only transferred to the nonbinary and multifaceted formation of nonauthoritative discourse. Significantly, Bakhtin expresses the spirit of this non-Manichaean multiplicity in terms of a triad of voices. He shifts Chalcedonian schemata twice, first to a Trinitarian structure and then to the world of the novel, the monologic authorial voice becoming a demonic paraclete.

Bakhtin then goes on to describe in greater detail the main features of the novel's projection of mediated agency as manifest both in the hero and the author himself. A structure inheres among the voices once the author's voice has been effectively subverted. Consequently, it is not the voices themselves, as individual entities, that become privileged but rather the interrelations among them. Yet in spite of this contextualizing and decentering—and perhaps even sabotage—of identity, each voice not only retains its individual integrity but can also be said to realize itself fully for the first time:

> Diversity of voices [*raznogolositsa*] and heteroglossia [*raznorechie*] enter the novel and organize themselves within it in a structured [*stroinuiu*] artistic system. This constitutes the distinguishing feature of the novel as a genre. . . . The social and historical voices populating language, all its words [*slova*] and all its forms, which provide language with its particular concrete conceptualizations, are organized in the novel into a structured [*stroinuiu*] stylistic system that expresses the differentiated socio-ideological position of the author amid the heteroglossia of his epoch.[56]

The considerable centripetal and centrifugal tendencies in the novel are mutually contrapuntal and yet never wholly cancel each other out; the clamorous disagreement among the voices is in fact highlighted by their organization into a structural whole. As Michael Holquist notes, "Bakhtin's conception of language is based on an a priori sense of opposition and struggle at the heart of existence, a ceaseless battle between centrifugal forces that seek to keep things apart and centripetal forces that strive to make things cohere."[57]

Only in the second chapter of "Discourse in the Novel," "Discourse in Poetry and Discourse in the Novel," however, does Bakhtin elaborate on the central term of his essay. There, he deftly shifts from one meaning of *slovo* to another, focusing once on the denotation of the term (the individual word or utterance) and then on its connotation (the hypostatic Word). A distinction is drawn in this pivotal essay between two manifestations of the word, on the one hand as a highly specific signifier and on the other as an abstraction:

> Discourse lives, as it were, beyond itself [*vne sebia*], in a living impulse toward the object [*v svoei zhivoi napravlennosti na predmet*]; if we detach ourselves completely from this impulse all we have left is the naked corpse of the word [*to u nas ostanetsia v rukakh obnazhennyi trup slova*], from which we can learn nothing at all about the social situation or the fate of a given word in life.[58]

Like Gumilev with his insistence that boundaries (*predely*) simultaneously demarcate and mortify the word, Bakhtin emphasizes that the strictly circumscribed or isolated word is destined for semantic obsolescence. Throughout his criticism Bakhtin accentuates the cognitive dislocation that occurs during the reading and writing of novels as discourse becomes alienated from itself and signifier temporarily separates from signified. As is made clear in the passage above, this cognitive process can either lead to a restoration of the link between the utterance and its historical and sociolinguistic context or to a widening of the chasm separating the two. What ultimately emerges from this discussion is a conception of the word that supplements the Saussurean categories of signifier and signified. Thus, in the term "discourse" (*slovo*),

Bakhtin, like Saussure, understands that the object or thing itself is arbitrarily linked and therefore fundamentally separate from its linguistic marker; unlike Saussure, Bakhtin believes that there does exist a realm of language study beyond that of the individual lexeme or even utterance, that which analyzes such units of expression in their dialogistic setting. It is precisely the wresting of the utterance from this setting, the decontextualization of the word, that renders it nugatory and lifeless, the object of a pedantic new paleology in language study. By using *slovo* in the sense of the isolated utterance (*dannoe slovo*) as well as in that of the Saussurian *la langue,* Bakhtin gives a thumbnail sketch of a difficult theoretical point. Unlike Saussure, Bakhtin believes that discourse (or *la langue*) is fractured by individual utterances that would fly apart were it not for the impulse toward dialogue that holds them together.

But the metaphorical freight conveyed by the excerpt above takes on additional baggage, and not just in its passage through the biblical subtexts as refracted through the Russian literary and philological context. Bakhtin also gathers material from the twin territories of theological exegesis and the biblical text itself. The image of the naked dead body of the word is strongly reminiscent of the unresurrected Christ, whose robes were taken by soldiers at the time of crucifixion. The strongly allegorizing Gospel of John has the most detailed description of this moment (19:23–24), the evangelist dwelling on the seamlessness of the tunic (Russian and Church Slavonic, *riza*) that the four soldiers wager for and the act's fulfillment of the scriptural statement "They shared my garments among them, and cast lots for my clothing" (Psalms 22:18). One has to go to Philo (whom several commentators believed to have influenced John) to find a more clearly stated and unequivocal interpretation of the divine word as vested with the garment of life, a conception corresponding more closely to Bakhtin's metaphor in the passage above from "Discourse in the Novel." Philo developed a conception of logos that was partially indebted to Stoicism in the latter's delineation of an inner and outer word. In one of his writings he states that "the most ancient Logos of the Existent is clothed with the world as with a garment . . . while the particular soul is clothed with the body."[59] According to Philo, the antemundane or inner logos is unbodied (Greek, *asomatos*) and naked and therefore not immanent in this world. One historian of early church doctrine sees in this attempted bridging of dualism (evident not just in Philo's treatises but also in the book of Job and the Apocryphal Wisdom of Solomon) an early precedent for the image of the soul as "house" in some of the Pauline epistles (for example, 2 Cor. 5:1; 1 Cor. 3:16) and John 1:14. Although the last of these biblical passages is usually translated as "[t]he Word became flesh and dwelled among us," a more correct translation of it would be "the Word became flesh and was tabernacled [Greek, *eskenosen*] among us."[60] Philo's conception of logos as a "cutter"—an entity that infinitely divides itself into opposites and yet remains whole—is one of the sources for both the image of Christ's indivisible garment in John 19:23–24 and the binary distinction of the Chalcedonian decision.[61] His thought also exerted a considerable influence on the conception of logos in Orthodox theology and a great deal of interest in his work was generated in Russian religious philosophy at the turn of the century. It is highly likely that Bakhtin was aware of certain aspects of Philo's theology either directly or through such conduits as the books and articles of Sergei Trubetskoi.[62]

Examples of the word as a Philonic tripartite matrix abound in Russian philosophy even into the early Soviet period. The most prominent of these is from Pavel Florensky in his unfinished work "The Structure of the Word [*Stroenie slova*]." Florensky begins with the Stoicist dichotomy of inner and outer word, which he then proceeds to elaborate into a triad of meaning, phoneme, and sound (*zvuk*), the second of these functioning as a link between the internal and external realms.[63] Florensky repeatedly draws attention to the theological overtones of these categories, explicitly referring to Philo's work as crucial precursor of the Christian doctrine of the triadic nature of meaning ("*troiakost'* smysla" [emphasis in original]).[64]

The metaphor of the soul or essence of humanity as a garment does occur in a much more explicit form in another of Bakhtin's earlier writings, *Problems of Dostoevsky's Art*. Although this reference occurs in a passage in which Bakhtin discusses dialogue and not novelistic discourse (*romannoe slovo*) itself, it becomes quickly apparent that the two concepts are, in fact, closely allied:

> An exceptionally keen sense [*oshchushchenie*] of the other person as *another* and of one's *I* as a naked [*gologo*] *I* presupposes that all those definitions which clothe [*oblekaiut*] the *I* and the *other* in socially concrete flesh [*plot'*]—family, social, and economic class definitions—and all variants on those definitions, have lost their authoritativeness [*avtoritetnost'*] and their form-shaping force. A person, as it were, senses [*oshchushchaet*] himself in the world as a whole, without any intervening stages [*instantsii*], apart from any social collective [*sotsial'nogo kollektiva*] to which he may belong.[65]

Here Bakhtin brings together many of the christological motifs already outlined. Particularly interesting and revealing here, however, are Bakhtin's variations on the theological topos. In this passage, existence or being takes on substance only when one interacts with an "other," not by partaking in some hypostatic category such as the divine Word. Although he is probably not referring to Shklovsky's "The Resurrection of the Word," Bakhtin's remark that we directly experience ourselves after such a transforming and transubstantiating event does recall the other critic's statement that we have lost all sense (*oshchushchenie*) of the world. What Shklovsky sees as an ideal of poetic and cinematic art Bakhtin views as the dialogical function in any kind of discourse, an oft-overlooked reality that did not pass Dostoevsky's notice.[66]

That Bakhtin has in mind the metaphor of soul as garment is signaled by the verb *oblekat'* (to clothe). The verb is used in a similar and particularly telling context in his *Problems of Dostoevsky's Poetics*. According to Bakhtin there, the real life of a language is experienced during the concurrent (although not necessarily unisonal) sounding of its constituent utterances. It is this interaction among speech acts and not their solitary vocalizations that ultimately assumes real significance, a transformation that Bakhtin describes in distinctly logocentric terms. A similar passage from the Rabelais book throws the image of the vested word into even sharper relief:

> Dialogic relationships are reducible neither to logical relationships nor to relationships oriented semantically toward their referential object, relationships *in and of themselves* devoid of any dialogic element. They must clothe themselves in discourse [*oblech'sia v slovo*], become utterances [*vyskazyvaniiami*], become the positions of various subjects expressed in discourse, in order that dialogic relations might arise among them. (*Problems of Dostoevsky's Poetics*)[67]

> Not only belles lettres but the utopias of the Renaissance and its conception of the universe itself were deeply penetrated [glubokoproniknuty] by the carnival spirit [karnaval'nym mirooshchushcheniem] and often adopted [lit., "clothed in" (oblekalis')] its forms and symbols. (*Rabelais and His World*)[68]

The wording in these quotations recalls Bakhtin's metaphor in "Discourse in the Novel" of the naked corpse of the word bereft of discourse: in all three passages the vested body is presented as a positive image. The statements bring to mind, moreover, the sanguinary transformation of the incarnational word (*logos* in the Greek text) portrayed in Revelation 19:13: "He is clad [Russian and Church Slavonic, *oblechen*] in a robe [*riza*] dipped in blood, and the name by which he is called is the Word of God [Russian and Church Slavonic, *Slovo Bozhie*]." As many biblical commentators have noted, the blood here may be that either of Christ or his suffering followers, and the grament may also refer to Philo's image of the logos of God as a high priest.[69] The use of the term "deeply penetrated [*glubokoproniknuty*]" from the second passage above is evocative of the hypostatic integrality posited by *perichoresis*, especially when juxtaposed with its highly marked appearance in a number of both Solovyov's and Bakhtin's works.[70] For Bakhtin, the carnivalesque and dialogic relations become genuine and integrated only through the Christ-like intercession of the word; they fully realize the stylistic and ideational possibilities of their antinomies only when they are arrayed in the garment of discourse. As the eschatological biblical subtext suggests, this exacerbation of conflict is both destructive and life-giving. Bearing in mind this probable biblical reference, one quickly realizes the potential ambivalence of both Dostoevskian polyphony and Rabelaisian carnival. There is a clear parallel between polyphonic discourse and carnival: both contain distinctive visions of the world without stifling them, providing a common envelope in which they can interact with one another. The garment of discourse metonymically comes to stand for that which it encloses: the vestment of the Word becomes the vessel itself.

Given that Bakhtin conceives of discourse primarily as a neutral container for subversive linguistic diversity, one could argue that it is a purely heuristic category, devoid of real identity or even real existence. In christological schemata, the situation in this regard is entirely different: the embodied presence of Christ is an absolute and indubitable quiddity. Perhaps the most telling example in relation to Bakhtin's portrayal of the naked body of the Johannine and Philonic word is Sergei Bulgakov's essay "Was ist das Wort?" This essay by the expatriate theologian and contributor to the politically controversial *Landmarks* collection of 1909 (which will be discussed in Chapter 3) was published in Prague in 1930 and manifests remarkable affinities with Bakhtin's own work later that decade. Bulgakov adduces as an axiom that although a word's essence is single or one, its expression is manifold and complex:

> Es ist augenscheinlich, dass dieses erste und grundliegende Axiom auf der Grenze der Linguistik liegt, die nur die konkreten, von Fleisch durchdrungenen und von Blut durchflutenen Worte kennt, mit den schon zu Worten gewordenen Klängen zu tun hat und dieses Fleisch des Wortes verschiedenen Schnitten gemäss erforscht.[71]

> (It is obvious that this first and fundamental axiom lies on the border of linguistics, which only knows the concrete words that are suffused with flesh and blood—concerning itself with sounds that have already become words—and which analyzes this flesh of the word according to different segments.)

What is interesting here is not only the possible echoes of this passage in Bakhtin's essay, but also the ways in which Bakhtin toyed with Bulgakov's image. Like Bakhtin and Shpet, Bulgakov believes in an internal structure of the word that is interconnected; for Bakhtin and Bulgakov in particular, this interconnection is almost organic in nature. The latter two writers, moreover, are extremely skeptical about the analytical reach of linguistics as a field of study: one only need think of Bakhtin's critical remarks about linguistics and stylistics in the first few pages of "Discourse in the Novel," where he characterizes them as blunt instruments incapable of bringing about any true analysis of a text.[72] It is these scholarly approaches that Bakhtin probably has in mind as the instruments of death in his description of the bare and unresponsive body of the word. In this context one cannot but think of Gumilev's description of the moribund word with its stultifying internal barriers of brute nature (*skudnye predely estestva*). Bulgakov similarly believes linguistics to be extremely limited. But he goes further than Gumilev in ramifying the internal structure of the word. In a strongly Philonic image, he asserts that the body of the word takes on life only when it undergoes a radical imbrication or involution into different and overlapping segments or cuts (*Schnitte*). As shall become evident later in this chapter when the chronotope essay is discussed, it is precisely this image of the substantiated and revived flesh and blood of discourse that Bakhtin holds sacred.

The christological subtext evident in these works can be traced to certain suggestive and, in some instances, more explicit antecendents in Bakhtin's essays before the thirties. Like many of his Russian contemporaries in literature and philosophy, Bakhtin recognized a reading of the term *slovo* that was both highly specific and yet was understood to mean much more than the isolated lexical unit. In its metapoetic and metalinguistic transformation, the divine Word becomes flesh only when it joins the mortal confraternity or human context. Bakhtin's description of the concretizing transformation of utterances into discourse is highly reminiscent of the patristic notion of the emptying or kenosis that eventually results in the deification of the flesh. As Saint Maximus the Confessor puts it, "Man, the image of God, becomes God by deification, he is full of joy at giving up all that pertains to him."[73] At the forefront of Bakhtin's work is the opposition to the traditional Saussurean dichotomy of the isolated utterance and language as a unitary and inclusive entity. For Bakhtin, it is imperative that the link between the two be reestablished, a restoration invested with an almost life-giving power. The metaphor of the "naked corpse of the word" is especially significant since it reinforces the christological paradigm in a way that is reminiscent of the Futurists, Gumilev, and Shklovsky. All of these writers highlight the moribundity, if not actual extinction, of meaning in much of contemporary language. In his essay "The Resurrection of the Word" Shklovsky states that things have essentially died in the transitional state represented by modern literature and culture and need to be resurrected in order for us to recover an experiential sense of the world: "Things have died, we have lost a sense of the world. . . . Only the creation of new forms of art can return man to an experience of the world, to resurrect things and kill of pessimism."[74] Shklovsky and others (such as the Futurists) ultimately tried to engage other aspects of the christological topos of the divine Word, incorporating occasional references to Christ, such as his martyrdom. But for many of them resurrection also had something of an eschatological flavor in its focus on the raising of the dead. Shklovsky's image of the graveyard of dead words quickly brings to mind another passage from the fourth synoptic Gospel: "[T]he hour is coming, when all who are in their graves shall hear His voice and shall come forth" (John 5:28–29).

In Bakhtin's hands, however, this imagery of resurrection and redemption is considerably more complex than can be found in the writings of his artistic contemporaries. In regard to Kruchonykh and Voloshin, for example, it is safe to say that the theological metaphor is colored with considerable self-consciousness and even portentousness. Many of the paradoxes of such images and even the history of the previous use and interpretation of them are woven into their appearances in "Discourse in the Novel." For all of his supposed piety, Bakhtin clearly takes these motifs less on face value and "faith."

THE ORCHESTRATED WORD

Bakhtin's first use of the term *slovo* in a metalinguistic and Johannine sense occurs in "Toward a Philosophy of the Act." As he outlines it in one paragraph, discourse has an intricate internal structure that operates in a dynamic rather than mechanistic way:

> Historically language grew up in service of participative thinking [*uchastnogo myshleniia*] and performed acts, and it begins to serve abstract thinking only in the present day of its history. The expression of a performed act from within and the expression of once-occurrent Being-as-event [*edinstennogo bytiia-sobtytiia*] in which that act is performed require the entire fullness of the word: its content/sense aspect (the word as concept [*slovo-poniatie*]) as well as its palpable-expressive aspect (the word as image [*slovo-obraz*]) and its emotional-volitional aspect (the intonation of the word) in their unity. And in all these moments the unitary full word [*edinoe polnoe slovo*] can be answerably valid, i. e., can be the truth rather than something subjectively fortuitous. One should not, of course, exaggerate the power of language: unitary and once-occurrent Being-as-event [*edinoe i edinstennoe bytie-sobtytie*] and the performed act that partakes [*pichastnyi*] in it are fundamentally and essentially expressible, but in fact it is a very difficult task to accomplish, and while adequacy is unattainable, it is always present as that which *is* to be achieved.[75]

Simply put, Bakhtin understands the ethical life as the union or harmony between one's word and deed. But before this can happen there must be a proper coordination and interaction between three parts of the word: its concept, image, and intonation. The first of these categories strikingly corresponds to the Stoicist inner or unspoken word (*logos endiathetos*) while the last echoes the spoken and exteriorized *logos prophorikos;* the word as image represents something of a transitional or mediational step of the word toward full concretization. The fact that the term image (*obraz*) also means icon—an art form commonly regarded in Orthodox teaching as a window onto the Divine—only reinforces Bakhtin's positioning of it as an ontological bridge between the unbodied content of an act and its performative or material manifestation.

The passage above requires some more paraphrasing and unpacking in order for it to be fully understood. According to Bakhtin, although the harmonization of consciousness and act is fundamentally immanent, the actual achievement of it is quite difficult. Bakhtin uses the adjective *prichastnyi* to describe the principal (if often unrealized) union between act and event, which suggests more of a fusion than a mere joining; the term also connotes a partaking in a communal or eucharistic sense (*prichashchenie*). Normally such a secondary meaning would not assume any prominence. In the context of describing the word as a three-link chain extending from the inner to the outer world with the middle link as a mediator between the two realms, it is almost impossible not to think of Trinitarian conceptions of the divine Word, all of which to a greater or lesser extent relied upon the Stoicist dichotomy. Seeing the divine Word as emblematic both of the physical world as a whole and its residents' potential for sanctification, Saint Augustine wrote that "[y]ou have already been made through the Word, but you need to be made anew through the Word."[76] Bakhtin certainly describes a similar striving toward a certain perfection through the medium of language; in a caveat that is almost patristic in tone, he notes that a complete realization of this ideal is virtually impossible.

The christological subtext underlying Bakhtin's conception of the word is fitfully evident in his work written during the fifteen-year period from "Toward a Philosophy of the Act" to "Discourse in the Novel" and the chronotope essay. In the fragmentary first chapter of "Author and Hero in Aesthetic Activity" Bakhtin concludes his analysis of a Pushkin poem with an involuted remark that does not appear in the first version of the same interpretation from "Toward a Philosophy of the Act:"

> [All] concrete and unitary [*edinstennye*] elements of a literary work (as well as their architectonic ordering in a single [*edinom*] artistic event [*sobytii*]) is realized around the person-hero's center of values. Now existence [*bytie*] has become thoroughly humanized [*splosh' ochelevechennym'*] in the single event [*v edinstvennom sobytii*]: everything that has meaning and existence here is but a moment in the co-eventness of the given person's life, his destiny.[77]

As in "Toward a Philosophy of the Act," here one can find both the architectonic motif linked with the christological one. Although the second of these motifs is not so obvious as the first, it is present nonetheless. The past passive participle *ochelevechennyi* (humanized) comes from the verb *ochelevechit'*, which means to take on human form. As the lexicographer Dal' notes, one of the prominent uses of this verb occurs in it reflexive form: "Gospod' ochelovechilsia" (God became human).[78] In this use it is almost synonymous with *vochelovechit';* in their theological connotations both of these words are almost certainly renderings or equivalents of the Greek *enanthropsis*, which is used in a particularly striking way by John of Damascus, the theologian most responsible for the development of the conception of *perichoresis.* In one of his treatises he writes that the term incarnation means "the same as if one said humanation [*enanthropsis*], signifies that the conjunction is with the flesh."[79] Thus, the architectonic image of the descent of Christ as morally paradigmatic (as asserted in "Toward a Philosophy of the Act") is also operative in the first chapter of his essay on the author and hero.

The imperfective form of the verb (*ochelovechivat'*) turns up in Bakhtin's next project "The Problem of Content, Material and Form in Verbal Art" (1924). There he writes that art unites the worlds of art and social humanity (*sotsial'noe chelovechestvo*), with humanity as the effective link between the two: "[Art] creates the concrete intuitive unity [*edinstvo*] of these two worlds, plac[ing] man in nature, understood as his aesthetic environment; it humanizes [*ochelovechivaet*] nature and naturalizes man." Although here Bakhtin does not use any of the term denoting interpenetration or *perichoresis,* the concept is vividly present in his description of the humanizing of nature and the naturalizing of the person. The fact that this quotation features a triad with an animate element as the mediator between two disparate worlds only enhances its theological flavor.

The christological metaphor as it has been outlined and treated so far in relation to Bakhtin is abundantly evident throughout "Author and Hero in Aesthetic Activity" as well as in the essay on content and form. Almost all of the instances of the metaphor in these two works represent at most slight variations of those in "Art and Answerability" and "Toward a Philosophy of the Act," essays that will be extensively treated in the next two chapters. The next stage in Bakhtin's development of this metaphor begins four years later, with *Problems of Dostoevsky's Art.* A number of theologically related terms appear in this book. In general, although these highly marked terms do not appear with the same frequency as in "Toward a Philosophy of the Act," they are illuminating nonetheless.

In *Problems of Dostoevsky's Art,* Bakhtin describes the convergence of life and death within the pale of discourse that becomes the hallmark of polyphony. But the utter controversion and disruption of time and space also represents an important feature of Trinitarian and eucharistic theology. Among the Russian religious philosophers such as Solovyov, this confusion of dimensional categories is effected through a modified version of the categorical imperative: in order to conceive of meaning, one must harken back to the paradigm of personal sacrifice as exemplified in the life of Christ, thus not only going beyond the strict boundaries of individual experience but also calling into question the very validity of the isolated consciousness. In his earlier study of Dostoevsky's art, Bakhtin more explicitly maps the ontological sequence that inevitably breaks down into consummate nonsequentiality:

> Plot [*siuzhet*] in Dostoevsky is absolutely devoid of any sort of finalizing functions. Its goal is to place a person in various situations that expose and provoke him, to bring people together and make them collide in conflict—in such a way, however, that they do not remain within this area of plot-related contact [*soprikosnoveniia*] but exceed its bounds [*predely*]. The real conections begin where the ordinary plot ends, having fulfilled its service function [*sluzhebnuiu funktsiiu*]. . . .
>
> In essence [*V sushchnosti*] all of Dostoevsky's heroes come together outside of time and space, as two beings in infinity [*kak dva sushchetva v bespredel'nosti*]. Their consciousnesses, each with its own world, intersect; their integral fields of vision intersect. At the points where their fields of vision intersect lie [*v tochke peresecheniia*] the culminating points of the novel. At these points also lie the clamps [*skrepy*] holding together the novelistic whole. They are external to the plot and cannot be subsumed by any of the schemas for constructing a European novel.[80]

According to Bakhtin, Dostoevskian time is distorted or bled into space and comes to be defined by a series of dramatic—one could say climactic—zones. Plot assumes the role of a stage director as well the stage itself, tentatively coordinating the players into contrapuntal positionings while serving as a backdrop for those same conflicts.

Bakhtin's double and metaphorically mixed description of the role of plot in the novel at first seems infelicitous and confused. Within the context of his argument, however, this characterization emerges as rhetorically useful and, in all likelihood, deliberate; the yoked, internally contrary image of plot as both person and place points up the impossibility of a truly delimited and clearly defined consciousness. The plot in Dostoevsky's novels represents an ultimately ineffective and superfluous impresario. Bakhtin's quasi-personification of *siuzhet* calls attention to the French origin of the Russian term, *sujet.* Bakhtin's *siuzhet* is patently both subject as topic or organizing principle (or even more suggestively, as topos [space]) and as apperceptive consciousness. In Bakhtin's view, as in Gumilev's, true life begins with rupturing the protective membrane of individual existence; both writers infuse the matrix of the multifaceted Word with a variant of the Husserlian conception of intersubjectivity. Just as the job of the stage director is inconceivable without the proscenium, so is the isolated subject guided by the impinging though nonetheless discrete presence of other consciousnesses. Unlike Husserl, however, Bakhtin is not interested in the diffused or utterly centrifugal intersubjectivity. According to Bakhtin, there is an element or link that goes about the business of bringing people together and causing them to interact with one another. In *Problems of Dostoevsky's Art,* this integrative function is carried out by the plot, which is portrayed metaphorically as a person; a similar mediating (if more sketchily described) role is played out by the word-image from "Toward a Philosophy of the Act." Clearly, the concepts of plot and discourse are quite different in Bakhtin's criticism and are hardly interchangeable. Nonetheless, one does get the sense that the two concepts are complementary, both being agents for universal affiliation or consolidation that are situated in an unstable but distinctly physical space between being and nonbeing. The christological ramifications of such conjoining become more evident when viewed in the light of Russian religious philosophy, particularly with its frequent analogy between collective responsibility and the paradoxical interdwelling yet separate hypostases of the Trinity. As the twentieth-century philosophical historian and priest Vasily Zen'kovsky explains, one can recognize the individuality of people while acknowledging their paradigmatically Trinitarian integrality to one another: "Only from the idea of consubstantiality [*edinosushchiia*] can we understand the separateness [*razdel'nost'*] or hypostaticness [*mnogoipostasnost'*] of people—the metaphysical persistence of individualism—and at the same time grasp their genuine unity [*edinstvo*]."[81] In a certain residual form and to varying degrees depending on the text at hand, this christological archetype underlies Bakhtin's category of language as mediator or consolidator.

Yet in spite of all this, there are good reasons for not interpreting Bakhtin's criticism as an expression of catacomb theology. Another strain of thought becomes evident upon close review of these images in his early work, one that is not wholly consistent with an explicitly Christian vision of the world. In the example from the 1929 edition of Bakhtin's Dostoevsky study, plot does not fulfill a soteriological role: in fact, given that it simply brings people into often confrontational contact, one hesitates to call it a mediator at all. A certain irony underlies Bakhtin's use of christology. Even allowing for the discretion needed in devotional matters during the Soviet period, he appears to be inordinately interested in its imagery and metaphors, perhaps even at the expense of its substance or status as credo. In particular, Bakhtin seems drawn to the vividly structural component of christology in its Russian Orthodox form. As will be demonstrated later, the Chalcedonian formula of the twin natures of Christ coexisting without confusion or separation (*nesliianno i nerazdel'no*) was particularly congenial to Bakhtin in his outlining of an ethical community in "Toward a Philosophy of the Act." From a structural point of view, the permeable or porous boundary between the members of the Trinity represents the truly distinctive marker of the Orthodox redaction of the doctrine: in a certain sense, it is the one paradigmatic feature that makes operational the Chalcedonian dynamic of interconnection and interrelation. The fact that the image of this open border is scantily referred to in patristic writings and is not described there in any detail is of no consequence: the Fathers were not modernists who (like Mayakovsky) would deliberately overcultivate a metaphor in all of its possible ramifications for dramatically ironic effect. Twentieth-century writers are, of course, a different matter. Bakhtin casts the novelistic word as christological primarily from a structural, rather than philosophical, point of view. At the same time, Bakhtin's numerous and glowing characterizations of novelistic discourse as salvific also indicate that his interest in the christological metaphor is far from being narrowly formalist and quite possibly carries some of the emotive bias of the theological source material on which he draws.

WORD AS EMBODIMENT

This multivalent understanding of *slovo* is echoed in several works by members of the Bakhtin circle as well as by Bakhtin himself. In *Marxism and the Philosophy of Language,* published five years before "Discourse in the Novel" was written, Voloshinov takes Saussure to task for the rigidity of his categories of *la langue, la parole,* and *langage* and invokes *slovo* as a concept whose various features would not only cover the same territory represented by these terms but would also be more functional in practical textual analyses: "[T]he material of behavioral communication [*zhiznennogo obshcheniia*] is preeminently the *word.*"[82] Naftali Prat, writing on the Russian Orthodox philosophy of language, observes that there are significant parallels between Voloshinov's treatment of the social dimension of language and Florensky's, Sergei Bulgakov's, and A. F. Losev's ideas on the ontology of the Word. For the "God-Seekers" the creation or instantiation of meaning occurs within the individual consciousness whereas for Bakhtin's colleague it is played out in society, the cosmos making itself felt through the objective social being.[83] What Bakhtin and members of his circle took from the theology of the Word was not just a specific structural paradigm (i. e., the relation of discourse to human or social reality) but also the very *idea* of structure, hypostasizing it into an architectonic metaphor. The Word thus becomes both edifice and event, a blend of time as well as space.

But the essay "Forms of Time and of the Chronotope in the Novel. Notes Toward a Historical Poetics" contains perhaps the most revealing set of correspondences and similarities to "Discourse in the Novel," which Bakhtin had finished two years earlier. The bulk of the chronotope essay was written in the late thirties; all that remained was the conclusion, which Bakhtin penned in 1973. In this essay he treats the reification and concretization of noncanonical voices in much greater detail than before. At several points throughout the essay, the chronotope is described as the concretizing center of the novel's various elements; it becomes the locus of the novelistic voices' embodiment or substantiation (*voploshchenie; priobshchenie*). Any pivotal event in a novel such as a climax brings to a head all of the distinguishing features of *slovo;* it both transcends and is pithily emblematic of the work as a whole. Bakhtin's multifaceted yet essentially consistent and unitary reading of the term *slovo* is eloquently illustrated by his varied collection of tropes describing it as an architectonic entity, a light-refracting prism, or as a loom that weaves the voices and the "words" (*slová*) into a common fabric. The inner contradictions of *slovo,* like the dissonances of Dostoevskian polyphony, are simultaneously pronounced yet mutually integrative and constructive.

This evolution in Bakhtin's critical lexicon can also be plotted in a philological comparison of the two essays. *Voploshchenie, oplotnennyi,* and *oplotnennost'*—crucial terms in both works—are derived from the root *plot'* (flesh). Famous interpretations of John 1:1 such as Augustine's have posited a narrative of linguistic ontology into the verse and its chapter as a whole, implying a tentative restoration of prelapsarian cognition and speech through the transubstantiation of the flesh described in the fourteenth verse. Both *voploshchenie* and *prichashchenie* connote transubstantiation and they and their derivatives crop up at key points in the argument of both "Discourse in the Novel" and the chronotope essay;[84] *oplotnennyi* and its derivatives appear primarily in "Discourse in the Novel." Bakhtin strove over a period of a few years to describe more forcefully the permutations of style within the novel, their ineluctable gravitation toward a transformational and vivifying act. The merely "reified" or "concretized" word of "Discourse in the Novel" is thus recast in the life-shaping mold of a substantive and substantiating event.

The rich yet shifting imagery of Bakhtin's terminology of concretization is brought to the fore not only by its sheer conspicuousness, but also by the example of the numerous references to the faculty of sight as the primary channel of apprehending and understanding it. Bakhtin's highlighting of this trope both calls attention to his difficult and eccentric terminology and provides a clue on how to understand it. In "Toward a Philosophy of the Act," the agent of the act is occasionally referred to as *sozertsatel'* (contemplation) and the purview of action as *krugozor* (horizon), both of which originate in *zret'* (to see) and its derivatives. Toward the end of the manuscript the references to seeing and vision become more frequent, so that the phenomena within the agent's purview are termed *sozertsaemoe* ([the] contemplated), apparently displacing the earlier present passive participle *perezhivaemoe* (experienced).

These nests of vision and sight metaphors represent the hatchings and early growth of Bakhtin's later concepts of the chronotope and dialogue. Several years later he stressed the "representational importance" of vision, positing an Husserlian equivalence between perception and the instantiation of phenomena. In the chronotope essay, Bakhtin attempts to move beyond the event (*sobytie*), that temporal and spatial category which played such a key role in "Discourse in the Novel" but which here he considers to be less than far-reaching:

> We cannot help but be strongly impressed by the *representational* [*izobrazitel'noe*] importance of the chronotope. Time becomes, in effect, palpable and visible; the chronotope makes narrative events [*siuzhetnye sobytiia*] concrete, makes them take on flesh, causes blood to flow in their veins [*obrastaiut plot'iu, napolniaiutsia krov'iu*]. An event can be communicated, it becomes information, one can give precise data on the place and time of its occurence. But the event does not become a figure [*obrazom*]. It is precisely the chronotope that provides the ground [*pochvu*] essential for the showing-forth, the representability of events [*izobrazheniia sobytii*]. And this is so thanks precisely to the special increase in density and concreteness of time markers—the time of human life, of historical time—that occurs within well-delineated spatial areas [*na opredelennykh uchastakh*]. It is this that makes it possible to structure a representation of events [*izobrazhenie sobytii*] in the chronotope (around the chronotope).[85]

For Bakhtin, only when time becomes reified into a kind of distinctly concrete space can we speak of the existence of consciousness and, concomitantly, morality or ethics. Here Bakhtin takes the conception of ethics he developed in "Toward a Philosophy of the Act" a few steps further. The event is now a stage or phase, albeit a pivotal one, in the construction of a system of aesthetics. Bakhtin's chronotope represents the transcendence of the mechanistic workings of the physical universe. If we conceive of the utterance as a vector of movement as understood by physics, then the chronotope becomes Bakhtin's most kinetic concept in explaining the workings of discourse, a term explaining the shift of insentient matter from the inorganic to the living. In this regard, Bakhtin's indebtedness here to Bergson is especially significant, although the Russian thinker has abandoned the former's estheticized atomism for a more rigorously Kantian vision. The fundamental unity of the ethical and aesthetic, suggested but never elaborated in the earlier essay, is subtly reinforced here inasmuch as the faculty of sight represents judgment as well as cognition for Bakhtin. In this essay ethics have been thoroughly fused with aesthetics: true vision is only possible within the chronotope, where to see is indeed to be. All of this is cast in the form of a transubstantiation: the word has finally become flesh. In a sense, Bakhtin's corporeal logos is itself a chronotope within his criticism, a metatheoretical trope that brings together the various motifs of his ideas into mutual relation.

Concrete suggestions of this fusion and the moral and critical judgment that arise from it can, upon closer inspection, be gleaned from "Toward a Philosophy of the Act." There, as well as in the chronotope essay, the direct and correspondent relation between the enhancement of the agent's vision and the concretization of the act is mapped out, although in not so great detail as in the chronotope essay. A juxtaposition of certain passages makes the reverberation of diction between the two texts even clearer:

> Only the value of mortal man provides the standards for measuring the spatial and the temporal orders: space gains body [*uplotniaetsia*] as the possible horizon [*krugozor*] of mortal man and as his possible environment, and time possesses valuative weight and heaviness as the progression [*techenie*] of mortal man's life, where, moreover, the content of the temporal determination [*vremennogo opredeleniia*] as well as its formal heaviness possess the value of rhythmic progression [*techeniia ritma*]. ("Toward a Philosophy of the Act")[86]

> In the literary artistic chronotope, spatial and temporal indicators are fused [lit., "a fusion takes place" (*imeet mesto sliianie*)] into one carefully thought-out, concrete whole. Time, as it were, thickens, takes on flesh [*sgushchaetsia, uplotniaetsia*], becomes artistically visible; likewise, space becomes charged and responsive to the [lit., "is drawn into" (*vtiagivaetsia v*)] movements of time, plot [*siuzheta*] and history. This intersection [*peresecheniem*] of axes and fusion [*sliianiem*] of indicators characterizes the artistic chronotope. . . . The chronotope as a formally constitutive category determines to a significant degree the image [*obraz*] of man in literature as well. The image of man is always intrinsically chronotopic [*sushchestevnno khronotopichen*]. ("Forms of Time and the Chronotope")[87]

In both texts the contract between the actor and the act is reestablished through an epiphanic and life-giving moment. Bakhtin's imagery throughout these three passages is extraordinarily vivid and evocative. Thus, the traditional and Kantian conceptions of time and space become undermined, each taking on the properties of the other as they lose their identities in a kind of ontological cross-dressing: space becomes insubstantial as time acquires substance and weight. As portrayed in the chronotope essay in particular, time and space generate the ethical agent of the action in all of his or her autonomy and answerability. But for Bakhtin the chronotope represents more than merely the crossroads of human experience, the point at which the confluence of various individuals takes on the definite identity of a shared experience: it is a force that creates. Bakhtin is quite specific in indicating that the concretization takes place within the chronotope and is not the chronotope itself, which is actually the force that enables the embodiment he describes. Significantly, the concretization of such experience only occurs during a crypto-Chalcedonian interaction (*peresechenie, sliianie*) among various consciousnesses. In a distinctly christological formulation, Bakhtin asserts that humanity's iconic image is concretized by the convergence of two, often disparate, realms. Yet again, Bakhtin subtly echoes the paradigm of a life reaffirmed through the dynamic—and almost kinetic—operation of the Trinity.

The word or discourse in itself is too neutral a category to describe the kind of intensely dialogic and interactive activity that Bakhtin is trying to develop at this point of his career. The chronotope represents both a person and the transubstantive event that inveigles him or her; in a certain very real sense, the person *becomes* the event. In his essays from the early twenties to the late thirties we see Bakhtin in the process of developing a distinct theory of language that entails dialogue as its key principle. By the time of the chronotope essay, a considerable branching out has taken place from the term of discourse he planted in "Towards a Philosophy of the Act." Bakhtin cultivates the Johannine and incarnational subtext of *slovo* in "Author and Hero in Aesthetic Activity," a much longer essay that represents a continuation of the philosophical fragment. In this context it is useful to return to the essay "The Problem of Content, Material and Form in Verbal Art" (written immediately after the unfinished project examining the relation between author and hero in art), where Bakhtin elaborates on the metaphor of incarnation and embodiment as almost nowhere else in his work. There, he brings out its various features in a way that makes it impossible for any reader not to be reminded of the image of intersubjective transubstantiation that is depicted in John 1:14.

> The cognitive constituent moment illuminates, as it were, the aesthetic object from within; like a sober stream [*trezvaia struia*] of water, it mixes with the wine of ethical tension [*napriazheniia*] and artistic consummation. But it is very far from condensing and solidifying [*sgushchaetsia i uplotniaetsia*] to the point that it becomes a determinate judgment. Everything is recognized but not everything is identified in an adequate concept [*poniatie*].[88]

Immediately after this passage Bakhtin refers to this possibility of a life-giving awareness as "all-penetrating" (*vsepronikaiushchee uznanie*), a telling example of the recurring motif of Trinitarian *perichoresis* in Bakhtin's work. The image of the cognitive moment as a purification through the water mixed in with the wine of ethical stress and artistic completion is strongly suggestive not only of the rite of communion, but also the desert streams of baptismal water mentioned in the Scriptures (Isaiah 35:6, 41:17–18; Jeremiah 2:13). However, as in "Toward a Philosophy of the Act," Bakhtin shies away from the prospect of a realizable perfection.

This theological subtext of the divine word reaches the ne plus ultra of expression in Bakhtin's 1940 essay "From the Prehistory of Novelistic Discourse," where he adduces the Gospels and the church fathers as virtual archetypes of the refracted or double-voiced word: "The primary instance of appropriating another's discourse and language was the use made of the authoritative and sanctified use [lit., word (*slovo*)] of the Bible, the Gospels, the Apostles, the fathers and doctors of the church."[89] This statement represents something of a culmination of Bakhtin's theological allusions, and is obviously highly significant as a confirmation of the broad range of theological literature implicit in earlier essays such as "Toward a Philosophy of the Act" and "Discourse in the Novel." As far as the Johannine references are concerned, "Toward a Philosophy of the Act," *Problems of Dostoevsky's Art,* and Voloshinov's *Marxism and the Philosophy of Language* constitute stepping-stones to Bakhtin's later works; they are studies of language in which Bakhtin decisively consolidates his terms describing the transformation of consciousness that occurs as a result of dialogic interaction.

"Discourse in the Novel" was written at the end of Bakhtin's ten-year fallow period, during which his arrest, exile, and illness doubtless made scholarly work very difficult. Bearing in mind this gap in his career, there are surprisingly few differences in terminology between the essay about content and form and "Discourse in the Novel," and those that can be found are in fact small. The christological metaphor of incarnation from the word emerges as a structural but not necessarily thematic dominant of Bakhtin's theory of language in the thirties. One gets the distinct sense that Bakhtin's incipient theory of polyphony is not entirely at home in this metaphor, which (in its guise taken from the theology of the church fathers) posits, after all, the grounding of the obstreperous many and pullulating words in the unitary Word. One also senses from his essays of the twenties and thirties and the later "Problems of Speech Genres" (1952–53) that Bakhtin in fact sees the Stoicist sequence or historical manifestation of language as reversed: for him, the multitudinous and particularistic words come first, followed by a unitary language with definite (if not inflexible) stylistic norms. By turning this traditional bifurcation of language on its head, Bakhtin works as much against traditional interpretations of the logos of John 1:1–14 as he does with it; in his hands, the word made flesh is distinctly superior to its disembodied ancestor, an idea that, in the patristic context, would be regarded as an example of the heresy of Arianism. For Bakhtin the corporeality of the word is paramount. This ambivalence would stay with Bakhtin whenever he evoked the metaphor, which begs the question of its ultimate suitability for his hermeneutical needs. As this period in his work comes to a close, perhaps the better question to ask is whether Bakhtin deliberately chose this metaphor as something of a device of Brechtian alienation (*Verfremdung*) or Russian Formalist "making it strange" (*ostranenie*), drawing the reader's attention to phenomena usually taken for granted. Certainly his innovations over the Stoicist and Johannine conceptions of the generative logos call attention to themselves and the contexts in which they appear. The possibility that Bakhtin may be pointing to a deeper ambivalence in discourse itself becomes more distinct in his landmark work on Rabelais. In his earliest work, however (examined in the next chapter) there is less evidence of this possible irony.

Chapter Two

Answerability and Ethics: Toward a Philosophy of Activism

Im Anfang war die Tat.
—Goethe, *Faust.*

The Formalists are imprinted with the seal of overripe clericism. They are Johannites. For them "in the beginning was the Word." But for us in the beginning was the act: the word appeared only after [the act], like a shadow made of sound.
—Leo Trotsky, *Literature and Revolution* (1924)

IF IN HIS study of Dostoevsky and essays of the twenties and thirties Bakhtin foregrounds a congested intersection of the theological motifs of Trinitarian interpenetration, Chalcedonian bisected unity, and embodiment of discourse, their actual manner of interaction remains unclear. In this chapter the precise nature of the christological interrelational dynamic and the terms and images Bakhtin uses to characterize it will be examined in greater detail. Particularly revealing of Bakhtin's development and fine-tuning of his epistemological terminology are the two different extant drafts of his textual analysis of Pushkin's 1830 lyric "For the Shores of a Distant Homeland," a treatment he undertakes as an application and demonstration of his philosophy of the act. The first version of Bakhtin's reading of Pushkin's poem occurs at the end of the extant manuscript of "Toward a Philosophy of the Act" and the second as a fragment of the first chapter of "Author and Hero in Aesthetic Activity." A discernible shift of emphasis occurs between these two analyses of the same poem: in the later draft, Bakhtin gravitates toward an emphasis on the uniting or synthesis of theoretism and estheticism. Bakhtin is not interested in the displacement or replacement of phenomenology by theology but rather in the confluence of the two. With his rhetorical and structural use of the Trinitarian paradigm, his discussion of how ethics operate in the real world is at times reminiscent of new wine poured into old vessels. Whether or not the transfer of new spirits causes the vessels of doctrine to break is a separate issue, which I shall deal with later. For Bakhtin, ethics and phenomenology are one and constitute the theology of experience.

THE ACT: A CONTEXTUAL MAP

In spite of Bakhtin's fairly consistent use of terms and concepts, the essay "Toward a Philosophy of the Act" fundamentally remains a fragment, full of underexplained assumptions and undeveloped ideas. The essay represents something of a workshop for Bakhtin, a place where he tried to forge a single approach to deal with questions of morality and personal responsibility; while doing this, he tried to respond to polemics that had occurred over the course of the previous decade. "Toward a Philosophy of the Act" is the second extant work by Bakhtin; like "Art and Answerability," it appeared (albeit many years later) in an obscure corner of the print medium. The fifty-odd pages of the later essay were published in—of all places—a 1986 yearbook on technology and culture issued by the Soviet Academy of Sciences. In stark contrast to the lapidary clarity of the earlier essay, "Toward a Philosophy of the Act" is undoubtedly the most difficult and expositionally roughest essay in Bakhtin's entire output. As Bakhtin's pupil and memoirist Sergei Bocharov maintains in his preface and commentary, on the basis of its clear provenance from the same body of materials as "Author and Hero in Aesthetic Activity," the piece can be dated from the early twenties, although the precise circumstances in which Bakhtin undertook it are unknown. Apparently several pages are missing from the extant manuscript, most conspicuously in the beginning. The handwritten copy is reported to be in poor condition and a group of three editors indicate throughout the published piece their conjectural readings of illegible words. As explained by Bocharov, the title of the originally unnamed essay was provided by the editors in what they perceived to be Bahktin's central concern in the piece.[1]

In addition to providing this useful account of the textual situation, Bocharov offers his own appreciation of the essay, asserting that it contains in embryonic form all of Bakhtin's major subsequent ideas.[2] Although the categorical sweep of this statement is open to question (particularly from the perspective of the so-called prosaics approach to Bakhtin represented by Gary Saul Morson and Caryl Emerson), a close reading of this incomplete work reveals that it does contain certain ideas and terms that, by the end of the thirties, Bakhtin was to develop into a more or less continuous conceptual matrix. From 1919 to 1924, Bakhtin's focus shifted from ethics to aesthetics, culminating in an attempt (in "Author and Hero in Aesthetic Activity") to synthesize the two disparate disciplines.

After discussing the various ethical ramifications of aestheticism, however, Bakhtin does proceed to a wide-ranging and detailed critique of regnant conceptions of ethics. He makes a distinction between two conceptions of ethics, the material and the formal,[3] the former roughly corresponding to aestheticism (*estetisizm*) and pragmatism and the latter to Kantianism and theoretism (*teoretizm*) in its broader manifestations. Bakhtin adduces Hermann Cohen and Heinrich Rickert as prime exponents of neo-Kantianism and states that both they and the movement as a whole straddle these two groupings. In all of these instances and in spite of the myriad differences of approach between these two philosophical camps, each ethical system in question is crippled by the fact that its "ought" (*dolzhenstvovanie*) is activated by forces external to the act (99). Whether the determining forces be biological, psychological, or those of Kant's categorical imperative, the participant of the act (*uchastnik postupka*) is stripped of responsibility for his or her conduct because nothing is generated from within (*iznutri*) the parameters of the event (*sobytie*). On the other hand, the person who takes full cognizance and responsibility for his or her mental activity realizes that thought does have existential consequences, and that thought and action must be conceived as an ontological pairing. As Bakhtin explains, the person who thinks participatively (*uchastno*) does not separate his or her act from its product (95). For the truly responsible person both the specific act and its action upon the world must be considered as one. Opposed to this are the ethics of neo-Kantianism, which represent a jerry-built edifice, a system with pretensions to a grand synthesis whose various elements are, in fact, not sufficiently integrated into a whole. As shown in the previous chapter, the idea of an integration as concretization plays a crucial role in Bakhtin's conception of the relation between self and other. The varied theological motifs he uses in "Discourse in the Novel" reinforce the equivalence between structuring and concretization.

Just how the various elements of the ethical act should be combined is not programmatically stated by Bakhtin. Whether this lacuna in argumentation is attributable to textual loss or actual authorial dereliction cannot be said for certain. A point of departure for reconstructing Bakhtin's full argument must be located in his emphasis on the physicality of time and space, which at times is virtually transmogrified into an animate corporeality. As he states at the beginning of part 1, disparate segments (or "patches" [*otrezki*]) of time and space acquire a single valuative center (*edinyi tsennostnyi tsentr*) only from within a subject's fully engaged (or communing [*prichastnoi*]) life (126). For Bakhtin, ethics presume a physical setting, a fully illuminated purview of action and consciousness in which the subject participates. Bakhtin stresses above all that ethics belong to subjective experience yet are nonetheless reified and real, a position tantamount to an abolition of the dichotomy of subject and object. It is useful to think of Bakhtin's conception of ethics in terms not just of physical or materialist phenomena but more specifically as an almost physiological process. The ethical dimension is generated during the act of reading as a result of the interaction between author and reader; it is the precipitant emerging after a reaction between two chemical compounds or the protective shell reflexively secreted by a fragile organism. The emergence of ethics occurs in a manner similarly automatic and inevitable given the right set of material circumstances.

In Bakhtin's hands, the particular mechanics of this process take on special significance. Moreover, they are realized not through contemplation of proscriptive morality but through the process of becoming, an incremental evolution that may be understood as defining Bakhtin's conception of "act" (*postupok*). Within this framework, Bakhtin's prosaic and seemingly simplistic assertion in this essay that the only viable philosophy is a moral one (124) becomes more understandable: for him, ethics are always generated from within being and never imposed from above. Thus, in Bakhtin's scheme philosophy emerges as a paradox: as the ontology that reproduces morality, it is the establishment and reification of rules and maxims that are always in the process of becoming.

Like many of Bakhtin's terms, the act seems to obscure matters as much as illuminate them. As far as the category of the act itself is concerned, it is difficult to say what exactly he has in mind or to which particular situations his conception of ethics may apply; many of his discussions in this essay are dense, cryptic, and refer to unspecified or ambiguous antecedents. Under such circumstances the best one can do is to reconstruct the overall argument on the basis of pronouncements throughout the essay and to worry only later about the possible applications of such abstruse theory, assuming that there is an underlying unity of arguments. Fortunately, a close examination of the essay not only reveals that a continuous conceptual pattern does exist, but also that it is extraordinarily well wrought. Thus, what Bakhtin has in mind when he uses such frustratingly vague terms like "passive" (*passivnyi*) and "passivity" (*passivnost'*) becomes clearer when seen within the emerging figure in the carpet. The delineation of immediately discernible links in the network of Bakhtin's terms represent the primary goal of this chapter. The bulk of Bakhtin's philosophical and aesthetic terms in this essay gravitate toward the act; it is a centrifugal configuration that will figure prominently in Bakhtin's subsequent work in spite of the fact that he subsequently abandoned the concept of the act itself as the stage-setting realm of ethical behavior.

Bakhtin's understanding of *postupok* is twofold, denoting behavior in general while connoting conduct, which is the movement or direction of a particular actor that is implicit in the locution "postupat' *kuda*" (to proceed *where*). Bakhtin characterizes the ethically informed act as a motion to and from the domain of the participating subject. He elucidates the kinetic properties of the act toward the end of the extant introduction. "The answerable act or deed," he writes, "is the final result or summation, an all-around definite conclusion." This act "concentrates, correlates and resolves [*stigivaet, sootnosit i razreshaet*]" the dichotomies of "sense and fact, the universal and the individual, the real and the ideal" within a "*final context*" (emphasis in original) that is unitary (*edinyi*) as well as unique (*edinstvennyi*). By entering into this grounding context, they contribute to the formation of its answerable motivation (*otvestvenn[aia] motivatsi[ia]*). "The performed act," he continues, "constitutes a going out [*vykhod*] *once and for all* from within possibility as such into *what is once-occurent* [*edinstvennost' raz i navsegda*]." Bearing all this in mind, one has no reason to fear that the philosophy of the act will "revert to psychologism and subjectivism" (103; 28–29). In his efforts to delineate a workable paradigm of the uniqueness and internal coherence of the answerable act, Bakhtin throughout the essay uses various derivatives of the Church Slavonic stem *edin-* (one), which felicitously highlights totality as well as separateness. The single act becomes the stage on which the unified drama of existential meaning is played out; it is the rendezvous point for sense, fact, and the actor who is engaged with them. The mystique that Bakhtin conjures around the act is enhanced by his unorthodox conception of ethics. By asserting that theoretism and pragmatism are thoroughly subsumed into one another, Bakhtin subverts traditional assumptions about ethics: "This moment can be expressed only in the form of a description of the concrete architectonic relationship [or, interrelation (*vzaimootnosheniia*)], but such a description is still unknown in moral philosophy" (138; 75). Consistent with the spatialist apprehension of the act delineated in the long passage above, Bakhtin asserts that his goal is to "construct" (*[po]stroit'*) an approach to ethics that would be consonant with what he calls a *prima philosophia* (87).

The Soviet Byzantologist and Bakhtin specialist Sergei Averintsev notes in his annotation to the text that this first or primary philosophy is an allusion to book 6 (E) of Aristotle's *Metaphysics,* in which this philosophy is said to consist of a triumvirate of the theoretical sciences: mathematics, physics, and theology. But there is an epistemological hierarchy even within these three crowning branches of knowledge, since in fact Aristotle reasons that theology must be assigned the preeminent position because of the ubiquity of the Divine;[4] theology therefore becomes the hypostasis of philosophy. As we shall see, although this preeminence is not explicitly acknowledged by Bakhtin, his insistence on ethics as *structure* echoes Aristotle's classification of these disciplines into a hierarchical arrangement. The first philosophy attempts to describe "not the world produced by the responsible act or deed", but rather "the Being-as-event [*bytie-sobytie*] as it is known" to that act; it comes to grips with "the world in which that act becomes answerably aware of itself and is actually performed [*v kotorom on otvetstvenno sebia osoznaet i svershaetsia*]." Such a primary philosophy cannot be constructed in an a posteriori manner: inasmuch as its descriptive project in itself renders the act answerable, it eschews the redundant task of building "universal concepts, propositions and laws about this world of the [already] answerable act (the theoretical, abstract purity of the act)." The first philosophy is, above all, a description, a phenomenology of the world of the act. From this it follows that the event cannot be analyzed according to a system-oriented method; it can only be "participatively described [*uchastno opisano*]" (105; 31–32). According to Bakhtin, the actor is beset by a paradox: he or she must aggressively cultivate a receptiveness to experience. In other words, the subject must not merely linger in a desultory fashion over the particular and prosaic but must actively focus on them; only thus can the subject be attuned to the complexities of the experienced world and navigate around the sirens of theoretical generalizations. In a similar conceptual turn, a few years later in his 1929 *Paris Lectures* Husserl glossed his own renowned concept of intentionality as the intense observance of and obeisance to the currents of phenomena, an imperative through which the subject strives to "reflect accurately the concrete contents of experience, precisely as they are experienced."[5] Bakhtin implies that such negative capability and capacity for apperception is the likely fruit of much discipline and effort. Bakhtin replaces the theology of Aristotle's hierarchy with his own phenomenological conception of ethics as the summit of epistemological science.

The centrality of ethics to this essay is underscored in the projected architectonics of the essay itself. Toward the end of the introduction Bakhtin divides his essay into four parts. In his outline the first part is taken up by a phenomenological examination of the structure of reality and the subject participating in it, what he calls the architectonics of the real and actually experienced (*perezhivaemogo*) world and not the merely contemplated one (122). The second part approaches ethics from the specific vantage point of the participating subject rather than from the perspective of the act's product, result or reality in its given and untransformed state. The focus of the third part is on the ethics of politics and the fourth on religion. What has survived in the manuscript is only the first part of Bakhtin's project, and that in itself is treated in a plainly incomplete manner. However, what clearly emerges from his outline and the extant fragments of the essay is Bakhtin's attempt to move away from positivist conceptions of ethics toward one that is situational yet would provide for individual responsibility and free will.

After listing these divisions (and in a gesture toward fusing the essay's structure and content), Bakhtin goes on to imply that they are not merely interfaces of the work at hand, but also of the world at large: the architectonics of this world recall those of Dante and the medieval mystery plays. In both mystery plays and in tragedy "the action is set in intimate proximity to the ultimate bounds [*granitsam*] of Being [*bytiia*]" (122; 54). In a deft rhetorical stroke, Bakhtin draws a parallel between the last (*poslednii*) part of his essay and the peripheral borders (*poslednie granitsy*) of existence. Toward the end of the manuscript he suggests that his attempt to fully restore ethics to the individual act is tantamount to giving the moral teachings of Christianity a rigorous and finely tuned phenomenological rendering, noting that such an effort has never been successfully undertaken (138). The relation of the proposed four parts of Bakhtin's essay is not so much hierarchical—although it does contain an element of that—as it is differentiated according to function, evoking the image of an edifice grounded upon experience (phenomena) and religion (noumena) and buttressed by aesthetics and politics.

Having all the hallmarks of a work in progress, the prolixity and technicality of "Toward a Philosophy of the Act" make for few lapidary or epigrammatic statements. Nevertheless, some striking images and turns of phrase do make their way into the mind of the reader, who inevitably comes to regret that Bakhtin never reworked this essay as he did his studies of Dostoevsky and Rabelais. In "Toward a Philosophy of the Act" Bakhtin describes the assumption of ethical responsibility as having a "non-alibi" for oneself. His elaboration of this idea leads to other images that do not seem related to the imperative of truly taking responsibility for one's actions. A closer look at the etymology of the word "alibi" helps us get closer to what Bakhtin is trying to say here. A term modified from the Latin *albius* meaning "elsewhere" or "in another place," the word is used juridically in French and German as well as in English and Russian. Considering Bakhtin's knowledge of all these languages—and, in "Toward a Philosophy of the Act," the vividly spatial images he marshals in describing the interaction between the subject and the world at large—it is hard to believe that he did not bear in mind the literal meaning of the term. To be mentally as well as physically *in propria persona* and not elsewhere requires effort and activity; at several points throughout the essay Bakhtin implies that wishing to be someone or somewhere else is an unfortunate and all-too-natural tendency. Bakhtin metaphorically characterizes the answerable deed as the physical incarnation of thought, throwing it into sharper relief by juxtaposing it with its opposite: "But what is also possible is non-incarnated [*neinkarnirovannaia*] thought, non-incarnated action, non-incarnated fortuitous life as an empty possibility." A life lived on the assumption of "my alibi in Being [*v bytii*]"—a life dictated by the opposing principles of either self-destructive denial or overweening self-interest—may indeed be free as far as license and the fluidity of agency are concerned, but ultimately "falls away into indifferent [*bezrazlichnoe*] Being that is not rooted in anything." The thought that is not realized by action remains "unincarnated," an empty possibility and an unfulfilled promise.

Bakhtin goes on to elucidate, in his characteristically oblique way, the true nature of unincarnated, irresponsible thought: "Any thought that is not correlated with myself as the one who is obligatively unique [*kak dolzhenstvuiushche edinstvennym*] is merely a passive possibility [*passivnaia vozmozhnost'*]. It could or could *not* exist, it could be different: its being [*bytiia*] in my consciousness has nothing compellent, irreplaceable [*net nuditel'nosti, nezamenimosti*] about it." The "emotional-volitional tone" of this unincarnated and responsible [*neinkarnirovannaia i otvetstvennaia*] thought will inevitably express this poverty of individual responsiblity, this state of being "unincarnated in answerability." "The only thing that transforms [this unincarnated thought] into my answerable act or deed [*otvetstvennyi postupok*] is the referral of it into the unitary and once-occurrent [*v edinyi i edinstvennyi*] context of Being-as-event through an actual acknowledgement of my actual participation [*uchastnosti*] in the latter" (114–15; 43–44). To have an alibi or an excuse for one's actions means not only to lack a definite or rooted place in existence, but also to living speechlessly, which for Bakhtin means to have no awareness of value, either of one's own or of society at large. Of all these commonly unacknowledged possibilities, the last is the most galling and paradoxical: the retreat into the self in fact does not create a more clearly defined identity, but in fact leads to a blurring and dissolution of it. Not to have an alibi in life therefore means to come to an awareness of one's own rootedness in existence, which is also to reinforce and concretize that space around the self. Thus, on a deeper level of Bakhtin's argument, the metaphors of incarnation and non-alibi are related: when the self or subject is fully commensurate with itself it becomes utterly fixed in a particular space and consequently more vividly "there," both cognitively as well as physically. For Bakhtin, importance of consciousness (*soznanie*) cannot be underestimated: it has the power of either effecting a rebirth of one's life or of attenuating it into an ephemeral epiphenomenon. Bakhtin's image of incarnation represents the ethical activization of a particular life.

But there is something else in the passage above that would give further pause to any reader. Bakhtin's term "unincarnated thought" (*neinkarnirovannaia mysl'*) carries with it more semantic weight than is immediately apparent. Like *voploshchenie* (embodiment), the Latinism *inkarnatsiia* can also denote concretization or transubstantiation in both a religious and metaphorical sense, although it would tend to have a more philosophical flavor. Bakhtin plays on both terms and their connotations throughout the essay, particularly on *voploshchenie* and related terms also derived from the root *plot'* (flesh). Especially important in this essay is the opposition between incarnated and unincarnated or, analogously, active versus passive. Bakhtin nonetheless makes certain distinctions between the apparent synonyms *voploshchenie* and *inkarnatsiia.* Two pages later he states that the participatory and incarnated consciousness (*uchastnoe inkarnirovannoe soznanie*) can be thought of as narrowly subjective only when it is placed in opposition to the consciousness of culture as a self-sufficient entity (119). The way an individual consciousness is able to relate to culture at large is, according to Bakhtin, a complex process consisting of various and seemingly antithetical stages or steps. The following précis of Bakhtin's argument highlights his belief that the consolidation and reification of the self do not necessarily lead to solipsism or moral relativism. It is within the space of the last few pages of the fragmentary introduction of "Toward a Philosophy of the Act" that Bakhtin explains why such a fortified individual consciousness is morally responsible and not selfish.

This part of the essay begins with a rather stark and uncompromising vision of the interaction between self and the world at large. According to Bakhtin, it is in the nature of humankind to pay no heed to the individual. Although values (*tsennosti*) as such are quite real, humanity as an historic phenomenon is ultimately incomprehending and indifferent to any one of its members: "What does an 'affirmed context of values' [*utverzhdennyi kontekst tsennostei*] mean? It means the totality of values which are valuable not for one or another individual [*individuum*] and in one or another historical period, but for all historical mankind" (117; 47). Between the individual and human lies a daunting chasm of incommensurability: "But I, the unique I [*ia edinstvennyi*], must assume a particular emotional-volitional attitude toward all historical mankind: I must affirm it as really valuable [*tsennoe*] for me, and when I do so everything valued by historical mankind will become valuable for me as well." The so-called reified or affirmed context of values is real only in the most static of senses. By referring to values as aggregates (*sovokupnosti*) rather than ethical systems or worldviews, Bakhtin implies that culture viewed in itself without reference to the individual is ultimately never more than the sum of its parts. The aspectual verbal pair *utverzhdat'-utverdit'* (to affirm, confirm; consolidate) and the related past passive participle *utverzhdennyi* (affirmed) arguably play into the spatial metaphor already discussed, but in an unexpected way. Although the aspectual pair *utverzhdat'-utverdit'* in modern Russian means to affirm or solidify in an almost exclusively figurative sense, older usage permits employment of these verbs in the concrete sense of building or affixing one object to another. Certainly the derivational origin of these words from the Common Slavic **tverd* (hard) was at first productive only in the context of material realia and culture. One gets the distinct impression here that the values of culture without reference to the individual represent inert and lifeless matter. Even in a passage as brief as this one, Bakhtin's contradistinction between ethics as viewed from the perspectives of the individual and society is graphically sketched out: the affirmation of value-oriented contexts creates an ordered but brittle and inflexible social world.

In what follows, Bakhtin elaborates this metaphorical distinction of animate versus inanimate matter, the former representing the human agent and the latter the inert societal reality that encloses him or her. According to Bakhtin, the first thing to remember is that hackneyed abstractions such as "humanity" or "man" have little resonance for the incarnated consciousness; for such a person, the distinction between *I* and *Other* is far more important than such generalities. Notwithstanding the indifference of abstract humanity to its constituent members, the individual all the same cannot help feeling the need to integrate himself or herself into those collectively shared values. But once the subject attempts to do this, it becomes a disembodied spirit (*razvoploshchennyi dukh*), a being who has lost all connection to the real world. Humanity in general is a shibboleth, an empty category that strips the subject of his or her concrete and compelling relation to the world. "Man-in-general does not exist [*Net cheloveka voobshche*]; *I* exist and a particular concrete *other* exists—my intimate, my contemporary (social mankind), the past and the future of actual human beings (of actual historical mankind)." All these moments go into the formation of "my non-alibi in Being" (117; 47). In endeavoring to relate to ideological abstractions the incarnated consciousness becomes temporarily etherealized and unsubstantiated. It is only when the subject is able to say that he or she stands in an emotional-volitional relation to humanity (*stoiu k nemu*), that words about values begin to shine with the light of actual value. Once again, Bakhtin uses a metaphor of spatial and concrete reality to describe the subject's relation to the world.

Bakhtin goes on to emphasize that the disembodied consciousness is diametrically opposed to this ethically responsible and cognizant subject. For the disembodied and detached subject [*dlia razvoploshchennogo bezuchastnogo sub"ekta*], all other lives and deaths "may be equal" (117–18). The death of the individual has scant significance from the perspective of the aggregate of humanity. Bakhtin counterbalances both the values of the isolated individual and his or her overall worth as an actor to those of humanity as a whole; he is not asserting that the Hobbesian and Leviathan-like mass interests of humanity are intrinsically bad, only that their range of vision is severely limited. This is not to say that unethical conduct does not exist at the level of mass psychology, only that the individual who insists on relating exclusively to mankind in the aggregate is perforce someone who is utterly anesthetized to the impact of the death of any one individual. Distinctly different from the person who serves the idea or ideal of people is the one who understands his or her unique place among others and the possibility of personal involvement with them. Far from being self-involved or narcissistic, such a person is capable of the kind of personal commitment or sacrifice that forms the basis of any truly ethical conduct. In other words, for Bakhtin there is no such thing as sacrificing oneself for humankind without detriment to one's own being. Considering the time and place of the writing of this essay—during a civil war in a privation-ridden socialist country striving to unite itself—such a claim for the autonomy of the individual can only be seen as going against the deepest ideological grain of the period.

What is implied in this tightly wound chain of reasoning is sprung in the seemingly tangential comment placed in parentheses at the end of this paragraph: "One should remember that to live from within myself, from my unique place in Being does not yet mean that I live only for my sake. For it is only from my own unique place in existence that *self-sacrifice* is possible, that is, the answerable centrality of myself can be a *self-sacrificing* centrality" (Liapunov trans., 48). Thus, the person who claims to serve the greater interest at personal expense is, in fact, the truly amoral and egotistical agent in all of this. Whether Bakhtin soft-pedaled his moral critique of the ascetic ideal of ideological zealot because he thought that it would not be tolerated by publishers or because he had not finished developing the idea in the draft will probably never be known. With collectivism unrealized at the time of this writing and the New Economic Policy already under way, it is not wise to assume that Bakhtin was then opposed to state policy as he almost certainly was during the Stalin period. Quite clear, however, is Bakhtin's remarkable illustration of ethical theory in the vividly negative person of the disembodied (*razvoploshchennyi*) and (*bezuchastnyi*) unconcerned agent, who emerges as a ruthlessly leveling judge of human lives. To such a person, all living matter is indeed insubstantial and so much interchangeable and ultimately disposable flotsam and jetsam.

Although the equivalence of "disembodied" (*razvoploshchennyi*) with an ethically myopic vision and the opposition of both to the "incarnated" (*inkarnirovannaia*) life is quite clear, Bakhtin's treatment of these categories is more nuanced and less rigidly dualistic than at first might seem. For one thing, there is the morphology of the term *razvoploshchennyi:* the negational prefix *raz-* denotes that something was once embodied and reified but then converted back to its former state of insubstantiality; in contrast, the term *neinkarnirovanyi* ("unincarnated") that crops up earlier in the essay suggests that which has never before been given concrete or realized form. There is much to suggest that the idea (encapsulated by *razvoploshchennyi*) of a shuttling back and forth between two ontological states is crucial to any understanding of the essay. In the first of the last two excerpts quoted above, Bakhtin states that any approach to the world in all of its own uniqueness [*ko vesmu eduinstvennomu miru*] must begin from "my own unique place [*s moego edinstvennogo mesta*]," in other words with an awareness and acknowledgment of personal uniqueness. Subsequently (he asserts), I become disembodied (*razvoploshchennyi*) and lose my obligative relation [*dolzhnoe nuditel'noe otnoshenie*] with the world, which as a result loses any reality or significance for me. While this latter step of ethical cognition is definitely regarded by Bakhtin as pernicious when it is becomes an end in itself, here he also seems to imply that humanity as an aggregate cannot be ignored and that any value-oriented stance toward it must begin with precisely such an alienation from the world-at-large. What is alluded to here by Bakhtin is something of an ethical correlative to the Formalist *ostranenie* (German,

Verfremdung), whereby the appreciation of an aesthetic universe is regained by a temporary separation from it. A little more textual excavation in "Toward a Philosophy of the Act" strips away some of the more distracting excrescences of verbiage to reveal a coherent and logical genealogy of ethics. As Bakhtin sees it, the act of becoming truly ethical in word and deed can never be instantaneous and requires an intermediate step of estrangement from the self. In other words, the participatory subject must recognize collective humanity's demands, which is not to say that he or she consents to live by them. Such recognition in fact always constitutes a seismic shift in consciousness, a new mode of cognition that has the effect of decentering and deflating the subject's potentially solipsistic world.

Several lines below the second of the segments quoted above there occurs a passage that represents a turning point in what remains of this essay. Here Bakhtin describes how passive and active modes of behavior are always oriented within a particular culture and need to alternate with each other in order for the individual to become ethically responsible. From this description of the self's ethical engagement in the world it becomes abundantly clear that Bakhtin is not advocating a retreat from the human community:

> Theoretical cognition of an object that exists by itself, independently of its actual position in the once-occurrent world from the standpoint of a participant's unique place, is perfectly justified. But it does not constitute ultimate cognition; it constitutes only an auxiliary, technical moment of such ultimate cognition. My abstracting from my own unique place in Being, my *as it were* disembodying of myself [*moe* kak by *razvoploshchenie*], is itself an answerable act or deed that is actualized from my own unique place, and all knowledge with a determinate context (the possible self-equivalent givenness of Being) that is obtained in this way must be incarnated by me [*dolzhno byt' inkarnirovano mnoiu*], must be translated into the language of participative (unindifferent) thinking, must submit to the question of what obligation the given knowledge imposes upon me—the unique me—from my unique place. That is, it must be brought into correlation with my own uniqueness or singularity on the basis of my non-alibi in Being and in an emotional-volitional tone. Thus knowledge of the content of the object-in-itself becomes knowledge of it *for me*—becomes a *cognition [uznaniem] that answerably obligates me* (118; 48–49).

Earlier in this segment of the essay Bakhtin established a correlation between theoretism and the natural and social sciences. Now Bakhtin explicitly connects theoretism—which is clearly what he has in mind by referring to the theoretical cognition of an object (*[t]eoreticheskoe poznanie predmeta*)—to the tendency (delineated in the preceding passage) of some people toward generalizations in which humanity and its attendant values (*tsennosti*) are viewed as a single entity at the implicit expense of the individual. What Bakhtin is saying about theoretism is rather interesting and, at first blush, unexpected.

The earlier evaluation of theoretism as pernicious was a veritable straw to grab at for readers struggling through this text. According to Bakhtin here, however, the theoretical *does* have its place in the subject's efforts to get its bearings in a bewildering and tumultuous world: it serves as a bridge linking the personal to the public that, however flimsy it may be, it has no choice but to cross. In other words, theoretism becomes calamitously deluding only when taken to an extreme. Bakhtin suggests as much earlier when he states that the faculty of critical reason is indispensable to the unitary subject's [*edinstvennogo sub"ekta*] moral orientation of itself within the event of unitary being [*v sobytii edinstvennog bytiia*] (91).

By far the most revealing connection that Bakhtin makes in this segment is between theoretism and alienation. As he explains it, although abstracting myself from my unique place in the world certainly represents a disembodiment, it too is a responsible and answerable act. Crucial here and tricky to render into English is the braking effect of the italicized *"as it were [kak by]"* (suggesting not only the "as it were" of Liapunov's translation, but also "something of" or "presumptive") before the term of disembodiment (*razvoploshchenie*). Why this qualified, *supposed,* or somehow mitigated disembodiment should in itself constitute a responsible act is, at first glance, extremely confusing in light of Bakhtin's previous characterization of disembodiment as an evisceration of ethical being. The statement becomes comprehensible only when the previous discussion about disembodiment is scrutinized more closely. There, Bakhtin states that the disembodied and unconcerned subject [*dlia razvoploshchennogo i bezuchastnogo sub"ekta*] is someone to whom all deaths *could be* of equal or commensurable significance. Although the qualifier in the earlier statement is not highlighted by Bakhtin, it is no less important than the *kak by* in the later one. Bakhtin is saying in both passages that disembodiment is not a final and irrevocable act and that, in fact, it is necessary in helping the individual come to terms with culture and society. In the latter of the two longer quotations above he asserts that the use of theoretical thought is perfectly justifiable as long as it is relegated to the service function of providing a "technical moment" leading to a higher form of knowing and is not perceived as an epistemological *summa* in itself. This "technical moment" is pure form, a lifeless and highly schematic structure: if it is recognized as such, it provides a cleared and raised deck or stage that affords a more integrated and panoramic view of knowledge, one that takes in both the theory of the social and natural sciences and the aesthetics of art. But to linger impassively on that purview of pure form—to render it an end in itself—results in emptiness and moral indifference.

At this point of our textual analysis it is useful to summarize the aspects of Bakhtin's conception of ethics that have been covered so far. Two approaches to knowledge have predominated in the worlds of learning and the arts, theoretism or theoretical cognition (*teoretizm; teoreticheskoe poznanie*) and aestheticism. While this dichotomy may be valid as an epistemological point of departure, if strictly enforced and if each category is cultivated to the point of monstrous overdevelopment, they result in a fundamentally passive attitude (*passivnost'*) toward values in a culture. Granted, when we first encounter certain principles there is a period in which our attitude toward them must be somewhat passive, insofar as we have not yet made sense of them by contextualizing them into our own lives. Nonetheless, although passivity does not denote a state of actual immorality, it does describe one of ethical apathy. Passivity attains its apotheosis in disembodiment (*razvoploshchenie*), which occurs when the socially generalizing tendencies of theoretism gain the upper hand. When this happens, however, one of two things may subsequently transpire. The first possible outcome is that the subject remains stuck in this state of ethical disembodiment or alienation, which means that he or she comes to see value solely in terms of abstract principles and not human lives. To be frozen in such a stage is to see the relentlessly structural edifice of theoretical knowledge as an end in itself, which is (to paraphrase Dostoevsky) to take a chicken coop for the Crystal Palace.[6] Writing in the aftermath of the Russian Civil War when thousands perished or gave their own lives for inflexibly held political principles, it is easy to see why Bakhtin was preoccupied by this particular ethical dilemma, the resonances of which are unmistakable in certain parts of "Toward a Philosophy of the Act." The second possible outcome is considerably more hopeful. The individual comes to understand general principles by going through a period of ethical readjustment during which he or she becomes *temporarily* disembodied, alienated, and passive. Either because the essay was never finished or due to a loss of a part of the manuscript, suggested by Bakhtin but unfortunately not elaborated by him is that the subject somehow manages to return to his or her incarnated or embodied self. It is only in this second scenario of multiple cognitive transformation that disembodiment can be regarded as a responsible (*otvestvennyi*) act.

The conception that remains somewhat undefined from this précis is that of "activeness" (*aktivnost'*). Although it presumably represents the opposite of *passivnost'* and thus brings about the embodiment or incarnation of values in the subject, its actual operation has not yet been directly observed. To be sure, Bakhtin does use the term more sparingly than *passivnost'*, and in contexts that are less rigorously explanatory. Nevertheless, it plays a role in Bakhtin's ethics that is no less important than that of *passivnost'*. From Bakhtin's actual use of this term it becomes eminently clear that he indeed describes the category in terms of images of embodiment. In Bakhtin's discussion, however, some of the nuances of *aktivnost'* are quite peculiar to itself and cannot be reductively thought of as characteristics that are simply antipodal to those of *passivnost'*. Before turning to this next term, however, it might be useful to meditate on Bakhtin's conception of embodiment or incarnation. Interestingly, the substantive *inkarnatsiia* never occurs in the text although *voploshchenie* (embodiment) and the verb *voploshchat'(sia)* (to embody) do. An examination of these terms and the differences among them is a necessary prelude to any analysis of Bakhtin's conception of activism or "activeness."

BAKHTIN AND KANT'S CATEGORICAL IMPERATIVE

Many earlier passages in the essay make a great deal more sense if taken in light of the symbiotic dynamic between ethical passivity and theoreticism outlined above. In all of these passages the move from a passive ethical stance to one that is more active is inevitably accompanied by certain images and metaphors of space. The following paragraph from the first few extant pages of the text brings all of the oppositional concepts discussed above into vital interaction. Kant's philosophy is presented here as the exemplar of the theoretical method toward ethics, and arguably he is the philosopher whose presence is most deeply felt throughout this essay. Here Bakhtin places him in the midst of a pitched battle:

> That my answerable self-activity [*aktivnost'*] does not penetrate [*pronikaet*] inside the content/sense aspect of a judgment seems to be contradicted by the fact that it is the *form* of a judgment (the transcendent [*transtsendentnyi*] moment in the makeup of a judgment) which constitutes the moment of our reasoning's self-activity, i.e., that it is *we* who produce the categories of synthesis. We shall be told that we have forgotten Kant's Copernican achievement. Yet is it really the case that transcendent self-activity is the historical and individual self-activity of my performed act, the self-activity for which I am individually answerable? No one, of course, will claim something like that. The discovery of an *a priori* element in our cognition did not open a way out from within cognition, i.e., from within its content/sense aspect, into the historically individual, actual cognitional act; it did not surmount their dissociation and mutual imperviousness [*ikh razobshchennosti i vzaimnoi ne pronitsaemosti*], and hence one was compelled to think up a purely theoretical *subiectum* for this transcendent self-activity, a historically non-actual *subiectum*—a universal consciousness, an epistemelogical *subiectum.* But, of course, this theoretical *subiectum* had to be embodied [*dolzhen byl . . . voploshchat'sia*] each time in some real, actual, thinking human being, in order to enter (along with the whole world immanent to him *qua* object of his cognition) into communion [*priobshchit'sia*] with the actual, historical event of Being as just a moment within it (86; 6).

Noticeable again is the component of movement in Bakhtin's metaphor of space. As he puts it, the problem with Kantianism is that its profound rationalism renders ethics far too mechanical, if not static. Kant's discovery of the a priori trascendental element in our understanding did not open up a channel connecting the realm of ideas as they are subjectively experienced and the empirical and historic world as it is actually lived. What we need is access into the historically and individually experienced act (*v istoricheski-individual'nyi poznavatel'nyi akt*) from inside [*iznutri*] our subjective understanding. In other words, rather than generalizing from a particular situation to see if a projected action would be ethical for other times, places, and people (as Kant does with his categorical imperative), one has to recognize the utter contingency and uniqueness of both the situation and the subject trapped in it. Certainly nothing could be farther from Kant's belief in moral absolutes than this situationist approach to ethics, which some might argue is no ethics at all. For all of its rationalist insistence on moral absolutes, Kant's categorical imperative is at least potentially applicable to particular situations; it is not at all clear how one could come up with an ethical decision from Bakhtin's insistence on the norm-disrupting flux of concrete reality and not fall into despair.

As will shortly become evident, Bakhtin's attitude toward Kant's moral philosophy is most complicated in terms of indebtedness and dissent. His respect for the philosopher is palpable in his reference in the passage above to Kant's Copernican deed of postulating transcendence as morally active. Bakhtin faults Kant, however, for conceiving of this transcendence as something of a renunciation of historic reality by maintaining a strict and, for all practical purposes, insurmountable barrier between the content or meaning of an act and its empirical and cognitive manifestation; elsewhere in the essay he directly attacks the idea of the categorical imperative as representing nothing but law in all of its formally pure but contentless manifestation.[7] But perhaps it is unfair to assume that Bakhtin is trying to forge here a practical philosophy in the same way that Kant explicitly does: there are indications that he is simply engaging in a descriptive account of the circumstances under which truly ethical decisions come about, a phenomenology of the act. Bakhtin's avowed interest in Bergson and Husserl makes a great deal more sense in light of his indirect approach to ideas, through experience. It would therefore be better to examine more closely *how* Bakhtin characterizes experience rather than *why*.

As implied by the doublet "dissociation and mutual imperviousness [*razobshchennost' i vzaimnaia nepronitsaemost'*]" in the passage above, one can see that Bakhtin characterizes the boundary separating thought from experience as something of an estranging chasm or a mutually impenetrable barrier. Diametrically opposed to this metaphysical stalemate is the brief scenario that Bakhtin sketches out at the end of this paragraph, which can be summarized thus. In practice, of course, every so-called theoretical subject has to become embodied (*voploshchat'sia*) in a live and thinking person so that the latter can join (*priobshchit'sia*) the historical and event-oriented being or existence (*istoricheski-sobytiinoe bytie*). Although these two categories represent disparate realms of existence, they do not exclusively divide up among themselves the entire knowable universe. In the last (and extremely convoluted) sentence Bakhtin delineates a third category, that of the subject (*sub"ekt*). Particularly notable here is the imagery Bakhtin uses to describe the bridge formed between the individual and the world. However, even more significant in this context is that the subject, the world of being that is the object of his or her immediate cognition, and the actual and event-oriented world all interact with one another when that subject becomes "embodied." Once again, we are confronted with a triad in Bakhtin's epistemology in which the subject transcends the solipsistic limits of individual experience by traversing or somehow interacting more fundamentally with the multiple levels of its personal experience, a fusion of self and phenomena that serves as an intermediate or mediating step toward coming to terms with reality.

In "Toward a Philosophy of the Act" Bakhtin makes certain distinctions among the closely related terms of *voploshchat'sia, priobshchit'sia* and the oft-used *prichastnyi* that are crucial for reconstructing his conception of ethics. The relationship between these terms is complex in the sense that they sometimes represent cognitive processes or transformations that are at odds with one another. *Voploshchat'sia* and *voploshchenie* is a case in point. Although in the following passage from much later in the essay Bakhtin points up the provenance of the latter term from *plot'* and echoes his use of it in the earlier discussion of Kant, here *volposhchenie* represents a more qualified ethical victory for the subject. Bakhtin precedes this passage with a discussion of the pathos that informs most conceptions of ethics, which assume an incommensurability between the world and the act of the subject. It is in these conceptions that "the living, compelling, and inescapable uniqueness of our actual life is diluted with the water of merely thinkable empty possibility." The consciousness laboring under these received ideas lives an attentuated life, one in which "[l]oving corporeality [*liubiashchaia plot'* (?) *Ed.*]" is declared to be utterly secondary and ephemeral, "valid only as a moment of infinite matter, towards which we are indifferent, or as an exemplar of *Homo sapiens*, or as a representative of [one's own particular] ethics, or as an embodiment of the abstract principle of the Eternal Feminine" (120; 51). The specifics of these statements interlock most revealingly with Bakhtin's evaluation of Kant quoted earlier. Important to bear in mind is Bakhtin's use of the term "theoretical subject" (*teoretichekskii sub"ekt*) from the polemic with Kant; it is a term that not only means theoretical subject in the sense of the moral agent speculatively posited by Kant, but also the person who is inclined toward what Bakhtin calls theoretism, the epistemological tendency to see certain set principles and absolutes as the only real values. It should also be recalled that there Bakhtin implies that such a subject will become embodied in some kind of actual and real experience whether he or she likes it or not. A similar situation seems to apply in the passage above.

But there is considerably more to this passage than merely a recapitulation of previous concerns. Here the flesh that is active with love is perceived by theoretism to be only a fleeting moment like any other, one that may be remarkable and more memorable than others but ultimately eclipsed and negated by the awareness of human experience as a classifiable and finite phenomenon, limited by mortality. That in the passage above Bakhtin is contemplating theoretism is signaled by the reference to humanity in generic terms, as *homo sapiens*. As has already been shown, Bakhtin explicitly connects this argument (with its pivotal use of the Latin term) to theoretism at another point of the essay: "[t]he totality of universal or general knowledge, on the other hand, defines man in general (as *Homo Sapiens*). That he is mortal, for example" (117–18; 47–48). All of these terms and arguments made in similar contexts throughout the essay refract through one another, ultimately projecting a single and clearly defined picture that can be described as the following: although embodiment (*voploshchenie*) is indeed an important concept, it does not represent the final stage or apogee that an individual can attain in his or her ethical development.

In this regard it is useful to recall Bakhtin's previous discussion of disembodiment in which he defines that reversive process as inevitable and even necessary whenever the individual tries to come to ethical terms with more than one other person; implied by Bakhtin in that formulation is that there exists a next step beyond a mere re-embodiment (or, as it would be put in Russian with the double meaning or reincarnation, *perevoploshchenie*). In what follows after the last excerpt quoted above, Bakhtin specifies what the next phase may be. When we reduce our lives to that of "man in general," we brutally equate our selves with something that is really nothing more than "one of the manifestations of the world's life." And yet this urge for dehumanizing abstraction is not without a certain service function. By recognizing such social imperatives as subjective in origin and not dictated by reality itself, we free ourselves to act from a position of truly independent agency: "[A]ll we need to do is to incarnate answerably [*otvetstvenno inkarnirovat'*] this very act of our thinking to its ultimate conclusion—to undersign it—and we shall turn out to be actual participants [*deistvitel'no prichastnymi*] in Being-as-event from within it, from our own unique place" (120; 51). Crucial here is the distinction that Bakhtin draws between incarnation and embodiment. The former is the fullest flowering of the act in all of its ramifications whereas the latter represents a partial realization of the act. When we incarnate rather than merely embody the act in our lives we put our signature on it (*podpisat'sia pod nim*), which is to say that it in a certain sense has the stamp of our individuality on it. But individuality does not mean absolute free license: we realize our individuality only when we become an integral part of a particular event. This event (*sobytie*) is therefore something of a "co-being," expressed in the very morphology of the Russian word as a fusion of the subject with being (*so-bytie*). In an earlier segment, Bakhtin emphasizes the obligative and binding nature of the signature that is placed under the truly responsible act: "[i]t is not the content of an obligation that obligates me, but my signature below it—the fact that at one time [*edinozhdy*] I acknowledged or undersigned the given acknowledgment" (110–11; 38).[8] Embodiment (*voploshchenie*) refers only to the change that an individual undergoes when he or she becomes consciously aware of the fact that all human lives are different; the actual deed of ethically integrating with others follows after this awareness, and is described by Bakhtin as both a partaking (suggested by *prichatnyi*) and an incarnation.

As Bakhtin says elsewhere in the essay—and in his inimitably prolix way—the act represents a genuine joining or communion (*deistvitel'noe prichashchenie*) that can be found in the categories of the participatory and active experiencing [*uchastno-deistvennogo perezhivaniia*] of the concrete uniqueness [*konkretnoi edinstvennosti*] (91). For Bakhtin it is not the reification of the individual that is ethically essential but the conjunctive union of him or her with others. With the movement of the metaphorically marked concepts of incarnation and communion to the forefront of "Toward a Philosophy of the Act," the christological subtext becomes more pronounced.

Traces of this subtext become more distinct when we cast a glance back to the curious yoking of the terms of disembodiment and mutual impenetrability (razobshchennost 'i vzaimnaia nepronitsaemost'). The correlations here between the topoi of Trinitarian interpretation (perichoresis [*vzaimoproni-knovenie*]) and terms such as *vzaimnaia nepronitsaemost* (mutual impenetrability) above are quite clear; previous allusions to the concept outlined in the introduction and the terms *voploshchat'sia* and *priobshchit'sia* in this passage with their secondary meanings of incarnation and communion throw the christological metaphor into even sharper relief here. Nonetheless, some may argue that Bakhtin's preoccupation with the particulars of experience notwithstanding, this entire triadic configuration of theoretism, aestheticism, and the subject is utterly chimerical and sterile from the perspective of practical ethics. In point of fact, Bakhtin's goal in this essay is more to illustrate the genesis of ethics than to provide a guide for conduct. The best way to achieve this goal is by breaking the Procrustean beds of philosophical and theological discourses and assembling from their fragments a new model for understanding experience.

BAKHTIN, SOLOVYOV, AND THE ETHICS OF AGENCY

The revision and extension of Orthodox theology into the disciplines of philosophy and ethics is one of the hallmarks of the "God-seeking" movement of Russian religious philosophy. Caryl Emerson has suggested that this movement as a whole and Vladimir Solovyov in particular had considerably influenced Bakhtin's conception of ethics.[9] In a otherwise straightforward encyclodepia entry on Kant that he wrote for the 1895 Brockhaus-Efron encyclopedia, Solovyov expresses particular approval of the categorical imperative's function as a rule that establishes a "kingdom of goals [*tsarstva tselei*]," one that brings about a "systematic conjoining of different rational beings by means of general laws that define their interaction [*vzaimodeistvie*]."[10] Solovyov believes that a modified version of Kant's categorical imperative could play an important role in bringing about a more organic and communal understanding of the rule of law, establishing a heavenly kingdom on earth. Not surprisingly, Russian nationalist interpretors of Solovyov have been especially intrigued by his redaction of Kant, rendering his version of the categorical imperative as something only accessible to the Russian people with their tradition of communality or *sobornost'*.[11] A particularly striking example of a christological vision of ethics comes from Solovyov's 1884 essay *The Spiritual Foundations of Life* (*Dukhovnye osnovy zhizni*). There he insists upon the image of Christ as a touchstone for morality in a way that least of all recalls such traditional hortatory guides as Thomas à Kempis's *Imitation of Christ.* Like Bakhtin, Solovyov defines morality in terms of the act (*postupok*). According to Solovyov, before deciding on an action, we need to elicit in ourselves the "moral image of Christ" as a check for our conscience (*proverka sovesti*), asking the following questions: Is this an action that He would perform or approve of? And would its completion (svershenie) consequently receive His blessing?[12] Solovyov's rule of thumb is clearly a christological reformation of Kant's categorical imperative. Kant formulated the moral axiom of the categorical imperative in his *Grundlegung zur Metaphysik der Sitten* (1785). As the German philosopher defines it, the rule consists of the following. Before embarking on a act within a particular situation, speculatively extend or apply it as a general law and see if it retains its positive moral value in different times and situations; if it does, the action can be deemed moral.

That Solovyov had Kant in mind when he wrote this becomes clearer when taken in the context of other works by the Russian writer. An examination of Solovyov's article on Kant is particularly revealing in this regard. In this article, the bulk of the section devoted to Kant's moral philosophy, is disproportionately taken up with a detailed summary of the categorical imperative.[13]

As important as that concept is for Kant, it does not constitute the whole of his moral teaching. Solovyov treats Kant's attitude toward religion in this same section, emphasizing not so much the pietism of Kant's background in its confluence with eighteenth-century rationalism as the particular importance of the image of Christ in his philosophy. Solovyov emphasizes the role of intercessor that Christ plays in mediating between the sufferings of the just man and those of mankind as a whole.[14] In other words, Christ becomes the crucial link uniting the individual to humanity as a whole, the incarnated *logos* emerging as the source of Kant's categorical imperative as well as of Solovyov's own (more explicitly christological) version of it. The resonances of this view of Kant to Solovyov's own philosophy of universal interconnectedness of "all-unity" or "all-oneness" (*vseedinstvo*) is quite audible both in his statement about the establishment of community through the categorical imperative and in his remarks about the moral image of Christ. Solovyov attempts to leaven what he see as the somewhat dry legalism of Kant's categorical imperative with a measure of organic communality in the form of the christological interdwelling of consciousnesses; he envisions soteriology as being in equal measure ethical and mystical. Bakhtin is likewise attracted to Kant's idea, stating that it "does include moments that are valid." Nonetheless, although he concedes that it "determines the performed act as a universally valid law," in its capacity as a law it is "devoid of a particular, positive content: law as such, in itself, or the idea of pre-legality, i.e., legality itself [*zakonnost'*] is the content of law" (100; 25). Both Bakhtin and Solovyov saw it necessary to respond to Kant, much as Russian Symbolist and Acmeists felt it necessary to wrestle with the ghosts of Pushkin and his pleiad in writing their own poems.

Between Solovyov and Bakhtin in "Toward a Philosophy of the Act" there are two striking similarities. First, the terminology: for Bakhtin as well as Solovyov the performance and completion (*svershenie; sovershit'sia*) of the isolated act (*postupok*) is crucial to any correct understanding of ethics; second, Bakhtin also implies that this ethics, in its fully realized and considered state, is compatible with Christian morality. Both Bakhtin and Solovyov have, moreover, a problematical relation with the Kantian legacy, criticizing it for its rationalism while availing themselves of the structural lever of an imperative that is obviously closely related to Kant's. As Bakhtin explains toward the end of the manuscript of "Toward a Philosophy of the Act," the interrelation between *I* and *Other* that informs every moral act is inadequately described by the neo-Kantian approach to ethics but already evident in the altruism of Christian morality (138). This statement, occurring several pages into part 1 and at the end of the extant manuscript, offers direct, if regrettably abbreviated, testimony to Bakhtin's assumption of an eventual convergence of ethics and theology. For Bakhtin, the seemingly incompatible realms of ethics and the protean particulars of daily experience that make up phenomenology are capable of a convergence in a modified version of the Christian ideal.

The link between Solovyov and Bakhtin becomes clearer only after a deeper excursus into the latter's conception of ethics. Many of the issues revolving around personal accountability are abundantly evident in Bakhtin's essay, only taken several steps further. For Bakhtin, the full acceptance of personal responsibility for one's actions means not to have an alibi or excuse for oneself. In "Toward a Philosophy of the Act" Bakhtin elevates the category of "non-alibi in being" to something of a reverse of Kant's categorical imperative: instead of basing any action on the speculation of someone else's doing it, one should acknowledge the total contingency and unrepeatable nature of one's actions within a particular point in time. As Bakhtin explains however, this realization about the uniqueness of one's experience, does not give way to relativism or moral lassitude. Here Bakhtin shuttles back and forth between the act as a unity and as an event *sans pareil,* concepts that are felicitously conflated in the Russian adjective *edinstvennyi* (single, sole, unique) and whose interrelation is almost impossible to render adequately in English:

> What underlies a unity of the answerable consciousness is not a principle as a starting point, but the fact of an actual acknowledgment of one's own participation in unitary Being-as-event [*svoei prichastnosti k edinomu bytiiu-sobyvtiiu*], and this fact cannot be adequately expressed in theoretical terms, but can only be described and participatively experienced. Here lies the point of origin of the answerable deed and of all the categories of the concrete, once-occurrent, and compelling thought [*konkretnogo edinstvennogo nuditel'nogo dolzhenstvovaniia*]. I, too, *exist* [*ia esm'*] actually—in the whole and assume the obligation to say *this* word. I, too, participate in Being in a once-occurrent and never repeatable manner [*prichasten bytiiu edinstvennym i nepovtorimym obrazom*]: I occupy a place in once-occurent Being that is unique and never repeatable, a place that cannot be taken by anyone else and is impenetrable [*nepronitsaemoe*] for anyone else. In the given once-occurrent point where I am now located, no one else has ever been located in the once-occurrent time and once-occurrent space of once-occurrent Being. And it is around this once-occurrent point that all once-occurent Being is arranged in a once-occurrent and never-repeatable manner. That which can be done by me can never be done by anyone else. The uniqueness or singularity of present-on-hand Being is compellingly obligatory. This fact of my *non-alibi in Being,* which underlies the concrete and once-occurrent ought of the answerably performed act, is not something I come to know of and cognize, but is something I acknowledge and affirm in a unique or once-occurrent manner (111–12; 40).

Bakhtin describes the uniqueness of the individual and his or her experience in terms that are vividly spatial. The actor or agent of the action occupies (*zanimaiu . . . nakhozhus'*) a unique, unrepeatable, and irreplaceable spot, point, or location (*mesto . . . tochku*) in existence, one that cannot be penetrated (*nepronitsaemoe*) or truly understood by another and around which sprawls unique existence or being (*raspologaetsia vse edinstvennoe bytie*). Developing the spatial metaphor more subtly, Bakhtin links contingency with this uniqueness in his assertion that one's non-alibi in existence forms the basis of, or literally underlies ("*lezhit* v osnove" [my emphasis]), the concrete and unique obligation. The spatial metaphor is, in fact, so strong here that even time becomes absorbed by space. The single moment of existence is, above all, a point and *space* in time.

In analyzing this passage (like many others), the reader gets the distinct impression that a great deal is suggested but at the last moment left unsaid. Bakhtin's relentless iteration of words of clear Church Slavonic and old Russian provenance such as the most conspicuous *esm'* ([I] am) and (again) variants of *edinstvennyi* (unique; unitary) gives a distinct oracular tone to the whole passage. At first glance, it would now seem we have come up against the first glaring inconsistency in Bakhtin's terminology and argument. Unlike the earlier passages where he sings the praises of an existence or way of life integrated with others, here he seems to be affirming the other extreme, the utter incommensurability of one human life with another. One need only to compare the *vzaimoproniknovennost'* (interpenetrability) that is implicitly raised as an ideal elsewhere with the zone Bakhtin describes here as "impenetrable" for others (*nepronistaemoe dlia drugogo mesto*)—the adjective of which is clearly a derivational cousin of the other term—to realize the extent to which Bakhtin consistently stresses an ethical equivalent of Trinitarian *perichoresis*. Thus, to some it may appear that Bakhtin wavers in the essay between espousing integration into humankind or asserting a presumably sad reality of mutual and unsurmountable alienation. In fact, however, impenetrability is not itself a negative category for Bakhtin: if anything, the imperviousness of my place in Being ensures the preservation of my identity. This vision of the valorized subject is quite distinct from that of Solovyov, who in one of his most famous essays turns Nietzsche on his head by asserting that individual perfection and divinization result in the dissolving of the ego, its grounding in the "all-oneness" (*vseeinstvo*) of the cosmos.[15] Bakhtin, on the other hand, argues for the coherence of the subject in its interrelation with the Other. His christological trope of intersubjective participation as both communal and communion-like (strongly suggested by the terms *prichasten* and *prichastnost'*) posits a resultant embodiment or reification; interestingly, it is the participants themselves who become transubstantiated, and without the aid of an externally existent divine hypostasis.

At this point one senses the strongly existential bent of Bakhtin's thought in its earliest phase. Although existentialism as a movement did not exist at the time Bakhtin wrote this, the affinities here are distinct and lend credence to the view (expressed well before the posthumous publication of the essay) that

Bakhtin anticipated it. Particularly telling in this regard is Bakhtin's elaboration of the individual's (as well as individual) experience as a point of departure toward larger epistemological questions. According to Bakhtin, ethical and political thinkers cannot come to grips with the uniqueness of individual experience by using theoretical terms (*teoreticheskie terminy*). Since earlier in the essay Bakhtin explicitly identifies theoretism with philosophy and the natural sciences (82), he does seem to be grappling with precisely the kind of all-embracing positivism that Lenin and Gershenzon (among many others from various segments of the Russian political spectrum) fought against. Gary Saul Morson has argued that "Toward a Philosophy of the Act" is the touchstone of Bakhtin's achievement: there more than anywhere else Bakhtin voices skepticism toward the ideology of philosophical and political world-views that are all-embracing and reductionist, attacking scholarly approaches to experience that clearly go under the rubric of theoretism.[16] While Bakhtin's criticism of sweeping generalizations that claim to comprehend the variety of experience is quite real, it cannot be an indictment of system-building as such for the simple reason that it, too, clearly represents an interpretive structure. This fact is perhaps obscured by the essay's nonlinear and, at times, seemingly associative manner of exposition. However, the reader has only to compare one part of the essay with almost any other to realize that, in spite of his divagations, Bakhtin consistently operates within a single conceptual framework.

Surprisingly, none of this emphasis on the individual subject leads to solipsism. According to Bakhtin, in order to truly recognize and realize one's individuality one must act: only then will the subject and his unique being (*edinstvennoe bytie*) truly join. What is given in any life is the fact of existence, a state that requires no effort or work and which is simply *there.* This recognition of the raw material of life as potential is, of course, mere passivity and brings about no substantive change. The true realization of the uniqueness of one's existence comes about through work or "activeness" (what Liapunov sometimes translates as "self-activity" [*aktivnost'*]); the fulfillment of this ethical imperative is assigned (*zadana*) rather than given. Now it becomes clearer what Bakhtin had in mind when he stated in "Art and Answerability" that everything one experiences and understands about art would have to be answered with one's life: the real fusion of art with life becomes an action (*postupok*) that is fundamentally no different from any other action where the individual interacts with the world.

BAKHTIN AND THE TRANSUBSTANTIVE ACT

Bakhtin describes this action in terms suggestive of the interaction between the various zones of human existence that occurs during communion; it is an event of distinctly Solovyovian properties in its foregrounding of a transubstantive moment. While the frequent iteration of *prichastnyi* (participant [to], partaking of) and *priobshchennyi* (joined; communal) in previously discussed passages by itself does not necessarily prove this, the essay's emerging argument about the necessity of true intersubjectivity reinforces the terms' eucharistic connotations. Similarly, while Orthodox Trinitarian turns of phrase such as "mutual impenetrability (*vzaimnaia nepronitsaemost'*) certainly amplify the theological leitmotif in the coded score of Bakhtin's lengthy disquisition on Kant (quoted above), the decisive stroke unveiling the subtext of christological sacrament is, significantly, the term "self-activity" (*aktivnost'*). As just shown, Bakhtin imbues this term in at least one instance with distinctly christological properties. A close examination of other uses of this seemingly neutral term in other parts of the essay yields unexpected riches. Earlier—a few pages after the beginning of the essay—Bakhtin submits the act of Christ's descent into Hell in association with other ideas and terms that fit snugly with several passages above and the assertion in "Art and Answerability" that the so-called inspiration (*vdokhnoven'e*) that ignores life is, in fact, not inspiration at all but a state of possession (*oderzhanie*):[17] "[P]ure empathizing [*chistoe vzhivanie*] as such is impossible." To truly lose oneself in another—two participants becoming one—represents an "impoverishment of Being." States of "passive" [*passivnoe*] empathy, possession and losing oneself have "nothing in common with the *answerable* act/deed of self-abstraction or self-renunciation." It is this self-renunciation [*v samootrechenii*] that "I actualize with utmost activeness and in the full uniqueness of my place in Being"; in its capacity as performance or accomplishment [*svershenie*], it encompasses Being-as-event. The descent of Christ represents just such a state of active answerability through self-renunciation; it is "a great symbol of self-activity" [*velikii simvol aktivnosti*]. "The world from which Christ has departed will no longer be the world in which he had never existed; it is, in its very principle, a different world" (93–94; 16). There is in fact something almost Pentecostal about this descent in its transformation of disparate humanity into communicants of the spirit of kenotic self-renunciation, into an actual community. The figure of Christ is above all a symbol for the disparate realms of experience, the paradigm of the individual whose entire life becomes thoroughly interpenetrated by the consciousness of guilt and answerability.[18] One does not abjure individuality when one gives oneself to another, but on the contrary preserves that uniqueness: the twain do not become one. By this point of our examination of "Toward a Philosophy of the Act" it has become clear just how important the Trinitarian model is for Bakhtin in describing the ethical workings among the three essential categories of existence, which are far deeper than the self/theoretism/aestheticism triangle submitted earlier. According to Bakhtin, the more fundamental triad in ethical being is the self, the Other, and the world that comes between them. The last of these comes between the two consciousnesses but is capable of being transformed into a unity or oneness (*edinstvo*) that mediates between them. The image of Christ is clearly more than an example of the kind of cultural process Bakhtin is arguing for; it is an exemplar of it.

In examining the passage above, one must mentally highlight the preposition "through" (*cherez*) because the English term lacks the vividly spatial meaning of the Russian that is crucial to Bakhtin's conception of ethics. The mere wafting of being (*bytie*) through a supine subject will not lead to his or her attainment of an ethical life. You must bestir yourself to engage being before it will touch you directly and can enter into your consciousness, becoming a constituent part of it for good; thus has Christ transformed the world by his appearance in it. It is now that the essential structural feature of Bakhtin's concept of interpenetrability (*vzaimoproniknovennost'; vzaimoproniknovenie*) becomes patent: the interaction among various consciousnesses represents not a short-lived interdwelling or possession of one by another, but the fundamental and permanent change of each. By this point of our examination of "Toward a Philosophy of the Act" it has become clear just how important the Trinitarian model in general and *perichoresis* in particular is for Bakhtin in describing the ethical workings among the self, the Other, and the world at large.

As evocatively referred to by Bakhtin, Christ as a paradigm for ethical being has implications that speaks not only to the individual agent's possible salvation but also to his or her place within a particular community. At a number of points in "Toward a Philosophy of the Act" Bakhtin refers to the agent as participant or *uchastnik* and the entire process of his engagement or embroiling in the ambient context as *uchastnost', prichashchenie,* or *priobshchenie.* As already pointed out, the latter two terms have the secondary meanings in Russian of communion or eucharist. If I do not recognize that my role as a participant in existence is comprehensible only from the inner perspective of my participativeness (*uchastnost'*), both my being and that of the Other will seem senseless and incomprehensible to me (95). In ontological terms, the integration of the subject with that which is not the self (what Bakhtin calls the "not-I") results in the solidifying and reinforcement of meaning. Bakhtin conceives of ethics as context without pretext, as an expression and assertion of human interconnectedness leavened with individual moral autonomy; his ethical system is a network of human associations that is ensured by the autonomy of each consciousness, which simultaneously integrates itself, as stay or support, into a larger edifice. Bakhtin's emphasis on "function" is therefore not, as it might seem at first glance, a reduction or minimalization of ethical answerability but rather an affirmation of its integrality within the organic ties that bind the human community.

One could argue, of course, that this vision of community as an intersubjective community owes more to contemporary developments in philosophy such as Husserl. In his commentary Averintsev acknowledges that Bakhtin was aware of Husserl's ideas at the time of writing "Toward a Philosophy of the Act" and that this influence is especially evident in the central position of experience (*perezhivanie* or *perezhivaamoe;* German, *Erlebnis*) in the essay's argument (157–58). He also stresses, however, that Bakhtin envisions the agent's responsibility in a way that differs from Husserl. A further comparison of Husserl with Bakhtin proves Averintsev to be justified in this view. For Husserl intersubjectivity has neutral, nonethical, and ultimately subjective beginnings; he notes, for example, that even Descartes used his own radical subjectivity as the starting point for his system, essentializing and externalizing his experience.[19] By attempting to merge the two opposing *Weltanschauungen* of Husserl's phenomenology with the Aristotelian imperative of constructing an ethical philosophy (to which experience would be subordinated), Bakhtin turns both philosophers on their heads. Bakhtin casts his cosmology from an essentially hylotheistic die, placing a premium not on the transcendence of earthly dross, but on its redemptive structuring in embodiment or concretization. Bakhtin links phenomenology and ethics by locating them both in the theological topos of Trinitarian interpenetration and its resultant embodiment, emphasizing the extent to which they share a deeper common ground. Insofar as the juxtaposition of the two philosophical modes suggests an attempt at the conditional resolution of an antinomy of thought, the connection he establishes between them also conjures up the paradigm of a Chalcedonian bisected unity that here is structurally separate or incidental to the incarnational aesthetics of experience he describes.

At this final juncture two apparently opposed images emerge as dominants in Bakhtin's discussion: on the one hand, the inanimate and inert represented by architectonics or structure and on the other the organic sentience that comes into being after a transformational event. Bakhtin uses a cluster of different concepts and terms to characterize this evolutionary leap, some theological and others philosophical. Among the latter is *vzhivanie,* which Averintsev in his commentary identifies as an approximate calque of the German *Einfühlung* (159). This term encompasses both the sympathy and the empathy that cement the interaction between reader and text and the relations among various consciousnesses. The moment of empathizing is always "followed by the moment of objectification, that is, a placing *outside* oneself of the individuality [*individual'nosti*] understood through empathizing [*vzhivaniem*], a separating of it from oneself, a *return* into oneself." Empathy and objectification of the self occur simultaneously and are inextricably interrelated:

> Pure empathizing is an abstract moment of the unitary act of aesthetic activity, and it should not be thought of as a temporal period; the moments of empathizing and of objectifying interpenetrate each other [*momenty vzhivaniia i ob"ektifikatsii vzaimno pronikaiut drug druga*]. I empathize *actively* into an individuality [aktivno *vzhivaius' v individual'nost'*] and, consequently, I do not lose myself completely, nor my unique place outside it, even for a moment. It is not the object that unexpectedly takes possession of me as the passive one. It is *I* who empathize actively into the object: empathizing is *my* act, and only that constitutes its productiveness and newness (93; 14–15).

For Bakhtin, the relation of subject to object is brought to its full fruition by effort or a kind of labor; the actor's gesture becomes productive in objective terms as well as indicative of his or her inalienable status as an autonomous and individual agent. The establishment of contacts among the participants of contiguous yet disparate acts constitutes an instant of nascent animacy if not transfiguration. Ethical answerability is generated through activity (of which aesthetics are one variety) and work. In the broader context of the essay, empathy (*vzhivanie*) emerges as the deliberately enacted force that can overcome the usual disembodiment (*razobshchennost'*) of human existence.

Bakhtin's highlighting of volition and deliberateness in human behavior as opposed to the deterministic reductionism is reflected in his emphatic usage of the term "active" (*aktivno*) and its derivatives throughout the essay. In this context, his reference to the descent of Christ into the fallen world as a paradigmatic symbol of directive action (*velikii simvol aktivnosti*) (94) is thrown into a new and highly revealing light. This particular christological image elegantly illustrates the inextricable link between kenotics and kineticism in Bakhtin's writings: the emptying and giving of oneself to the Other paradoxically occurs just as one is crossing the border from non-being to life. It is within this drama that the rapprochement between ethics and religion (drawn by Bakhtin at the end of the introduction) is played out: the wine-soaked bread of communion is both metaphor for Christ as a divine yet human and isolated being and metonym for humanity as a corporeal aggregate or entity of humanity. The descent of Christ into the world of mortality is a symbol of his constituency in humankind as well as his connection with the eternal; it is ultimately a symbol of interconnection. Incarnational theology provides a framework for understanding the formal and material dimensions of the human community; according to Bakhtin, it unites that which has been separated by contemporary approaches to ethics.

The paradigm of communion in all of its ritualist and ideological ramifications goes a long way in explaining the process whereby ethics is integrated into daily life. Early on in his discussion of the relation between ethics and aesthetics Bakhtin adduces confession (*ispoved'*) as a corrective to aestheticized worldviews. Although Bakhtin's polemic with Bergson is not altogether clear, it appears that he sees him as a representative of aestheticism on the basis of his unresolved dichotomy between intuition, which focuses on the inalienable essence of an object, and analysis, which, inasmuch as it concerns itself with symbols, always compares the object with something else (87; 91–92). Bergson describes this process as "[t]he *sympathy* by which one is transported into the interior of an object in order to coincide with what there is unique and consequently inexpressible in it."[20]

Both sympathy and intuition are important for Bakhtin for another reason as well: the Husserlian *vzhivanie* (empathy) clearly runs parallel to Bergson's conception of sympathy and explains Bakhtin's subtly expressed favoring of aestheticism over theoretism. The confessional mode provides the loophole through which works of literature can attain a status that, as Bakhtin stated in "Art and Answerability," is answerable to life and not merely to the literary tradition; it is a mode that constitutes a fundamentally moral orientation in existence (*nravstvennaia orientatsiia v edinstvennom bytii*) (92). Confession represents an opening and a consolidation of separate consciousnesses or monads, starting with the formation of the inchoate link between two beings and subsequently the strengthening of mutual support within the architectonics of a community. In its role as the prelude to communion, confession clears the ground for a foundation of communal identity.

But the potential for confession in Bakhtin's scheme is more than merely as a preliminary or subsidiary to something else. While humbling him- or herself, the confessor reaffirms inclusion within a particular doctrinal or confessional fold, in the sense of the Russian *ispovedovanie* (creed). The terminology in Bakhtin's essay is built around morphological and derivational variations on a small group of verbal stems, a scholar's palette that paints a tense balancing act between isolation to integration, individualism, and communitarianism: incommensurability (*nesoobshaemost'; razobshchennost'*) versus joining (*priobshchenie*); a qualified participation (*uchastnost'*) versus communing (*prichashchenie*).

In the atomistic universe of the human community that Bakhtin sketches in "Toward a Philosophy of the Act" ethics represent the forces of gravity that give it its shape and internal cohesion. Like any collocation of matter such as a molecule or organism, the community is brought into existence only when its potential constituents attempt to move beyond their immediate space toward contact with one another. Community does not come about through the triumph of a particular will or by the imposition of specific tradition or precedent. Bakhtin describes this negative tendency in his critique of what he calls material ethics (*material'naia etika*), certain varieties of which point to a hypostasized tradition of accepted texts and textual interpretations as touchstones for personal conduct and belief such as legal texts, preconceptions about the rule of law and legality, and the supposedly divinely inspired texts of the religious canon (99). Bakhtin was fully aware of the cynicism and Nietzschean pragmatics of ideological claques, a fact reinforced by his persistent but formalistic and highly syncretic application of christological markers to his outline of a phenomenological ethics. Such loci of affiliation and influence resemble Stanley Fish's interpretive communities or the political scientist Benedict Anderson's imagined communities. All such groupings operate on the principle of exclusion and closure rather than interconnectedness; for some of these, as Edward Said points out, the repercussions can be geopolitical in nature. The symbol of Christ offers in ethical terms precisely a transcendence of such boundaries. What really interests Bakhtin in the figure of Christ is his interstitiality and liminality, his position of being poised between the states of conjunction with others and separation from them. Christ represents a sociological principle which, as important as it is, most pointedly does not constitute a confessional frame of reference. The idea of a specifically or denominationally Christian society (in the sense the T. S. Eliot understands it) does not interest Bakhtin in the least.

AMALIA RIZNICH AND HER LOVER: DIALOGUE EMBODIED

Bakhtin cultivates the christological subtext practically to the very end of the extant essay. After the more philosophical segment that constitutes roughly two-thirds of the surviving text, Bakhtin pauses to offer a close reading of Pushkin's famous poem dedicated to Amalia Riznich in order to apply his ethics of action to the portrayal of the separated poet and his lover in that work. Two versions exist of Bakhtin's interpretation of the poem. The earlier version appears in the incomplete first chapter of "Toward a Philosophy of the Act"; Bakhtin's revision of his analysis of the Pushkin poem occurs in a fragment of the first chapter of "Author and Hero in Aesthetic Activity" and was also published posthumously.[21] Bakhtin's reading of the poem in both versions follows more or less the same pattern, although some of the differences between the two are significant from the perspective of the christological metaphor and its subsequent development in Bakhtin's criticism.

Death certainly hovers over the lyric itself, which borders on the elegiac. Pushkin wrote the piece in 1830 as a belated response to the news of the death in Italy of his Odessa love Amalia Riznich in 1825. Tolstoy regarded it as a consummate example of the poetic art,[22] and one Pushkin scholar has recently stressed the speaker's pathos and sense of irreparable tragedy.[23] In the lyric's twenty-four iambic tetrameter lines the poet recalls his last and bittersweet meeting with Riznich, who had promised him that they would meet again in Italy. But in the last (and most memorable) stanza the poet envisions her death in the vividly pellucid clime of Italy and mysteriously vows to wait for her kiss nonetheless:

> But there—alas!—where the sky's vault
> Shines with bright radiance,
> Where the waters slumber beneath the cliffs,
> You have fallen asleep forever.
> Your beauty and your sufferings
> Have vanished in the grave—
> And the kiss of our meeting has vanished as well . . .
> But I am waiting for that kiss—you owe it to me . . .[24]

Although this final strophe figures prominently in both versions of Bakhtin's interpretation, it is particularly important in the earlier one. In "Toward a Philosophy of the Act" Bakhtin emphasizes the importance that the realization of death has for both players in Pushkin's poem, the analysis of which he prefaces with a detailed and vivid description of the cognitive and sensual reawakening of the subject as he or she becomes ethically aware:

> Only the value of mortal man provides the standards for measuring the spatial and temporal orders: space gains body [*uplotniaetsia*] as the possible horizon of mortal man and as his possible environment, and time possesses valuative weight and heaviness [*tsennostnyi ves i tiazhest'*] as the progression of mortal man's life, where, moreover, the content of the temporal determination as well as its formal heaviness possess the validity of rhythmic progression [*znahimoe techenie ritma*] (131; 65).

Here, as elsewhere, the ethically significant moment represents the attainment of consciousness that Bakhtin likens to the organic beginnings of life with its growth and differentiation of tissue and gradually increasing flow of fluids. Certainly the concept of enfleshment is present here. Particularly significant here, however, is the fact that this process is portrayed as somehow more than an embodiment (*voploshchenie*), a term that never occurs in either version of Bakhtin's analysis of the Pushkin lyric. As delineated by Bakhtin earlier in the essay, what is important is not so much embodiment in and of itself but its periodicity, the fact that periods of alienation or disconnectedness (*razobshchennost'*) are necessary for true ethical understanding. This process of cognitive dissociation is vividly demonstrated in Pushkin's poem, making Bakhtin's choosing of it as an illustration of his ethics all the more understandable: by the time the poet has come to an understanding of Amalia Riznich, she has in death lost all substance.

Indeed, on the same page as the passage above, Bakhtin claims that he picked Pushkin's poem because he sees in it a paradigm of the kind of structural interplay between two sets of concrete and value-oriented contexts (*dva tsennostnykh konteksta, vse tochki*) that signifies the truly ethical action (131), which is certainly consistent with Bakhtin's earlier description of ethics as a going beyond the boundaries of one's own existence toward a particular other. As is evident from the two passages above and previous statements made by Bakhtin, a syllogistic chain of reasoning about ethics emerges: (1) only the person who is aware of the unique significance of each death can ethically connect with an Other, (2) only the person who connects with an Other becomes truly alive, and (3) only the person who is aware of death becomes truly alive. Bakhtin's transubstantive metaphor operates only when one person comes into contact with at least one other.

Bakhtin's use of the aspectual verbal pair *uplotnit'sia-uplotiat'sia* (to consolidate; solidify; compress) is particularly revealing in regard to this metaphor. Russian dictionaries derivationally link this verb not to *plot'* (flesh), but to *plotnyi* (compact, dense; strong).[25] Dal', however, has speculated on the possible derivation of *plotnyi* itself from *plot'*.[26] Here Bakhtin is clearly trying to combine both the ideas of density and fleshiness in his use of the verb. Analyzing Pushkin's lines "My hands, growing ever colder, / Strained to hold you back [*Moi khladeiushchie ruki / Tebia staralis' uderzhat'*]," Bakhtin writes—with, one might add, grandiloquent pleonasm—that the poet is trying to bring her closer to that unique spatial (*edinstvennomu prostranstvennomu*) and concrete center that all at once comprehends and consolidates (*uplotniaet*) the ideas of motherland, foreign land, distance, and the eternity of oblivion (133). From this double and somewhat unusual use and extension of the verb, Bakhtin is clearly trying to underline that the ethical moment is not just a physical consolidation, but also a creation of new meaning from the qualities and people who are thus brought together.

In "Toward a Philosophy of the Act" Bakhtin devotes an entire section to the last stanza of Pushkin's poem that does not at all appear in the later version. The prominence here of the term *prichastnost'* and Bakhtin's elaboration of the transubstantive metaphor merge most revealingly in his commentary:

> The experiencing of Italy as event includes, as a necessary constituent moment, the actual unity of Italy in unitary and once-occurrent Being [*edinstvo v edinom i edinstvennom bytii*]. But this unitary Italy gains body (is invested with flesh and blood) [*oplotnevaet . . . obrastaet plot'iu i krov'iu*] only from within my affirmed participation in once-occurrent Being, in which the once-occurrent Italy is a constituent moment. But this event-context of my unique participation [*sobytiinyi kontekst edinstvennoi prichastnosti*] is neither closed nor isolated. . . . Through the hero's participation [*prichastnost'*] in Being from his unique place the unitary and self-identical Italy has become consolidated [*uplotnilas'*], for him, into a foreign land and—again, for him—into the homeland of his beloved. For she is valuatively affirmed and found by him, and consequently, her entire evaluative event-context (in which Italy is her homeland) is affirmed and founded by him as well. And all other possible facets of the event of once-occurrent Italy that is correlated with valuatively affirmed

human beings, i.e., the Italy of all mankind, enter into the composition of his participative consciousness [*prichastnoe soznanie*] from his unique place in Being (135; 65).

Once again, the curious verb *uplotnit'sia* (to take on flesh) reappears; in juxtaposition with *oplotnevat'* (to become enfleshed, engorged) and *prichastnost'* (communion, joining) its homonymic convergence with *plot'* (flesh) is all the more highlighted. In his analysis of Pushkin's lyric, Bakhtin highlights communication as a communion stripped of its ritualistic demands. The transformation of logological embodiment as a thoroughly ex cathedra act is merely one of many examples testifying to Bakhtin's unorthodox sublimation of theological themes into a pointedly non- (and even anti-) institutional context. It is no wonder that even the political and official realities of Russia and Italy get lost in the dynamic interrelation that Bakhtin describes above.

In the later version of Bakhtin's interpretation of this poem in the incomplete first chapter of "Author and Hero in Aesthetic Activity," the analysis of this passage is considerably shorter and almost completely lacking in many of the terms listed above. In the later fragment Bakhtin speaks only of how Pushkin's description of nature represents simply a plot-oriented joining ("*fabulicheskoe* priobshchenie") with nature and that the natural metaphors are anthropomorphic in character and join nature with human fate (*priobshchaiut prirodu chelovecheskoi sud'be*).[27] The use of the verb *priobshchat'* and the noun *priobshchenie* can be regarded as residues of the same transformational and transubstantive metaphor that figures so prominently in "Toward a Philosophy of the Act." The only use of the verbs *uplonit'sia-uplotniat'sia* (consolidate; solidify) in the later version of the Pushkin interpretation occurs in a comment about the first line of the poem in which Bakhtin asserts the equivalence (also articulated in the previous essay) of the ethics of transubstantive reciprocity: the idea of distance (*dal'*) in the lyric takes on weight and substance (*uplotniaetsia*) as the poet tries mentally to reach out to his lover.[28]

In contrast, the situation is viewed as far less tragic in the analysis of the poem offered in "Toward a Philosophy of the Act." There, the interaction between the poet and his lover is relatively worry-free: together (and with a complete and unproblematic equality) they form one center of meaning without sacrificing themselves as subjects. The relationship is indeed presented as an ethical paradigm, but one achieved without pain or even special effort. As Bakhtin puts it midway through this earlier version of his reading of Pushkin's poem, there is an interpenetration and unity of events (*vzaimoproniknovenie i edinstvo sobytii*) that occurs with a value-oriented separation of contexts (*pri tsennostoi nesliiannosti kontekstov*) (132). Significantly, the patently Trinitarian *vzaimoproniknovenie* (interpenetration) and Chalcedonian *nesliiannost'* (nonconfusion; nonconvergence) do not occur in Bakhtin's discussion of the same lines in the fragment of the first chapter of "Author and Hero in Aesthetic Activity." Perhaps this is because he sensed that his reading of the poem posited an ethical relation between poet and beloved that was altogether too easy and seamless. In both versions Bakhtin describes the estrangement as completely offset by the poet's spectral self traveling to Italy. Probably realizing that this interpretation lacks any truly tragic component—that it in fact is *not* an example of the attainment of an ethical orientation through the temporary separation (*razobshchennost'*) that he outlines in "Toward a Philosophy of the Act"—Bakhtin disassociated it from the material of that essay and reworked it for another essay, deemphasizing the soteriological overtones.

Bakhtin's variant treatments of Pushkin's poem, as similar as they are, reflect the shifts that his thought was undergoing at that time. The differences in terminology between the two essays are emblematic. In "Toward a Philosophy of the Act" Bakhtin emphasizes the consolidation and solidification of consciousness that occur during the aesthetic event, whereas in "Author and Hero" he focuses more on the dialogic interaction between reader and author. In "Toward a Philosophy of the Act" meaning is associated with the faculty of sight. To see is to create and, in a certain sense, to be; being (*bytie*) becomes inclusive and integrative as it is transfigured into the event, once again pointing up the morphology of *[so]bytie* (event) as "co-being." In the fragment of the first chapter of "Author and Hero in Aesthetic Activity," Bakhtin goes further, describing the lovers of Pushkin's lyric as an embodiment of the ethical event of co-being, an extension of ideas that clearly approximates the notion of dialogue that he began to develop a few years later in *Problems of Dostoevsky's Art* (139). For Bakhtin, ethical issues are inextricably linked questions related to a community, which can be as large and inclusive as a reading audience or restrictive as a meeting between lovers. Over the span of the early twenties Bakhtin moves toward a nascent theory of dialogue in which he attempted to demonstrate the essential unity of ethics and aesthetics. In his writings from this period, an idiosyncratic social vision prevails, albeit one politically unaffiliated.

The christological metaphor in both its transubstantive and Trinitarian aspects is remarkably prevalent and, one could argue, obtrusive in "Toward a Philosophy of the Act." The Trinitarian—and, more specifically, Chalcedonian—formulation of one-yet-separate (*nesliianno i nerazdel'no*) that appears with considerable and telling frequency in this work will be examined in greater detail later. That Bakhtin attenuated these images for his subsequent essays indicates that he himself might have become uncomfortably aware of the extent to which these images had exaggeratedly insinuated themselves into his work; living in a society that was becoming increasingly antireligious, perhaps he felt the need to mute his use of them for purely practical reasons. Nonetheless, as will be shown later, the christological metaphor never completely left his writings and even manifested something of a recrudescence late in his career. In all his writing he always effects a transfer or shift—one is tempted to say a translation—of this metaphor into a thoroughly humanized setting. In a very real sense, Bakhtin inverts the Johannine conception of the conception of the word: for him, as for Trotsky—and this is the only area in which the critic and the revolutionary would agree—the act comes first, the word proceeding from it as its concretized efflorescence. As we shall see in the next chapter, Bakhtin's disagreement with revolutionary ethics is actually informed by the same skepticism toward preexistent political modes of discourse as well.

Chapter Three

The Russian Intelligentsia: Bakhtin's Ideological Critique

> We were all, to some extent, "flying Dutchmen"; we were one of the branches of the Russian intelligentsia. For all the differences among our characters, we were united in this search for truth and in our shunning of worldly goods . . .
> —Maria Veniaminovna Yudina

THROUGHOUT his life Mikhail Bakhtin considered himself to be a literary critic only in the most secondary and even incidental of ways. In the recently published 1973 interview with Vladimir Duvakin, Bakhtin states that from his university days he has remained more of a philosopher than a philologist, adding portentously, "I am a philosopher [*filosof*]; I am a thinker [*myslitel'*]."[1] Given the accent on rigid specialization that pervaded the Soviet educational establishment and scholarly world, it is hardly surprising that he was soon pigeonholed into the category of literary critic (*literaturoved*). Yet for the generation of those studying and teaching at universities prior to and immediately following the Revolution, making one's bed in such narrow and Procrustean professionalism was not necessarily compulsory or inevitable. Continuing to reflect on his Petrograd student years, Bakhtin notes with approval the interdisciplinary organization of philosophical study under the pre-Soviet dispensation.[2] There is a great deal about Bakhtin's work written during the twenties that suggests a discernible influence from other disciplines such as philosophy, which has led a few scholars to claim that some of these early works are either deliberate hybrids or fortuitous mongrels. Thus, Gary Saul Morson has made the case for the fragment "Toward a Philosophy of the Act" as primarily a treatise on ethics. The term "interdisciplinary" would perhaps be misleading here with its assumption of a deliberately cultivated eclecticism; up to the end of his life Bakhtin assumed a natural connection between fields in the humanities and the social sciences, even when the rage for compartmentalization had become all-engulfing in the Soviet educational system. Certainly the interest in linguistics in conjunction with literary studies in his writings from the fifties to the seventies is plain for all to see, as is the preoccupation with history in the Rabelais book and with philosophy in the longer extant version of "The Author and Hero in Esthetic Activity." In the various notes he wrote in 1970–71, he begins a section about dialogue with the heading of "Sketches on Philosophical Anthropology."[3]

While university faculty members before the Revolution on the whole were certainly more conservative than the many students who believed that knowledge had no meaning unless it could be applied to redress political and social wrongs, a number of them exhibited surprisingly heterodox leanings. Some teachers at Russian universities found themselves drawn to various segments of the political spectrum and wrote on a wide variety of subjects or adopted interdisciplinary approaches to their particular fields. An excellent example of such engaged and polymath mentors was Aleksei Alekseevich Ukhtomsky, whom Bakhtin's close friend Yudina characterizes in her personal recollections of the man as a believing Christian, theologian, and philosopher as well as a biologist by profession; she singles out his theory of the "dominant" in organic structure as something that can be considerably expanded and applied to areas of study other than physiology.[4] During the twenties in Saint Petersburg Bakhtin heard one of Ukhtomsky's lectures about the dominant, which is widely believed to have influenced him in forming his theory of the chronotope. Another academic who galvanized students with his erudition and wide range of interests was the Polish émigré Tadeusz Zielinski, Bakhtin's professor of classics at the University of Saint Petersburg, to whom in the same memoirs Yudina jokingly refers to as "our center of Classical philology."[5] In the circles of Bakhtin and his friends, there was a real sense that epistemological as well as political barriers were falling, that the realms of knowledge and experience were coming together into an unprecedented and dynamic mutual relation with each other.

To be sure, the long hand of government control could certainly be felt in the years preceding the cataclysmic events of 1917 to 1918, particularly in the attempts to restrict the university enrollment of women and Jews. Nonetheless, there were many like Yudina (who was Jewish) who were able to work around some of these strictures. The actual and direct guidance of what was taught and how varied greatly in those years. One only has to compare the curriculum and composition of Russian university faculties shortly before the Revolution with those after it to realize the comparative freedom or at least flexibility of the former; the post-glasnost documentation attesting to the decimation of Slavistics in the Soviet Union during the Stalin years is particularly telling.[6] While reminiscing about his early student years Bakhtin repeatedly insists that the university bureaucracy was far from draconian, having in fact a rather flexible attitude toward the students. In answer to Duvakin's questions about political measures taken by the administration of the University of Saint Petersburg against its students, he dryly states that "[t]here were no specific repressions at the university before the Revolution; those began later, when the new power arrived."[7]

As far as the students were concerned, the liberalization of the higher education system in Russia after the death of Alexander III in 1894 created an atmosphere conducive to various kinds of political and social ferment. Very quickly the schools in Moscow and Saint Petersburg became a hotbed of specifically radical and anarchist activity. In the Duvakin interviews Bakhtin recalls politically motivated fights that would erupt in corridors at the university, stating parenthetically that the administration generally chose not to get involved in them.[8] One of the more scathing contemporary accounts of the radicalized student body was A. S. Izgoev's account in the famous *Landmarks* (*Vekhi*) collection of 1909. On the other hand, the views expressed by the left-leaning students were hardly unique; in a peculiarly Russian fashion, such sympathies were, in fact, felt by the variously professioned members of the intelligentsia throughout society and tinctured with a zeal that was almost messianic and millenarian in its ascetic and single-minded devotion to an uncompromising vision. The Russian intelligentsia of the teens and twenties had inherited more than a little of the clericalism and sublimated religiosity of its nineteenth-century counterpart, the members of which had been ironically referred to as *popovichi* (sons of priests) on account of their literate if indigent class background. In her unpublished memoiristic notes about her student years in Saint Petersburg during the late teens and early twenties, Yudina vividly describes the unity of the artistic, professional, and scientific groups in their idealistic empathy with the revolutionary events: "Our youth (and that of many, many people involved in art, science, and practical life) was inspired by selflessness, poverty, and the distant rumble of civil war in the far-flung corners of our country." But it is at this point that an element of self-criticism creeps into Yudina's reminiscence. One could also characterize this experience, if you like, as "inspired by romanticism, by a firm and organic idealization of events, people, and each other. At the center of each and every one of us there resided a search for the truth"; each in his or her own way, was able to iterate the poet Aleksandr Blok's lines "I hear the sound of the turning pages of history."[9] Curious in this romantic recollection is its vicariousness: the contemplation of everything from a safe distance is actually a precondition for the Russian *intelligent*'s pursuit of truth, allowing each to embark on a unique and idiosyncratic spiritual quest. As Yudina herself practically admits, such an idealistic intellectual peregrination would certainly be stymied by direct involvement in the political upheavals of the day. In another part of her memoirs she admits that her immersion in musical study left her far from revolutionary thematics, although she felt "like a fish in water" empathizing with the suffering poor and surrounded by the danger and upheavals of those events.[10] To some, this image of insouciant and privileged idealism may seem less than endearing. In one revealing anecdote, Yudina describes her political involvement as having been limited to learning how to use a rifle, which once accidentally went off. Although the shot went through all four floors of the institute, she adds (with evident relief) that no one was hurt (9–10). When all is said and done, Yudina and many of her idealist contemporaries espouse what might ironically be termed an ethic of politically committed spectatorship.

This stance was common to the liberal and even revolutionary intelligentsia in general and was shared by members of Bakhtin's circle. In precluding action that would put political ideals into practice it was, to say the least, a highly problematic position to maintain. As the poet Andrei Bely provocatively put it in 1909, in the final analysis the Russian intelligentsia is nothing more than an intellectually privileged caste, incapable of any practical or constructive activity in spite of its readiness to sacrifice itself for the people.[11] In one of his unpublished poems preserved in the National State Library at Saint Petersburg, the gifted poet and novelist Konstantin Vaginov (another important member of Bakhtin's circle during the Saint Petersburg years) gives an almost classically succinct expression of the intelligentsia's contradictory self-perception of entitlement, self-denial, aestheticism, and broad sympathy for revolutionary events tempered by its outsider status as a chronicler. Vaginov mourns that although "[w]e were born for munificence and glory," for us now there awaits only "the fate of sputtering springs"; thus they became "nightingales against our wills / Where life has gone 'tis our fate to sing / About fallen cities, about hope / And about love, frothing like wine."[12] Bakhtin himself seems to have been aware of the difficulties inherent to such ideological voyeurism, categorically stating in one of the 1973 interviews that not only did he take no part in the revolutionary events of the Russian capital, he was also "completely apolitical" except for his dislike of attempts at reforming the university system, which he considered to be adequate for making a person "learned and prepared for life."[13] The image of Bakhtin that emerges from the Duvakin interviews is unquestionably that of a conservative, although pointedly in the more literal rather than ideological sense of the word.

Although the agitational aspect of progressivism left Bakhtin cold, he was not entirely unsympathetic to the cognate vision endorsed by many eclectic thinkers such as Yudina, who endorsed the prospect of a new knowledge of culture cutting across disciplines and professions. Judging from his self-definition as thinker rather than a mere investigator of language, Bakhtin himself was not immune to the oracular self-importance typical of his circle and class. Arguably, elements of this transgredient epistemology do cast shadows in many of Bakhtin's works, particularly in his three earliest extant writings, which has led many commentators to describe them as possessed of a revolutionary agenda. With the exception of the first piece, all of these works were left unfinished by Bakhtin: "Art and Answerability," "Toward a Philosophy of the Act," and the partially surviving draft of the first chapter of "Author and Hero in Aesthetic Activity." In these early writings there is a distinct confluence of philosophy, literary theory, textual criticism, and, in a more submerged yet ascertainable form, politics and theology. Bakhtin is ultimately a defender of the conditional autonomy of areas of knowledge, whether they be phenomenological or abstract, suggesting that such interrelation does not necessarily disrupt the conceptual integrity of the fields coming into mutual play. This synthetic interaction occurs only within the individual consciousness entering into a dialogic relation with those fields. Bakhtin's emphasis on the individual's shaping of knowledge is a far cry from the primacy of the social asserted by the radical intelligentsia. In spite of this apparent antinomy, however, the intelligentsia itself valued the same notion insofar as it applied specifically to themselves as the annointed prophets of the new order; it was a conceit with distinctly religiose (as opposed to religious) aspects. In these early works Bakhtin grapples with this valorization of the individual consciousness or personality (*lichnost'*), using it as a foil to adumbrate his own conception of the same term. At that time of Russian intellectual history, it was a term that was often invested with self-consciously vatic, if not overtly theological, dynamics.

"ART AND ANSWERABILITY": THE BIRTH OF THE BAKHTINIAN SUBJECT

Bakhtin inauspiciously published his first piece, a short, meditation-like essay, in the pages of a provincial art journal. "Art and Answerability" appeared in 1919 in the Nevel journal *Art's Day* (*Den' iskusstva*) during Bakhtin's stay in that town. The years that followed—and particularly the period from 1920 to 1924—were for Bakhtin highly fruitful in terms of handwritten volume but utterly fallow in publications. This one-and-one-half-page essay and the much longer "Author and Hero in Aesthetic Activity" and "Toward a Philosophy of the Act" overlap somewhat in terminology and share a number of deeply felt concerns. The latter two essays were written a few years later but remained unfinished. As documented in Chapter 2, Bakhtin's indebtedness to both neo-Kantianism and Kant himself is especially evident in all of these essays, as is the prevalence of certain key terms. One of the most prominent of these is *lichnost'*, which in Bakhtin's hands corresponds to the English terms *personality* or *individual consciousness*, but which arguably takes on philosophical significance and even theological resonance. "Art and Answerability" emerges as the most polished and accessible of these essays. It possesses a manifesto-like clarity that is rare for Bakhtin and was written at a time when the Russian presses were deluged with programs and broadsides for all sorts of political and literary projects.

And yet, when this piece is examined on its own terms, the apparent clarity quickly shades off into an opacity. The article is certainly provoking in its ambiguity; it is not altogether clear what audience Bakhtin is writing for and with whom he is polemicizing. On the one hand, certain anticipations can be gleaned here of the anti-Formalist arguments put forth nine years later in Medvedev's *The Formal Method in Literary Scholarship,* particularly the critique of the Formalists' privileging of structure over the social function in a literary work. On the other hand, Bakhtin's insistence on the importance of personality (*lichnost'*) at first seems out of place in a Marxist context, expecially his argument that all knowledge acquires meaning only within the purview of the individual perception: "The three domains of human culture—science, art, and life—gain unity [*edinstvo*] only in the individual person [*v lichnosti*] who integrates them into his own unity [*priobshchaet ikh k svoemu edinstvu*]."[14] Bakhtin here also takes pains to indicate that the paramount ethical status of the category of *lichnost'* does not lead to solipsism. Clearly, more than one set of sources need to be posited for this early piece.

The essay begins with a particularly gnomic statement, one that seems self-sufficient and only tenuously connected with what follows. This opening paragraph stands out almost as an unelaborated argument or a thesis from another work:

> A whole is called "mechanical" [*mekhanicheskim*] when its constituent elements are united only in time and space by some external connection and are not imbued [*proniknuty*] with the internal unity of meaning. The parts of such a whole are contiguous and touch each other, but in themselves they remain alien to each other.[15]

This theoretical gambit is developed more fully in the essay that Bakhtin was to write in the early twenties, "Toward a Philosophy of the Act." For the time being, a closer look at "Art and Answerability" is in order. This aphoristic essay represents one piece of a larger plan underlying Bakhtin's seemingly immature and derivative early work.

Without actually naming names or movements, Bakhtin questions the mutual segregation of life from art. Bakhtin insists on the reciprocal and symbiotic functioning of these two categories, not on the supremacy of either. The consequence of any subordination and privileging of life over art (or vice versa) would be the impoverishment of both: "When a human being is in art, he is not in life, and conversely. There is no unity between them and no inner interpenetration [*edinstva i vzaimoproniknoveniia vnutrennogo*] within the unity of an individual person [*v edinstve lichnosti*]."[16] To a much greater extent, Bakhtin develops this notion of the interpenetration yet mutual integrity of the aesthetic and the real in his later writings, particularly in both editions of his Dostoevsky study, where the voice of each character fundamentally clashes and changes those of others.[17] Granted, the dichotomy of life and art does not figure in Bakhtin's work on Dostoevsky. However, nothing illustrates more clearly the interaction between thought and act than Bakhtin's later argument that the agonistic relation that the Dostoevskian hero experiences with other characters' points of view occurs as much (if not more) within his own consciousness as during his actual contact with them.

But, as noted earlier in this study, the term interpenetration (*vzaimo-proniknovenie*) in Bakhtin's work is also a distinct reminiscence of *perichoresis,* the interaction of the components of the Trinity. And yet in this particular context the theological reference may not be alone in underlying the term as a concept. In his 1817 *Enzyklopädie der Philosophischen Wissenschaften im Grundrisse,* Hegel aphoristically states that "[t]he *inter-penetration of universality, particularity, and individuality* in the Concept reappears in the teleogical inter-penetration of individual, particular, and universal concerns and realms of life, which serve each other mutually as ends and means."[18] Bakhtin uses the term in a somewhat similar way, contentiously arguing for the interaction between the particular and the universal that Hegel takes as a given. Yet there are also interesting differences between Bakhtin's and Hegel's notions of interpenetration, not the least of which is that Bakhtin sees a dichtomy whereas Hegel believes that the process comes into play precisely when there is a nonbinary and therefore nondialectical relation among certain categories. A closer look at this essay goes a long way in clarifying not just the disparate subtexts of this term, but also the animus that informs the essay as a whole.

There are clear indications that at least a part of Bakhtin's polemic in "Art and Answerability" is directed toward perhaps not so much or not only at Formalism but also toward contemporary literary movements. Although he does not single out any particular writers or trends, his statement on this score is highly suggestive:

> This union, however, may become mechanical, external. And, unfortunately, that is exactly what most often happens. The artist and the human being are naively, most often mechanically united in one person [*v odnoi lichnosti*]; the human being leaves "the fretful cares of everyday life" and enters for a time the realm of creative activity as another world, a world of "inspiration, sweet sounds, and prayers." And what is the result? Art is too confident, too audaciously self-confident, and too high-flown, for it is in no way bound to answer for life. And, of course, life has no hope of ever catching up with art of this kind. "That's too exalted for us"—says life. "That's art, after all! All we've got is the humble prose of living."[19]

Bakhtin seems to be far more supportive of life in its demands for an art accountable to it than for a life that is worthy of art; the overall tenor of this passage suggests that the rift between these two sides is asymmetrical, the self-preoccupied world of art primarily culpable for their mutual incommensurability. These statements emerge as possible allusions to the Marxist critique of putatively hermetic and bookish poetic movements such as Symbolism, Acmeism, and even Futurism; it was a stance that was later to harden into official Soviet dogma. In a typical entry of a contemporary Russian guide to Marxism, the Party theorist Umansky wrote that the more widely a literary work casts its net over the social world and accurately captures the actual relations of life, the more valuable it is aesthetically. According to Umansky, literature is only literature when it is not divested of social meaning.[20]

Nonetheless, problems remain with this interpretation of "Art and Answerability" even if one were to posit Bakhtin's particular version of this uncompromising view as doctrinally sophisticated and less vulgar and simplistic. On a deeper conceptual level, there is much in the essay to suggest that Bakhtin evenhandedly sketches out the life/art dichotomy, a fact obscured by his somewhat greater elaboration of the deficiencies of the doctrine of art-for-its-own-sake. The most direct proof of this maintained symmetry can be found in the primary poetic allusion in the text. The first two quotations in the passage above are extracts from the last four lines of Pushkin's 1828 poem "The Poet and the Rabble [*Poet i tolpa*]." Through this allusion Bakhtin not only effectively reinforces the identification of poetry with art and prose with life, but also points up the perception of these values as perfectly antipodal. In Pushkin's piece, the poet and the rabble can only execrate each other in their attempt at a dialogue, each scornfully and unyieldingly replying to the statements of their interlocutor. The last word in "The Poet and the Rabble" belongs to the poet, quoted above. Several lines below this passage Bakhtin gives a pithy summary of the strife attending this division: "The poet must remember that it is his poetry which bears the guilt for the vulgar prose of life, whereas the man of everyday life ought to know that the fruitlessness of art is due to his willingness to be unexacting and to the unseriousness of the concerns in his life."[21] In the poem the rabble and the poet hysterically insist on their independence and self-sufficiency, each resorting to a shrillness of rhetoric that points up the absurdity of their extremist positions.

Bakhtin is undoubtedly responding to the tendency in contemporary Pushkin criticism to take sides with one of the two speakers in the poem;[22] he asserts that both are in fact dependent on each other, whether they care to admit it or not. This conclusion is qualitatively different from saying that each must deliberately pay homage to the other in order to approach some sort of golden mean: what Bakhtin is describing is the actual or existent interdependence of roles, the *acknowledgment and exploration of which* would liberate language. Thus, consciousness is important only insofar as it sets into motion the interaction of the political and aesthetic. The Marxist idea that consciousness—be it enlightened or false—is crucial as a constant behavioral mover and political category in itself is therefore very far from the concerns of "Art and Answerability," to say nothing of the Chernyshevskian imperative of relegating art to life.

Bakhtin reinforces this sense of symmetry by returning to the role played by the individual consciousness. Ultimately, poetry and prose, art and life, emerge as equals whose encounter on the neutral meeting-ground of *lichnost'* is not only mutually enriching, but transformational: "The individual [*lichnost'*] must become answerable through and through: all of his constituent moments must not only fit next to each other in the temporal sequence of his life, but must also interpenetrate [*pronikat'*] each other in the unity [*v edinstve*] of guilt and answerability [*viny i otvetstvennosti*]."[23] Bakhtin's conception of the interrelations between life and art hinges on ethical concerns; the subordination of one of these categories to the other results in a kind of fetishistic self-preoccupation and nihilism. In his view, the synchronic approach to this conflict would restore the factor of individual accountability and perhaps even the issue of morality to the debate.

Bakhtin's insistence that ethics are born of the individual consciousness's mediation between art and life seems unusual and novel in a number of respects. Because of the schematic and at times obscurely aphoristic statements in "Art and Answerability," much of Bakhtin's reasoning along these lines is, at best, implied and needs to be constructed or speculatively extended. His argument appears to be the following. Ethics emerge as something of a synthesis of the isolated subject in contact with another subject, who is initially perceived by the original subject as merely an object. Only after negotiating the demands between life and art and acknowledging the existence of others can this original autonomous consciousness come into full possession of responsibility:

> But what guarantees the inner connection of the constituent elements of a person [*lichnosti*]? Only the unity of answerability. I have to answer with my own life for what I have experienced and understood in art, so that everything that I have experienced and understood would not remain ineffectual in my life. But answerability entails guilt, or liability to blame. It is not only mutual answerability [*vzaimnuiu otvetstvennost'*] that art and life must assume, but also mutual liability to blame [*no i vinu drug za druga*].[24]

The key terms in this passage are person (*lichnost'*), answerability or responsibility (*otvetstvennost'*) and guilt (*vina*). When a person pays simultaneous tribute to life and art and properly aligns the demands they make, he or she becomes ethically empowered, accepting responsibility in general and, if need be, culpability or guilt in particular. The correct understanding and reception of art is therefore essential for any moral stock-taking or coming to terms with oneself. The symbiotic joining of art and life within the individual consciousness represents judgment as well as epiphany, conscience as well as delight. This equivalence and absolute interdependence that Bakhtin establishes between life and art transcends the formulations of his Formalist and Marxist contemporaries.

In the concluding remarks of his essay Bakhtin posits an absolute, even interchangeable, relation between life and art. In their draconian and isolationist manifestations, these two perspectives doom themselves to stifling and dessicated hermeticisms, voided of content in the banishing of a life-giving context. The claims advanced for the supremacy of life over art curiously take on a certain paradoxical self-referentiality as formidable as that of any aesthetic doctrine. Above all, the exoteric stock-taking that life and art need to engage in requires effort and work:

> The true sense, and not the self-proclaimed sense, of all the old arguments about the interrelationship [*o vzaimootnoshenii*] of art and life, about the purity of art, etc.—is nothing more than the mutual striving of both art and life to make their own tasks easier [*vzaimno khotiat oblegchit' svoiu zadachu*], to relieve themselves of their own answerability. For it is certainly easier to create without answering for life, and easier to live without any consideration of art. Art and life are not one, but they must become united [*edinym*] in myself—in the unity [*v edinstve*] of my answerability.[25]

One is initially tempted to see in this passage a vision of life and art forming a collective or union that labor in the field of the individual consciousness, creating a set of values that transcend the mechanical means of production. In fact, since none of the schemata embedded in "Art and Answerability" are distinctly Marxist, such a reading is highly speculative and metaphorical, as is Holquist's parallel of the work of Bakhtinian dialogue to recent medical research attesting to the intensification of body processes during conversation.[26] As interesting as such comparisons are as extensions of Bakhtin's thought, they do not settle the issue of his actual relation to Marxism. Bakhtin's insistence on the moral imperative of life rendering proper tribute to art finds no counterpart in and is not readily adaptable into contemporary Marxist theory. While suggestions of reversing the traditional Marxian relation between base and superstructure can be gleaned from the writings of the Frankfurt School, it is practically nonexistent in most manifestations of Soviet Marxism. In any event, the subordination of base to superstructure that signaled an important shift in twentieth-century Marxist thought is not being submitted by Bakhtin in this essay; the task put forth here is the integration of all human activity, in which each thought is potentially tantamount to or identical with a physically actuated event. In this essay Bakhtin sketches out a sociology of mental activity.

Yet for all this anthropomorphizing of art and life, what is singularly absent from this picture is the materialist background essential for a truly politically radical reading of this essay. The prominence in "Art and Answerability" of the terms person(ality) (*lichnost'*), interpenetration (*vzaimoproniknovenie*), and unity (*edinstvo*), with their amplified connotations of reified identity and transcendent intersubjectivity, impart a more sanguine, millenarian, yet curiously synchronic and ahistorical, quality to the tense negotiations and depredations between life and art—one not easily assimilable to the dialectical materialism that dominated Russian Marxism from the 1880s with figures such as Plekhanov and arguably continued to the end of the Soviet period. Taken together, Bakhtin's prominent use of the verb *pronikat'* (to penetrate/permeate) together with the terms interpenetrability and unity strongly suggests the topos of Trinitarian *perichoresis* and interdwelling. Structurally speaking, the vocabulary of perichoresical interpenetration is used here to describe what is in fact a Chalcedonian dynamic. According to Bakhtin, the regrettably sporadic interaction between the individual and public spheres of life in the essay occurs only within *lichnost'*. Bearing in mind the derivation of *lichnost'* and viewing all these terms together as a single conceptual constellation, one is immediately struck by its analogous relation to the Chalcedonian configuration of the human and divine natures co-inhabiting in the hypostasis or person (*lik, litso*) of Christ. In an audacious move, Bakhtin first fully fuses the bridged duality of Chalcedonian dogma to the interpenetration and overlapping of Trinitarian unity and then retrofits the entire doctrinally hybrid paradigm onto the secular issue of the relation between the public and private. It is precisely the *dual* nature of interpenetration that interests Bakhtin, something that is lacking in Hegel's use of the term. Even though the term dialogue is not used in this essay, its inchoate presence is powerfully felt. Bakhtin's conception of dialogue emerged from the idea of an interpenetrative unity.

More than twenty-five years later while teaching at Saransk, Bakhtin wrote a touching guide to students engaging in university-level research for the first time, a very short and deceptively transparent series of encouraging suggestions that are remarkably resonant with "Art and Answerability." The "active engagement in [the] subject matter" of a scholarly book is "the most important precondition for the productive reading" of it, Bakhtin writes. "The greater and more insistent are our demands towards the book, the more will it speak to us. It does not care for indifferent readers and does not respond to them. The true, engaged work on a book is not a passive appropriation but a living and passionate dialogue with it." Bakhtin goes on to say that true scholarship is not simply an isolated and impotent cerebration but in fact represents a balance of thought and action:

> In the course of independent study one must never forget about praxis [*o praktike*]. It is essential that all theoretical principles be linked to life, so that they may render to themselves an account in their possible practical application. Naturally, this should not be done in a simplistic or vulgar way, for some principles in scholarship do not have any immediate application and obtain it only through other principles of a given discipline. But the emphasis on praxis is the indispensable condition for the productive mastering of any scholarly book.[27]

Bakhtin subsequently elaborates that a book's scholarly apparatus is that which takes us beyond "the text of the book" and that "[t]he reading of a book without the painstaking and full use of its scholarly apparatus [can only be] unproductive and inadequate." The image of the book in this piece is clearly homologous to the category of art from the 1919 essay, as is scholarly apparatus to "life." Bakhtin has shifted the entire art versus life dichotomy to the domain of literary and hermeneutic activity. The text of art—the book—has, furthermore, been given additional importance by becoming the facilitator of thought into action. In his notes to his students, Bakhtin asserts the written word—in all its profound contectedness to other utterances—as that which ultimately resolves the conflict he describes in "Art and Answerability." His 1958 piece is as much a metacritical mediatation as it is a series of helpful suggestions to his students: the image of the scholarly book is an allegorical trope for the conception of multivoiced discourse he described years before in *Problems of Dostoevsky's Art* and "Discourse in the Novel."

Because Bakhtin wrote "Art and Answerability" during a time when the alternation between intense violence and cynically manipulative propaganda was a part of daily life, it is perhaps not altogether surprising that he was unable then to envision language itself as a redemptive force. The 1919 essay is a poignant testament to a hoped-for but unattained spiritual as well as aesthetic transformation of a new age. The ethically creative role of art and, more specifically, the attempt to define the relation between social reality and thought as experienced by the individual consciousness still reverberated in the air from recent and often bitter polemics. As Bakhtin wrote at the beginning of his essay, a whole is mechanical when its components are not "imbued with the internal unity of meaning." It is a principle easily applied to "Art and Answerability" itself, revealing the essay to be lapidary in composition and possessed of a finely tuned terminology. Anything but mechanical, the deeper operations and ramifications of Bakhtin's arguments are not immediately visible. A deeper look into the concept of *lichnost'* as it was understood by Bakhtin's contemporaries and friends does much to clarify these inner workings.

PERSONALITY AS REVOLUTIONARY HYPOSTASIS

The attempt to define the individual consciousness in relation to its social surroundings gained wide currency in the philosophical, political, and theological discussions that took place during the decade preceding the Revolution. The essential validity of the term *lichnost'*—or, at the very least, its importance as a methodological point of departure—was acknowledged even by certain opponents of the controversial *Landmarks* collection, a polemic that will be discussed in the next section of this chapter.[28] In contemporary theological debates, the term crops up in Berdiaev's other essays and in the moralist doctrine of M. M. Tareev (1866–1934), where it acquires special significance. Tareev was controversially known for his aggressively antimystical conception of theology, which concentrated almost exclusively on ethics and the importance of experience for the individual Christian. He argued for what he called "inner [*vnutrennee*] Christianity," a conception that depended absolutely on the autonomy of the individual consciousness. For Tareev the very essence of Christianity resided in the absolute importance of both religious good and the sanctity of the individual (*lichnost'*).[29] The idea that the individual consciousness is supreme and yet beholden to an ideal of reponsibility was important for both ends of the political spectrum but had special poignancy for writers interested in issues of theology.

Perhaps the most crucial nexus between these overlapping conceptions of *lichnost'* and Bakhtin's own can be found in the work of one particular "God-Seeker" who did not contribute to *Landmarks*. The theologian, priest, scientist, and contemporary of Bakhtin Pavel Aleksandrovich Florensky (1882–1943) treats the operations of the individual consciousness in terms very similar to Bakhtin's. In a chapter on the Trinity from his eccentric and abstruse treatise *The Pillar and Foundation of Truth* (1913), Florensky discusses *lichnost'* in the context of the Trinity. In a chapter titled "Remarks About Triunity" ("Zametki o troichnosti"), he divides the individual consciousness into three kinds of what he calls "life activities" (*zhiznedeiatel'nosti*): the corporeal (*telesnaia*), the emotional (*dushevnaia*), and the spiritual (*dukhovnaia*), and goes on to characterize them as an organic and even productive entity: "The isolated *personality* ["otdel'naia *lichnost'*"] is likewise constructed in a triune manner [*troichno*], and each of its psychological movements is trichotomous [*troiako*] in nature, inasmuch as it maintains a relation to *mind, will, and emotion* [*k umu, k vole, k chuvstvu*]."[30] Both Bakhtin and Florensky assert the tripartite structure of personality, a point not lingered over in traditional Eastern Orthodox theology. In "Art and Answerability" Bakhtin adduces science, art, and life as the three domains of human culture and claims that they become activated only when they are joined to the integral unity (*edinstvo*) of the individual consciousness. Between the schemes of these two writers, a series of analogous triads emerge. Bakhtin's category of life (*zhizn'*) has certain affinities to Florensky's category of corporeal activity and emotion (*chuvstvo*); his category of learning (*nauka*), to Florensky's of mind (*um*); and Bakhtin's concept of art (*iskusstvo*) to Florensky's spiritual activity and will (*volia*). For both Bakhtin and Florensky, the individual consciousness (*lichnost'*) is virtually an organic entity in itself, consisting of a triple internal structure differentiated according to function. For Bakhtin, however, this trichotomy is external and action-oriented whereas for Florensky it is primarily emotive and internal. The difference is revealing. Bakhtin jettisons some of the more traditional baggage of triadic thought, veering away from the phenomenology that is defined by essences rather than by experience itself. It was a movement that culminated in what he had outlined in "Toward a Philosophy of the Act."

Nonetheless, additional parallels in the terminologies employed by Bakhtin and Florensky flesh out their notions of *lichnost'*, which emerge as relatives in a conceptual family tree. The emphasis that Bakhtin places on the interconnectedness of all human activity and thought is also evident in the methodology employed by Florensky, for whom the terms *edinosushchie* and *edinosushchnost'* (consubstantiality) owe as much to Solovyov's "all-oneness" (*vseedinstvo*) and Khomiakov's *sobornost'* as to traditional theology. As Florensky states in *The Pillar and Foundation of Truth*, the terms can be applied not just to the interrelations within the Holy Trinity, but also to those in the created world.[31] Clark and Holquist point out that Florensky and many of his contemporaries interested in theology attempted to synthesize the humanities and the hard sciences into a single scholarly and even philosophical approach.[32] In light of the assertion in "Art and Answerability" that the three domains of human culture find expression only in the individual consciousness, this attempt at elaborating a grand epistemological scheme must have been congenial to Bakhtin as well.

Clark and Holquist have noted a number of other suggestive parallels in the thought of these two Russian contemporaries. Both writers stress the communality yet irreducible duality of all existence, a shared being reflected in the prominence of the Russian prefix "*so-*" in their critical vocabularies.[33] This is certainly evident in "Art and Answerability," particularly in that essay's foretelling of the confluence of life and art. As Clark and Holquist rightly point out, however, these similarities between the two writers ought not to obscure the differences. Florensky is generally drawn toward external rather than internally generated discourse, highlighting the harmonious coexistence of self and Other[34] rather than the potential of their noncorrespondence or incommensurability, which Bakhtin recognizes as a very real possibility. This crucial difference is most vividly expressed in "Art and Answerability," where life and art do not surrender themselves but instead render accounts to one another in a delicately balanced and almost contractual way.

The general similarities between Bakhtin and Florensky are most clearly manifest in their attempts at the formation of a new science. In spite of his training as a priest, Florensky claimed to be unmoved by mysticism and metaphysics and more interested in applying and assimilating the gains made in philosophy into both the human and the natural sciences. This certainly seemed to be the case after the Revolution with his increased involvement in Soviet science. In a letter to a friend in 1922, Florensky makes his disposition abundantly clear: "[I am] developing a monist world-view, one entailing an ideal, concrete and labor-oriented relation [trudovogo otnosheniia] to the world. . . . As a matter of principle, I remain hostile to spiritualism, abstract idealism and metaphysics of that sort."[35] Bakhtin's insistence on the opacity and ultimate meaninglessness of the concept of inspiration parallels Florensky's on the demystification and devalorization of the humanities. As Bakhtin states in his early essay: "Nor will it do to invoke 'inspiration' in order to justify want of answerability [*bezotvetstvennosti*]. Inspiration that ignores life and is itself ignored by life is not inspiration but a state of possession [*oderzhanie*]."[36] Like Florensky, Bakhtin is interested in the specific manifestations rather than speculative origins of concrete phenomena.

The subliminal presence of a theological category such as the Trinity in "Art and Answerability" on at least two levels actively demonstrates the essay's critical principles of forging a truly interdisciplinary and synthetic approach to knowledge: first and most obviously by virtue of drawing terms from a different field such as theology, and, second, through the programmatic content of the particular variant of theology to which his criticism had marked affinities, namely, Florensky's application of church doctrine to epistemology and matters traditionally not directly linked to traditional religious teaching.

Elsewhere in Florensky's writing, *lichnost'* is characterized as embodying both the wide gamut of everyday experience and its ideal essence in a manner that throws into sharper relief Bakhtin's theologically informed use of it. In his 1922 essay "Iconostasis" Florensky makes a series of distinctions among person or being (lit., "face" [*litso*]), visage (*lik*) and person or individual consciousness (*lichnost'*). The first of these categories consists of the raw material of corporeal reality: " The person [*litso*] is he who we see in our daily experience, the being who represents the reality of this world."[37] The visage, on the other hand, represents the realization of the ontological potentialities of the being (*litso*); it is manifestation of ontology ("*lik* est' proiavlennost' ontologii"), the result of a transformation that takes place within the individual consciousness (*lichnost'*). In other words, the last of these constitutes the arena where being assumes its embodied and individualized form, God's image becoming embodied both in it and in life (*voplotit' v zhizni, v lichnosti*), as well as in the particular person (*v litse*). It is only then that "the person [*litso*] take[s] on clarity in its spiritual structure."[38] Particularly significant here is the portrayal of the individual consciousness (*lichnost'*) as a kind of border or retentive surface for the emerging picture of human activity in its totality and gained significance. Florensky in fact throughout this essay uses metaphors drawn from the visual arts—and in particular from icon painting—to illustrate the kind of ontological possibilities described above.[39] For him, the realization of the spiritual possibilities of the individual consciousness is accompanied by a concretization and sharper definition of its constituent parts. Florensky alludes to this capability elsewhere in *The Pillar and Foundation of Truth*, in his discussion of sophiology or the study of wisdom: "Sophia is the great root of [God's] creation in entirety; She is the ideal consciousness [ideal'naia *lichnost'*]."[40] Both Bakhtin and Florensky stress the potentially transformative and revelatory status of the individual consciousness. The transcendental potential of *lichnost'* emerges as being of great import for both of them. In their emphasis on the concrete over the metaphysical, the full activization of the subject over mere existence, they delineate a concept of personality as revolutionary hypostasis, as an entity that is able to change its environment only after it itself has become embodied. However, this implicitly valorized conception of the subject was not altogether congenial to the reigning self-image in contemporary Russian intellectual life.

"LA TRAHISON DES CLERCS RUSSES": THE INTELLIGENTSIA AT THE BORDERS OF SOCIALISM AND IDEALISM

The *Landmarks* (*Vekhi*) controversy from exactly a decade before "Art and Answerability" embodies many of these issues with particular acuity, and Bakhtin himself seems to echo many of its arguments against the conception of individual agency adhered to by many members of the prerevolutionary progressive intelligentsia. The contributors to this 1909 collection of articles included both political and legal commentators such as P. B. Struve and M. Gershenzon along with a number of philosophers and theologians associated with "God-seeking" (*bogoiskatel'stvo*), among them N. A. Berdiaev, S. N. Bulgakov, and S. L. Frank. The spotlight that these writers threw on the dynamics of the inner life and its interaction with social reality casts a distant gleam on Bakhtin's early essays, particularly on his conception of the individual consciousness (*lichnost'*).

Any linking of Bakhtin to this book is inevitably fraught with political and ideological implications. The collection's critical thrust was directed by disenchanted Russian liberals and certain conservatives against the radical intelligentsia. Most of the contributors held the intelligentsia responsible for the disastrous outcome of the 1905 revolution and its dispiriting aftermath. For many years in the Soviet Union, the collection was considered to be something of a classic in the anti-canon of reactionary nationalist literature. For many otherwise sympathetic contemporaries, the affiliation and voiced support of certain contributors (such as Bulgakov) for the Russian Orthodox Church undercut the project's credibility. Some contributors, however, effectively restored certain political and philosophical terms and arguments to public discourse.

For the most part two views about *Landmarks* have predominated, essentially falling along political fault lines. The first identifies *Landmarks* with the political center and far right, calling into question both the veracity of and motives behind its analyses. Most of the contemporary responses—or rather rebuttals—fall within this camp, bluntly expressing disagreement and outrage with the positions taken in the collection.[41] The most politically coherent and representative of this perspective is Lenin's review of the collection, a piece that became the touchstone for virtually all of the Soviet historiographic appraisals that followed.[42]

The second perspective places *Landmarks* in the developing tradition of Russian liberal thought that began with Chaadaev and stresses that the problem is less with the intelligentsia's putative radicalism and more with the ideological contradictions that riddle its movement. As one adherent of this view has put it, *Landmarks* was first and foremost concerned with "the irresponsible behavior of the intelligentsia."[43] Thus, in his positive review of the collection Andrei Bely accuses the intelligentsia of being a "spiritual bourgeoisie" as amply demonstrated in its frenzied response to the critical articles.[44] According to this view, the Westernizer legacy is at least as important to the writers of *Landmarks* as the Slavophile one, as evinced in their indebtedness to Solovyov's radically skeptical stance toward religion as institution, particularly in its contemporary Russian manifestation as nationalist bulwark.[45] It is this second interpretation of *Landmarks*—for many years in the minority—that is most productive in understanding the first ten years of Bakhtin's work.[46] Like *Landmarks,* Bakhtin was preoccupied with what may be termed the internal contradictions of Russian political activism.

In spite of the various and at times nonconvergent perspectives of the *Landmarks* contributors, the first article of the collection, Berdiaev's "Philosophical Verity and the Truth of the Intelligentsia," does sound out some of the central concerns of the group. Berdiaev focuses on the inconsistencies that riddle the radical intelligentsia's worldview. For the typical *intelligent*, the evidence of social injustice is undeniable and therefore constitutes truth or at least the most prominent luminary in its constellation. On the other hand, truth also exists in more diffuse and nonpolitical manifestations that are ultimately subordinate to political and class struggle; consequently, the conception of knowledge, learning, and the arts as self-sufficient realms is viewed as not only frivolous but morally irresponsible.[47] Furthermore, as almost all the contributors of *Landmarks* note, the radical intelligentsia denies the importance of *lichnost'* or the autonomous consciousness.

As Berdiaev points out in his essay, the supreme irony of the intelligentsia's idolatry of the social is that while they minimize the importance of individual moral autonomy, they themselves rely on a highly subjective conception of class conflict, one in which every social group ceases to be a locus of economic forces in the Marxian sense but instead becomes anthropomorphized into a player in a drama or game:

> For the most part, economic materialism is an objective doctrine; it places the objective principle of production, as opposed to the subjective principle of distribution, at the center of society's life. This doctrine sees the essence of human history in the creative process of vanquishing nature in the economic creation and organization of productive forces. It should be said that there was a healthy seed in Marxism's objective-scientific aspect. . . . Generally speaking, economic materialism and Marxism were misunderstood among us: they were interpreted "subjectively" and adapted to the traditional psychology of the intelligentsia. On Russian soil, economic materialism lost its objective character: the productive-constructive factor was pushed into the background and the subjective class-oriented aspect ["*sub"ektivnaia-klassovaia* storona"] of social democracy stepped out into the foreground.[48]

He extends this line of reasoning to its logical and oxymoronic conclusion by stating that the intelligentsia's radicalism hinges on a "subjective sociology (13). Traces of the Marxist phase that Berdiaev himself went through are clearly evident in this critique. For Berdiaev, as for Bakhtin, the utter renunciation of the sphere of the inner life leads to the paradoxical result of a solipsistic social theory, where the revolutionary elite becomes, in its capacity as an agitational service class and bellwether, the sole repository of licensed subjectivity.[49] Both writers submit a conception of the primacy of perception that includes social accountability. Berdiaev's intelligentsia and the unnamed myopic targets of Bakhtin's essay do not attempt or, apparently, even see the need for such a synthesis.

Even more revealing, however, is the emphasis that Berdiaev places on the moral autonomy of the individual consciousness. Toward the end of his article, he points up the inherent contradictions of the intelligentsia's project and in particular the chasm separating its theory from its practice. The critical remarks in his summation treat the very minor—and, according to Berdiaev, hardly extant—role played by ethics in the views of the intelligentsia, where responsibility and free will are ultimately rendered void by the overriding concern in demonstrating social culpability: "Indeed, our intelligentsia cherished *freedom* and professed [or preached (*ispovedyvala*)] a philosophy in which there is no room for freedom; it cherished the *individual* ["dorozhila *lichnost'iu*"] and professed a philosophy in which there is no room for the individual [*v kotoroi net mesta dlia lichnosti*]."[50] As with Bakhtin, the crux of Berdiaev's discussion of ethics turns on the category of *lichnost'* and the maintenance of its structural integrity and overall viability.

Other contributors to the collection make similar, even more dyspeptic comments about the intelligentsia's willful neglect of the individual. Struve, for example, highlights what he deems to be the hallmark of the socialist worldview, the wholesale denial of personal responsibility (*lichnoi otvestvennosti*).[51] The crux of almost every essay in this collection turns on the category of *lichnost'* and the importance of preserving it. Bakhtin's "Art and Answerability" is strongly reminiscent of these discussions, but devoid of ideological posturing.

In the final paragraph of the essay, Berdiaev makes clear that these contradictions amount to nothing less than a total, if unintended, abrogation of individual responsibility. Like Bakhtin, Berdiaev makes the assertion that any assumption of responsibility entails the acceptance of possible guilt. While the moral quandary that the intelligentsia has found itself in is partly the result of the traumas inflicted upon it by the Russian autocracy, it has another source as well. In a distinctly Dostoevskian turn, Berdiaev asserts that the intelligentsia's rejection of God has only led it to to a new idolatry, of the human; it has also robbed its members of the sense of guilt (*vinovnost'*) and deadened their instinct for truth. Only our consciousness of guilt will bring us to the new life; only then will we be free from both the external knout as well as inner slavery; only when we assign to ourselves responsibility or answerability (*otvestvennost'*) for our actions and cease to blame external forces for everything that goes wrong. It is then—and only then—that the new soul of the intelligentsia will be born (*naroditsia*).[52] By using the colloquial verb *narodit'sia* (to be born), Berdiaev inserts a shrewd Russian pun into this last assertion: to a Russian ear and in the context of the essay, the verb echoes the term *narod,* meaning "(the) people" in the sense of the suffering masses. The intelligentsia and the people are in fact separated by a chasm, one made paradoxically all the wider just when the former believes that it is selflessly toiling for the latter; conversely, the intelligentsia is able to join in some kind of solidarity with the people only when it admits its culpability, undercutting its oxymoronic self-image as a progressivist elite. Thus does Berdiaev in a single deft stroke delineate his view of the estranged relationship between the intelligentsia and society at large. Bakhtin's and Berdiaev's essays end on a manifesto-like note that sketches out a hoped-for renascence of ethical responsibility in contemporary Russian thought; in both cases answerability (*otvestvennost'*) and culpability (*vinovnost'; vina* in Bakhtin's essay) are inextricably linked. The similarity in tone and terminology between Bakhtin's essay and Berdiaev's is perhaps too patent to be coincidental. Both essays were written in the shadow of revolutionary events whose repercussions were still deafening, painful, and difficult to reckon with; each deals with the dissonant role played by the intelligentsia in a potentially new social order: for Berdiaev, this group constitutes the radical intelligentsia, and for Bakhtin, the literary intelligentsia.

Other essays in the collection besides Berdiaev's highlight this reading of the individual consciousness (*lichnost'*) as the repository of human creative energy. In his article on the ascetic heroism of the Russian radical, the theologian Sergei Bulgakov outlines the reasons for the Russian intellectual's revulsion toward this philosophical category. Nowhere else in this collection is the intelligentsia's problematical conception of morality addressed so bluntly:

> Extremely unpopular among the intelligentsia are the concepts of *personal* morality ["*lichnoi* nravstvennosti"], personal self-improvement [*lichnogo samousoveshenstvovania*], and the development of the *individual* ["vyrobotki *lichnosti*"] (and vice versa, the word *social* has a special, sacramental character). Although the intelligentsia's world outlook constitutes the extreme assertion of the individual [*lichnosti*], the worship [lit., self-deification (*samoobozhestvleniie*)] of the individual in its theories, the same intelligentsia persecutes the same individual mercilessly, wiping away all influencing trace of it on the environment and the elemental forces of history (in accordance with general teaching of the Enlightenment). The intelligentsia refuses to admit that the individual possesses a vital creative energy. (emphasis in original).[53]

The intelligentsia preaches, it sanctifies and anathematizes; it has absorbed all of the hierarchical passions of entitled clericalism with none of its will for self-examination and possible reform. At best, the *intelligent* gropes in a fog of unwitting egoism; at worst, he or she is prone to authoritarian and fundamentally undemocratic drives, deeming no individual consciousness worthy of survival except his or her own. The view that reverberates throughout *Landmarks* concerns the Russian intelligentsia's spiritual provenance, one influencing its members arrogating to themselves the privileges of a priestly caste, embittered in its literate isolation and lowly status while sublimating a kind of self-righteous piety. According to Berdiaev and Bulgakov, it is a particularly lethal combination, one that can lead to despotism.

Similarly, Gershenzon asserts that the intelligent's *lichnost'* is fractured into consciousness (*soznanie*) and will (*volia*) is propelled by a desire not for self-sacrifice, but for a self-sufficiency that need not answer to anyone;[54] in the last piece in the collection, Frank asserts that the ultimate goal of the intelligentsia is at least the effacement of personality, if not the sacrifice of all moral considerations on the altar of utilitarianism.[55] These views differ in a number of particulars regarding the problematical status of individual identity in Russian socialist thought, but all concur that the operative status of the individual consciousness becomes stymied or debased. In his article "Creative Self-Cognition [*Tvorcheskoe samosoznanie*]" from *Landmarks*, Gershenzon identifies consciousness and personality as the two primary components of cognition, the former being governed by the will and the latter by an irrefrangible inner voice. The problem with the current state of the intelligentsia, claims Gershenzon, is that the two are no longer synchronized; the task—and a difficult one, at that—is to attempt to harmonize them. There should be a constant interaction (*vzaimodeistvie*) between consciousness and cognisant personality (*chuvstvennoi lichnosti*) in their constant struggle and minute-by-minute mutual balancing. Unlike the delusion under which the intelligentsia labors, this represents an egocentrism of consciousness in the highest sense of the word (*"[e]to v vysshei smysle slova egotsentrizm soznaniia"*). Gershenzon invests the full realization of *lichnost'* with an almost transubstantive status, characterizing the entire hoped-for event as a kind of incarnation: "[U]niversal flesh is actually transformed into individual hypostasis [*v lichnoi ipostasi*], for this flesh [*plot'*] is one in all, and any essential change in an atom is an irrevocable cosmic act."[56] His understanding of the individual consciousness is remarkably consonant with Florensky's in a number of respects, not least of which is the conception of the simultaneous concretization and self-transcendence of the individual consciousness. Although these ramifications are not elaborated in Bakhtin's "Art and Answerability," they remain tantalizingly and subtextually present.

With the current anathema in literary theory against reifying the subject, perhaps it is useful to delve into the ideology of the Russian subject as espoused by Bakhtin's contemporaries. As already mentioned, *Landmarks* was notable in part for representing a religiously oriented view of Russian affairs that was neither nationalistic nor Leninist, its contributors critical at times of certain manifestations of Russian nationalism as well as socialism. In a certain sense, the concept of the isolated consciousness becomes a refuge from conceptions of valorized communities, a place where true identity can be gauged separate from the deterministic fantasies of systems of political thought. By using it to refer only to the individual, the *Landmarks* writers use *lichnost'* as a foil to the nationalist construct of a people as a single or collective consciousness distinct from others. Nonetheless, a certain Russophile tendency does make itself heard, even in the concept of *lichnost'*. This ambivalence is especially evident in Bulgakov's essay in the collection, which vacillates between extolling and implicitly criticizing the tradition of

Russian heroism. In a particularly intense form, the work of Bakhtin's friend and mentor Aleksandr Aleksandrovich Meier (1875–1939) also reflects this ambivalence about the term and its political ramifications.

Meier is a fascinating figure in his own right, and has received a great deal of attention lately primarily because of his association with Bakhtin. Meier was actively involved in the Saint Petersburg Religious-Philosophical Society, whose meetings were conducted at the residence of Ksenia Anatolievna Polovtseva. The papers of the Society are kept in the Polovtsev family archive at the National State Library in Saint Petersburg. These documents consist of membership lists, minutes of meetings, and correspondence and presentations of members. The collection is useful in elucidating two issues. First, it confirms that although Yudina and Meier were members, Bakhtin perhaps never was: not once, in fact, is his name mentioned in the entire collecton. Second, certain documents contained there make it clear that the society was politically left-leaning and that Meier in this regard was one of its more charismatic participants. But Meier's politics were highly eccentric, even in the motley political circles that fed on the controversies and upheavals that accompanied the revolutionary events in Saint Petersburg. Born to an uprooted German Lutheran family in Odessa, Meier cultivated an intensely devout religiosity in his writings and recorded speeches. Although he was arrested for socialist agitation during his student days, he was perhaps more of an apocalyptic Bakuninite than he was a consistent adherent of Marxism, a fact that has led some to call him a mystical anarchist. Meier conceived of individual identity as organically linked to nationhood, so much so that the latter entity in fact is defined by the individual. A manichaean struggle unfolds in every culture between the pagan and the Christian, the former representing social fragmentation, idolatry, and destructive anarchy whereas the latter ushers in a truly collective society by establishing dynamic connections between its disparate members. Of the two, only the Christian aspect of culture is truly creative and revolutionary as a principle.[57] But Meier's conception of the Christian is itself imbued with a Nietzschean and anarchist feel and in his scheme the creators (one is almost tempted to say "artists") and the true revolutionaries are interchangeable and constitute something of an elite: only they are able to define the significance of the new national identity.

In the manuscript of a presentation he gave at the society on 16 January 1918 called "On Class Struggle" (*O klassovoi bor'be*), Meier fuses socialism, Solovyovian God-manhood, and Christianity in a bold if not entirely successful venture. He asserts on the one hand that the ideal of God-manhood is an assertion of identity or *lichnost'* (*Ideal bogochelovechestva est' utverzhdenie lichnosti*) which in turn demands the ideal of social interaction ("*lichnost'* trebuiut ideal obshcheniia"),[58] the cleaving unto a greater entity. "Nations must be baptized," Meier asserts. In our revolutionary society there already exists baptized humanity, that is, redeemed individuals (*iskuplennye lichnosti*). But the collective ideal has yet to be truly fulfilled. For that we need a "new Israel," an even newer humanity, a church (*Tserkov'*). It is only in such a collective society that the isolated individual (*individuum*) will become more of an real consciousness ("kazhdyi individuum v takom kollektive bol'she *lichnost'*"), entering into communion with the person (*lichnosti*) of Christ.[59] The unredeemed person—referred to derisively by Meier as the "individual"—is capable of self-transcendence and true identity or personhood only by joining to the person of Christ. Therefore, *lichnost'* essentially denotes the personality in its organic relation to a particular community (which may be a nation or nation-state) and not the particular consciousness as delineated by the *Landmarks* writers. Nevertheless, the conception of *lichnost'* in *Landmarks* does contain an element that gravitates toward intersubjectivity: as Gershenzon points out in the passage quoted above, the changes occurring within the hypostasis of the individual personality have repercussions in the world at large. Perhaps the only essential difference between Meier and Gershenzon is that the christological setting of this transcendence of the ego is implicit in the latter and explicit in the former.

Yet surely even more significant is the nationalist coloring of Meier's essay, unlike anything that can be found in *Landmarks*. The metaphor of the revolutionary transformation of an entire nation as a kind of baptism is certainly a powerful image, both in the light of Russian religious nationalism (with its significant messianic component) and the tense political situation at the time Meier wrote. In the same city the morning following Meier's talk, Lenin disbanded the Constituent Assembly, which some had considered the last chance for a democratic forum in Russia. Later that month Aleksandr Blok unforgettably recorded his impressions of these events in "The Twelve," a poem that begins by ironically highlighting the rallying cry "All power to the Constituent Assembly!" and ends with a band of apostle-like revolutionaries being led to victory by a figure who may or may not be Christ. Like Meier's "On Class Struggle," Blok's poem raises the thorny issue of what and who constitutes representation and leadership during a revolution. Both in this essay and in others, such as "The Religious Meaning of Messianism" (written four years before), attempts were made to come to terms with this dilemma by emphasizing the socially transformative role of the messianic ideal itself.[60] The specter of political pretendership looms behind many of his efforts in this direction, a concern that only his friend Bakhtin fully addressed.

Nonetheless, from the meeting minutes of the Religious-Philosophical Society ones sees that Meier gradually distanced himself from this idea precisely because of the curdling in it of Russian nationalism into chauvinism and the kind of arguments advanced against it in the *Landmarks* collection. In a meeting devoted to the theme "On the Church" on 1 March 1922, Meier notes with chagrin that the only real reason he believes in Orthodoxy is simply because he was born in Russia. The dictation of religious belief by the accident of one's birth represents not a Christian ideal but a pagan one, the triumph of the tribe over the individual: the primacy in the choice of faith is transferred to one's ancestors. Meier juxtaposes such arbitrary affiliations with the example of Saint Augustine, who chose his faith *against* the reigning religion of Rome and his ancestors. But we Russians, Meier argues, have merely fallen into faith, narcissistically considering this to be *our* God, the God of our nation ("potomu-chto eto *nash* Bog, Bog nashego naroda"). Only Christianity in the deeper sense transformed the isolated individual into a truly and responsibly acting subject ("V zhizni otdel'nyi chelovek ne iavliaetsia *lichnost'iu;* tol'ko khristianstvo delaet ego *lichnost'iu*").[61] This statement is compelling both for its substance and its echoes of Meier's earlier essay. Bearing the latter in mind, one sees that Meier now views Russia as one of the pagan and "unbaptized" peoples he mentions in "On Class Struggle," one of those who do not truly understand the salvific revolutionary ideal. Apparently, intervening political events had disillusioned Meier in his view of political messianism, particularly in its Russian manifestation that drifts toward despotic nationalism. For Meier, Saint Augustine emerges as an ideal of the moral autonomy, culminating in the attainment of Christian personhood or *lichnost'*: he renounced the faith of his ancestors after a painful search, a decision that brought him into contact with a community that was not defined by national borders or ethnic differences.

In an essay he wrote the following year, Florensky strikes some similar notes. He launches into a devastating critique of Russian piety, asserting that some of it is based on the solipsistic tendency of assigning native qualities to Orthodoxy as a belief, transforming it into an idolatry of the nation or *narod*.[62] Inasmuch as Florensky's and Meier's conceptions of *lichnost'* assume an ethical as well as an avowedly spiritual transformation, they cannot be made to retrofit the politicized conceptions of personality in nationalism and revolutionary socialism. The pathos and violence of this period is perhaps best captured by the coincidental remarks that Julien Benda made about French intellectual life during the mid-1920s in his classic *La Trahison des Clercs.* He makes clear that political passions are, in origin, religious ones, and that intellectuals have increasingly asserted themselves as priestly proselytizers and schismatics. Much of Benda's argument is uncannily reminiscent of those put forth with such astringency in *Landmarks:*

> Today political passions show a degree of universality, of coherence, of homogenousness, of precision, of continuity, of preponderance, in relation to other passions, unknown until our times. They have become conscious of themselves to an extent never seen before. Some of them, hitherto scarcely avowed, have awakened to consciousness and have joined the old passions. Others have

> become more purely passionate than ever, possess men's hearts in moral regions they never before have reached, and have acquired a mystic character which had disappeared for centuries. All are furnished with an apparatus of ideology whereby, in the name of science, they proclaim the supreme value of their action and its historical necessity. On the surface and in the depths, in spatial values and in inner strength, political passions have today reached a point of perfection never before known in history. The present age is essentially the age of politics.[63]

While all the contributors to *Landmarks* touched upon such issues, it was especially Meier and Gershenzon who, in exploring them, effectively criticized the Russian intelligentsia's inconsistency and irresponsible idealism. As one scholar has noted, Bakhtin sees this reified cognicizing subject as interacting with various voices within a particular culture whereas Meier only sees the subject as pitted againt the cosmos.[64] In a effort that has no counterpart to the work of the *Landmarks* contributors, Florensky, or Meier, Bakhtin soon attempted to extend the conception of *lichnost'* more substantially into the social sphere. As we shall see, he does this by exploring in great depth the highly specific structural implications of the theological associations of *lichnost'*. In contrast, the efforts in this direction undertaken by those other writers are jejune, examples of what Bakhtin refers to in "Discourse in the Novel" as authoritative discourse's special, magisterial script of received wisdom.[65]

THE REDEMPTION OF INDIVIDUAL EXPERIENCE IN "TOWARD A PHILOSOPHY OF THE ACT"

In "Toward a Philosophy of the Act" Bakhtin resumes his discussion about the problematical relation between art and life, only this time grounding his terms more firmly in a philosophical context. The similarities between the arguments expressed in *Landmarks* and those espoused by Bakhtin become more clear-cut here. Now the loosely fitting categories of art and life from "Art and Answerability" are filled out with the concepts of "theoretism" (*teoretizm*) and "aestheticism" (*estetisizm*).

Given the ambitiousness of Bakhtin's enterprise in the later essay, it is inevitable that aesthetics and politics would occupy subordinate positions in this scheme. In fact, he asserts that it is precisely the elevation of those two cultural domains above all others that has led to the crisis in contemporary philosophy.[66] Echoing "Art and Answerability," Bakhtin asserts that the overevaluation or fetishising of either life or art drives a wedge into cognitive understanding, producing a rift between the objective content (*soderzhanie*) of an act and the actual experience of the subject's participation in and cognizance of the event (*sobytie*). The alienation of the act's product from the act itself results in a breakdown of communication and even of communicability, leading to a fundamental incommensurability (*nesoobshchaemost'*) (92). As aesthetics and politics attempt to ground and totalize knowledge in themselves, knowledge inevitably becomes compromised. Thus, for Bakhtin the crisis in contemporary philosophy is essentially an epistemological crisis.

It soon becomes clear, moreover, that politics constitute a part or subset of a much larger and even more insidiously omnivorous doctrine, what Bakhtin labels theoretism, discussed in the last chapter. For Bakhtin, the task of philosophy should be to steer away from the Scylla of aestheticism and the Charybdis of theoretism. Bakhtin points to the thought of Henri Bergson as an attempt to bring together philosophical contemplation on the one hand and intuition on the other. Nonetheless, Bergson ends up, like many others, overevaluating subjective experience, leading to what Bakhtin calls the aesthetization of life (*estetizatsiia zhizni*) (91). Bakhtin argues that this occurs because the Bergsonian approach to philosophy—which, in spite of its attempt to synthesize, is ultimately emblematic of aestheticism—is informed by a specific, if highly provisional and passive, conception of ethics (92). Aestheticism conceives of ethics in extremely situational and at times positivist terms, reducible to the immediate context and contacts at hand. According to Bakhtin, the primarily subsidiary role played by ethics in such a conception is responsible for the impoverishment of contemporary philosophical systems. Since Bakhtin believes epistemology and ethics to be inextricably linked, they are equally impacted on by the crisis in contemporary philosophy, which is where politics comes in. Regrettably, Bakhtin does not get around to examining the political component of theoretism, an analysis that would have tested the applicability of his conception of ethics to specific problems and perhaps have clarified his own chimerical and much-debated political views.

While the beginning of the extant essay obviously does not represent the actual beginning, even in medias res Bakhtin clearly pursues an argument that resonates with the central distinction between art and life in "Art and Answerability." The style here, however, is infinitely more convoluted and, one senses, intentionally obscure. Whether this approach is due to a greater complexity of ideas or to the fact that the work remains unfinished is unclear. A quotation of the first part of this sentence gives a good idea of the denseness and prolixity of the rest of the essay, which the translator Vadim Liapunov renders masterfully while clearly making an effort toward conceptual clarification:

> Aesthetic activity as well is powerless to take possession of that moment of Being which is constituted by the transitiveness and open event-ness of Being [*sobytiinosti bytiia*]. And the product of aesthetic activity is not, with respect to its meaning, actual being in the process of becoming, and, with respect to its being, it enters into communion [*priobshchaetsia*] with Being through

> a historical act of effective aesthetic intuiting [*deistvennogo esteticheskogo intuirovaniia*]. (82; 1)

As almost nonsensically elliptical as this passage might at first seem, there is a series of assumptions at work within it that makes a synoptic reading possible. While the precedent of this sentence is not known, presumably Bakhtin had already made clear that being (*bytie*) in and of itself is not necessarily a vital (and vitalist) category. Working within Bergsonian categories, Bakhtin undoubtedly distinguishes between being that is protean and alive (in a virtual if not actual organic sense) and inert and immutable being. The product of aesthetic activity belongs to the latter category: it is all artifact, an excrescense of a living process or activity (*deistvitel'nost'*) that may have pretensions to transcendence but that ultimately remains finished, complete and therefore immured within itself. But even in the inertness of its own being aesthetic activity may fuse with the kind of being that changes or evolves, although this can occur only through a particular act of intuiting that is aesthetic in nature but which is not always present in aesthetic activity. In other words, intuiting is the loophole that aesthetic activity potentially has at its disposal to become more than itself, to join with a being that is truly significant because it is alive. At the end of this sentence Bakhtin implies that historical or linear time is somehow transcended as a result of this joining; although the act may be located within a single point of historical time, it plumbs the full depth of that moment and the "open event-ness of Being" that is characteristic of it. Bakhtin's insistence on the importance of intuiting (*intuirovanie*) rather than intuition (*intuitsiia*) is also revealing: for a lover of the Heraclitean flux of nature such as Bakhtin, the process or actual operation of *being* intuitive is more important than the mere capacity for it.

Much of this is resonant within "Art and Answerability," particularly because of the insistence in both works that the realm of aesthetic activity transcend and thus transform itself. In the earlier essay, however, Bakhtin did not indicate how this can be accomplished; here, he seems to grope for a clarification of the precise means of transcendence. The original dichotomy of art and life makes its appearance in the later essay as well; the terms that Bakhtin uses to describe that dichotomy here, however, differ in some crucial respects from the ones evident in "Art and Answerability." The central epistemological distinction that Bakhtin makes throughout the later essay is between aestheticism and theoretism, these new terms being more precise in what they describe and at the same time more inclusive than the shopworn "art" and "life." Unlike the earlier opposition, this new one is distinctly cognitive, expressive of particular ways of viewing the world. Aestheticism represents not just the finished products of art but also the aesthetic activity that produced them as well as the propensity of looking at the world from a solipsistic perspective; theoretism comprises not just life itself as we experience it but also those rational steps at system-building that we take to apprehend it, such as in the learned disciplines of the natural and social sciences. As it turns out, theoretism is no less immune to overweaning subjectivism than is aestheticism.

The finer shades of meaning will become more visible as our discussion progresses. The following passage occurs in the next paragraph after the sentence just quoted. Although this passage is clearer, it too is written in what, at least at first, seems to be a needlessly involuted style even for its difficult subject matter:

> [T]wo worlds confront each other, two worlds that have absolutely no communication with each other and are mutually impervious [*ne pronitsaemye*]: the world of culture and the world of life, the only world in which we create, cognize, contemplate, live our lives and die or—the world in which the acts of our activity are objectified and the world in which these acts actually proceed and are accomplished once and only once [*edinozhdy deistvitel'no protekaet, svershaetsia*]. An act of our activity, of our actual experiencing, is like a two-faced Janus [*dvulikii Ianus*]. It looks in two opposite directions: it looks at the objective unity [*edinstvo*] of a domain of culture and at the never-repeatable uniqueness [*edinstvennost'*] of actually lived and experienced life. But there is no unitary and unique plane [*no net edinogo i edinstvennogo plana*] where both faces [*oba lika*] would mutually determine each other in relation to a single unique unity [*k odnomu edinstvennomu edinstvu*]. It is only the once occurrent event of Being in the process of actualization [*sobytie svershaemogo bytiia*] that can constitute this unique unity [*(e)tim edinstvennym edinstvom*]; all that which is theoretical or esthetic must be determined as a constituent moment in the once-occurrent event of Being, although no longer, of course, in theoretical or esthetic terms. (82–83; 2)

On the face of it, the world of culture corresponds to the world of art described in the earlier essay and to the category of the aesthetic (*esteticheskoe*) mentioned in the last sentence of this quotation; the world of life is clearly the descendant of the same term used by Bakhtin a few years before and is linked to the theoretical (*teoreticheskoe*). Unlike in his previous essay, however, here Bakhtin portrays the two categories to be more incommensurable with one another. The style of Bakhtin's Russian in the passage above is almost grotesque in its redundancies and scholastic opacity: while "never-repeatable uniqueness [*nepovtoriaemaia edinstvennost'*]" clearly refers to the unrepeatable uniqueness of human experience, the meaning of such turns of phrase as "single unique unity [*odno-edinstvennoe edinstvo*]" seem almost deliberately obfuscatory in their tautological structures, a sense only heightened by Bakhtin's persistent repetition of them. A number of these stylistic flourishes are highly marked by their derivation from the Church Slavonic stem *edin-* (*one*), which is sometimes tautologically reproduced in both a noun and its modifier (*edinstvennoe edinstvo*). Bakhtin deliberately compounds this verbally incantatory effect by playing *edin-* off its more prosaic East Slavic stem *odin-*. The conflation of *odno-edinstvennoe* (single unique) and the arresting use of the thoroughly bookish *edinozhdy* (once) instead of the modern *odnazhdy* are clearly cases in point, as are the archaic and likewise Slavonic *svershaetsia* (accomplished) and *svershaemyi* (actualized) instead of *sovershaetsia* and *sovershaemyi* and *lik* (face) instead of *litso*. The love of variation that Bakhtin confessed to at the end of his life almost fifty years later is certainly evident here.[67]

Nevertheless, the plethora of such terms in one place still begs the question of the rhetorical or expositional purpose that might be served by using such terminology. If any part of this passage can be said to be highly marked by virtue of an almost egregious stylization—and therefore signaled by Bakhtin as something of a nodal point—it has to be the gnomic statement that the twin figures of theoretism and aestheticism there do not share a single and unique plane (*edinogo i edinstvennogo plana*) where both Janus faces (*lika*) can mutually define one another in relation to one unique unity (*vzaimno sebia opredeliali by po otnosheniiu k odnomu-edinstvennomu edinstvu*). This constitutes the first clear-cut textual echo of "Art and Answerability." A quick look at that essay reveals a very similar interplay between Church Slavonic and East Slavic forms, although not so strong as in "Toward a Philosophy of the Act." Vadim Liapunov's translation of the earlier essay's final sentences effectively renders this stylistic variance by juxtaposing Latin and Anglo-Saxon roots to each other: "Art and life are not one [*ne odno*], but they must become united [*edinym*] in myself—in the unity [*v edinstve*] of my answerability."[68]

As in that piece, a triad appears in "Toward a Philosophy of the Act," only in an entirely different place. In 1919 Bakhtin identifies three areas of human culture: science, art, and life, which he claims can find union (*edinstvo*) only within the individual personality (*v lichnosti*), who joins them (*priobshchaet ikh*) to its own unity (*edinstvu*). In the later essay Bakhtin has redrawn the boundaries separating these categories: now art corresponds to theoretism, whereas science and life itself both go under the rubric of life. In other words, while the unity of the individual constituted something of a fourth category before, now the two categories are discussed as a *tertium non datur*, incommensurable without a third, and the mysterious single-unitary unity (*odno-edinstvennoe edinstvo*) becomes the *tertium quid* or the third and mediating element between the other two. In this essay Bakhtin outlines the complex relationship between lived experience and abstract knowledge.

To truly act answerably or responsibly means to make that knowledge not just a part of that experience, but to transform it into an experience itself.

BAKHTIN AND "LANDMARKS" ON RUSSIAN PRETENDERSHIP

What still remains unclear after all this abstruse tinkering with theological and ontological structures is the actual relevance they have to the ethical concerns pointed up by the Russian editors in the title they provided for the piece. Although many of the further ethical ramifications of "Toward a Philosophy of the Act" were explored in the previous chapter, a recapitulation of some of Bakhtin's terms and concepts is nonetheless helpful at this point. In spite of the fact that here (as in "Art and Answerability"), Bakhtin never names his opponents and possible polemicists, it is easy to see that the issue may be the deterministic positivism that was much discussed from the turn of the century in Russia up to at least the mid-1920s. Early in his career Lenin made the distinction between belief in the historical dialectic and the fetishistic preoccupation with objective reality as a totally determining force: "When demonstrating the necessity for a given series of facts . . . the objectivist always runs the risk of becoming an apologist for these facts; . . . a materialist discloses the class contradictions and in so doing defines his viewpoint."[69] In "Critical Self-Cognition" Gershenzon shrewdly traces the philosophical roots of some members of the intelligentsia to the certain tendencies in Russian history toward political acquiescence and quietism. He sees in the intelligent's insistence on material improvement more than a trace of the peasant complacency that is easily assuaged by immediate creature comforts. Coexisting with this are the almost confessional dynamics of their political faith, which, "like any other, essentially require[s] heroic action." Because few are capable of truly heroic action, the majority of devotees periodically gather and pay lip service to the creed, becoming in effect its laity. "In our radical politics," Gershenzon continues, "the entire rank-and-file intelligentsia was made up of such laymen: one had to recognize oneself as the true son of the church and to periodically participate in its symbolism for society to be satisfied and for one's conscience to be lulled." Such passive and pharasaical piety resulted in a profound fatalism, one in which autocracy (*samoderzhavie*) was blamed for "all the filth and disorderliness of personal and social life," one through which the individual (*lichnost'*) was "not held responsible" (*bezotvetstvennoi*).[70] Many of the terms used by Gershenzon are strikingly similar to Bakhtin's. Like Bakhtin, Gershenzon sees moral responsibility or answerability (*nravstvennaia otvestvennost'*) as being intertwined with attitudes toward systems of belief, whether it be political or religious. As it turns out, the attitudes of many Russians toward politics, ethics, and religion curiously come from the same source: it is precisely because the faith of the Russian people is one of slavishness and not actual belief that they do not understand the concept of answerability for one's actions. Joining a particular creed (*priobshchaetsia k vere*) is not enough. Like many of the other contributors to *Landmarks,* Gershenzon views ethics as being inextricably linked to the idea of the viability of the individual personality. Both Bakhtin and Gershenzon assert that any moral theory that tends to view and excuse most human behavior because of extenuating circumstances must reckon with considerable ethical consequences in its wholesale abrogation of answerability. Like Bakhtin—and more clearly than any of the other contributors to the *Landmarks*—Gershenzon specifically views the individual as being answerable for his or her actions.

The christological subtext of "Toward a Philosophy of the Act" throws the parallels between Bakhtin's essay and *Landmarks* into sharper relief. Many of the contributors to the 1909 collection saw elements of messianism in the political activity of the intelligentsia, the presence of which could only be paradoxical given the latter's anticlericism and atheism. Some of the ethical categories referred to by the *Landmarks* writers seem to converge with Bakhtin's. One of these is the figure of the "pretender" (*samozvanets*) in Russian history and its correlative in the contemporary intellectual life of the country. In "Heroism and Asceticism," Bulgakov's contribution to *Landmarks,* an acid sketch is drawn of the age-old antinomian streak of a certain kind of upheaval in Russia, one tending toward a rage for anarchy on the one hand or a readiness to recognize pretenders (*samozvantsy*) on the other. To paraphrase Bulgakov via Bakhtin, both of these contrarious tendencies—one unconditionally rejecting authority and the other yearning for it—are really flip sides of the same Janus-faced coin. As Bulgakov puts it, this devastating nihilism (*razrushitel'nyi nigilizm*) underlies the intelligentsia's worldview and is very far from a truly revolutionary spirit or a principled political dissent.[71]

According to Bulgakov, what is deeply characteristic of the Russian revolutionary spirit is its profound dualism; it is equally at home in the ascetic refuge of an anchorite as it is in the belligerent marauding of the Cossacks and the peasant uprising. The Russian intelligentsia does not understand the depth and inveteracy of these simultaneous and utterly conflicting inner drives of the Russian masses; and yet (as Bulgakov makes clear elsewhere in the essay), in its zeal to build an earthly City of God (*Grad Bozhii*) the intelligentsia reveals itself as no less prone to the mystical revolutionary spirit that occasionally descends upon the Russian people themselves.[72] Thus, the intelligentsia labors under a double alienation, not only from those it claims to represent, but also from itself; their striving toward a political solidarity with the masses masks their actual solidarity with them on a deeper psychological level. As in his essay "Was ist das Wort?" Bulgakov here is highly attuned to the presence of internal contradictions within a particular phenomenon, a sensitivity that he elsewhere openly (and with palpable respect) admits having acquired in his study and appreciation of Marxism.[73] Bulgakov believes that there is a distinction to be made between productive and sterile forms of inner contrariety. The particular relation of the intelligentsia to the Russian working class and peasantry is clearly terminal and nonproductive, an utterly unbridgeable incommensurability. The logos doctrine represents a political ideal of tempered interaction that the intelligentsia falls woefully short of.

Bakhtin touches perspicaciously on some of these dilemmas of the Russian intelligentsia in "Toward a Philosophy of the Act," although many of these observations are almost pushed out by the conceptual density of the piece. The motif of the pretender occurs not just in this essay, but also many years later in *Rabelais and His World* and *Problems of Dostoevsky's Poetics*. In all three works Bakhtin uses the term in a patently pejorative way, referring to the delusive and egotistic efforts of certain literary characters to take upon themselves the sins of the world and thereby supposedly alleviating them. In "Toward a Philosophy of the Act" Bakhtin describes this term as an ethical and not a literary archetype. In this essay the pretender is someone who is ethically purblind, lost in a miasma of self-centeredness that is all the more pernicious for his unawareness of it. Taken together, the following two segments from the essay represent a single and coherent delineation of the same psychological complex, relating it in a particularly illuminating way to the category of *lichnost'*. According to Bakhtin, the moral imperative cannot be attained in a Kantian or generalizing way, by abstracting the situation entirely from oneself. One needs in fact to begin this process from within, with a clear acknowledgement of one's particular situation in the world: "[t]he 'ought' [*(d)olzhenstvovanie*] becomes possible for the first time where there is an acknowledgment of the fact of as unique person's [*edinstvennoi lichnosti*] being from within that person; where this fact becomes a center for answerability—where I assume answerability for my own uniqueness [*edinstvennost'*], for my own being" (113; 42).

Pursuing this thought, Bakhtin later asserts that "[p]articipation in the being-event of the world [*prichastnost' bytiiu-sobytiiu mira*] in its entirety does not . . . coincide with irresponsible self-surrender to Being, to Being possessed by Being." In that scenario, "the passive moment in my participation [*passivnyi moment uchastnosti*] is moved to the fore," reducing the "to-be-accomplished" self-activity (*aktivnost' zadannaia*). The pathos of Nietzsche with his nostalgia for Dionysian excess stems precisely from such ethical passivity. He goes on to describe the illusory nature of this abandonment of the self:

> The actually experienced fact of my actual participation [*perezhivaemyi fakt deistvitel'noi prichastnosti*] is impoverished here inasmuch as affirmed Being takes possession of the one who affirmed it [*chto utverzhdennoe bytie zavladevaet utverdivshim*], that is, empathizing into one's actual participative Being [*vzhivanie v deistvitel'noe uchastno bytie*] leads to the loss of oneself in it (one cannot be an imposter [lit., "pretender" (*samozvantsem*)]), to the renunciation of the ought-to-be uniqueness of oneself [*k otkazu ot svoei dolzhenstvuiushchei edinstvennosti*]. (119; 49)

The state of possession (*oderzhanie*) causes subjects to view themselves from the perspective of that which possesses them and not from themselves and their possible relation to other consciousnesses. The only thing they have to empathize with is the experience of possession itself in which their identities are already dissolved. It is thus that answerability for one's actions becomes impoverished. The wholesale abstraction from the self ultimately leads to a place where the entire perceived world becomes the experience of abstracting oneself, where there is nothing but an eternal return to the self; it is a world where there is no "outside."

Thus, like the *Landmarks* contributors, Bakhtin believes that true self-sacrifice involves a respect for the individual consciousness (*lichnost'*) and not a denial of it, and that what often seems to be selfless is really a thoroughgoing nihilism and preoccupation with the self. Both he and they define and make use of this concept in a defensive, even embattled way, as if justifying its moral validity. Like those other writers, Bakhtin defines ethical responsibility (*otvestvennost'*) as inextricably linked with that of the individual; the state of Dionysian possession he describes is similar to the anarchic violence that Bulgakov mentions, and it is especially significant that both writers view that situation in political terms as the abdication of responsibility inherent to pretendership. Furthermore—and more substantially—the category of *lichnost'* is, for both Bakhtin and the *Landmarks* contributors, imbued with christological qualities. The second of the excerpts above with its terms "empathizing" (*vzhivanie*) and "participation" (*prichastnost'*) becomes more comprehensible in light of the theological concept of interpenetration as evinced in other parts of the essay; because it is one-sided (*odnostoronee*), Nietzschean Dionysianism cannot fundamentally interact with other realms of existence (*bytie*) and becomes an obstacle to any genuine communing involvement (*prichastnost'*) with others. As already shown, the conception of the tripartite division of the individual consciousness was developed by Florensky four years after the publication of *Landmarks*, a trichotomy that has certain possible echoes in "Art and Answerability." By the time Bakhtin wrote "Toward a Philosophy of the Act," he had effected a distinct fusion of the philosophical connotations of *lichnost'* with their theological nuances of triunity and Trinitarian interpenetration.

But it is in the two quotations in the passage above that the precise point of intersection between Bakhtin's early work and *Landmarks* can be seen more clearly. Yet another link between "Art and Answerability" and "Toward a Philosophy of the Act" can be seen with the term *oderzhanie* (state of possession), which Bakhtin used in the first essay in reference to ex nihilo poetic inspiration and here to describe the Nietzschean abandonment of self to Dionysianism. Averintsev glosses Bakhtin's reference to Dionysianism as a possible reference to the preoccupation with Nietzsche that was evident in the work of poets such as Viacheslav Ivanov (161). Thus, it would seem, Bakhtin implicitly puts Dionysianism under the rubric of aestheticism. In fact, however, here he could also be alluding to theoretism. By the time he wrote this essay, Russian interest in Nietzsche had gone well beyond fin de siècle decadence and deeply into political radicalism. In his *Landmarks* essay "The Ethic of Nihilism," Semyon Frank caustically takes note of what he perceives to be a most peculiar fusion: "At present, everything has become confused: the Social Democrat is discussing God, studying esthetics, fraternizing with 'mystical anarchists,' losing his faith in materialism and reconciling Marx with Mach and Nietzsche."[74] There is the distinct sense in Bakhtin's description of the aestheticism/theoretism dichotomy that the two categories are essentially two different sides of the same coin. It was an awareness that seemed to be shared by some of his contemporaries.

The confluence of the christological metaphor in relation to politics and the image of the pretender are most abundantly realized in the following passage from "Toward a Philosophy of the Act." As Bakhtin explains here, there is a distinct difference between genuine communion and ritualism. In terms that are highly reminiscent of Bulgakov's demystification of the intelligentsia, Bakhtin describes how the pretender—the one loudest in proclaiming his or her individuality—is in fact more enslaved than anyone else to the hollow ritual:

> To orient an act or deed within the whole of once-occurrent Being-as-event [*edinstvennogo bytiia-sobytiia*] does not mean at all that we translate it into the language of highest values, where the concrete, real, participative (unindifferent) event [*uchastnoe sobytie*] in which the act orients itself immediately is only a representation or reflection of those values. I participate in the event [*ia personal'no prichasten sobytiiu*] personally, and every object or person with which I have to do in my once-occurrent life participates personally. I *can* perform a political act or religious ritual in the capacity of a representative, but that already constitutes a specialized action, which presupposes the fact of my having been actually able to have performed it. But even here I do not definitely abdicate my answerability in person; on the contrary, my representative and empowered status in itself takes into account my personal answerability. The tacit presupposition of life's ritualism is *not* humility, but pride. One has to

> develop humility to the point of participating in person [*personal'noi uchastnosti*] and being answerable in person. In attempting to understand our whole life as secret representation [*predstavitel'stvo*] and every act we perform—as a ritual act, we turn into imposters and pretenders [*samozvantsami*]. (121; 52)

The pretender is the one who is excluded from oneness with others; it is he who is permanently alienated from those for whom he claims to speak. Bakhtin's assertion that one needs to commune with the event in order to commune with others does not, however, constitute a swallowing-up of identity in the manner of Khomiakov's *sobornost'*. Bakhtin stresses the preservation of individuality in the face of such interrelation with others, the adverb *personal'no* (personally) emphasizing the almost physical presence of the agent participating in the action. There is much about this passage that resonates deeply with the pathos of the Russian intelligentsia from its inception at the end of the eighteenth century up to Bakhtin's day. The allusion to the striving of the pretender for representation (*predstavtil'stvo*) of others is highly suggestive of the intelligentsia's crypto-megalomania, described by Bulgakov and the other contributors to the *Landmarks* collection. This rage for representation also takes on a more somber hue in the context of the Russian Civil War during which Bakhtin wrote the essay.

Bakhtin links many of these insights in a paragraph a few pages later. There, he notes that economic materialism is correct to the extent that it focuses so much attention on the product of the act; the motives that issued that product, however, cannot be deduced from the relic that it is, for "the product in its validity walls itself off from the actually performed act in its actual motivation." Only the act itself can give us that information. "The contemporary crisis is, fundamentally, a crisis of contemporary action [*postupok*]." Bakhtin finally outlines what that crisis represents in its contemporary setting:

> The theoretical and esthetic worlds have been set at liberty, but from within these world themselves it is impossible to connect them and bring them into communion with the ultimate unity, i.e., to incarnate them [*priobschit' ikh k poslednemu edinstvu, inkarnirovat' ikh*]. Since theory has broken away from the actually performed act and develops according to its immanent law, the performed act itself, having released theory from itself, begins to deteriorate. All the energy of answerable performing is drawn off into the autonomous domain of culture, and, as a result, the performed act, detached from that energy, sinks to the level of elementary biological and economic motivation, that is, loses all its ideal moments: that is precisely what constitutes the state of civilization. The whole wealth of culture is placed at the service of the biological act. Theory consigns the performed act or deed to the realm of brute Being, drains it of all the moments of ideality in it and draws them into its own autonomous self-contained domain, that is, totally impoverishes the

> actually performed act. This is the source from which Tolstoyism and all forms of cultural nihilism draw their impelling inspiration. (123; 55)

As before, Bakhtin here underscores the close association between aestheticism and theoretism, one that undermines the supposed opposition between these two ways of thinking. In this passage Bakhtin returns to his earlier treatment of "art versus life" that he put forth in "Art and Answerability"; his treatment of the dichotomy now, however, is considerably more sophisticated. Here, he hints at the ethical consequences of such approaches to knowledge. His indictment against reductionism in economics, its encroachment on other fields, and his explicit identification of the progressive intelligentsia at the end of this paragraph are astonishing even considering the time and place of their writing, and certainly would have been unpublishable even during Khrushschev's "thaw," the next significant period of liberalization. This part of Bakhtin's essay is particularly close in sentiment and argument to Frank's article in *Landmarks* about the ethics of nihilism.[75] For Bakhtin, both the politically informed scholarship of his day and forms of political activity itself were found to be ethically wanting because of their insistence on the supremacy of life over art or of the irrelevance of the latter to the former. The christological terminology of "Toward a Philosophy of the Act" and "Art and Answerability" is the means by which Bakhtin expresses the nature of this interrelation between different forms of human activity; as in *Landmarks,* it is also the rebuttal to the the new clericalism embodied in intelligenstia's conception of the revolutionary elite, a category that Lenin himself played no small role in developing. Aleksandr Meier was all too aware of the tensions lying in wait from inside this notion of the socialist elect. Bakhtin and the *Landmarks* writers take this notion of the individual (*lichnost'*) as revolutionary hypostasis and adapt it, applying it to ontology and epistemology as a whole and therefore making what was once a class-bound category into a general principle. In "Toward a Philosophy of the Act" Bakhtin holds out for a more hopeful future, one where the individual and society can interact in a way that bespeaks mutual respect. Bakhtin believes the categories of participant (*uchastnik*) and communicant (*prichastnik*) do not significantly differ: the genuine taking part in the body politic transforms the individual rather than obliterating him or her. Like the contributors to *Landmarks,* Bakhtin implicitly argues for the return of the individual and personality to philosophical discourse. Bakhtin wrote his first two essays during the uncertain and difficult period between the 1905 revolution and the death of Lenin; his calls for the rethinking of human culture outside of the positivistic confines of the social sciences and literature went unheard at that time but have found a more receptive audience now.

The problematical interrelation between art and life that Bakhtin focused on at the beginning of his career was both a glance into the recent Russian past and an attempt to break out of the vicious ideological circle that pitted politics and aesthetics against each other. Naturally, on account of its brevity, his "Art and Answerability" could only pose the problem in the most schematic of ways. It has already been demonstrated that in his somewhat equivocating first article Bakhtin outlines a balance between the concerns for social accountability and individual autonomy not because he pursues the Aristotelian ideal of a golden mean but because he believes that only such a balance will lead to more fruitful work in both literature and literary scholarship. In his second extant essay Bakhtin examines the transformation of these two epistemological stances within the individual act. The affinities between Bakhtin and *Landmarks* becomes even clearer when viewed in the light of this defense of the individual's moral autonomy.

In this essay and "Art and Answerability" Bakhtin endeavors to restore the categories of the individual personality (*lichnost'*) and, inextricably linked to it, the viability of ethics. As already seen, Bakhtin's arguments significantly run the same course as many of those espoused by the *Landmarks* contributors and Florensky, particularly in regard to the interaction between the individual and society. For all of these writers the self-abnegating ideal of the radical intelligentsia was myopic and self-contradictory. To them the intelligentsia's attack on the idea of individualism was not all it seemed to be: it concealed a profoundly egotistical and quasi-messianic view that the *intelligents* had of themselves and their historic mission; according to the contributors to the 1909 collection, the *intelligents'* putative veneration of the suffering people contained its own obverse or opposite in the form of a certain condescension and even contempt toward the same people whom they claimed to be representing.

Like the *Landmarks* writers, Bakhtin locates much of the difficulty in discussing ethics with the passion for ramification that dominates philosophical discourse; he believes that contemporary approaches to philosophy are hobbled by their strict dichotomizing of theory and aesthetics as mutually exclusive and noncorrelating categories. This disciplinary compartmentalization transforms theory and aesthetics into two realms poised against each other, like neighboring countries without diplomatic relations. The bulk of "Toward a Philosophy of the Act" constitutes a brief for a closer interaction between these two disciplines. A close examination of the form that this interrelation would take reveals that Bakhtin conceives of it in terms of an absolutely symbiotic association that would nonetheless not result in a merging of the two; he envisions a situation in which both would preserve their fundamental individual identities, describing this interdisciplinary dynamic using the Chalcedonian dictum of conditional or mitigated fusion. As we shall see in Chapter 4, however, this productive state of an almost organic mutual relation is not without its own complications that stem from the core of Chalcedonian doctrine itself.

Chapter Four

"Without Confusion or Separation": Bakhtin and the Chalcedonian Ideal of the Divided Union

> Dostoevsky's world is profoundly *pluralistic.* If we were to seek an image toward which this whole world gravitates, an image in the spirit of Dostoevsky's own worldview, then it would be a church as a communion of unmerged souls, where sinners and righteous men come together; or perhaps it would be the image of Dante's world, where multi-leveledness is extended into eternity, where there are the penitent and the unrepentant, the damned and the saved. . . . [T]he image of a unified spirit is deeply alien to him.
> —*Problems of Dostoevsky's Poetics* (1963)

IT HAS often been said that commonly held notions of dialogue were irrevocably changed by Bakhtin. As one critic provocatively put it in 1983 when Bakhtin's writings on language were still being rediscovered in the West, "Bakhtin's linguistics is an *anti-linguistics,* a systematic questioning and inverting of the basic premises and arguments of traditional linguistics."[1] Never again will we see communication merely as a mechanical exchange of information: if the terms used to describe this act (such as concretization [*uplotnenie*] and enfleshment [*oplotnenie*]) are any indication, it has now become an event that changes the consciousnesses of its participants, lending them a fuller social and even corporeal existence in the world. As demonstrated earlier in this study, the Johannine subtext of discourse as transubstantiating logos comes into play through the root from which these terms are derived ("flesh" [*plot'*]). In the last two chapters we also caught a glimpse of how Bakhtin's transformative model of dialogue is also grounded in later christological paradigms such as the interdwelling or interpenetration (*perichoresis*) of the Trinity's hypostases and the doctrine concerning the twin natures of Christ, propounded at the Fourth Ecumenical Council at Chalcedon. In this chapter I shall examine more closely Bakhtin's references to Chalcedonian doctrine and its ramifications for his conceptions of dialogue and carnival.

Even a brief reminder of the innovations wrought by this ecumenical council throws into sharp relief their potential relevance for Bakhtin's theories. According to the Chalcedonian decision of 451, both the human and the divine natures of Christ coexist immutably and without separation or division (Russian, *v dvukh prirodakh, neslitno, neprevrashchenno, nerazdelimo, nerazluchimo;* Greek, *en duo physesin asynchytos, atreptos, adiairetos, achoristos*).[12] As outlined by the drafters of the decision and their contemporary Pope Leo II (from whom they adapted many of the terms used in his famous *Tome* to Flavian) the formula was adduced as doctrinally linked to Johannine transubstantiation, which they saw as a curative to the extremes of Nestorianism and Monophysitism. Surely the belief of the Word made flesh (John 1:14) makes untenable both the Nestorian view of Christ as a being forever riven by two irreconcilable natures and the Monophysite assertion of the subsuming or absorption of the human into the Divine![13] Or so the reasoning went. In point of fact, the decision resolved little in matters of widespread belief, and Monophysitism in particular (together with its doctrinal opposite of Arianism, which stressed the humanity of Christ and was generally perceived as being more patently heretical) continued to flourish in many parts of Christendom. The Monophysites saw Christ as only "seeming" to be human, like the angel Raphael in the Apocryphal Book of Tobit who eventually reveals himself to the family he helps as having maintained earlier nothing but an illusion of mortality such as theirs: "What appeared to you was a vision" (Tobit 12:19). Translated into the secular terms of phenomenology, the Monophysite position is utterly irreconcilable with Bakhtin's conception of identity and agency, since any playing of roles other than one's own position in existence constitutes pretendership or impostership. Monophysitism is also inimical to any conception of dialogue, since it assumes the impossibility of sustained interaction between parts of one's being and instead posits the assimilation, and therefore disappearance, of one into another. As will be discussed later in this chapter, Bakhtin even polemicizes with what may be considered a contemporary version or descendent of Monophysitism in the philosophy of Vladimir Solovyov.

In the present context, the Russian locution *nesliiano i nerazdel'no* (or its variant *neslitno i nerazdelimo*) assumes a special importance. This opaque turn of phrase (which literally means "not merged yet undivided" and will subsequently be referred to as the Chalcedonian formula) is not an idiom in Russian and is recognizable only as a product of the ecumenical council's decision; it assumes a surprisingly high profile in Russian philosophy and literature from the turn of the century to the twenties. Bakhtin iterates this phrase (or patent variants of it) in several crucial moments of his work, from his earliest writings to *Problems of Dostoevsky's Poetics.* Moreover, Bakhtin renders this theological subtext explicit by using Chalcedonian terms in relation to the topos of interpenetration, thereby reenacting the confluence of the doctrinally separate yet mutually supportive notions of interpenetration or *perichoresis* (which was not a part of the council's decision) and the twin natures of Christ. For Bakhtin, dialogue represents just such a coexistence and inseparable interaction of identities, an event possessed of transubstantiating qualities.

Up until this point, it could be argued that as interesting as such resonances may be, they are more suggestive than substantive. Unlike the two natures of Christ, the voices within Bakhtin's theory of the Dostoevskian word are more—perhaps even irreconcilably—agonistic and antagonistic to one another in a way that the twin natures of the council's decision seem not to be. There is, in fact, considerable evidence that Bakhtin was not satisfied with the presumption of harmony arising from diversity that he expressed in the short and almost sermonistic piece "Art and Answerability": in his essays of the thirties such as "Discourse in the Novel" and "Forms of Time and the Chronotope in the Novel" he seems more at home with an interactive diversity than with a centrifugal reining-in. What is important here, however, is not Bakhtin's agreement with or belief in the doctrine espoused by the ecumenical council but the possibility that he echoes its doctrines in his paradox of diversity within unity. The real issue is Bakhtin's indebtedness to the particularly Russian and nineteenth-century religious and philosophical concept of communality or "all-oneness" (*vseedinstvo*), a connection postulated by Steven Cassedy as well as Clark and Holquist but that has remained essentially unexplored.[4] The Chalcedonian subtext offers the most irrefutable proof of Bakhtin's engagement in the aesthetic implications of christological categories. At the same time, Bakhtin's relation to this subtext is complex and even problematic. While he clearly makes use of Chalcedonian terms and concepts in his theory of dialogue, his deracination of them from their doctrinal context bespeaks a certain ambivalence. One is tempted to say that Bakhtin enters into a dialogic relation with the Chalcedonian dogma of interrelation. The similarities and affinities between Bakhtin and religious philosophers such as Solovyov and Meier emerge with particular clarity here, as does the realization that the sources of Bakhtin's christological metaphor are probably at least in part funneled through the conduit of these later and more unconventional glosses on theology and not taken exclusively from the hermeneutic well of the church fathers. And yet, Bakhtin navigates through all these versions of the Chalcedonian formula without running aground, in "Art and Answerability" (1919) setting out on a journey that, in *Problems of Dostoevsky's Poetics* (1963), results in his own map of this treacherous doctrinal territory. Unlike his Russian contemporaries, Bakhtin returns to the original doctrine, producing his own careful reading of what it means in practical terms.

THE TWIN NATURES OF MODERN RUSSIAN THOUGHT

The fourth ecumenical council occurred on the cusp of one of the most difficult periods of Byzantine doctrinal history. During the sessions of the council there were numerous attempts to mediate the Monophysite controversy, many of which were informed by Leo II's assertion that Christ consisted of two natures in conjunction. The final decision represented something of a mediation between the Nestorian and Monophysite positions, asserting that the human and the divine come together in the person and hypostasis of Christ but remaining conditionally separate as natures. Not surprisingly, this drafting left few satisfied and the meetings themselves were often accompanied by catcalls such as "Down with the Nestorians!"[5] This sense of what might at best be called a Scholastic paradox and at worst an unresolved conflict became an important and problematic element in the council's legacy. It was precisely the tense equilibrium of the interrelational paradigm delineated at Chalcedon that attracted many fin de siècle Russian writers, its formulation about the twin natures becoming an important symbol for them. In his book *Russia and the Universal Church,* Vladimir Solovyov explicitly refers to the council and comments extensively on the ontological and cultural implications of its most famous declaration. The influential poet and philosopher-mystic Nikolai Minsky in his 1905 book *The Religion of the Future* uses the Chalcedonian formula to denote the positive value of antirationalism, embedded in the council's insistence on the coexistence and interdepedence of opposites. Minsky believed that modernity's dyad of rationalism and mysticism (acknowledged as a positive conflation since the time of Kant) was in fact anticipated in the assertion at Chalcedon of the complete and utter harmony between the human and divine natures of Christ.[6] According to Minsky, although reason and the unknowable "do not merge [*ne slivaiutsia*] with each other, they are inconceivable one without the other."[7] The phrase also appears in at least one essay by the poet Aleksandr Blok, who uses it to refer to the ambivalence of the artist separated from the world yet still maintaining a foothold in it.[8]

But in this period it is Solovyov's writing that is most significant in influencing Bakhtin's use of the formula. Solovyov uses the formula himself in his essay "Beauty in Nature" to describe the unconvergent yet inseparable union of matter and light (*nesliiano[oe] i nerazdel'n[oe] soedineni[e] veshchestva i sveta*).[9] A similar dichotomy takes hold in another essay, "The General Meaning of Art." There Solovyov sketches out the spiritual development of mankind in distinctly evolutionary terms. Solovyov explains that the individual human consciousness represents the culmination of the natural process in a double sense (*v dvoiakom smysle*): first, as a manifestation of beauty, and second, as the most cognizant being in nature. As a result of this dual identity, the subject can itself become a mover ("*deiatelem*" [Solovyov's emphasis]) in the world, coming closer to fulfilling the universal ideal of the complete mutual penetration (*polno[e] vzaimno[oe] proniknoveni[e]*) and unconstrained solidarity of the spiritual and material, the ideal and the real, and the subjective and objective.[10] For Solovyov, this activated consciousness represents not only the epitome or emblem of the interconnectedness of the universe: it in fact becomes an agent actually capable of changing the surrounding material reality. Given Solovyov's direct and explicit use of the Chalcedonian formula, there can be little doubt that the dichotomies he outlines correspond to the divine and human natures of Christ and that the mutual penetration (*vzaimnoe proniknovenie*) he mentions is at least in part reminiscent of *perichoresis.* One can easily see how such modified Nietzscheanism became an important part of the postrevolutionary cult of man as creator and transformer or artist of nature, a notion philosophically central to the Five-Year Plans and the Soviet space industry. Many of the ideas of "God-manhood" developed by Solovyov and, to a more significant extent, his contemporary Nikolai Fyodorov (1828–1903) were in fact subsumed into Soviet philosophy, where they uneasily coexisted with Marxist terms and categories.

Several passages in Solovyov's work manifest his interest in the Chalcedonian paradigm from a perspective simultaneously theological, philosophical, and sociological. Elsewhere in "The General Meaning of Art" Solovyov speaks pejoratively of what he calls the impenetrability of egoism (*nepronitsaemost' egoisma*) and opposes to it the paradisiacal state of interpenetrability (*vzaimo-pronitsaemost'*), where individuals find themselves in others and each sees himself or herself in everybody else (*vse nakhodiat sebia v kazhdom, i kazhdyi—vo vsekh drugikh*) (1:391). In this last statement Solovyov is patently alluding to John 6:56, a verse that forms one of the cornerstones of both the doctrine of transubstantiation and the Chalcedonian council ("He that eateth my flesh and drinketh my blood, dwelleth in me and I in him" [King James Version]). Later in the essay, Solovyov states that the light of reason (*svet razuma*) has to embody artistically the conscious meaning of life (*soznannyi smysl zhizni*) into a new reality, one that is more harmonious with it (1:394). This light reveals the pervasiveness or ubiquitous penetrability (*vsepronitsaemost'*) of idealist principles such as beauty and equality among people (1:397). Solovyov quite explicitly brings together his various borrowings from traditional christology as espoused in doctrines such as the Eucharist and the decisions of the ecumenical councils to provide a matrix for his philosophical system of "all-unity" (*vseedinstvo*), a vision of a humanity as a single organism constituted by porous cells. Although his conflation of a quasi-biological metaphor and christological schemata is unusual, it almost seems inevitable in the secularized context within which Solovyov operates.

Closer to Bakhtin's time, this hybridization of the (pseudo-)scientific and the sacred is amplified by Nikolai Lossky in his 1915 extended article "The World as an Organic Whole." Lossky mingles Chalcedonian and perichoresical motifs in his use of terms such as *sliianie* (merging) in tandem with interpenetrability (*vzaimopronitsaemost'*) and impenetrability (*nepronitsaemost'*) in describing the operations of the intersubjective universe, a place where each agent or actor represents an atom or *substantia.*[11] In an article he wrote seven years later, Lossky argues against vitalist theories of contemporary biology that posited the idea of a Bergsonian life force coming from within the atom or *substantia.* He asserts that, on the contrary, the principles of attraction and repulsion are in fact ubiquitous and a balance exists in nature between them, between the impenetrability of the body (*nepronitsaemost' tela*) and its no less innate drift toward consubstantiality (*edinosushchie*) with a larger whole.[12] The last of these philosophical terms is distinctly theological in provenance, a translation of the Greek *homoousia* (lit., same essence) that is used to describe the internal coherence of the Trinity.

Many years later, Lossky returned to this terminology in his book *Dostoevsky's Christian Understanding of the World,* which he wrote in exile in the early fifties. Unlike his 1922 article "On Contemporary Vitalism," Lossky now explicitly acknowledged the theological provenance of his organicist theories. There are certain striking parallels between Lossky's Dostoevsky book and *Problems of Dostoevsky's Poetics.* As described by Bakhtin and Lossky, there are structural affinities or parallels between the Dostoevskian word and the Chalcedonian one. For both scholars, Dostoevsky's language is bifurcated but not binary; like the theologians at Chalcedon, Bakhtin conceives of this discourse as a dyad whose members exert a powerful and fundamental influence upon one another. Bakhtin's memorable term for such refracted or socially impacted speech is the "word with a sideward glance" (*slovo s ogliad'koi*),[13] which is essentially another version of this union and is consistent with Chalcedonian doctrine's stipulation of the enfleshed Johannine word as the common and binding matrix of the twin natures of Christ. Lossky stresses a similarly dynamic interaction between self and other, linking kenosis or emptying out of the ego to Orthodox Trinitarianism with its emphasis on the conditional or mediated autonomy of each hypostasis. Similarly, as Bakhtin explains Dostoevsky's world, giving oneself wholly to each and all undividedly and without reservation (*bezrazdel'no i bezzavetno*) is the highest good; there, the law of *I* merges (*slivaetsia*) with the law of humanism, these opposites mutually annihilating each other in their convergence (*v slitii*).[14] With their repeated use of terms such as *edinosushchie, nerazdel'no* and derivatives of the verb "to merge" (*slivat'/slit'*), there can be no doubt as to Lossky's and Bakhtin's Chalcedonian frame of reference. In his book on Dostoevsky, Lossky states the *I* enters into a close relation with Christ as Word (*slovo*) and

Logos; he even calls this close link a partial consubstantiality ("chastishnoe *edinosushchie*" [Lossky's emphasis]). In Bakhtin's writing about Dostoevsky, a strikingly similar integrative unity takes place in the head of the novelist's hero. Thus, in Dostoevsky's "Poor Folk" the word (*slovo*) spoken by Makar Devushkin is inextricably linked to those of other characters. As Bakhtin puts it, the hero's word about himself is built on the basis of the incessant influence of another's about him, the selfish principle of "I for myself" shading off into "I for another."[15] Both editions of Bakhtin's Dostoevsky book are full of Chalcedonian reverberations, the most conspicuous being his famous statement that the archetypical image of Dostoevsky's world is that of a church, a single meeting-place for the disparate and unmerged souls (*kak obshchenie nesliiannykh dush*) of sinners as well as the righteous.[16] It is a highly significant allusion to the Chalcedonian formula, the full signifiance of which will become evident at the end of this chapter. Years later, in his 1973 interview with Duvakin, Bakhtin fondly recalled Lossky as a teacher at the university but when asked whether or not he had read *Dostoevsky's Christian Understanding of the World*, he answered no. It is entirely possible, of course, that Lossky read the 1929 edition of Bakhtin's book and was himself influenced by it; several passages from it certainly seem to resonate in Lossky's 1953 study.[17] As just demonstrated, however, the Chalcedonian terminology was already firmly in place in Lossky's writing, years before *The Problems of Dostoevsky's Art* was published. The philosopher simply funneled the same organicist and Bergsonian concepts from his epistemological writings into his literary criticism. It is the Bergsonian transformation of the Chalcedonian model in Lossky's early philosophical work (familiar to Bakhtin) that may have influenced the critic.

But perhaps the most striking feature of all these allusions to the Fourth Ecumenical Council from Solovyov to Lossky is its political ramifications. In the final analysis, what they and Bakhtin share in their adaptation of the Chalcedonian ideal is the principle of the relation between the individual and society, stressing the need for an equilibrium between the respective demands of each. On the face of it, it is a social ideal that seems both banal and self-evident. The distinction between the ontological subject and the citizen is, however, a revolutionary notion in a society steeped in the statist and autocratic traditions of post-Petrine Russia, which many have seen as undergoing a particulaly robust development in the Soviet period. At first blush, one is especially surprised in finding this idea retrofitted into a paradigm drawn from ecclesiastical history. All the same, in the conceptual vividness of its structural model this conjunction of rarified spirituality with the gritty realities of political life and civil rights somehow seems highly appropriate. The renowned American leftist I. F. Stone once stated that doctrines such as the Eucharist, Trinity, and the virgin birth had been "crystallized long after the Gospels and [are] not relevant to their ethical teachings."[18] And yet in the Russian context it is precisely through the lens of christological doctrine that distinctions between different kinds of ethical categories emerge most clearly. This fusion of theological and political frames of reference in delineating a social philosophy represents what might be called the twin natures of Russian thought. Like the human and divine within the Chalcedonian formula, they interact closely with each other in the definition of an all-inclusive inquiry into material reality, one whose inner contradictions are as productive as they are profound.

One of the more striking uses of the Chalceonian formula in this heterodox and surprisingly politicized vein—and one that approaches Bakhtin's own understanding of the Chalcedonian formula—occurs in Aleksandr Meier's 1918 unpublished essay "On Class Struggle," discussed in the previous chapter of this study. Meier's essay has additional importance because it represents something of a link between Bakhtin's and Solovyov's treatment of the Chalcedonian ideal. While Solovyov often adduces the formula *nesliianno i nerazdel'no* as the watchword of utopia, it is Meier who explicitly imbues it with specific political meaning, taking Solovyov's distinctive but idealistic and rarified treatment of it several steps further. Meier makes extensive use of the Chalcedonian formula to describe the ideal workings of the classless society. In Meier's scheme, this formula and the theologically related concept of "interpenetration" (Russian, *vzaimoproniknovenie;* Greek, *perichoresis*) come to represent how each group or cadre merges with others while maintaining its integrity within society. As mentioned in the previous chapter, it is likely that Bakhtin knew this essay from his friendship with Meier and his possible attendance of the meetings of the Saint Petersburg Religious-Philosophical Society where it was first read.

At the beginning of the essay Meier describes the truly creative (and therefore revolutionary) act as a necessarily incomplete or conditional fusion of cerebration and activism, a tense yet highly beneficial equilibrium:

> Society as a whole always creates. But it seems to me that true creation takes place only when the thought [*zamysel*] is not separated from its deed [*ispolnenie*]. In the creative process the thought is inherently inseparable [*nerazdelen*] from the deed. That is characteristic of the creative act. The creative act disappears whenever the thought is estranged from the deed. The dissociation of thought from deed now characterizes the uncreative act. However, there is also no creativity where there is a complete merging [*slitnost'*], where there is no particular task to be done, such as in instinct. The inseparable yet unmerged [*Nerazdel'noe i nesliiannoe*] presence of thought and deed is true creativity. When they are merged [*slity*] there is still no creativity; when they are separated [*razdeleny*], it has already gone. At this time, the inseparability and non-convergence [*nerazdel'nost' i nesliiannost'*] of the creative act is present

> within the individual mind; in society [however] it is still absent. The collective activity of humanity is still insufficiently creative. The isolated individual may still strive towards creativity. But in the realm of the material—in culture, in the social management of collective creation—it is practically non-existent: there the thought and the deed are separated [*razdeleny*]. [Our current situation represents] the mortification of creativity.[19]

Unlike Bakhtin himself, Meier believes that true creative activity hinges on something very much like the Marxian abolition of the division of labor. And yet, the anomalous nature of Meier's communardism is pointed up by the fact that for him this division is not between classes, but between thinkers and doers in a very broad sense; in fact, there is no recognizable component of class criticism in this or any other essay by him. One is struck, in short, by the overweening idealist nature of Meier's political stance. Meier's elevation of Chalcedonian dualism into an ideal cannot be doubted. The tenor of these comments, moreover, dispels any question as to the nature of Meier's relation to his theological reference; the remarks are reverent to their reference and do not carry even the slightest overtone of detached trope-mongering or irony. Nonetheless, the conflation of doctrinal christology with revolutionary ethics emerges as an uneasy alliance.

This positive valuation and pasting of a page from doctrinal history into the highly charged and politicized present is deliberately reinforced by Meier throughout the essay, as if to point up the singularity of what could be called his agitational christology. A few pages later, he reasserts that merging of intent and performance in the truly creative act must occur in order for the distinction between thinkers and performers to disappear. We stand, Meier states, before a daunting task:

> Here we see the road to the creation of a collective subject [*kollektivnoi lichnosti*]. Not the external state of being separated [*razdelennost'*], but a complete inseparability [*nerazdel'nost'*] of the aspects of thinking and doing [*razuma i ispolneniia*] is what characterizes the subject. On the stage of social life, the path of the subject is possible only under the condition of the full merging [*polnogo sliianiia*] of the aspects of thought and deed [*zamysla i ispolneniia*] in one individual. How can we proceed with the liquidation of the currently-existing separation [*razdeleniia*] [of people] into thinkers and doers? Not, of course, by mechanical means, not through the reconciliation and cooperation of separate groups [*razdelennykh grupp*].[20]

Particularly important both in this excerpt and the one preceding it is the distinction between the adjective "separate" (*razdel'nyi*) and the participle "separated" (*razdelennyi*). For Meier, the latter is utterly insidious, denoting the enforced separation or sequestering of one kind of human activity from another; the former, highly marked as a lexeme from the Chalcedonian decision, represents the contigent or mediated separation needed for the personal and the public to coexist fruitfully. Personality needs to be guided by the faculties of both the thinker and the doer, simultaneously; the idea that there should be separate groups of people specializing in these activities is odious to Meier. Implicit in this disquisition is the notion that thinking and doing naturally belong together. The famous yoked dichotomy from the Chalcedonian council is used as a point of reference for Meier's conception of revolutionary ethics, the christological schemata becoming thoroughly internalized into the mental state of the true political activist. One could call Meier's thought a kind of practical Christianity if its actual recommendations for social transformation were not so difficult to extract from the mythologized conflict he establishes between archetypes of the thinker (*zamyslitel'*) and doer (*ispolnitel'*). Nonetheless, in spite of this uncertainty in the area of application, one is struck by the sheer originality and conceptual brilliance of Meier's interweaving of church dogma with a highly politicizied version of Solovyov's conception of "God-manhood." In an interview conducted for this study, Sergei Bocharov stated that Bakhtin once described Meier to him as both a social democrat and a traditional Christian, praising him for his principled stands and political loyalty.[21] Bakhtin remembered Meier for the unconstrained eclecticism of his thought, for the ability to believe both politically and religiously without (to borrow a Chalcedonian turn of phrase) confusion or division.

Something very much like Meier's description of the transformation of person into deity can be found in various versions and potencies in the writings of the movement of Russian religious philosophy that was inspired by Solovyov and continued in emigration as late as the sixties. Significantly, in his otherwise meticulous and dispassionate history of Russian theology the scholar-priest George Florovsky registers an unmistakable dislike of these adaptations of traditional religious thought by the laity of the Russian intelligentsia, claiming that their work has more in common with Western European Romanticism than with Orthodoxy.[22] From the Florovskian perspective, the supremacy of the subject is a relic of the German philosophical tradition in particular and is irreconcilable with the older tradition of Russian religious thought. Solovyov himself was never able to transcend this radical subjectivism, his insistence on an individual's binding membership in the "all-unity" (*vseedinstvo*) of the cosmos notwithstanding. The fact that much of Russian thought professes to be collectivist or Marxist is, from this point of view, not a contradiction of the idolatry of the individual subject: as the contributors of the 1909 collection *Landmarks* themselves point out with considerable self-awareness, much of Russian political radicalism is constituted precisely by the oxymoron of subjective sociology. Many thinkers such as Solovyov, Sergei Bulgakov, and Nikolai Berdiaev had, in fact, been at one time or another Marxists; drawn to certain aspects of the notion of "God-manhood" and "God-building" were Marxist writers, theorists, and soon-to-be pillars of the Soviet cultural establishment such as Maxim Gorky and Anatoly Lunacharsky.[23] In the eclectic political thought of Meier and Solovyov, the entire social universe is ideally transformed into precisely such a cognicizing subject, which makes it possible to conceive of society as (in Meier's words) a collective subject or person (*lichnost'*). Society becomes in essence nothing more than the macrocosm of the idealized individual consciousness. In the Russian context, collectivism and phenomenological solipsism or individualism are cut from the same cloth, a strange conjunction that is yet another example of the double or twin nature of Russian thought in its political and axiological modes. That the Chalcedonian formula exerted such a strong attraction for these thinkers is hardly surprising: they were drawn to it as a principle partly because it illuminated so much of the inner workings of their own thought and intellectual biographies. The sense of contradiction, paradox, or even dread of logical inconsistency was never far behind such ruminations about the divided union of God-manhood. As Solovyov put it at one particularly contentious debate with a group of scholars, our salvation is guaranteed only by the work we do in society; at the same time, we also should bear in mind that the church and state are *already* equivalent to the divine and human natures of Christ, which of course should never be viewed as either separate or fused but in harmonious interaction.[24] But is not the separation of corporeal existence and the afterlife initially highlighted by Solovyov precisely an example of non-fusion and alienation? While Solovyov's and Meier's extensions of the Chalcedonian formula are ingenious, their idiosyncratic selectiveness and conceptual innovations also stretch the substance of the original doctrine to its breaking point.

THE CHALCEDONIAN FORMULA IN BAKHTIN'S EARLY WORK

Bakhtin's first clear reference to Chalcedonian doctrine occurs in this politically sublimated version typical of Russian thought from Solovyov to Lossky, one based not on the dichotomy of the divine and the human but on the opposition between the demands of the social order on the one hand and the individual act on the other. In the shrewd analogies wrought by this redaction of the formula, reason and civilization are tantamount to a cold deity (indifferent to its minions), and the specifically individual corresponds to the human nature. At the beginning of "Toward a Philosophy of the Act," Bakhtin states that the theoretical and aesthetic perspectives on life can be brought into better coordination with one another only within the act or deed itself:

> An act must acquire a single unitary plane to be able to reflect itself in both directions—in its sense or meaning and in its being; it must acquire

> the unity [*obresti edinstvo*] of two-sided answerability—both for its content (special answerability) and for its Being (moral answerability). And the special answerability, moreover, must be brought into communion [*dolzhna byt' priobshchennym*] with the unitary and unique moral answerability [*edinoi i edinstvennoi nravstennoi otvetstvennosti*] as a constituent moment in it. That is the only way whereby the pernicious non-fusion and non-interpenetration [*durnaia nesliiannost' i nevzaimoproniknovennost'*] of culture and life could be surmounted.[25]

In this passage, the doublet of "non-fusion and non-interpenetration" is unquestionably Chalcedonian in provenance. Once again, peculiar to the Russian expression of this doctrine—and abundantly in evidence here—is its sense of paradox bordering on dualism, its vision of a bisected union. Although Bakhtin does not use the term "without separation" (*nerazdel'ny*), his substitution of "non-interpenetration" in its place reinforces the subtext nonetheless because of its reference in turn to the idea of *perichoresis*, which posits the interdependence and the interpenetration of the three parts of the Trinity. The desired transformation of aesthetic activity and life that Bakhtin describes entails precisely this dynamic of a thoroughgoing interaction. In a statement that effectively reenacts the conflict addressed by the Chalcedonian decision, Bakhtin yokes "non-interpenetration" with "non-fusion" as terms of contrast and paradox as much as of equivalence. Bakhtin clearly takes a dim view of the tendencies toward isolationism and hermeticism that oppose this conditional integration, implying that fusion (*sliianost'*) and mutual penetrability (*vzaimoproniknovennost'*) are qualities that are needed for the transformational process to take place. This possible implication and the fact that Bakhtin attaches the stigmatizing label "pernicious" to non-fusion only reinforces the subtext of the Trinitarian doctrine. The Chalcedonian formulation is more than a rhetorical tool that Bakhtin avails himself of in order to communicate effectively the actual set of relations that his terms have with one another: it is a touchstone of truth for a world of souls separated from each other in their custom-made prisons of mutual incommensurability. The issue is not that Bakhtin actually believes in the religious doctrine of "without division or separation" but that he considers it important enough as both a poetic and structural model to play with and against.

The parallels between this essay and "Art and Answerability" are thrown into sharper relief with the prominence here of the concept of answerability or responsibility (*otvetstvennost'*). The echoes of the earlier essay in "Toward a Philosophy of the Act" are striking. The Russian phrase "[to] acquire unity" (here *obresti edinstvo* and in "Art and Answerability," *obretat' edinstvo*) are used in both essays to describe the integration of life and art into a whole, differing only in Russian verbal aspect as do the verb forms *priobshchat'* from the earlier essay and the past passive participle *priobshchenny[i]* derived from *priobshchit'*, both meaning to join or bring together. Bakhtin's account of the workings of answerability in the quotation above is, however, considerably more nuanced than anything in his first published essay. When Bakhtin wrote in 1919, he considered answerability to be the upshot or synthesis of the joining of art and life; now *every* aspect of human life and work is imbued with responsibility. Thus, what he now calls special or specific answerability (*spetsial'naia otvetstvennost'*) corresponds to the cultural or aesthetic approach to life while moral answerability (*nravstvennaia otvetstvennost'*) arises from theoretism or life as such. Only when the latter is joined (*priobshchenny[i]*) to the former can they find meaning and transcendence. At this point some of the shades of meaning in Bakhtin's multiple terms describing answerability begin to modulate and move in unison with one another on the same plane, like a pantomime or Javanese puppet show. While the aspectual pair *priobshchat'-priobshchit'* means to join or conjoin, Bakhtin's repeated and loaded use of the term (referring to the responsible action that ultimately integrates and gives meaning to the disparate facets of existence) suggests that he has something much greater in mind than an alliance-like linkage or a mere supplementation. As Liapunov recognizes in his translation, the secondary use of the verb is ecclesiastical, referring to a priest's act of administering communion or, in its reflexive or intransitive form with the suffix *-sia,* to the act of receiving of communion. This sense of a noumenal or rarefied process taking place is enhanced by particular Church Slavonicisms that proliferate throughout "Toward a Philosophy of the Act," such as the archaic *lik* used to refer to the respective "faces" (or facets) of aestheticism and theoretism in relation to a greater whole or unity, which echoes the doctrine of the consubstantiality (Greek, *homoousia;* Russian, *edinosushchie*) of each member of the Trinity. Special and moral answerabilities are portrayed here as ultimately being commensurate and equal in their integrality to one another; likewise, since the greater whole (*edinstvo*) comes about only in the interaction between the two types of answerability, it too is dependent on and inextricable from them in equal measure. The fealty that all three have to one another put them on the same footing in the eyes of a possibly greater unity. The Chalcedonian principle guarantees that this unity will preserve the autonomies of its constituent elements.

This conconceptual eclecticism becomes foregrounded by examining Bakhtin's own variation on the lexemic phrase "without division or separation." Certain other terms that are closely related to the Chalcedonian formula in its traditional theological context—accompanied by the sort of philosophical backdrop sketched out by Meier—turn up at significant junctures in Bakhtin's works. The presence and persistence of these other terms, often linked directly to *slovo* in the sense of discourse, effectively rules out the possibility that his use of the formulation was based entirely on idiosyncratic adaptations of the Chalcedonian statement such as Minsky's. The most crucial of these related terms from the perspective of Bakhtin's criticism as theory is "interpenetration." In "Toward a Philosophy of the Act," the term tellingly occurs with the noun "non-fusion" in Bakhtin's discussion of Pushkin's lyric poem to Amalia Riznich, which he sees as a literary example of full ethical reciprocity between the self and Other: "What we have here is an interpenetration [*vzaimoproniknovenie*] and unity of events, while the contexts remain valuatively different, i.e., they do not fuse together [*pri tsennostnoi nesliianosti konteksktov:* lit., in the presence of a valuative non-fusion of contexts]" (132; Liapunov trans., 68). In juxtaposition with terms such as *slovo* (in its various metaphysical connotations already mentioned) and "without division or separation," the theological subtext of interpenetration is thrown into strikingly sharp relief: Bakhtin is undoubtedly referring to the patristic concept of *perichoresis* that figures in a number of post-Chalcedonian discussions of the Trinity. The christological provenance of the idea of interpenetration in the present context is highlighted by the Chalcedonian echoes that Bakhtin clusters around it.

In "Toward a Philosophy of the Act," Bakhtin's elaboration of "the pernicious non-fusion and non-interpenetration" of high culture and life is particularly resonant with Meier:

> My active deed affirms *implicite* its own singularity and irreplaceability within the whole of Being, and in this sense it is set, from within itself, into immediate proximity to the borders of that whole and is oriented within it as a whole. This is not simply an affirmation of myself or simply an affirmation of actual Being, but a non-fused and undivided [*nesliiannoe i nerazdel'noe*] affirmation of myself in Being: I participate in Being as its sole actor. Nothing in Being, apart from myself, is an *I* for me. In all of Being I experience only myself—my unique self—as an *I*. All other *I*s ["vsiakie drugie *ia*"] (theoretical ones) are not *I* for me, whereas my own (non-theoretical) *I participates* [*ia prichastno*] in once-occurrent Being: I *exist* [*ia esm'*] in it. Furthermore, what is also given here in a non-fused yet undivided form [*nesliianno i nerazdel'no*] is both the moment of my passivity and the moment of my self-activity. [1] I find myself in Being (passivity), and actively participate in it [*ia aktivno emu prichasten*]; [2] both that which is given to me and that which is yet to be achieved by me: my own uniqueness is given, yet at the same time it exists only to the extent to which it is really actualized by me as uniqueness—it is always in the act, in the performed deed, i.e., it is yet to be achieved; [3] both what *is* and what *ought* [*dolzhenstvovanie*] to be: I *am* [*ia esm'*] actual and irreplaceable, and therefore *must* actualize my uniqueness. . . . The ought becomes possible for the first time where there is acknowledgment of the fact of a unique person's being from within that person [*priznanie fakta bytiia edinstvennoi lichnosti*]; where this fact becomes a center of answerability—where I assume answerability for my own uniqueness, for my own being. (112–13; Liapunov trans., 41–42)

Like Meier, Bakhtin longs to see the fusion of thought and deed (or, as the latter also puts it in "Toward a Philosophy of the Act," "theoretism" and "aestheticism") in the same individual. Both critics recognize this undertaking as an ambitious one, necessitated by a time of social crisis. Its difficulty of fulfillment notwithstanding, it is an essential task of the utmost importance. In this light, Bakhtin's reiteration of the Church Slavonic *ia esm'*—which Liapunov offers in brackets as being equivalent to the Latin *ego sum*—emerges as doubly shrewd: first, to emphasize the ontology of the self's existence (since Russian, unlike Church Slavonic, does not have present-tense forms for the verb "to be"), and second, to remind the reader of the theological and ecclesiastical provenance of the locution *nesliiannoe i nerazdel'no*.

It is at this point that the precise orientation of Bakhtin's use of the Chalcedonian formula becomes more distinct: the formula occurs in places of his work that suggest not just an awareness of Solovyov's use of it, but Meier's as well. In Bakhtin's hands the formula serves as evidence not only of his interest in theology, but also of the political interpretation of it by Russian thinkers of both his and the older generation, among people for whom the dividing line between revolutionary politics and religious idealism was becoming increasingly blurred. Like Meier, Bakhtin uses the Chalcedonian formula to denote the transcendence of hermetic individualism; unlike Meier, he is also aware of the incompatibility of collectivism with this enterprise, which seeks abolition of the discrete identity rather than its mediation in its interaction with others. As Bakhtin saw it, the "Great Experiment" of the Bolshevik state drove a wedge between the cognicizing subject and society, rendering the two utterly separate and unmerged. The consequences of such an act are, according to Bakhtin, in ontological terms as unexpected as they are contradictory to the ideal of a classless participatory democracy. In a brief but tantalizing note titled "Man Before Mirror" dated 1943, Bakhtin speaks of "[the] falsehood and lying that inevitably emerge in [one's] interaction [*vo vzaimootnoshenii*] with oneself. . . . [Then] it is not I who looks from inside to the world without, but I who look at myself with the eyes of the world, with foreign eyes: I am possessed [*oderzhim*] by the Other." The abolition of the private realm is really a reassertion and reification of the imperial and narcissistic subject, whose habitat has simply been shifted from that of the individual to the society as a whole. In a statement pointedly referring to the self-policing of Stalinist state by its citizens, Bakhtin goes on to say that the absorption of the I into Other is precisely what makes it possible for me to spy on my own witnessed image (*zaochnyi obraz*), a strangely tautological act that results from the naïveté of merging oneself and the Other [*naivnost' sliianiia sebia i drugogo*] in the mirror-image.[26] In the spirit of the Chalcedonian formula, Bakhtin is critical of any utter fusion or merging (*sliianie*) that erases difference. Needless to say, the obsessive and gratuitous acts of epistemological redundancy he describes above reinforce such erasure and are not what Meier had in mind in his outlining of the collective subject's robust body politic.

THE AMBIVALENCE OF LAUGHTER: THE CHALCEDONIAN LEGACY IN BAKHTINIAN CARNIVAL

Operating within the strictures of the Soviet censor, Bakhtin naturally could not be explicit with the theological provenance of such references, much less their ramifications as a political critique. Nonetheless, the similarities between Bakhtin's description of the Dostoevskian hero's interactive word and Lossky's vision of Dostoevsky's world as communality achieved through the agency of an ego-piercing and bodied-forth Christian logos are too striking to be ignored. The issue is hardly that of Lossky's study of Dostoevsky influencing *Problems of Dostoevsky's Poetics,* although, as will be seen later in this section, some of Lossky's other work informed by the Chalcedonian topos may very well have had that effect on Bakhtin. What is new in the second edition is, of course, the sections devoted to carnival. It is there that Bakhtin formulates his own distinctive version of the Chalcedonian formula, one transcending in complexity the earlier Russian models he relied on.

The references to the Chalcedonian divided union and *perichoresis* in the 1963 edition of the Dostoevsky book have several significant parallels to Solovyov's own elaboration of these concepts in terms of aesthetics, especially evident in the essay "The General Meaning of Art." A comparison of "The General Meaning of Art" and Bakhtin's book testifies, however, to an influence that is leavened with a considerable measure of polemicism. The following are two oft-cited statements in *Problems of Dostoevsky's Poetics* that until now have never been discussed in terms of these sources:

> In Dostoevsky's artistic thinking, the genuine life of the personality [*podlinnaia zhizn' lichnosti*] takes place at the point of non-coincidence between man and himself, at his point of departure beyond the limits of all that he is as a material being, a being that can be spied on, defined, predicted aside from its own will, "at second hand." The genuine life of the personality is made available only through a *dialogic* penetration [*"dialogicheskomu proniknoveniiu"*] of the personality, during which it freely and reciprocally reveals itself. (79; Emerson trans., 59)

> People who in life are separated by impenetrable barriers [*razdelennye nepronitsaemymi bar'erami*] enter into free familiar contact on the carnival square. The category of familiar contact is also responsible for the special way mass actions [*massovy(e) deistv(a)*] are organized, and for free carnival gesticulation, and for the outspoken carnivalistic word. (164; Emerson trans., 123)

The wording and even the immediate network of ideas here is strikingly similar to Solovyov. Furthermore, Bakhtin's reference to those separated by the impenetrable barriers of hierarchy (*razdelennye nepronitsaemymi bar'erami*) both lexically and conceptually echoes not only Solovyov's anathematizing of egoism, but also Meier's conjuring of the Chalcedonian ideal as a counterweight to alienating separateness or *razdelennost'*, the tendency to assign the tasks of thinking and doing to different people. According to Solovyov, in the ideal social order the carapace of self-centeredness would dissolve, the impenetrability of egoism would be abolished and a ideal social order would come into being, an all-encompassing brotherhood as each person sees himself in others.[27] Solovyov argues for what he calls the mutual solidarity and equilibrium between the part and the whole (*vzaimna[ia] solidarnost[']* *i ravnovesi[e] chastei i tselogo*), warning against the evil represented by both anarchic particularism and despotic unions.[28] Elsewhere Solovyov idiosyncratically defines personality or the individual consciousness (*lichnost'*) as the potential for the realization of a unlimited reality.[29] Both Bakhtin and Solovyov take considerable care in pointing out that their visions of ethical interrelation are not anti-individualistic. In fact, Solovyov (like Bakhtin) does not believe that this devoutly-to-be-wished abolition of the barriers of ego or class would annihilate the individual's personality. Solovyov's emphasis on the concept of diversity (*raznoobrazie*) is an excellent example of this, as is Bakhtin's valorization of the individual consciousness in the first of the two passages quoted above and in "Toward a Philosophy of the Act." Very much like Meier, Bakhtin emphasizes the actual civic ramifications of this divided union. In contrast, for Solovyov the interacting subject never leaves the rarefied upper regions that the community of ideal souls inhabits. Unlike either thinker, Bakhtin brings the Chalcedonian and interpenetrative subject fully into the realm of social coexistence and practice.

The parallels between Solovyov and Bakhtin assume an even higher profile in a theological light. In the works of both writers the vocabulary of interrelation is couched in christological terms. In a manner suggestive of the interdwelling of the Trinity's hypostases, Solovyov's utopia has each person dwelling within others and they in him or her with diversity nonetheless left intact; similarly, Bakhtin's concepts of polyphony and heteroglossia have Trinitarian properties in their dynamics of interaction tempered by separateness. The case for Bakhtin's possible indebtedness to Solovyov would, however, have to allow for some important conceptual differences between the two writers. In Bakhtin's book *perichoresis* is more radically subjectivist than anything in Solovyov. His subjectivism is, however, fundamentally different from Solovyov's. There is nothing of the anthropomorphist or pantheist in Bakhtin, and all of his terms denoting interconnection or interrelation refer strictly to what occurs among people or to the dialogic operations that develop within the individual consciousness of the author. Unlike Solovyov, Bakhtin uses theological terminology to demystify social relations rather than link them with the unseen ether in which the cosmos is suspended: it is only the mass ritual of the carnivalistic word that can overcome these barriers. Although Bakhtin shies away from Solovyov's cosmological imagery and does not foreground the theological provenance of his terms, he clearly takes the Chalcedonian formula more seriously than Solovyov because he implicitly acknowledges both its devotional aspect as well as its doctrinal substance. For Bakhtin, the carnival square is a sacred site, a fact that he points up by describing it as the place for "mass actions" (*massovy[e] deistv[a]*). The Russian term *deistvo* is hardly neutral or generalized and in fact suggests a ritualized action in the sense of a ceremony or public performance. But in what is his most radical departure from the lopsided Chalcedonian dualism of Russian thought represented by Solovyov's influential writing, Bakhtin insists on a balance between the forces of assimilation or "all-oneness" and separateness. A life consisting of unimpeded intersubjectivity, unrelieved by illuminations of difference and moments of mutual nonpenetribility, is nothing more than a police state, one where the activities of surveillance and coercion—spying, defining, and predicting aside from one's own will—are abstracted into political principles. It is precisely this horrifying total commensurability that Bakhtin describes in his 1943 fragment "Man Before Mirror." For all his idiosyncratic applications of the Chalcedonian formula, Bakhtin (unlike Solovyov or Meier) rigorously emphasizes the idea of symmetry that was central to the dualism of the original doctrine.

This brings us finally to the mixed nature of the christological metaphor in *Problems of Dostoevsky's Poetics*. The organic and even biological component of this metaphor is quite strong and seems irreconcilable with the image of the novelistic word as a Christ-like mediator. At this point another model for the perichoresical interpenetration in Bakhtin's work emerges more clearly. Henri Bergson asserted the continuity of nature and the interaction of atoms with one another as a defining characteristic of the flux of material reality. In *Problems of Dostoevsky's Poetics*, Bakhtin's characterization of polyphony as an intersubjective and interpenetrating phenomenon seems to come straight from the pages of Nikolai Lossky's 1922 *The Intuitive Philosophy of Bergson*. Lossky summarizes Bergson's atomism in the following manner: "Not only are different motions inseparable [*nedelimy*], but the material world as well does not become differentiated into 'independent bodies, with strictly defined contours.' Bergson sympathizes with [Michael] Faraday's idea that each atom 'occupies a coherent space through which gravitation is dispersed,' that 'all atoms mutually penetrate each other' [*vse atomy vzaimno pronikaiut drug druga*]."[30] In "Toward a Philosophy of the Act," Bakhtin praises Lossky's book on Bergson while also voicing his own disagreements with the Belgian philosopher. Bakhtin sees Bergsonianism as a typical expression of contemporary phenomenology. Such philosophical approaches to life ultimately succeed only in aestheticizing its subject, as they attempt to integrate the world of theory with the internal, phenomenological unity of experience: "A characteristic of contemporary philosophy of life, which endeavors to include the theoretical world within the unity of life-in-the-process-of-becoming, is a certain aestheticization of life." Nonetheless, in a Chalcedonian turn of phrase, Bakhtin goes on to say that theoretical and aesthetic elements are successfully merged in these phenomenological conceptions: "As a rule, the theoretical and esthetic elements are fused [*slity*] in . . . conceptions of life" such as Bergson's.[31] Thus, although it might seem that such a model as Bergson's with its pseudoscientific trappings would cancel out the possible theological subtext of Bakhtin's work, the actual textual situation suggests a conflation between the tropes of the divine economy defined at Chalcedon and Bergsonian atomism. In his 1939 book *The Ineffable: An Ontological Introduction to the Philosophy of Religion,* the émigré Russian philosopher Semyon Frank blends Bergsonian categories with christological and Chalcedonian terms in a way that is unmistakable.[32] Certain passages in Frank's book bear an uncanny resemblance to "Toward a Philosophy of the Act," which of course he could not have read. Nevertheless, his adaptation of christological categories is certainly provocative from the perspective of traditional theology and patristics. Bakhtin's and Frank's use of the Chalcedonian formula and the related concept of *perichoresis* to refer to social interaction is somewhat problematical from a doctrinal point of view inasmuch as they avail themselves of christological markers without actually forging a theological method or even a religious philosophy. There are some (like George Florovsky) who have considered such appropriations to be misguided and irreverent, if not sacrilegious.

Interestingly, Solovyov had little use for Bergsonianism. Writing in the 1890s during the height of the movement (but without actually naming it or any of its adherents), he makes a series of barbed comments that throw into sharper relief the differences between his attitude and Bergson's toward corporeality. Solovyov's professed disagreement ultimately reveals the extent to which he is closer to Bergson than he would care to admit; in contrast, Bakhtin's criticism of the philosopher is more insightful and substantial. Solovyov sees in Bergson's atomocentricism a fundamental contradiction. The philosophical metaphor of an atomistic universe that is mediated or given meaning by the life force (Bergson's *élan vital*) is, according to Solovyov, spatially and ontologically incorrect: the life force does not counter or offset matter—interacting with from outside—but suffuses all of it, steeping it in its essence. By attempting to locate the guiding forces of attraction and repulsion within the atoms themselves, Bergson unwittingly sees them animistically, as repositories of a crypto-pantheistic world soul; his philosophy is tainted by the residue of a pantheistic spirit even as he claims to locate life exclusively in brute matter.[33] Solovyov's criticism of Bergson must, however, be conditioned with a crucial caveat: the universal soul is present throughout matter but is still a separate quality or essence that is not inherent to it. Thus, matter in and of itself is for him a neutral and amoral force, which leads to the conclusion that Solovyov's disagreement with Bergson is not so fundamental as he would have us believe. Solovyov cannot brook the idea of matter having meaning in and of itself; for him it needs to be subsumed and redeemed by a deeper meaning; there is no question that his hostility to it is more profound than anything that can be found in Bergson. Solovyov is a Monophysite in his thinking, emphasizing the transcendent meaning conferred upon matter by divine afflatus; Bakhtin's approach, on the other hand, is more profoundly Chalcedonian in its orientation, foregrounding the conditional union of entities in consecrated space.

The confluence of Bergsonianism and christological images in Bakhtin becomes more comprehensible in light of the Russian critic's emphasis on human interaction. Unlike Solovyov or even Bergson, Bakhtin is not interested in the goings-on of the inanimate universe because in fact he does not perceive them as being in themselves problematical; he adapts Bergson's idea of atomic clashing and interpenetration to the world of human contact, where each individual personality corresponds to an atom in Bergson's scheme. It is at this point that Bakhtin's divergence from both Solovyov and Bergson becomes especially evident. In a diary entry from 1940, Bakhtin criticizes Bergson's conception of laughter as being thoroughly undercut by its foundation on the feelings of despair and the fear of death. According to Bakhtin, laughter and the comedic in fact have as their base a simultaneous awareness of the positive and the negative; Bergson, however, is only interested in the negative insofar as he considers laughter to be essentially a rebellious response to the mechanical soullessness of material reality. For Bakhtin, laughter is more than merely a despairing response to the abyss:

> Bergson's whole theory knows only the negative pole of laughter. Laughter is a touchstone, and the comic represents unconstraint. The difficulty in analyzing the truly comic and humorous stems from the fact that the negative and positive are merged indisunitably [*neraz"edinimo slity*] in it, and that one cannot draw a clear boundary between them. The main thought [of Bergson] is true: life laughs at death, over the dead mechanism. But the organic *matter* [*"materiia"* (emphasis in original)] of life in laughter is positive.[34]

As far as matter is concerned, Bakhtin agrees neither with Bergson nor with Solovyov, since both view it as external to human experience: For Bakhtin, the matter of organic life is thoroughly subsumed into laughter. In a clear lexical reference to the Fourth Ecumenical Council with the pointedly awkward phrase "merged indisunitably" (*neraz"edinimo slity*), Bakhtin imbues laughter and the comedic with the Chalcedonian virtue of joining without fully conflating or dissolving two antipodal forces, in this case life and death. Laughter possesses a salvific function, redeeming the human by placing it in contact with that which it fears. What is curious and revealing is that an inversion of the traditional Chalcedonian hypostases takes place: here, matter becomes divinized, a kind of Godhead, redeeming the individual. In Bakhtin's scheme, organic matter becomes immortal and the human consciousness profoundly perishable. Upon reflection, this apparent inversion of christological thematics is not so iconoclastic as it might seem. By preserving these essences or natures but redefining each in terms of the commonly perceived properties of its twin, Bakhtin gives a brilliant demonstration of the Chalcedonian ideal of tempered interrelation. Bakhtin's references to the formula of "without separation or division" reflect an actual meditation on the dynamics and overall signifiacnce of the christological doctrine itself. Solovyov's reliance on this locution is in contrast jejune and self-serving, a mere conceptual peg convenient for hanging his disembodied cosmology of self.

Although *Problems of Dostoevsky's Poetics* was written quickly in 1961 immediately after Bakhtin sketched out his revisions of the 1929 edition in "Toward a Reworking of the Dostoevsky Book," it was published only two years later. Variants of all the christological terms already outlined occur throughout the 1963 edition. These are too numerous to quote exhaustively and only a few representative examples will be given with references to other points of the text where such terms can be found. Occasionally, such theological subtexts in Bakhtin's work are almost as patent as in Lossky's. In the 1963 book Bakhtin uses the Chalcedonian formula to describe how mockery and exaltation are inextricably merged in carnival laughter, "in which mockery and triumph, praise and blame are inextricably fused [*nerazdel'no slity*]."[35] This is a modified but unmistakable rendering of the Chalcedonian formula, derision/abuse and triumph/praise taking the place of the twin human/divine sides of Christ's being. Carnival becomes the emblem of reconcilability, an aesthetic counterpart to the Christ figure in the age of the novel. Although the noun interpenetration (*vzaimoproniknovenie*) does not occur in *Problems of Dostoevsky's Poetics,* several other closely related terms such as interaction (*vzaimodeistvie*), interrelation (*vzaimootnoshenie*), and dialogic penetration (*dialogicheskoe proniknovenie*) clearly fulfill the same conceptual role.[36] Bakhtin uses this latter terminological cluster to refer to the interaction among the voices of polyphony in a manner highly reminiscent of Trinitarian *perichoresis*.

The second edition of *Problems of Dostoevsky's Poetics* draws in all of these terms scattered through Bakhtin's writing into a single and continuous conceptual weave, underlining in particular the integrality of *perichoresis* in maintaining the human divided union of the marketplace or carnival square. Here Bakhtin takes the opportunity to give a thoroughgoing treatment of ideas that he had left undeveloped because of personal travails and the practical impossibility of publication during the Stalin era. The christological metaphor is in fact so manifest here that one almost wonders how the book got through the censors. After all, the late fifties and early sixties marked a period of renewed agitational activity in the Soviet Union against religion in general and the Russian Orthodox Church in particular.[37] Yet, as might be perceived from the representative example above of his use of term discourse or word (*slovo*) in this book, Bakhtin's theological metaphor curiously coexists with other and completely nontheological tropes (most significantly those drawn from biology and sociology) that undoubtedly masked it. At first glance, it seems hardly possible to reconcile the tableau of the word as the embodied Word of God among people with that of an organism symbiotically coexisting with its immediate environment. Bakhtin's abundant yet idiosyncratic use of this metaphor brings us into renewed contact with the vexed question of his personal attitude to religion and its reflection in his work. If Bakhtin was a believing Christian, how could he juxtapose images taken from his own faith with ones drawn from the presumably rationalist and reductive natural sciences? For all of his purported piety, Bakhtin conjoins christological terms with images and contexts that almost suggest a burlesque of incarnational theology. All of this would seem to point to the unorthodoxy of an Orthodox believer.

Lingering on this thought brings to mind the possibility that Bakhtin's unusual treatment of such sacrosanct images is perhaps his demonstration of carnivalistic discourse with all its characteristic inversions. It is a conclusion all too easy to draw. Based on the textual evidence, these images were undoubtedly important for Bakhtin on a philosophical level that parallels a possible confessional one. The persistence of inversion in these tropes vis-à-vis their source material is only initially troubling if we examine his orchestration of them, which is too meticulous and conceptually acute to be merely an example of parody or anticlerical burlesque. Bakhtin adapts christological images and metaphors in a way that ultimately calls attention to the structural complexity of their source material, and a closer look at his work reveals an intense engagement of the theological paradigms themselves that makes Solovyov's and even Meier's references to them seem superficial, pedantic, and aleatory by comparison. In the studies of Dostoevsky and Rabelais that Bakhtin reworked for publication during the sixties, carnival emerges as savior and redeemer, as mediator but—in complete consistency with Chalcedonian doctrine—not necessarily reconciler between good and evil, laughter and the seriousness of official culture.[38] That tense equilibrium between high and low cultures is no less an unresolved problem in Bakhtin's criticism than it was at Chalcedon, where the Monophysite controversy was, in the final analysis, unsuccessfully addressed. Bakhtin's innovation over Meier is that he does not idealize or blithely gloss over the implications of the Chalcedonian notion of "not fused yet not separate"; Bakhtin possesses a more tragic vision, acknowledging that every interaction with others involves a potential surrender of identity and individuality. Certain aspects of this are elaborated in the various notes and drafts for his dissertation on Rabelais, where (as Mikhail Ryklin notes in his controversial essay "Bodies of Terror: Theses Toward a Logic of Violence") carnival is imbued with a kind of crypto-Stalinist drift toward the collectivization of consciousness. The subtler elements of this recapitulation of religious thought will be addressed in the next two chapters about Bakhtin's famous study *Rabelais and His World.*

In his references to theological doctrine, Bakhtin points up or replays the conflicts and disparities of that older tradition, transposed to a more topical and politicized setting. In his criticism he enacts a kind of aesthetic and ideological correlative to the christological paradigm. Bakhtin's references to the ontological dualism of Chalcedonian doctrine take on a certain political significance when read in light of the realities of Soviet life. Nothing could be further from a paradigm of opposing yet interacting natures—one allowing for the possibility of social transformation—than the rigidly hierarchical political order under which he lived. It was precisely this ideal that Solovyov and especially Meier had in mind; it was a model that Bakhtin himself in *Problems of Dostoevsky's Poetics* pointedly juxtaposed to the image of people separated (*razdelennye*) by impenetrable barriers. For Bakhtin, a person emerging from professional and political exile to rewrite this book, such an image of isolation undoubtedly had all-too-real significance for him. As both editions of the book reveal—spanning the periods of early Stalinist rule to the end of the Khrushchev era—for Bakhtin, the idea of the bureaucratic state as the only structure with any integrity and viability was utterly repugnant. Bakhtin asserts that Dostoevsky's world is "profoundly *pluralistic,*" and "deeply alien" to the "image of a unified spirit," calling it a church in which "the communion of unmerged [*obshchenie nesliianykh dush*] souls" takes place, "where sinners and righteous men come together." To great effect—and as if to call attention to the Chalcedonian nature of this plurality—this statement is an almost incantatory reiteration of one highlighted earlier that the chief feature of Dostoevsky's novels is "a plurality of independent and unmerged [*samostoiatel'nykh i nesliianykh*] voices and consciousnesses, a genuine polyphony of fully valid voices."[39] Bakhtin's implicit equation of the image of the church with the carnivalistic square is yet another vivid example of the joining of contraries that informs Chalcedonian doctrine; the image is perhaps less than surprising coming from a period of Soviet history when many Orthodox believers were significantly harassed, the church indeed becoming something of a liminal space. In a profoundly anti-Solovyovian vein, he emphasizes the interactive yet separate mutual relations of community, stressing that community is characterized as much by the constituative diversity of its disparate participants as it is by its impulse toward human connection and self-definition. In a brilliant rhetorical twist, Bakhtin transfers the Chalcedonian ideal of the unmerged yet separate human and divine natures of Christ to the exclusive and secular realm of the human sphere, foregrounding the idea of community as a forever divided union. Such a coexistence between the righteous and the unclean is both necessary and desirable, for the consquence of erasing it would be to do away with the respective identities of these groups. As far as group identity is concerned, it should be noted that Bakhtin believes that the group interacts with the larger community in a way that is no different from the individual's involvement with it; for Bakhtin, there is no sense in which the subject is subordinate to the group or that it, any more than the group, should be enjoined to dissolve its identity in the community at large. Considering the time and place in which Bakhtin wrote, such ideas were bound to be especially poignant.

Chapter Five

Carnival and Embodiment in *Rabelais and His World*

The nations want peace,
And long will their yoke not shatter.
Has hope's ray disappeared?
But no—Happiness is what we will relish,
Communing through the bloody cup—
And I will say, "Christ has risen."
—Pushkin, "To V. L. Davydov"

IN 1939 Bakhtin wrote the first version of his monograph on Rabelais (then titled "Rabelais in the History of Realism") for submission as a dissertation at the Gorky Institute of Literature. The interference of the war and his own peregrinations from Savalevo to Saransk prevented Bakhtin from expeditiously submitting his work, which he was able to do only in 1946. Unfortunately, additional delays were in store for him. The actual awarding of his degree was to come only in 1952, and then with the recommendation by members of the reviewing committee that he receive a candidate's degree instead of a full doctoral one because of the "formalistic" and insufficiently political nature of his work.[1] To think of the events that took place during this twelve-year interval is mind-reeling: the aftermath of Stalin's purges, the Stalin-Hitler pact, the German invasion of the Soviet Union in 1941, and the beginning of the Cold War read like a devil's litany. Yet none of this left any overt mark on Bakhtin's longest work; the revisions of the dissertation made for the 1965 first edition are quite minor, mostly taking the form of an expansion of certain points and a pruning of the footnotes.[2] The deeper marks made by that difficult period of Soviet history on Bakhtin's work will be examined in Chapter 6. For now, it is sufficient to look into the charges of the "formalist" methodology of the final published version of his study of Rabelais, what has been come to be known in English as *Rabelais and His World* (more accurately, The creation of François Rabelais and folk culture of the Middle Ages and the Renaissance). For the sake of brevity, this final version of his study will be referred to as *Rabelais and His World*.

A close examination of Bakhtin's arguments and terms in this book reveals a striking continuity with his previous works. In fact, *Rabelais and His World* represents a watershed in Bakhtin's career, a vantage point from which a backward look gives a highly coherent view of his development up to that point. All of the terms he used in previous years such as boundary (*predel*), discourse (*slovo*), and various Chalcedonian motifs appear in this book as well, with one fundamental distinction: here they are more tightly interwoven into a single conceptual scheme than ever before. Never before had there been such a distinct sense in his criticism of each concept or term playing out a specific role in relation to others. If taken in an strictly methodological sense (i.e., untainted by the Soviet-era stigmatization of the term), it is indeed quite true that Bakhtin's study of Rabelais is profoundly formalist: with its highly consistent yet varied and modulated terminology, the study is almost a meditation on the very idea of a literary critical system. Bearing this in mind, it is no wonder that his dissertation defense in 1946 went so poorly. Maria Teriaeva, the most hostile member of the committee, accused Bakhtin of "narrow formalism" and of writing a thesis that had a "reductive" character. Not surprisingly, her warnings against the snares of reductionism did not prevent her from exclaiming, "[w]e do not find in this dissertation the principle of a political approach to literary criticism!"[3]

The following examination of Bakhtin's Rabelais book is admittedly itself formalist in bent to the extent that it closely interrelates the various terms as they appear in the work. In a certain sense, I treat *Rabelais and His World* as a literary work in its own right, finding a certain pattern of imagery throughout the book that has a considerable metaphorical dimension; these sophisticated and idiosyncratic terms are always marshaled by Bakhtin in order to serve his argument. Much of the methodological internal unity in *Rabelais and His World* comes into even sharper focus if viewed through the lens of the christological imagery outlined in previous chapters. Bakhtin's tightening of the circle enclosing these topoi leads to some striking adaptations and juxtapositions of theological concepts and motifs. But my approach is formalist only in its point of departure and not in the conclusions that it eventually sets into motion. As will become apparent here and in Chapter 6, the nature of some of these textual echoes and connections eventually burst the hermetic bubble of the text and reach out to the political context in which Bakhtin wrote in ways that are unusual and, in some cases, unsettling. Needless to say, these extrinsic ramifications of Bakhtin's Rabelais study are not the ones that Teriaeva and other hostile members of the committee had in mind.

THE FRUIT AND FLESH OF THE GROTESQUE BODY

Because of its prominence as a cornerstone concept earlier in this study, the first term that will be explored under these new circumstances is that of discourse (*slovo*). Given the inclusive and protean nature of this term as demonstrated earlier, it serves a good point of departure toward Bakhtin's more specific and less flexible categories. A closer look at various parts of chapter 5 of the Rabelais book ("The Grotesque Image of the Body and Its Sources") reveals additional links between the perpetual becoming (*stanovlenie*) of the grotesque body to the topos of the communion-like moment described in "Discourse in the Novel." At the beginning of the chapter Bakhtin grapples with previous scholarly definitions of the grotesque, taking particular issue with G. Schneegans's *Geschichte der Grotesken Satyre* (1894). Schneegans adduces examples of various kinds of the grotesque, among them one from the Italian commedia dell'arte that he claims is representative of the clownish grotesque. A Harlequin is talking with a stutterer who cannot get out a difficult word (*odno trudnoe slovo*). Paraphrasing Schneegans, Bakhtin describes how the stutterer gasps, sweats, and convulses like a woman in labor (*kazhetsia, chto delo idet do rodovykh muk i spazm*) and finally the impatient Harlequin butts him in the stomach with his head, shocking the difficult word into birth ([it] is "born" [*rozhdaetsia*] at last [emphasis in original]).[4] In Bakhtin's view, although it is Schneegans himself who in the retelling of this sketch explicitly evokes the image of impeded speech as childbirth, the German scholar actually sees nothing inherently valuable in this scene of grotesquerie, only a "degradation of the high style" (309; 344); Bakhtin, on the other hand, asserts that this story in fact represents the positive meaning of the "generating lower stratum" of the body (*rozhdaiushchii niz*).[5]

Using Schneegans as a foil, Bakhtin proceeds to delineate his own conception of the comic word engendered by the grotesque body. According to Bakhtin, we must emphasize or foreground the fact that it is the word that is being born (*[p]odcherknem, chto zdes' rozhdaetsia imenno slovo*); what was once "a highly spiritual act is [now] degraded and uncrowned by the transfer to the material bodily level of childbirth, realistically represented." But, this transfer (*perevod*) is far from being the attenuation of the high style envisioned by Schneegans; it signals, in fact, a transformation of the perceived world, one through which the body's hierarchy is turned on its head, the "lower stratum replac[ing]" the upper. But what Bakhtin has in mind here is more a convergence than a mere transposition of values. As with subsequent quotations from *Rabelais and His World*, Bakhtin's distinctive and important highlighting of certain terms will be restored to Iswolsky's translation:

> The word is localized *in the mouth and in the head (thought)*; from there it it transferred to the *abdomen* ["pereneseno v *zhivot*"] and is pushed out under the impact of the Harlequin's head. This traditional gesture of *the head ramming the abdomen* [*golovoi v zhivot*] or *the buttocks* [*zad*] is essentially topographical. Here once more we have the logic of opposites, the contact [*soprikosnoveniia*] of the upper and lower level. . . . [T]he entire mechanism of the word is transferred from the apparatus of speech to the abdomen. An objective analysis of this brief scene [*v etoi malen'koi stsenke*] discloses the fundamental and essential traits of the grotesque. It [*stsenka*] reveals a great wealth and fullness of meaning, worked out to the smallest detail. It has at the same time a universal character; it is a miniature *satyrical drama of the word* [*satirova drama slova*], of its material birth, or the drama of the body giving birth to the word. (309; 343)

Bakhtin rhetorically takes the metaphor of childbirth to the furthest possible extent; in a certain sense, he takes it more seriously and fully than Schneegans does. Some of the images that Bakhtin uses are especially revealing in this regard. Particularly striking in this passage is the virtual personification of the word uttered by the grotesque body: the word is not only born, but lives and dies only to be born again, and even moves from one place of residence to another. Bakhtin's use of the term transfer (*perevod*) is most revealing in regard to this dominant metaphorical underpinning of the harlequinade described by Schneegans. Although Iswolsky's translation of the term as "transfer" is correct as far as it goes, the secondary meaning of *perevod* as "translation" is also important for Bakhtin in the present context; since the high and the low strata interact in movements that are completely dissimilar from one another, the uttered word serves as an interpreter and even mediator between them.

A closer look at this passage reveals that Bakhtin is offering other possible meanings of the word as a newborn being. The presence of a costumed figure and the fact that Harlequin plays something of a role of a midwife to the word immediately leads to a realization of the intense theatricality of the comic word. There are echoes here of the crucial section of *Problems of Dostoevsky's Art* (1929) where Bakhtin describes the novelistic word in highly theatrical terms, evoking the jostling of the various voices of the characters on the stage of the novel. If anything, the repeated use of the term "scene" (*stsenka*, which can denote either a segment of a performance or the stage itself) together with the term "contact" (*soprikosnovenie:* lit., "touching") makes the theatrical metaphor even more explicit than in Bakhtin's first Dostoevsky book. The word (*slovo*) is the offspring of the body born during the comic or carnivalesque moment. In a certain sense the high and the low are the parents of the uttered word, and its birth jarringly occurs within full public view. Interacting with these motifs of public performance is a curious fact that has gone unnoticed by all commentators writing about this book: the word was "once a highly spiritual act." In what sense is the unborn word a spiritual phenomenon? Bakhtin clearly does not have in mind here the discourse of high style, which of course all too concretely *exists,* defined in fact by its consummately non-oralist language in the form of textual artifacts and ossified ritualism. But in Johannine logology, what is the unbodied word if not the spirit? In a revealing parallel to Chalcedonian theogony, it is the coming together of thought and appetite (spirit and body) that gives birth to the word. That new word represents a mediator, even intercessor.

Opposed to Bakhtin's synthetic vision is the idea of mutual and utter impenetrability of thought and experience. For the Russians struggling from the thirties to the fifties against the triple scourge of Stalin's purges, the Second World War, and the Cold War, such isolationism and rigorous boundary-drawing became an ethical touchstone if not an unfortunate necessity on both the personal as well as geopolitical stage. As delineated by Bakhtin, however, carnival ignores the hard-and-fast distinctions of spatial boundaries (*karnaval ne znaet prostranstvennykh granits*).[6] This idea and the varied terminology of restrictive borders or dividing lines opposed to it are reiterated time and again by Bakhtin: derivatives of the words *granitsa* (border, boundary), *rubezh* (border, verge, dividing line), *predel* (limit, or often other variants formed from the stem *del* such as *delenie* [division] and the Chalcedonian *razdel'no* [undivided]), and occasionally the terms *mezha* (boundary, boundary-strip) and *mezhdu* (between) reverberate throughout the book, sometimes taking on an almost incantatory quality in concentrating in one place a wide range of such terms, together with their numerous derivatives. Many of these moments take place at crucial theoretical junctures of Bakhtin's analysis of Rabelaisian laughter. In a shrewdly drawn parallel, Clark and Holquist note that the effacing or blurring of demarcations or limits of various spheres of existence was espoused by both Bakhtin and Rabelais:

> This breakdown of the border between stage and gallery, between actors and audience, in their respective ages is a key to the obsessive concern in the work of both writers for the breakdown of borders of all kinds. Each is fascinated by unusual combinations, mixings, the interpenetration of elements regarded at other times by less heterodox contemporaries as mutually exclusive.[7]

As will shortly be demonstrated, the theological dimensions of "interpenetration" or *perichoresis* are reproduced at several points of *Rabelais and His World* with such varied if clearly related terms as interrelation (*vzaimootnoshenie*) and mutual orientation (*vzaimoorientatsiia*). The crossing of boundaries is, however, extraordinarily complex and paradoxical for Bakhtin, a process whose internal contradictions become more conspicuous toward the end of the book as he warms to his concluding remarks on Rabelais.

The first significant cluster of these terms of separation and containment occurs in the same chapter devoted to the subject of the grotesque body. When Bakhtin arrives at the point where he begins to describe the grotesque body itself, the rich yet ultimately academic prose that dominates much of *Rabelais and His World* suddenly takes wing. "The *grotesque body*, as we have often stressed, is a *body in the act of becoming* [*stanoviashcheesia telo*]. It is never *finished*, never *completed;* it is continually *built [stroitsia], created [tvoritsia] and builds and creates [stroit i tvorit] another body.*" It is a body that is both devourer and devoured, endlessly "swallow[ing] the world" and swallowed by it ("telo eto *pogloshchaet mir i samo pogloshchaetsia mirom*"), overwhelming its surroundings as much as it is overwhelmed by them. The verb Bakhtin uses here, *pogloshchat'*, means to absorb or overpower as well as to devour. It is in both senses of the verb that Bakhtin goes on to describe the recrudescence of the lower bodily stratum of the body:

> This is why the essential role belong to *those parts* [or, places (*te mesta*)] of the grotesque body in which it *outgrows* [*pererastaet*] *its own self, transgressing its own body* [*vykhodiat za sobstvennye predely*], *in which it conceives a new, second body: the bowels* [*chrevo*] *and the phallus.* These two areas play the leading role in the grotesque image, and it is precisely for this reason that they are predominantly subject to *positive exaggeration*, to hyperbolization; they can even *detach themselves from the body* and lead *an independent* life, for they hide the rest of the body, as something secondary (The *nose* can also in a way detach itself from the body). Next to the bowels and the genital organs is the *mouth,* through which enters the world to be swallowed up. And next is the *anus.* All these *convexities and orifices* have a common characteristic; it is within them that the *confines* [*granitsy*] *between bodies* [*mezhdu dbum'ia telamia:* lit., between two bodies] *and between the body and the world are overcome:* there is an interchange [*vzaimoobmen*] and an interorientation [*vzaimoorientatsiia*]. (317; 351–52)

The grotesque body is above all a breaker of boundaries, whether it be those of its own size or of abstract categories such as time and space; it conflates (and therefore confounds) properties and functions usually perceived as separate. Gargantua swallows the world and the world swallows him; likewise, the mouth and the anus become virtually interchangeable. Taken in the context of similar terms denoting interrelation from Bakhtin's other writings, one easily sees that Rabelais's world represents the Chalcedonian ideal of consubstantiality pushed well past the limits of seemliness, not to mention conventional piety.

But there are deeper reversals at work in this passage than the ones explicitedly enumerated by Bakhtin. For one thing, in Russian the word *chrevo* (bowels) has the additional, more archaic and biblical, meaning of womb. The presence of the term in this context is extremely felicitous for

Bakhtin's purposes, effectively pointing up the surrealistic confluence of function characteristic of the grotesque body's organs; it is a telling ambiguity that is inevitably lost in Hélène Iswolsky's translation of the word. Another such paradox is the paronomastic yoking of the verbs "to build" (*stroit'[sia]*) and "to create" (*tvorit'[sia]*), the former verb connoting a gradual and organized development whereas the latter, bookish one describing a more mysterious or at least less rationally comprehensible process. By using these verbs in both their transitive and reflexive forms (the latter signaled by the suffix *-sia*), Bakhtin characterizes this process as one that is as much an act of the grotesque body's self-creation as it is the engendering of another body. Ultimately, perhaps the most significant instance of contrariety in this passage is the one that almost escapes notice for its sheer manifestness: namely, that the grotesque body is described as immortal while simultaneously being defined by a monstrous corporeality. Here, in a telling inversion, the flesh is eternal and transcendent whereas the spirit is not even deemed worthy of mention, precisely because of the latter's status as a pure and unembodied entity that is utterly preexistent (and therefore extrinsic) to the world Bakhtin describes. But the absence of the spirit at this juncture of Bakhtin's discussion of the grotesque has far greater significance than the exit of a supernumerary player. By investing the corporeal with the eternal, Bakhtin fully subsumes the spirit (referred to earlier in chapter 5 of his book) into the body; in a certain sense, the spirit *becomes* the body. The metaphor of transformation as a giving birth is crucial to understanding this translation of the spiritual into the corporeal.

Perhaps it is this paradox that Bakhtin has in mind when he speaks in the passage above of overcoming the boundaries between two bodies and the body and the world: being infinitely divisible, absorbent, and suppurating, the grotesque body becomes the ultimate representation of the interaction between the self and other or the self and world. Bakhtin then proceeds to expand on the implications of phenomenological interconnectedness that he refers to with the mention of interchange (*vzaimoobmen*) and interorientation (*vzaimoorientatsiia*). "Eating, drinking, defecation and other elimination [*i drugie vydeleniia*] (sweating, blowing of the nose, sneezing), as well as copulation, pregnancy, growth, old age, sickness, death, physical torment [*rasterzanie*], dismemberment [and being] swallowing up by another body" are all *"acts of the bodily drama"* [*akty telesnoi dramy*]. *"[A]ll these acts [akty],"* Bakhtin continues, *"are performed on the confines* [*na granitsakh*] *of the body and the outer world,* or *on the confines of the old and the new body.* In all these events *the beginning and the end are closely* [*nerazryvno:* lit., inextricably] *linked and interwoven"* (317; 352). The acts of the body's drama are played out on the interface between it and the world at large. What began earlier as a theatrical metaphor, however, ultimately subverts the idea of theatricality, or at least becomes transformed into a Brechtian one: the drama and the spectators join at the barrier traditionally separating them, thereby obliterating the entire ritualistic setting. In the final analysis—and against all dramatic convention—time itself is confounded, beginning and end merging indistinguishably. But for all his assertion of the permeability of the borders (*granitsy*) between body and world, old and new, Bakhtin does not question the fundamental existence of those separators of experience.

The theological formulation "without separation or division" (*nesliianno i nerazdel'no*) discussed in the previous chapter inevitably comes to mind, as does the ancillary doctrine of *perichoresis* that asserts the close interaction between the human and divine, balancing the isolation that mortality entails with the intergration into the eternal. Other sections of *Rabelais and His World* in which Bakhtin describes the participation of the self in carnival manifest to varying degrees this dynamic of transcendence in terms that are remarkably reminiscent of the theological formulations concerning the Trinity and the Eucharist. The following discussion explores these correspondences and echoes.

Over the next several pages of chapter 5 of *Rabelais and His World,* Bakhtin elaborates in various ways on the "openness" of the grotesque body. Some of the nuances of Bakhtin's conception of the grotesque body can be inferred from his description of the aesthetic that he opposes to it, the "new canon" (*novyi kanon*) that has dominated the visual and literary arts over the past four centuries. In describing this anticarnival aesthetic Bakhtin throws into sharper relief some of the features of carnival itself:

> The new bodily canon, in all its historic variations and different genres, presents an *individual expressive body, one that is entirely finished, completed, strictly limited* [*otgranichennoe*] *and closed* [*zamknutnoe*], *something that is unadulterated* [*nesmeshannoe*] *and shown* [*only*] *from the outside.* That which protrudes, bulges, sprouts, or branches out (when a body transgresses its limits [*vykhodit za svoi granitsy*] and a new one begins) is eliminated, hidden, or moderated [*smiagchaetsia:* lit., softened]. All orifices of the body are closed. The basis of the image is *the individual, strictly limited mass of the body* [*otgranichennaia massa tela*], *its massive and opaque facade* [*ego massivnyi i glukhoi fasad*]. *The opaque surface and the body's "valleys"* [*ravnina tela*] acquire an essential meaning as the border [*granitsa*] of a closed individuality [*individual'nost(')*] that does not merge [*neslivaiushcheisia*] with other bodies and with the world. All attributes of the unfinished world are carefully removed, as well as the signs of its inner [*vnutritelesnoi:* lit., inner bodily] life. (318; 354–55)

Here Bakhtin cautiously examines what might be called the sociology of the grotesque body; now borders (*granitsy*) take on new and clearly political meanings only touched upon by Bakhtin earlier. Although the term "body politic" does not have a ready equivalent in Russian, at certain revealing points of *Rabelais and His World* Bakhtin explicitly yet with revealing circumspection draws the parallel between the grotesque body and society at large. Thus, in regard to certain travesty satires, Bakhtin states that "it is interesting to note *the combination of the dismemberment of the body and of society.* This is a travesty of the widespread mythical concept of the origin of various social groups from various parts of a god's body" (351; 388–89). In this metaphorical sense, clearly acknowledged by Bakhtin, the term *granitsa* becomes activated in both of its primary Russian meanings: denoting boundary generally and a nation's border specifically.

What clearly emerges from all of this is the fact that *granitsa* is a neutral term whose fundamental existence as a filter-like boundary is not questioned; the effluvia from the grotesque body never corrode or dissolve the membrane that they traverse. The terms *otgranichennyi* (limited, or more literally, "cut off") and *ogranichennost'* (limitedness) are, however, clearly pejorative for Bakhtin. The inevitable conclusion—one that is hardly surprising and that has been noted by, among others, Holquist and Clark[9]—is that Bakhtin favored open societies over closed ones. Yet certain aspects of the terminology that Bakhtin uses to describe these two diametrically opposed kinds of politicized bodies are revealing in ways that are perhaps less expected.

Bakhtin imparts some fine-tuning and sharper focus to these distinctions in his continuation of the comparison and contrast between closed and open bodies, the "new canon" that attempts to deny (or at least co-opt) carnival's remaining the focus of his analysis. The linguistic norms of official and literary speech are defined by the anathema against everything that represents the open body, whether it be "fecundness" (*oplodotvorenie*), pregnancy, or birth, among other things. But in what sense are these archetypal physical movements opposed to official and literary speech? The answer (not explicitly provided by Bakhtin) certainly lies partly in the fact of *orality:* the language of officialdom will have no truck with a mode of discourse that is defined as a bodily manifestation. The official canon is opposed to everything that is connected with the makeshift and unfinalized state of the body (*vse to, chto sviazano s negotovost'iu i nezavershennost'iu tela*) in all the inner dynamics of its corporeal life (*s ego chisto vnutritelesnoi zhizn'iu*). "There is a sharp line of division [*chrezvychaino rezkaia granitsa:* lit., extremely sharp dividing line] between familiar speech and 'correct' language [*pristoinoi' rech'iu:* lit., decent speech]" (320; 355).[10] Once again, it becomes clear that Bakhtin finds the idea of borderlines (*granitsa*) problematical only when they are utterly opaque and impermeable. Here, he moves from the political concerns of the previous passage to ones that are both literary as well as political. Speech becomes official and respectable when it is placed in a state of hermetic isolation and self-sufficiency, willfully contemptuous to and ignorant of other forms of speech. As in many other parts of the book, the terms Bakhtin uses to describe the grotesque body are consistently organic: "fecundation," "pregnancy," and "childbirth."[11] In this context, the term "dividing line" (*granitsa*) is revealed as having the potential to be an interface or even a membrane; in other circumstances, of course, it may become ossified into a restrictive and impenetrable carapace.

In aggregate, many such terms used by Bakhtin take on a certain significance that they would not have in isolation. *Oplodotvorenie* (translated by Iswolsky as "fecundation") seems in many ways remarkably similar in both sense and even sound to the term *oplotnennost'* (denoting the state of enfleshment) that appears in "Discourse in the Novel," written by Bakhtin only a few years before he began his dissertation on Rabelais. These are derived from *plod* (fruit) and *plot'* (flesh). To be sure, important differences exist between the conceptual underpinnings of these two terms: *Oplodotvorenie* denotes fertility and the potential for becoming whereas *oplotnennost"* refers to the actual concretization of the abstract. Taken together, however, these variant denotations describe an important dynamic in Bakhtin's analysis of Rabelais: in order for a consciousness to become fully realized, it must become material. The parallel between flesh of the body and the fruit of the earth is important in ways that go beyond Bakhtin's conflation of them in his chapter on grotesque body. In addition to the description of the Last Supper described in John 6:52–58 and the famous christological formulation "And the Word was made flesh [*plot'iu*] and dwelt among us" of John 1:14, the lexemes "fruit" and "flesh" in reference to the body of Jesus appear in two other verses from the New Testament:

> Blessed art thou among women, and blessed is the fruit of your womb [Russian and Church Slavonic: *plod chreva*]. (Luke 1:42)
>
> Be patient therefore, brethren, unto the coming of the Lord. Behold, the husbandman waiteth for the precious fruit [Russian and Church Slavonic: *ploda*] of the earth, and hath long patience for it, until he receive the early and latter rain. (James 5:7)[12]

The parallelism and occasional identification of "fruit" and "flesh" is, for a variety of reasons, particularly resonant to the Russian ear. When uninflected, the final *-d* of *plod* is devoiced into a [t], effectively transforming the biblical dyad into an iterative phonetic doublet whose only distinguishing marker is the palatalization of the last consonant: *plot/plot'*. The Russian word for fruit (*plod*), moreover, has the secondary meanings of fetus or the young of animals and, as Dal' points out in his exhaustive nineteenth-century Russian lexicon, certain derivatives of the *oplodotvoriat'-oplodotvorit'* verb family (to fecundate) can refer to the conception and nascency of animals as well as plants.[13] In light of the close identification of the earth with the grotesque body throughout chapter 5 and Bakhtin's emphasis in his retelling of *Pantagruel* on the animality of Rabelais's eponymous hero, the subtextual linking of *plod* and *plot'* remains pronounced even when stripped of its biblical component. Together with the paradoxical yokings of ingestion/cannibalism and defecation/birth that are distinctive of the grotesque body, Bakhtin's associative chain of *oplodotvorenie* (fecundness), *beremennost'* (pregnancy), and *rody* (childbirth) inevitably evokes the image of the belly/womb (*chrevo*) that bears the fruit/flesh of carnival in its fusion of body and earth. Although the possible biblical subtext is certainly not central to Bakhtin's conception of the grotesque body, its presence beautifully reinforces his argument that the interchangeability or convergence of body functions is central to the logic (or some might say illogic) of Rabelais's world.

It is at this point of investigating Bakhtin's critical vocabulary that the particular relations between terms such as *granitsa* and *predel* begin to take on critical mass. Rereading the book with a view at clarifying this analytic lexicon, we find that certain patterns or constellations of terms inevitably emerge. In the introduction to *Rabelais and His World* Bakhtin sketches in a comprehensive yet condensed way the arguments of the subsequent chapters of the book. A look back at his précis-like account of his dissection of the grotesque body in Rabelais is extremely useful in making sense of all the particulars of that crucial chapter:

> The unfinished and open body (dying, bringing forth [*rozhdaiushchee*] and being born [*rozhdaemoe*]) is not separated [*ne otdeleno*] from the world by clealry defined boundaries [*chetkimi granitsami*]; it is blended [*smeshano*] with the world, with animals, with objects. It is cosmic, it represents the entire material bodily world in all its elements. It is an incarnation of [*voploshchaet v sebe:* lit., "it embodies in itself"] this world at the absolute lower stratum, as the swallowing up [*pogloshchaiushchee*] and generating [*rozhdaiushchee*] principle, as the bodily grave and bosom, as a field which has been sown and in which new shoots are prepared to sprout. (26–27; 34)

That the grotesque body is emblematic of concrete reality as a whole is prevalent as a working assumption throughout chapter 5 but is never put so succinctly as it is here. The mixed vegetative and zoological metaphor that Bakhtin uses at the end of this passage retroactively reinforces the *plod/plot'* analogy that is implicit in his discussion of the *oplodotvorenie* (fecundness) of the grotesque body. But after finishing this pithy paragraph, one immediately realizes how interrelated all these terms are and the great extent to which they anticipate others that will turn up later for more extensive treatment. The term *voploshchaet* (embodies), while clearly a figure of speech, conceptually and even phonetically parallels *oplodotvorenie:* together, the two represent the *corporeal/vegetative* dichotomy. In the last sentence of the paragraph, Bakhtin metaphorically evokes the images of the fauna and flora of the world of the body (*telesnyi mir*), again playing on the *plod/plot'* analogy that is subtextually present in the fifth chapter. Most prominently of all, Bakhtin insists on the absence of well-defined borderlines between the open body and the world as such, which in itself is described in highly unitary though multifaceted terms. In effect, Bakhtin enacts the argument or substance of this passage through the overall tenor of its lexical style.

Only now does the importance for Bakhtin of the concept of embodiment (*voploshchenie*) and other members of its immediate morphological family (that is, those with the prefix *vo-*, including other derivatives of *plot'*) become clearly manifest. In the illuminating context of the passage above and the treatment of Rabelais in chapter 5, certain apparently gnomic statements later in the introduction become more transparent. One of the more conspicuous of these occurs roughly two pages before the conclusion of the introduction as Bakhtin winds down his discussion of the folk culture of laughter, proceeding to characterize what he calls the second, festive life of the Middle Ages. As he sees it, the "striving toward renewal and a new birth, 'the thirst for a new youth' pervaded [*pronikali:* lit., penetrated or permeated] the carnival spirit" of the medieval world; they "found a multiform expression [*mnogoobraznoe voploshchenie:* lit., multiform embodiment] in concrete sensual elements of folk culture, both in the forms of ritual or spectacle and in literature" (57; 66).[14] As in the previous passage from the introduction, the moment of embodiment (*voploshchenie*) represents a coming to or leaving of life, a moment when the multifaceted richness of human existence is briefly intensified. This transformation is accompanied by an action of perichoresical penetration, the transformation made possible only by impingement from the outside. Only during the crossing of phenomenological barriers does carnival take place. As already shown, Bakhtin often emphasizes the paradox of such a moment, its simultaneous representation of eating and being eaten, of being born and dying. The notion of embodiment or enfleshment emerges as the essence of such contrariety and therefore of the institution of carnival as a whole.

A quick reference to another point of Bakhtin's introduction bears out the importance that this term has for Bakhtin's conception of carnival. About fifteen pages earlier Bakhtin discusses the use of masks at carnival time. As he describes it, the metaphysical connotations of donning a mask are richer than one might expect:

> Even more important is the theme of *the mask*, the most complex and multivalent [*mnogoznachashchii*] theme of folk culture. The mask is connected with the joy of change and reincarnations [*perevoploshchenii*], with gay relativity and the merry negation of uniformity and similarity; it rejects conformity to oneself [lit., rejecting one's identification (*tozhdestva*) with oneself]. The mask is related to transition, metamorphoses, the violation of natural boundaries

> [*s narusheniem estestvennykh granits*], to mockery and familiar nicknames. It contains [*v maske voploshcheno:* lit., in the mask is embodied] the playful element of life; it is based on the peculiar interrelation [*vzaimootnoshenie*] of reality and image, characteristic of the most ancient rituals and spectacles. (39–40; 48)[15]

Once again, the term embodiment (*voploshchenie*) and its variants are used to describe the transformation of identity or physical being. Since Bakhtin uses it to describe the ontological source of carnival (i.e., the grotesque body) rather than the institution itself, the mask (the totem of carnival) becomes metonymically transformed into a particularly pungent or intensified essence of that source—hence Bakhtin's characterization of the mask as connected with the joy of change and reembodiment (*perevoploshcheniia*)[16] and his statement that the principle of play is embodied in it. Significantly, in the passage above the concept of a border or dividing line (*granitsa*) also comes into play, consistent with the emphasis throughout the book on the necessity of breaking tightly delimited expectations and assumptions of behavior during carnival time and reflected here in the imperative of transgressing one's own identity.[17] From all of this it becomes clear that the concept of embodiment is linked to carnival in all its bewildering yet wonderful multiplicity and iconoclasm. Like any biological entity, the membranes of the grotesque body's organs are constantly permeated and flushed through while it remains alive. *Voploshchenie* and its various derivative terms represent the integrated functioning that always occurs at the moment of life.

The term appears at several telling points throughout the book. One of these occurs in chapter 5 when Bakhtin describes the significance of Pantagruel for Rabelais and for the history of laughter in particular:

> We must not forget that urine (as well as dung) is *gay matter,* which degrades and relieves at the same time, transforming *fear into laughter.* If dung is a link between body and earth (the laughter that unites them), *urine is a link between body and sea.* This is why the little devil Pantagruel, who in the mystery play is the *incarnation* [*voploshchenie*] of the sea salt element, becomes in Rabelais' novel the *incarnation* [*voploshcheniem*] *of the gay element of urine.* (Pantagruel's urine, as we shall later see, possesses certain curative properties.) *Dung and urine lend a bodily character* [*otelesnivaiut*] *to matter, to the world, to the cosmic elements,* which become closer, more intimate, *more easily grasped* [*i telesno-poniatnym:* lit., more easily understood by the body] for this is the matter [*materiia*], the elemental force [*stikhiia*], born from and excreted by [*porozhdaemye i vydeliaemye:* or born and extruded by] the body itself. *It transforms cosmic terror into a gay carnival monster.* (355; 370–71)

However unmentionable or seemingly peripheral it might be, bodily waste serves as a reminder of the inescapable corporeality of our existence. Excrement and urine are also emblems of physical change and transmutability, of precisely the "gay relativity" (*veselaia otnositel'nost'*) of carnival and the grotesque body that is so important for Bakhtin. What Bakhtin calls here "gay matter" is a clear analogue to that relativity; whether such matter be located between the body and the earth or the body and the sea, it too is above all a mediator and link (*zveno*) between various strata of existence. Here, as before, the functions of secretion, excretion, and the separation from the mother's body after birth are viewed as parallel, if not interchangeable, functions. The use of the past active participle *vydeliaemye* (excreted) reinforces this confluential paradigm: besides deriving from a verb that denotes both secretion as well as excretion (*vydeliat'*), it also has the literal morphophonemic meaning of "to separate (from)" ("*vy*-deliat'"). Also salient is Bakhtin's emphasized use of *voploshchenie* twice in the paragraph; he patently draws attention to the root of this word (*plot'*) by giving it special emphasis in a context where the term *telo* (body) and its derivatives (*otelesnivaiut . . . telesno-*) figure prominently as well. By focusing on the various functions of the body, carnival becomes the epitome of all change and thus, paradoxically, comes to represent the very concept of the transformation and transcendence of the imprisoning ego, a function that is, of course, traditionally assigned to spiritual revelation. In a certain sense, for Bakhtin the body and its flesh are *in themselves* transcendent of the self and therefore fulfill something of a spiritual function, dispelling the isolated individual's dread of the cosmos (*kosmicheskii uzhas*) and reestablishing his or her link with it.

In chapter 7 ("Rabelais' Images and His Time"), the last in *Rabelais and His World,* Bakhtin uses the term *voploshchenie* in contexts similar to the ones above, but contextualizes it in his entire approach to Rabelais and branches out more extensively into other spheres of the French writer's work and times. The bulk of the chapter is taken up by a select examination of topical references in Rabelais. The last third of the chapter, however, consists of a conclusion that is perhaps the best in all of Bakhtin's writings; there, Bakhtin effectively brings together and interrelates his various insights and critical terms on Rabelais. The entire chapter is also valuable for distinctly echoing and clarifying certain aspects of incarnational aesthetics treated in his earlier essay "Discourse in the Novel."

In the historical section of chapter 7, Bakhtin uses *voploshchenie* in his discussion of Rabelais's politics, which he claims were progressive for the time. The appearance of the term is unexpected insofar as his previous usage of it centered on the antinomian and anarchic aspects of the carnivalesque that are presumably unassimilable to any activity of the ruling culture. Rabelais's politics represented the "most advanced and progressive positions"; to him, "[r]oyal power" was the embodiment [*voploshcheniem*] of the principle of the national state, one that was new and to which the immanent future belonged (452; 500). Two pages later, at the beginning of his conclusion for the chapter and the entire book, Bakhtin sums up this line of thought about the relative progressiveness of Rabelais's politics. Interestingly enough, the progressive political principle of the national state is linked to carnival, for Rabelais's historically transitional "contemporary reality [*sovremennaia deistvitel'nost'*] . . . is best seen in the light of popular-festive images." Being a product of contemporaneity, carnival naturally partakes of this mediated and adulterated situation: in itself it does *not* represent the progressive ideals. Thus, "in this light even the best perspectives of reality appear limited [*ogranichennymi*] and remote from the people's ideas [*idealov:* lit., ideals] and aspirations, embodied [*voploshchennykh*] in popular-festive images" (454; 502). Once again, the remarkable consistency of Bakhtin's terminology is fully evident: the term limited (*ogranichennyi*) is used pejoratively and embodied/embodiment (*voploshchennyi/voploshchenie*), positively. The full political ramifications in the Soviet context of Bakhtin's assertion that Rabelais took a position progressive for his time by supporting a national government will be treated later; of more immediate interest and significance is the fact that as in many other parts of the book, *voploshchenie* represents an integration of various spheres of existence at carnival time whereas the adjective-noun pair *ogranichennyi/ogranichenie* figures as its opposite, the partitioning or separation of those dimensions of being. Toward the end of the book Bakhtin thus brings these two terms into relation with one another. In his last chapter in general and in the conclusion in particular he tightens the circle around the various terms that figure so prominently in his treatment of carnival, bringing them into a clear-cut conceptual scheme with a topography all its own.

Before the full ramifications of Bakhtin's usage of *voploshchenie* can be clarified, a short tour through other sections of chapter 7 needs to be made. Some of Bakhtin's ferreting out of contemporary allusions in *Gargantua* unexpectedly leads to more general and theoretical insights into the literary manifestations of the carnivalesque. At one point in his historical treatment Bakhtin attaches three levels or planes (*plany*) of meaning to the Picrochole war described in *Gargantua.* The first is the strictly topical, consisting of the reasons and pretexts for going to war that prevailed in sixteenth-century Europe; the second is the actual treatment and transformation of the topos of war in Rabelais's work; and the third consists of the interaction between war and the "gay relativity" of the carnivalesque. But Bakhtin finds the third plane to be the most interesting and productive in terms of cultural study because it is there that the popular-festive life is located:

> The third, popular, dimension is also *individual and concrete,* but this is the *broadest, all-embracing, universal individuality.* At the same time, the festive popular images reveal the *deepest meaning of the historic process, which extends not only beyond* [*vykhodiashchii daleko za predely:* lit., beyond the

> limits (of)] *contemporary events in the narrow sense but beyond Rabelais' entire epoch.* These images reveal the people's view concerning war and peace, the aggressor, political power, and the future. In the light of these views, formed and defended over thousands of years, we discover the *gay relativity* of events as well as of the entire political problem they presented. In this gay relativity the *distinctions* between the just and the unjust, the right and the wrong, the progressive and the reactionary *are not lost* [*ne stiraiutsia:* lit., not effaced] *in the cross-section* [*v razreze*] *of the given epoch and the immediate contemporary reality,* but these distinctions *do lose their absolute character, their one-sided and limited seriousness.* (447–48; 494–95)

As demonstrated earlier, the grotesque body is infinitely divisible and is relentlessly partitioned and fragmented at carnival time; in a certain sense, people and events partake of the grotesque body and yet, for all its indubitably physical nature, its quantity almost supernaturally never diminishes and its essence remains intact. Here, the same dynamic applies, with the folk perspective standing in for the grotesque body.

But the passage above is also significant for bringing into sharper focus than anywhere earlier in the book Bakhtin's conception of borderline or *granitsa.* Here, as before, the highly marked term "limited" (*ogranichennyi*) plays a key role in defining the tendency opposing carnival. In this context, distinctions (*razlichiia*) and limits (*predely*) emerge as analogues to the motif of the border (*granitsa*); as elsewhere in *Rabelais and His World,* going beyond boundaries (*vykhodiashchii za predely*) is considered essential by Bakhtin. Unlike before, however, here Bakhtin insists that these distinctions should not be erased in the face of relativity (*razlichiia ne stiraiutsia*); in fact, as he asserts here, those borders of existence need to be preserved but made permeable, not abolished altogether. The virtual substitution of the term *predel* for *granitsa* is highly significant: the overall context is also highly reminiscent of John Chrysostom's homilies on the Johannine divine word, particularly his characterization of the divine word as "unlimited" (Russian, *bespredel'no*), which will be examined in greater detail in Chapter 7 of this study. Although the term interpenetration (*vzaimoproniknovenie*) does not occur in the Rabelais book as it so conspicuously does in "Toward a Philosophy of the Act," the interaction between the various levels that Bakhtin describes in the passage above is very similar to interpenetration of consciousnesses that Bakhtin outlines in that work. As already shown in the previous chapter, Bakhtin's use of the term and its derivatives is almost certainly informed by the Trinitarian *perichoresis* or interpenetration of hypostases, a notion that was much more fully developed in the passage above from chapter 7 of *Rabelais and His World.* The popular and festive point of view is a reifying moment in time, one that brings together various planes of existence. It is no accident that Bakhtin refers to three levels of the Picrochole war in *Gargantua;* like certain Trinitarian conceptions of the

Word, this tripartite scheme makes a distinction between higher and lower levels of existence that ultimately points to a more complex reality.

At this point, the extent to which Bakhtin's terminology is consistent throughout *Rabelais and His World* becomes palpable. Viewing Bakhtin's criticism itself from a hermeneutic and textological perspective, one is struck by his varied yet effective use of repetition of certain phrases and concepts that taken together remind the reader of a single methodological approach at work. Bakhtin prefaces the following passage (which also occurs in chapter 7, a few pages before the one just quoted) with yet another statement about the limited perspective (*ogranichennost'*) of even the progressive circles in French society to which Rabelais belonged. From the point of view of popular culture in Rabelais, wider perspectives have always opened up that stretch beyond (*bolee shirokie perspectivy, vykhodivshee za predely*) the limited progressiveness (*ogranichennoi progressivnosti*) of his epoch. "Rabelais' basic goal," Bakhtin continues, "was to destroy the official picture of events":

> He strove to take a new look at them, to interpret the tragedy or comedy they represented from the point of view of *the laughing chorus of the marketplace.* He summoned all the resources of sober popular imagery [*trezvoi nardonoi obraznosti*] in order to root out [*vytravit'*] of all notions about contemporary life the official lies [*ofitsial'nuiu lozh'*] and narrow [*ogranichenniu:* lit., limited] seriousness dictated by the ruling classes. Rabelais did not implicitly believe in the word [*slovo*] that his time "said and imagined about itself"; he strove to disclose its true meaning for the people, the people who grow and are immortal. (439; 485)[18]

There are a number of remarkable things about this seemingly straightforward expository passage. By bringing the terms *ogranichennyi, ogranichennost'*, and *predel* into close contact with one another in the statement about the people's point of view going beyond limited progressivism, Bakhtin effectively establishes a parallel between the root terms *granitsa* (border) and *predel* (limit). Also conspicuous here is a strong appreciation of corporeality, particularly of the faculty of sight focusing on a highly theatrical setting of events. Thus, from the people's vantage point, vistas are opened that go beyond boundaries inaccessible to those of other social forces; Rabelais attempts to ruin an official picture of things and illuminates a tragedy or comedy taking place on the public square with a laughing chorus of people. By exposing the official culture for its stiltedness and artificiality, it is popular imagery that de facto becomes "sober," completely reversing their conventionally perceived or allotted roles. Thus, Bakhtin believes that the role-reversals of carnival represent nothing less than transformations of embodiment, a fundamental and substantive change of being and not just a ritualistic gesture sanctioned by the social contract.

In addition to the relation of carnival to embodiment, other connections with various seemingly unrelated ideas put forth earlier in the book become more evident as well. In the passage above, the theatricality of the public square is conveyed more explicitly than anywhere else, and the implicit evocation of a stage also brings to mind the derivational origin of marketplace or square (*ploshchad’*), which (as the etymologist Vasmer notes) is *ploskii* (flat).[19] The linkage of *ploshchad’* to *ploskii* ultimately reinforces the horizontality of the carnival world that Bakhtin adduces as a countervailing idea to the hierarchical verticality of the medieval worldview. The very prominence of the phonemic triad [*plo*] in Bakhtin’s terminology certainly brings to the fore of the reader’s attention the varied gamut of meanings and ramifications of these words with this combination of sounds: ***plot’*** (flesh), *vo**plo**shchenie* (embodiment), *o**plo**tnenie* (reification, enfleshment), *o**plo**tnennost’* (enfleshment), ***plod*** (fruit), *o**plo**dotvorenie* (fecundation), ***plo**shchad’* (square). Significantly, the vegetative metaphor used in a more patent form earlier is present here as well, albeit residually, in Bakhtin’s assertion of the necessity of uprooting or exterminating (*vytravit’*) official lies and the image of the growing mass of people (*rastushchii narod*). The contiguity of the term *slovo* (word, discourse) with *ogranichennyi* and *predel* is also suggestive, reminiscent of the multifaceted word described by Bakhtin in "Discourse and the Novel." Granted, here it is the word of the epoch that is severely limited, which clearly has little to do with the sublime novelistic word that Bakhtin describes in the earlier essay. It must be remembered, however, that in “Discourse and the Novel” Bakhtin makes an important distinction between the novelistic word in the sense of logos and “words” (*slová*), the latter corresponding to precisely the kind of myopic and solipsistic utterance about oneself that he describes in the passage above. Toward the end of *Rabelais and His World* a strong sense of methodological continuity is projected retrospectively not only to that book’s programmatic introduction, but also as far back as Bakhtin’s essays of the preceding few years.

“BOUNDARIES AND BORDERS, FISTICUFFS AND QUARRELS”: THE LIFE OF CARNIVAL ON THE EDGE

All we have seen notwithstanding, certain crucial links in the genealogical pattern of Bakhtin’s work still seem unclear and insufficiently mapped, both between *Rabelais and His World* and his earlier essays as well as those connecting the various chapters of Rabelais study itself. On the page following his statement about Rabelais’s support of the principle of national government, Bakhtin makes a few provisos about the full meaning of such a political stance in the light of the folk culture of laughter. Although there is no doubting the novelty, progressive historical significance, and earnest sincerity of that particular political position, Bakhtin seems to be saying that it is severely limited by the constrictions of class and its own seriousness. As he characterizes it, the last word of the epoch overlaps with Rabelais's but is not fully congruent with it:

> The last word [*slovo*] of the *epoch, sincerely and seriously* asserted, was not *Rabelais'* [*own*] last word ["poslednim slovom *samogo Rable*"]. However progressive, our author knew the limits [*meru*] of this progressiveness. And although he spoke seriously of such things, he knew the limits of this seriousness. *Rabelais' own last word is the gay* [*veseloe*], *free, absolutely sober word of the people,* which cannot be bribed with the help of the *limited progressiveness* [*ogranichennoi meroi*] accessible to the men *of his time.* This gay word of the people opened far wider perspectives, even though the positive outlines of the future were still dimly utopian. *All that was definite* and *completed* ["Vsiakaia *opredelennost'* i *zavershennost'*"] within the epoch was in some way *comic* [*smeshnymi*], insofar as it was *limited* [*ogranichennymi*]. But laughter was *gay* while all that was *determined and finite* ["*ogranichennaia* opredelennost' (i potomu *zavershennost'*")] was about to die [*umiraia i razlagaias'*: lit., was dying and decaying (or falling apart)] and to grow into *new possibilities* ["prorastala *novymi vozmozhnostiami*]. (453–54; 501)[20]

A number of motifs of carnival as described earlier in the book make their brief appearances here. As before, paradox reigns supreme. Thus, the last word of Rabelais is gay and free yet sober; and the irreproachably serious becomes ludicrous. Yet again, the limited (*ogranichennost'*) is linked with that which is finished (*zavershennost'*). Bakhtin's deliberate metaphorical mixing of the animal and plant worlds is evident here as well, where in the last sentence his description of the overdetermined world as dying and decaying rubs shoulders with the growth into new possibilities; "grow" is the operative verb of the latter process (*prorastala*), imagistically equating physical growth from the earth with the transcendence of the self at carnival time. Although the flawless modulation of all these terms and images with one another is consistently maintained throughout the book, by this point of the book it is aggressively extended and developed.

It is here that the structure of Bakhtin's reasoning and the terms that form its foundation begin to emerge. Among other things, the centrality of the term discourse or word (*slovo*) to Bakhtin's approach is forcefully made in the passage above. Bakhtin's earlier statement in the same chapter about not taking an epoch at its own word about itself quickly comes to mind, as does its implied corollary of the existence of more than one kind of word, some more inclusive and transcendent than others. Presumably there exist various kinds of words that may to a greater or lesser extent represent the voices of carnival; in the passage above at least three such words can be distinguished.

First, there is the sincere word of the progressive forces in sixteenth-century France, one of whose most prominent members was Rabelais; second, is the "last word" of Rabelais, which transcends the more limited one of his progressive brethren and overlaps with the third, what Bakhtin calls the "gay word of the people" (*veseloe narodnoe slovo*). Conceived pictographically, we would see three circles: the first and second overlap, as well as the second and third. The first circle has no direct contact with the third, its experience of carnival is secondhand at best. Rabelais's word may partially coincide with that of the people but, being a final word, it is necessarily limited (*ogranichennyi*) and therefore ultimately plays the role of signifier to the signified of carnival, the vividness of its representation notwithstanding. The most transcendent category and the largest circle is, naturally, the third, which almost eclipses the other two in scope, longevity, and overall significance. What emerges here is a triad of languages with Rabelais's word playing a mediator-like role between the other two. Such a configuration is christologically suggestive, particularly in light of the emphasis on the conditional autonomy of the Trinity's hypostases that is dominant in Orthodoxy. One need only think of Sergei Bulgakov's essay "Was ist das Wort," where the body of language is described as riven by cuts (German, *Schnitte*) and mortified when it ceases to be perceived as an dynamic and integrated whole. For both Bakhtin and Bulgakov, these are lines that inscribe the body without sectioning or dismembering it, delineating regions of multiple intersections and congruence. But Bakhtin takes this image a few steps further, conflating the biological feature of symbiosis and the theological doctrine of *perichoresis* in his description of linguistic interaction.

The level of interaction and engagement between these three manifestations of language described above is profound. While there is no gainsaying the self-evident truth that this dynamic between the three languages and their attendant social worlds is fundamentally antihierarchical, Bakhtin's subsequent and more detailed treatment of such linguistic interaction is more involuted than one might expect. Stepping back for a moment from Bakhtin's text, we find it useful to think of the various metaphors or scenarios of linguistic inversion. Two models of the crossing of boundaries between high and low types of literary speech spring to mind. The first conception that may account for such linguistic reversals is the one of "diglossia" posited first by West German Slavists during the late 1960s and early 1970s to account for the presence of the vernacular in medieval Russian literature. According to them, there actually existed side-by-side two linguistic and literary cultures in pre-seventeenth-century Russia: one was the Church Slavonic used in sermons and in the Chronicles, while the other, more East Slavonic standard, reflected daily usage, exemplified in legal documents such as the "Russian Law" (*Russkaia Pravda*) and mercantile ones like the Novgorod Birch Barks.[21] Occasionally reversals of style could be discerned in certain texts, although always in a somewhat modest and limited form and depending on the political situation of a particular period. This scheme, however congenial to Bakhtin it might initially seem to be because of its assumption of high and low cultures that speak in coherent languages of their own and intermittently influence each other, is ultimately too static and inflexible for him in its vision of well-defined communities of speakers. Bakhtin's conception of community, while certainly overlapping with class, is not fully coterminous with it; carnival, after all, provides the loophole that permits the participant temporarily to escape social distinctions.

The second, and metaphorically more vivid and theatrical, model to describe this reversal is at least tangentially suggested by Bakhtin at the end of *Rabelais and His World,* where he quotes Dmitri the Pretender's dream (from Pushkin's "Boris Godunov") of falling into a crowd. It is a model based on the image of an insurrection, the dethroning or overthrowing of the high by the low. But this manifestation of reversal, however radical and dramatically subversive, ultimately lacks nuance in describing a universe that is not at heart Manichaean. This model cannot easily brook the presence of a third voice, such as the one posited earlier by Bakhtin as belonging to Rabelais and his "last word"; with its whole view of the world as dualistically dominated by high versus low, any third element would either be viewed as a *tertium quid*—defined in terms of the other two regnant categories—or simply ignored. In reality, these gambits are not so dissimilar: in neither is the third force of Rabelais's last word considered on its own terms. Furthermore, if the third is simply defined as that which is middle or intermediary, in its fulcrum-like position it remains unmoved and inert during any reversal between high and low. The dualistic universe here is two-dimensional indeed, strictly defined by the distance between antipodes of order and rebellion. In their recent panoptic study of Bakhtin, Morson and Emerson take to task the Western view of Bakhtin as "a Bakunin of our time" and convincingly argue that the Bakuninite equation of destruction as creation is irreconcilable with the ideal of ethical responsibility implied in the writings of Bakhtin and his circle.[22]

But other essays by Bakhtin need not be resorted to in order to see the deficiency of a linguistic model that operates on the asssumption of agonistic inversion between speech norms, its assertion of coexistence and interaction notwithstanding. The most glaring internal contradiction of this model can be quickly discerned in the light of *Rabelais and His World* alone: it is a conception that reinforces precisely the verticalism of the medieval worldview that Bakhtin decries. Furthermore, to be workable for Bakhtin such a model would have to be modified from a finite line determined by two endpoints to a circle where the third point would not occupy the stationary center but would lie alongside it with high and low on the circumference, all three equally susceptible to a change in position. In other words (even stranger still) one would have to adapt the model to fit a spatially determined metaphor originating in the Middle Ages: the Wheel of Fortune, the *locus classicus* of which appears in the *De Consolatione Philosophiae* of Boethius. Clearly, this model does differ significantly from the one of diglossia by being kinetic, imagistic, and even pictorial rather than rigidly classificatory. Both, however, hinge on an overweening dualism in their pictures of language change. There can be little doubt that Bakhtin would have found neither congenial to his approach. Bakhtin's linguistic triad is, in fact, a rather sprawling entity in the image of the word's inscribed body sketched out by Bulgakov, with its overlapping and criss-crossing lines and its regions that have areas of adjacence and convergence as well as separateness and otherness. The multiple folds and sheer surface volume of the grotesque body that Bakhtin describes render it a mirror-image of Bulgakov's logos as an involuted and layered text. Although Bakhtin sees language as having different yet interconnected parts, he regards it as centrifugal only in the sense he sees multiple yet overlapping centers of influence, much like the gravitational pull exerted by different masses. Bakhtin's adaptation of the Trinitarian and Chalcedonian paradigms was inevitably selective and idiosyncratic; in a certain very real sense they were devoid of devotional and doctrinal content in and of themselves. Although admittedly speculative, the comparison of Bakhtin's conception of the human universe with Boethius's is suggestive in revealing the conditionally centrifugal and almost antitheocentric drift of the Russian critic's work.

And yet we would do well to consider the possibility that Bakhtin's Copernican conception of language development is theologically grounded while *also* being centrifugal. This unexpected affiliation becomes clearer after examining in greater detail Bakhtin's other statements about linguistic and cultural change. The linguistic triad just discussed reappears in a more fully wrought and less abstract form at the beginning of the conclusion of the chapter and book, a few pages after Bakhtin's outlining of the three worlds of humanism, Rabelais himself, and the culture of laughter. As if bearing out what he implied earlier, now Bakhtin manifestly demonstrates that the clash among high, middle, and low levels of language indeed does not always take the form of a simple inversion. In this passage he describes the clash between classical Latin, medieval Latin, and what he calls the national language. Although the scheme Bakhtin now uses to describe language's development at the time of Rabelais is suggestively spatial, the process is more thoroughgoingly antihierarchical than the mere descent of the top and assumption of the bottom:

> Thus we see that the interorientation [*vzaimoorientatsiia*] of the vernacular and medieval Latin was complicated by an intersection [*vzaimoorientatsiei i*

> *vzaimooveshcheniem:* lit., interorientation and (mutual) illumination] of the latter with classic Latin. *One line cut through the other* [*Odna mezha peresekalas' s drugoiu mezhoiu*], and Cicero's Latin threw light upon the true nature of medieval Latin, whose character was actually perceived for the first time. Up to that moment medieval Latin had been used without awareness of its ugliness and limitations [*ego urodlivogo i ogranichennogo litsa:* lit., its ugly and stunted face]. (466; 516)

Bakhtin stresses here the significance of the interrelatedness of all linguistic phenomena. The paradoxical fact that (as described by Bakhtin) in Rabelais's day the chronologically and culturally distant model of Ciceronian Latin played the unexpected role of a mediator between medieval Latin and contemporary French indicates that reversal occurs not just between high and low, but among high, low, and middle. It is especially revealing that Bakhtin does not specify in his highlighted statement what borders of which languages intersect with the others; apparently, as they were spoken and read during Rabelais's age all three languages had inevitably been affected. The metaphors in this passage are vivid, memorable and built on certain of those used earlier: once again, the linguistic forces are personified as players, although here they are deftly personalized as well into people who mix with one another, the figure of medieval Latin even individualized with a misshapen face. The figure of Ciceronian Latin is singled out as well as an almost supernatural source of light, although the concept of mutual illumination (*vzaimooveshchenie*) implies that all three languages are at least capable of illuminating one another. Here it is not the national language that causes the foundation of the church's language to tremble; in a certain sense, the mediating force of Ciceronian Latin becomes more important than the polar opposition represented by the other two languages.

As Bakhtin describes in greater detail on the following page, the interaction among these three languages and the integrality of each to the other two becomes evident upon closer examination. The evolution of a language does not teleologically proceed in the manner of an historical dialectic toward an end that altogether does away with the upper levels of the hierarchy; the real evolution of language is not so much antihierarchical as it is progressively heedless of hierarchy. While this distinction may appear to be minor, it is important here given Bakhtin's belief in the cumulative process of the trickling into one another that occurs between the leaky containers of different language levels.

The following description of this process of interpenetration across porous boundaries is Bakhtin's most revealing in the entire book and will be quoted in its entirety. Given the length of the paragraph, it will be broken down into two parts. In the passage directly below, Bakhtin continues his discussion of the jostling of one level of speech against another, particularly in regard to medieval Latin:

> In this process of mutual clarification, an exceptional self-awareness was developed by *living reality*, that is, by all that was new and had not existed formerly: new objects, new concepts, new points of view. [*The new reality*] *achieves an exceptionally acute consciousness as the boundaries* [*rubezhi*] *of time, epochs, world-views and day-to-day life are distinctly apprehended* [*otchetlivo proshchupyvaiutsia*]. The flow of time could have never been so sharply and clearly felt within the confines [*v predelakh*] of a single, gradually evolving language system. Within the confines [*v predelakh*] of medieval Latin, which levels all things, the *marks* [*sledy: traces*] *of time* were almost entirely effaced; here consciousness seemed to live on in an eternal, unchanging world. In such a system it was particularly difficult to look around in time and space, that is, to become aware of the peculiar traits of one's own nationality and homeland. (467; 517)[23]

What Bakhtin is saying here is considerably more complex than that medieval Latin was a dead language deleterious to the growth of a national language and consciousness. True, the older language is something of an artificial phenomenon that is not allowed to be affected by changing usage. Bakhtin communicates here a vivid sense of it as a linguistic curiosity, zealously preserved in a scholastic hothouse and assiduously kept free of all other possible influences. His use of the phrase "within the confines [*v predelakh*]" is particularly revealing in that it comes into play with previous and contrasting uses of the term where Rabelais's language is said to go *beyond* certain boundaries (*vykhodiashchii/vykhodivshii za predely*); medieval Latin is therefore clearly representative of a language that deliberately stays within its perceived limits. But this is not to say that medieval Latin cannot positively affect the spoken language of early sixteenth-century France. In fact, the petrified archaisms of medieval Latin somehow serve to offset the modern national language and to give its educated speakers a clearer sense of what is genuinely new and their own and what is not. Thus, willy-nilly, the borders (*rubezhi*) will clash, the older and more archaic language influencing the formation of the vernacular and becoming embroiled in modernity whether it likes to or not.

In the rest of this keystone passage Bakhtin continues his meditation on borders and boundaries, playing on various senses of the terms to the point where the paragraph seems to reach beyond the immediate study of Rabelais himself. "*It is on the brink" of the[se] three languages* [*No na rubezhakh trex iazykov*]," Bakhtin stresses, that the awareness of time (in its cultural manifestations) takes on "exceptionally sharp and varied forms." It was precisely this awareness [*soznanie*] that was able to see itself "*on the boundaries of epochs and philosophies*" [*na rubezhe epokh i mirovozzrenii*], for the first time embracing vast dimensions embraced and measuring the flow of time; it was able to acutely sense its present in contradistinction to its past ("ono smoglo ostro oshchutit' *svoe segodnia, ego nepokhozhest' na vchera*"), its limits (*granitsy*) and perspectives. "This interorientation [*vzaimoorientatsiia*] and mutual clarification [*vzaimoosveshchenie*] of the three languages suddenly disclosed *how much of the old was dead and how much of the new was born.*" Contemporary reality was finally able to be cognizant of itself [*(s)ovremennost' osoznala sebia*], seeing its face in the "mirror of comedy" (467–68; 517). The kind of linguistic and cultural intersection that Bakhtin describes here brings about change not only among the languages involved, but also in individuals like Rabelais, who suddenly finds himself in the middle of such an historical crossroads. Yet again in Bakhtin's writing, the sense of the physical space or site of a certain action unfolding is very strong and the principal categories are personified as actors on the scene. Thus, it is consciousness (*soznanie*) itself that sees, feels, and acts, all of which it does while standing on the threshold (*rubezh*) between different epochs and ways of viewing the world. One of the events it witnesses is the fight of forces like Matthew Arnold's ignorant armies clashing by night or like multiple vectors colliding with one another, irrevocably changing the direction of each. It is only after taking in this encounter that the consciousness becomes transformed into contemporaneity (*sovremennost'*); only then that the human agent can truly understand what is genuinely expressive of and novel about the present moment. The highly synchronic and trichotomous operation of language presented here is residually reminiscent of the chronological transgredience of the Johannine word, where a new "generation" paradoxically blends with the one that preceded it.

Several pages later, Bakhtin expands on this metaphor of a fateful meeting at the crossroads of a national culture. By this point, the tintinnabulation of the terms Bakhtin uses to describe Rabelais's language reaches something of a high pitch:

> We see *at what a complex intersection* [*peresechenii rubezhei*] *of languages, dialects, idioms, and jargons the literary and linguistic consciousness of the Renaissance was formed.* The primitive and naive coexistence of languages and dialects had come to an end; the new consciousness was born not in a perfected and fixed linguistic system but at the intersection [*na mezhe*] of many languages and at the point of their *most intense interorientation and struggle* [*napriazhennoi vzaimoorientatsii i bor'by*]. Languages are philosophies—not abstract but concrete, social philosophies, penetrated by a system of values inseparable from living practice and class struggle. This is why *every object, every concept, every point of view as well as every intonation found their place at this intersection of linguistic philosophies* and was drawn into an intense ideological struggle. In these exceptional conditions, *linguistic dogmatism or naiveté* [lit., linguistic or communicative dogmatism (and) communicative naïveté] became impossible.

> The language of the sixteenth century, and especially the language of Rabelais, are sometimes described as naive today. In reality the history of European literature presents no language less naive. Rabelais' exceptional frankness and ease are anything but that. The literary and linguistic consciousness of his time was aware of its media [*svoi iazyk:* lit., its language] not only from the inside but also from *the outside, in the light of other languages;* it was able to sense *the limits* [*granitsy*] *of its language,* to see it as a specific and limited *image* [*obraz*] in all its relativity and humanity. (470–71; 520–21)[24]

What Bakhtin calls here the "literary and linguistic consciousness [*soznanie*] of the epoch" corresponds to the "contemporaneity" (*sovremennost'*) described by him a few pages earlier. The formation of this consciousness is not an easy one: it comes about through conflict between different levels of society and language, none of which remain the same afterward. The new consciousness is like a spark produced by the friction of the various languages, dialects, and argots upon one another: the grinding of one face against another changes the contours of the surfaces as well as generating energy. That a distinct consciousness is born at this moment of intersection (*peresechenie*) is borne out by certain metaphorical traces; about halfway into the quotation an important shift occurs where Bakhtin switches from sociological to cognitive and behavioral classifications, from worldviews (*mirovozreniia*) to naïveté (*naivnost'*) and unconstraint, spontaneity (*neprinuzhdennost'*), or ease. During the course of this passage Rabelais's language has become more than just a language: it is now invested with thought and feeling. In a word, it has been given life.

Proceeding with this vivification of Rabelaisian language, Bakhtin enhances certain distinctions reflecting that language's new status as animate and conscious. According to Bakhtin, spontaneity or ease is more characteristic of Rabelais's language than naïveté. The contradistinction between the attributes of unconstraint and naïveté in particular deserves a pause for thought. At the end of chapter 1 ("Rabelais in the History of Laughter"), Bakhtin ends his bibliographical survey of Russian translations of Rabelais with the comment that only the 1961 Liubimov translation captures Rabelais in all his inimitable familiarity and spontaneity (*neprinuzhdennost'iu*); in chapter 2 ("The Language of the Marketplace") Bakhtin takes issue with Veselovsky's description of Rabelais as a naive and irreverent village boy, asserting instead that his is not a naive gaiety (*naivnoe vesel'e*), but a popular and festive gaiety and an ancient youthfulness (*drevniaia molodost'*) like that of Heraclitus's "playing boy" who rules the physical universe. Given the meticulous consistency with which Bakhtin uses his terms and the clear correspondences between these various statements, it is safe to conclude that *neprinuzhdennost'* is associated with or is considered a related character trait to "popular-festive gaiety" and "ancient youth." Once again, we find ourselves in the precipitous territory of Bakhtinian paradox: in an image that clearly bears a family relation to the terracotta laughing and pregnant hags that Bakhtin in his introduction takes as emblematic of grotesque realism, the language of Rabelais ultimately belongs not to the French writer himself (whose own word, after all, is limited and finite [*poslednee*]) but to the unconstrained yet ancient lord-child of the universe.

Particularly significant from the perspective of these textual allusions to other parts of the book is the distinction that Bakhtin makes in the last sentence of the paragraph above, which almost gets lost in the thicket of his highlighted remarks. We have already established that Bakhtin values the crossing of borders and limits (rendered variously as *predel, mezha,* and, in the passage above, as *rubezh* and *granitsa*). Up until this point, however, it has not been completely clear who or what would transgress these constrictions. Finally, in the conclusion of the book, this has been made clear: it is language. But language alone cannot transcend itself; in and of itself it is limited (*ogranichennyi*). A literary and linguistic consciousness is born out of language only after the latter comes into chafing contact with other levels of culture. The analogy between the formation of consciousness and the procreative act is not accidental. For Bakhtin, the passage from one realm of culture to another represents a moment of conception and nascency.

Bakhtin pursues this generational metaphor over the next two pages in ways that are not always obvious but which, taken together, effectively fill out the lacunae and interstices of its form. This is the point where the Marxist ramifications of Bakhtin's discussion of the class struggle between languages and ways of life become brittle and break, for the final stage of the intense discord between them unexpectedly leads to conjunction. If the creating consciousness (*tvoriashchee soznanie*) lives "in one language only" (*v odnom i edinstvennom iazyke*), or if it partakes of [*prichastno:* lit., communes with] several languages that "coexist but remain strictly divided [*razgranicheny*] without struggling for supremacy," one cannot overcome the profound dogmatism of officialdom under which the linguistic thought labors. "It is possible to place oneself outside one's own language only when an essential historic *change of the languages* [*smena iazykov*] occurs," when, so to speak [*tak skazat'*], these languages adapt or adjust themselves [*primeriaiutsia*] not only to each other but also to the world at large ["i *k miru*"]," as the facets [*grani*] of time, culture, and social groups are simultaneously beginning to be felt. It was just such a period of dialectical tensions that made the "ideological radicalism of Rabelaisian images" possible (471; 521–22).[25] Yes, discord and struggle are indispensable for the true and healthy development of a language, but they are not ends in themselves. Here Bakhtin shrewdly uses the term "creative consciousness" to denote both the consciousness that comes into being at the crossroads of history (which he discussed shortly before and which would still be in the reader's mind) and Rabelais himself. As it turns out in this particular case, in early sixteenth-century France Rabelais was precisely that point of intersection where a new consciousness was conceived; in a certain sense, a second Rabelais emerged like Gargantua himself from his mother's ear in the sixth chapter of *Gargantua* and in whose spirit we use the term "Rabelaisian." It is this Rabelais who is personified as a consciousness and who stands outside of the language that engendered him.

In this regard Bakhtin's use of *smena* (change) is particularly revealing. The term broadly refers to the change of languages, yet its multiple meanings in Russian suggest much more: languages not only change, they sometimes replace one another, perhaps in the manner of one generation by another. Such change takes place, Bakhtin continues when, "so to speak" (*tak skazat'*) languages match up (*primeriaiutsia*) with one another. Given the slightly colloquial flavor of the Russian "so to speak" in an otherwise stylistically overripe passage of scholarly prose, the phrase serves as the rhetorical equivalent of a railway switch signaling an important turn of argument or a particularly important stop. While *primeriaiutsia* is difficult to translate and Bakhtin himself seems to imply that he is resorting to circumlocution, there is no question that the verb here (as in its more straightforward uses without the reflexive prefix *-sia*) refers to some kind of matching up, orienting, and adjusting in a highly concrete sense. The nuances of all of this are, of course, completely lost in any English translation.[26]

What is clear, however, is that languages come to relate to one another and the world in a way that is analogous to physical contact and that results in a succession of languages. In other words, the encounters between languages, at first confrontational, somehow segue or shift to alliances or unions. The gradual discerning of the surfaces or facets (*grani,* of which the term *granitsa* is a diminutive) of time periods, cultures, and social groups within each language contributes to the creation of a new creative consciousness. This incipient awareness or cultural identity undergoes something of a gestation period during which its ontogeny recapitulates its phylogeny, its early development replaying the provenance of almost Darwinian contestation that preceded the close interaction necessary for its conception. Given Bakhtin's description of this disarming of contestants in a culture, there is hardly a Russian ear that would not hear a little bit of *primiriáiutsia* (they reconcile) in Bakhtin's *primeriáiutsia,* especially with the accentual vowel reduction of *e* [ě] in the latter to [i]. It is a clever pun, one that effectively foregrounds the point being made here about the confluence of languages and testifying to the orality of Bakhtin's writing. Bakhtin's metaphor of language as a conscious entity or life produced as a result of language interaction is deeply embedded even in a thoroughgoingly theoretical passage like the one above.

Bakhtin's further pursuit of this line of thought is unabashedly teleological; nonetheless its end had been anticipated and tantalizingly hinted at at various points earlier in the book. In the subsequent discussion he switches from the subject of the birth and growth of language consciousness to deal one last time with previous scholarship on the carnivalesque, and once again he trains his sights on German work on the subject. The book at hand is Dieterich's 1897 study of Pulcinella, the Italian version of Punch and Judy. Many of the terms and their distinct usages that made cameo appearances or took leading turns earlier make their farewell appearance here, and with special flourish. That Bakhtin's propensity for stylistic flamboyance and baroque ornateness reaches something of an apogee here should not distract from the highly logical and interconnected series of ideas that are presented in a unprecedentedly condensed form. Dieterich focuses on the specifics of the "antique comic art [*drevnego smekhovogo iskusstva*]" of southern Italy. Paraphrasing Dieterich, Bakhtin states that comic forms such as farces and buffoneries are characteristic of a *"mixed culture* [*smeshannoi kul'tury*]." Since Greek, Oscan, and Latin cultures and languages touched or came into contact with each other (*soprikasalis'*) and were "interwoven" (*perepletalis'*) in southern Italy, the patrimony of Pulcinella is complex. Imperial Rome itself had already possessed a mixed culture. The figure of Pulcinella "arose out of the depths of the peoples, *at the very point where peoples and languages were constantly merged* [*smeshivalis'*]" (471–72; 522). What Bakhtin calls earlier the "interorientation" (*vzaimoorientatsiia*) among languages is asserted yet again, although here the geopolitical ramifications rather than those of merely the national culture are alluded to as well. Regionally and ethnically, the "mixed culture" (*smeshannaia kul'tura*) that Bakhtin speaks of in this excerpt is a multiple entity and not simply that which consists of various estates within a single society. But the dynamics in this new, more global situation do not fundamentally differ from those before; only the scale has changed. As before, various manifestations of culture come into direct and distinctly physical contact in which they become embroiled with one another perhaps more than they would like. Bakhtin's use of the metaphor of weaving is particularly evocative here.

Other terms stand out by virtue of their juxtaposition and phonetic—and even morphophonemic—similarity. One cannot help thinking that Bakhtin was playing upon the words *smeshannyi* and *smekhovoi*, particularly since the mixed culture is indeed the one where laughter is able to flourish. Taken in the context of the rest of chapter 7, Bakhtin seems to be drawing a parallel between the cultural mosaic of what is presumably pre-Risorgimento southern Italy and the stratified society with its multiple types of speech. This parallel becomes more visible with a quick glance to the point several pages earlier where Bakhtin describes the limited and closed perspectives of the progressive Renaissance as being in themselves comical (*smeshnymi*) in juxtaposition with the corporeality of folk imagery.[27] As it turns out, even the earnest and the serious, by virtue of contrast, can play a comic and carnival role. In a certain sense, variety and differentiation within the body politic are indispensable to the efflorescence of the carnivalesque. This crucial link in Bakhtin's line of reasoning is more than implied in the passage above, especially when contemplating the interplay between the trisyllabic terms *smekhovoi* and *smeshannyi*. In fact, a triple chain of terms emerges here, with the last link not just a morphophonemic and thematic subtext but also something of phonetic composite of the previous two: ***smekhovói—sméshannyi—[smeshnói]***. Finally Bakhtin has provided for the reader an indestructible connection between laughter and the celebration of difference within unity, and has done it in the numerical form of three-in-one. This configuration appears plainly, of course, in Bakhtin's historical comments on the growth of the comic in that part of Europe, where he asserts that three spirits of the comic live in the breast of every southern Italian. The various levels and terms of Bakhtin's argument are audibly in tune with one another here, carefully orchestrated to foreground the evolution on language that he is describing.

Picking up momentum, Bakhtin next brings all the central tenets of his defense of carnival to a magisterial close, his most substantive comments about the comic word framed by his respectful but critical appreciations of two German scholars, Schneegans in chapter 5 and Dieterich in the conclusion. Never has Bakhtin's reiteration of certain phrases and terms been so concerted and concentrated within a paragraph. Confronted with this critical vocabulary as never before, the reader comes to the vivid awareness of just how important indeed it had been for Bakhtin's arguments throughout the book:

> Dieterich's opinion can be summed up as follows: The peculiar and extremely *free humorous language* [*vol'noe smekhovoe slovo*] of Sicily and southern Italy, the similar media [*slovo*] of the Attelanae and later of Pulcinella's own linguistic clownery, were born *on the confines of languages and cultures* [*na mezhe iazykov i kul'tur*], which not only were in direct contact [*neposredstvenno soprikasalis'*] but were in a certain sense interwoven [*perepletalis' mezhdu soboiu*]. We believe that their emergence and development *on these linguistic boundaries* [*na mezhe iazykov*] had exceptional significance for the *universalism of humor and radicalism* [*smekhovogo universalizma i radikalizma*] represented by these forms. The link of these forms with a *multiligual world* [*s mnogoiazychiem*], as pointed out by Dieterich, seems to us extremely important. In the sphere of literary and artisitic creation it is impossible to overcome *through abstract thought alone*, within the system of a unique language [*odnogo-edinogo i edinstvennogo iazyka:* lit., of a single, unique and unitary language], that deep dogmatism hidden in all the forms of this system. The completely new, self-criticizing, absolutely sober, *fearless* and therefore *gay*

> life of the image can start only on linguistic confines [*na mezhe iazykov*]. In the system of one language, closed to all others, the image is too strictly imprisoned to allow that "truly divine boldness and shamelessness" which Dieterich finds in the farce of southern Italy, in the Attelanae (as far as we can judge of them), and in Pulcinella's folk humor. We repeat, another language means another philosophy and another culture but in their concrete and not fully translatable form. The exceptional freedom and pitiless gaiety of the Rabelaisian image were possible only on the confines [*na rubezhe*] of languages. (472–73; 522–23)

Each national culture has its own "word of laughter" (*smekhovoe slovo*). Analogous to this festive national word (and, in a certain sense, included in it) are other words that are smaller in scope such as those of the Attenelae and emblematic comic figures such as Pulcinella. In these instances, however, the precise manner and sequence of how such localized words came into being need to be reconstructed from Bakhtin's remarks. A close examination of the section where Bakhtin describes the development of these words—the first half of the paragraph above—yields surprising and amusing results: being a lover of inversion and the vision of a world turned upside down, Bakhtin charts the genesis of these words in reverse chronological order. The essential prerequisite for their coming into being is a multilingual milieu (*mnogoiazychie*) perspicaciously pointed out, Bakhtin acknowledges, by Dieterich. The languages and their cultures touched upon (again, *neposredstvenno soprikasalis'*) and then interwove (*perepletalis'*) with those of others, after which the particular words arose (*voznikli*) on the boundary (*na mezhe*) dividing the differing sociolinguistic realms that originally engendered them. Thus are singular carnival words with highly distinct comic voices born under the protectorate of the single and macrocosmic comic word of the nation.

That this is an image of birth and corresponds to the nascent new consciousness described earlier is left to little doubt in the second half of the paragraph. Thus, the existence of these emergent comic words is characterized as a new and absolutely sane, gay (*veselaia*) and fearless life of the image that begins on the boundaries of languages. The new comic word comes about only after the interaction between different languages and cultures in a way distinctly similar to mating. None of this could ever occur within the confines or limits of a closed and utterly unitary language; unlike the actual biosphere and the animal kingdom within it, Bakhtin's literary universe is completely intolerant of parthenogenesis. The Rabelaisian image Bakhtin speaks of at the end of the paragraph above is constituted by literary productivity as motivated by a transgredient cultural multeity. With the assonant characterization of official language as single, unique, and unitary (*od[in]-edin[yi] i edinstvenn[yi]*), Bakhtin evocatively dramatizes how this generous abundance of cultural activity breaks away from the grip of obsessive linguistic centripetality.

But there is an additional depth to the imagery here that not only enhances the metaphor of conception but also has special resonance for a Russian of Bakhtin's time. Bakhtin uses here the term *mezha* (boundary-strip) with startling frequency in place of the more usual *rubezh*, *granitsa*, or *gran'* to denote border or boundary in the sense of a partition between different classes, cultures, or languages. Only one of these latter terms is used here, and then only once (*rubezh* at the end of the paragraph). On the other hand, *mezha* appears three times, once where Bakhtin almost drolly uses it in a highlighted form in the same sentence with the obviously related preposition *mezhdu* (between). In short, the reader ends up with the distinct impression that the term plays a special hermeneutical role here that the other synonyms cannot fulfill. The connotation separating *mezha* from the other words is that of a border dividing plots of land, a meaning that was richer in the prerevolutionary period but certainly—and for many not without bitterness—would have not been lost on a Russian living during the collectivization sweeps pushed forward by Stalin. But as evinced by some of the proverbs recorded by Dal', the word's usage before the Revolution was also laced with contention and anger, no doubt partly in response to the insufficiency of tsarist land reform: "Mezha—sviatoe delo" (The boundary is a sacred thing); "Mezha—i tvoia i moia" (The boundary—yours and mine); "U kogo silka, naidet za mezhku nivku" (He who looks, will find [a field beyond the boundary]); and the pithily philosophical "Mezhi da grani, ssory da brani" (Boundaries and borders, fisticuffs and quarrels). Dal' also lists the memorably metonymic and cynical "na mezhe zhenit'sia" (to marry a boundary) for marrying a woman with property as a dowry.[28] What becomes clear from all of this is Bakhtin's reason for resorting to the term: relating as he does in the passage above both the geopolitical and the societal manifestations of the comic word, nothing could be more felicitous than *mezha* for characterizing both the wars between estates (in all senses of that word) and nations.

With these final comments, Bakhtin's case for the carnivalesque perceptibly winds down to the end, but not without a quick look back at Schneegans's description of the birth of the carnival word. Rabelais's art is characterized by the "*freedom of laughter* [*vol'nost' smekha*]" as illuminated by the traditions of popular-festive forms, one "raised to a higher level of ideological consciousness, *thanks to the victory over* [*preodolenie:* lit., overcoming of] . . . [the most stubborn and hidden] *linguistic dogmatism.*" It was an overcoming made possible only through the conditions of those intense processes (*ostrykh protsessov*), contemporary with Rabelais, of "interorientation (*vzaimoorientatsii*) and mutual clarification (*vzaimoovseshcheniia*) of languages." The life of language at the time "enacted that same drama: *simultaneous death and birth, the aging and renewal* of separate forms and meanings" as well as entire worldviews (473; 523). Like any visitors to or participants in carnival, we are now, as T. S. Eliot put it in *The Four Quartets,* back at our beginnings. That carnival becomes to those partaking in it simultaneously death and birth, aging and renewal is due entirely to the interorientation and mutual illumination of different kinds of speech and *Weltanschauungen.* The key to carnival is in its role as the ultimate mediator of humanity.

In *Rabelais and His World* we are confronted with the same complex of ideas that were so abundantly present before; once again, discourse (*slovo*) is invested with soteriology, with a christological subtext. This subtext is in fact more profound here than in any other work written by Bakhtin because it is so tightly woven into the fabric of his analysis of Rabelais; in earlier efforts such as "Toward a Philosophy of the Act" and "Discourse in the Novel" it is easier to isolate these motifs because of the highly rhetorical use made of them. In the Rabelais book it is impossible to say where the secular and sacred begin and end in Bakhtin's terminology. There are two levels of this ambiguity in *Rabelais and His World.* First, and most obviously, his discussion of carnival hinges on the idea of the conflation of the officially sacred and the popular profane; second, Bakhtin's discussion itself of the interaction among different language levels at Rabelais's time reverberates with the theological *loci classici* of *perichoresis* and the Chalcedonian ideal. Although Bakhtin's romance of the boundary and (permeable) barrier is evident in almost all his criticism, it is certainly never more prominent than it is here. The divisions that now become porous, allowing for interpenetration and synthesis, are no longer simply individuals, but entire categories of experience. In series of complex puns that fit his methodological purposes beautifully, the earth (fruit, *plod*) joins with flesh (*plot'*) in carnival and laughter (*smekh*) becomes the emblem of cultural joining and commingling: *smekhovoi, smeshnoi* (humorous); *smeshannyi* (mixed). As shown in this chapter, all of these motifs come into play in *Rabelais and His World,* interacting in a manner strikingly resonant with Bulgakov's "cuts" (*Schnitte*) and Gumilev's *predely* (limits), both demarcating a distinctly Johannine body of the word. In Bakhtin, the boundary is no longer a mathematically perceived line, lacking space or depth: it now metonymically *becomes* the region it demarcates, at various points of its surface fusing with others and hence producing the abundantly convoluted and porous topography that makes up the grotesque body. Clearly, no other physical image could have been more felicitous in accurately rendering Bakhtin's conception of Rabelaisian discourse as a Chalcedonian and interpenetrative union of interlocking realms of cultural life.

In spite of all this, Bakhtin's own attitude toward such theological concepts is still difficult to ascertain; even murkier are the contemporary political ramifications of his theory of carnival, particularly in regard to the borders dividing up the cosmos. In *Rabelais and His World* Bakhtin at one point suggests a connection between carnival and the historical phenomenon of formation of the national state in Europe. One can certainly see that a crypto-Chalcedonian interaction and interrelatedness among individuals are in some sense congruent with the ideals of modern citizenship. Nonetheless, since carnivalistic celebration does not sit well with the demands of the polity, Bakhtin's statement about the confluence of carnival with progress and modernity seem at best unclear and at worst unconvincing. But if we bear in mind that Bakhtin highlights carnival as an intersubjective phenomenon—as an event of corporealizing communion with a macrocosmic and collective entity—then its affinities with civic duty and societal responsibility become less obscure. The questions that then remain are these: Ideologically speaking, what particular vision of social agency does Bakhtin implicitly advance? Or at least, what kind is most consonant with the vision presented in the Rabelais book? The ramifications of carnival—its reaching out and dwelling among social and political relations—will be treated in Chapter 6.

Chapter Six

The Word Made and Unmade: Rabelais, Bakhtin, and Stalin

> [P]olitical passions are realism of a particular quality, which is an important element of strength in them: They are *divinized* realism.
> —Julien Benda

> For murther, though it have no tongue, will speak
> With most miraculous organ.
> —*Hamlet*, II.ii.593–94

IN THE late sixties and early seventies, it was Bakhtin's landmark study of Rabelais that caught the attention of non-Slavist scholars. *Rabelais and His World* was first published in the Soviet Union in 1965 and translated into French and English over the next few years;[1] counting the two versions of his Dostoevsky study, it was Bakhtin's third book to appear in print. Bakhtin's investigation of folk laughter and carnival in *Gargantua* and *Pantagruel* was hailed in the West as something startlingly new with its focus on carnival, a cultural institution that had been deemed by traditional critics as unworthy of attention because of its mockery of high seriousness. There can be little doubt that Bakhtin esteemed folk culture with its celebration of the body over and against the culture of the church and state in Rabelais's time. The patent anticlericism of much of this book has been regarded as particularly significant in this regard. In this sweeping view, the church is a particularly egregious culprit in its attempts to nullify the demands of somatic existence; it plays a crucial role in promulgating and supporting the humorlessness of the hierarchical culture. Carnival periodically relieves the tension induced by the institutional repression of the body.

Notwithstanding this clear veneration of carnival, it is at this point of the delineation of Bakhtin's conception that trouble develops. Although carnival does indeed represent the recrudescence of the body, as an institution it is ultimately co-opted by the culture that repudiates it, serving as something of a safety valve for the libidinous impulses that afflict the body politic. Therein lies the central paradox of carnival, one not stated by Bakhtin but certainly implied by him and recently noted (with some chagrin) by Marxist scholars in the West.[2] All of this suggests that Bakhtin may have been more ambivalent about carnival than has been previously supposed, or that at the very least his vision of it might have been as an ancillary institution within a particular society rather than one that represents a potential and all-embracing utopia. Bakhtin closes his magisterial first chapter ("Rabelais in the History of Laughter") with an anticlimactic discussion of Russian translations of *Gargantua* and *Pantagruel.* Bakhtin singles out Liubimov's translation (published in 1961) as "remarkable" and "almost completely adequate." It is only thanks to this translation that "Rabelais has begun to speak in Russian, with his unique familiarity and spontaneity, with his immeasurable depth, with his comic imagery. It would be impossible to overestimate the importance of this event."[3] This coda-like statement asserting the significance of Rabelais for the Soviet Union of his time somehow seems highly suggestive: any reader of this passage would immediately query what possible import or overall relevance could the translation of a non-Russian classic have for a Russian in the stringent political atmosphere of a post-Khrushchev Soviet Union. It is important to bear in mind that in 1964 Bakhtin amplified and rewrote what was originally his dissertation from the early forties. But the philosophical and political implications of the Rabelais book are evident on other levels as well; specifically, it is in what might be called the theological subtext of *Rabelais and His World* that many of Bakhtin's political insights can be found. As will soon become evident, Bakhtin's diagnosis of the body politic of his time is profoundly critical and contentious.

THE SACRAL CHARACTER OF CARNIVAL

In his rebuttal to the committee at his dissertation defense on 15 November 1946, Bakhtin insisted to his opponents that he did not depoliticize carnival in his thesis. "In carnival I did not have in mind something cheerful. Not at all. Death is present in every carnivalistic image. Speaking in your terms, it is a tragedy. But it is not tragedy that becomes the last word [*poslednim slovom*]."[4] Carnival is nothing if not ambivalent. On the one hand, by purging people of their fear and trembling before authority in its many guises, it brings them closer to a more unconstrained and organic sense of community. On the other, the individual is defined by more than simply his or her relation to official culture, and the banishment of fear as a dread of punishment or execution does not, in itself, open up reservoirs of fellow-feeling and joyful communality. The awareness of death represents only a part of the essence of carnival, whose final word ultimately signifies an affirmation of the life principle. In this sense, there is no question that the operation of carnival is redemptive and salvific.

But this represents only one perspective opened up by the ontological dimensions of carnival. In *Rabelais and His World,* we are also confronted with the tableau of the collective's regeneration being ensured by the demise of the individual, his or her body enriching and renewing the infertile soil of the whole. The vegetative metaphor that Bakhtin uses here is highly suggestive of the transubstantiational model insofar as the topos of the renewal of the earth has occasionally been viewed as a kind of cosmological counterpart or equivalent of communion. Since the purification and progress that communion effects is short-term, a repetition and recurrence of the action becomes essential. For it to remain deathless, the collective body needs to partake regularly of its eucharistic meal of perishable individual bodies. Both of these perspectives on carnival, the positive and the negative, stem in one way or another from the theological implications highlighted in the previous chapter.

On the face of it, there is a a great deal that supports the laudatory perspective on carnival. Toward the end of chapter 3 ("Popular-Festive Forms and Images in Rabelais") Bakhtin unequivocally asserts the progressiveness of carnival: "The progressive leaders of the Renaissance participated [*prichastny*] directly in this [*unofficial folk*] culture and above all in its popular-festive, carnivalesque aspect" (274; 301). Given the ritual nature of carnival that is emphasized in this chapter of the book, the term *prichastny* which means as much to commune with as it does to participate in—has a reverberent quality here that suggests a more profound partaking of a custom or tradition than a straightforward participation or simple involvement. As in "Toward a Philosophy of the Act," the reader inevitably thinks of its derivational cousins *prichastit'sia* (to take communion) and *prichashchenie* (communion, joining). In his subsequent elaboration of carnival Bakhtin stresses its life-giving and transformative power:

> Carnival (and we repeat that we use this word in the broadest sense) did liberate human consciousness and permit a new outlook, but at the same time it implied no nihilism; it had a positive character because it exposed the abundant material principle, change and becoming, the irresistible triumph of the new immortal people. This was indeed a powerful support for storming the stronghold of the Gothic age; it prepared the way for a new, free, and sober seriousness. This is the very same carnivalization of consciousness [*karnivalizatsiia soznaniia*] that we spoke of earlier, the complete liberation from Gothic seriousness, so that roads could be built toward a new free and sober seriousness. (274; 301)[5]

Here carnival is characterized as reestablishing the link between the individual, the community, and the universe that surrounds them both. To be sure, certain shibboleths of Soviet literary scholarship stand out here and there ("nihilism," "a powerful support for storming the stronghold of the Gothic age," "progressive leaders," and so forth). Bakhtin's discussion of carnival in the context of the metamorphic and liberating transition from the Middle Ages to the Renaissance insists on the joyful integration of modernity's human diaspora.

In instances too numerous to discuss exhaustively, Bakhtin himself characterizes participation in carnival as a moment of transcendence out of the self and into a larger fellowship. The more significant and revealing passages—those that most fully reflect his central positions and definitions—will be touched upon in the following discussion. In the introduction to *Rabelais and His World* Bakhtin covers many of his arguments treated in the subsequent chapters of his book. There he defines carnival as the second life of a people, the first represented by the official culture of the church and state: "Carnival is the people's second life, organized on the basis of laughter. It is its *festive* [*prazdnichnaia:* lit., holiday] *life*" (8; 13). The paradox that carnival takes on a ritualistic, even systematic form (as implied by the word "organized" [*organizovannaia*]) while representing unofficial culture should not be glossed over here. At another point of the introduction, Bakhtin vividly describes the freedom and the carnival's universality. Carnival ignores spatial boundaries or limits (*prostranstvennykh granits*); it has, furthermore, its own way of measuring time as well as space, being "subject only to its laws, that is, the laws of carnival *freedom* ["karnavel'noi *svobody*"]." That is why it "has a universal spirit; it is a special condition [*osoboe sostoianie*] of the entire world, of the world's revival and renewal, in which all people take part [*kotoromu vse prichastny*]" (9; 12). Carnival represents a synchronization of the self and cosmos, a spiritual integration that some view as missing from modern-day life, an absence implied by Bakhtin with his specific and repeated identification of carnival with the Middle Ages and the Renaissance. The issue of alienation is, furthermore, explicitly acknowledged by Bakhtin. As he describes it, carnival temporarily dissolves the celebrant's usual alienation from others, the individual becoming seemingly reborn in his or her relations with them.[6]

Thus, carnival is sacral and communal (in both senses of the word) without being institutional. It is carnival's extrinsic relation to any institutional framework that accounts for the anticlerical nature of Rabelaisian laughter. One of the most important manifestations of carnival that Bakhtin discusses in the book are the traditions connected with the celebration of church holidays. In a passage that is identical both in his dissertation and in the 1965 edition, Bakhtin takes issue with A. N. Veselovsky's description of Rabelais as an obstreperous village boy who bursts out from the house into the spring air, splattering mud on passersby as he runs: in fact, asserts Bakhtin, Rabelais could be described as a boy only in a highly metaphorical sense; his art more accurately embodies Heraclitus's image of the "playing boy" who oxymoronically represents an ancient youthfulness (or the youthfulness of antiquity).[7]

According to Bakhtin, the one thing that Veselovsky does get right about Rabelais is the sense of springtime renewal as the dominant of the metaphor of the village boy. Spring is "the season . . . correctly chosen in Veselovsky's picture: this is truly a springlike carnivalesque, Paschal [*paskhal'nyi*] laughter." In this image one could say that "these forms of gay Shrovetide cynicism [*maslenichnogo veselogo tsinizma*] are transferred to a historic spring, to the new era." What needs to be revised is the image of the obstreperous boy. To Veselovsky, "[h]e is the symbol of youth, of immaturity and incompleteness." In fact, however, "Rabelais' youth is the youth of antiquity, the 'playing boy' of Heraclitus [and] [f]rom the historic point of view, Rabelais' cynicism belongs to the most ancient stratum of his novel."[8] Bakhtin believes spring celebrations to be the archetypes of carnival and the Rabelaisian spirit, specifically singling out Easter and Shrovetide as events of particular importance. In fact, spring represents the open-ended and unfinished quality of social reality in toto; to use a Bakhtinian turn of paradoxical phrase, the restive boy of spring stands for perpetual nascency. This emphasis is significant for a number of reasons; the reasons for Bakhtin's finding Heraclitus's image of the playing boy so congenial will become apparent later in this chapter.

In describing the rich tradition of pre-Lenten celebrations that Rabelais availed himself of, Bakhtin is clearly drawn to the season of spring as an emblem rife with philosophical implications that transcend the geographical, cultural, and historical borders. Particularly significant in the context of the passage above is that Easter traditionally figures as the most prominent holiday in the Eastern Orthodox calendar. Arguably, in explicating the significance of the entire Easter experience—from its very different stages of Shrovetide, Lent, and Easter itself—in terms of a movement toward a renewal that is as much personal as it is universal (and of a building, mutual coinherence of the two), Bakhtin betrays a traditional bias of Orthodoxy. In one passage that appears only in the introduction to his dissertation, Bakhtin imbues festive laughter with distinctly Chalcedonian properties. "In Gothic laughter it is impossible to say where its negative aspect (destructive mockery) ends and its positive, affirmative side (gay, triumphant laughter—*'risus paschalis', 'risus nataliis'* according to medieval terminology) begins inasmuch as both poles are merged [*slity*] in it into an inseparable unity [*nerazryvnoe edinstvo*]."[9] One sees more clearly the internal dynamics of Bakhtin's carnival by bearing in mind the thematics of the Fourth Ecumenical Council at Chalcedon, which of course is particularly important for Orthodox doctrine.

But the absence in Russian culture of real carnival as defined in *Rabelais and His World* is surely not without significance. There are those who have argued that besides the rich literature of carnival from Western European folk culture, Bakhtin's theory of carnival also has a number of Russian precedents. Many of these specifically Russian subtexts and ramifications of Bakhtin's carnival are rather elusive. The renowned Russian medievalist Dmitri Likhachev has asserted that examples of Bakhtin's vision of carnival as "the world upside down" can be found in Russian literature from at least as far back as the seventeenth century, often taking the form of parodic and blasphemous inversions where the flesh takes the place of spirit in the hierarchy of religious values.[10] Likhachev adduces the so-called Kaliazin Petition, a blasphemous parody of the Lord's Prayer written by the monks of the Kaliazin monastery in the late seventeenth century, as one such literary example of an "antiworld" of religious doctrine, one in which the world is turned inside out. With no connection to the classical patrimony of comedy represented by Aristophanes and Plautus, humor in Russian literature developed almost exclusively in terms of the culture of the church. To be sure, such an inversion of values is fully consistent with the transformational scheme outlined in "Discourse in the Novel," where the flesh becomes the word in a kind of inversion of Johannine logology. But Likhachev's view has been vigorously and convincingly argued against by Iurii Lotman and Boris Uspensky. According to them, Bakhtinian carnival is impossible in the period and culture Likhachev discusses: "Russian medieval Orthodox culture is organized on [the principle of] the opposition between holiness and satanism. Holiness excludes laughter."[11] Laughter in Russian culture is therefore often perceived as satanic, the obliteration of the line between spectator and performer inspiring fear in the audience by introducing the element of possible violence to one's person. Such were the participative theatrical events staged by Ivan the Terrible, which often resulted in executions of those forced to take part in them.[12] Here, death *is* the last word. It is no wonder that at Bakhtin's dissertation defense Nikolai Brodsky attacked Bakhtin for seeing a carnivalistic saturnalia in Dostoevsky's graveyard phantasia "Bobok." "That is not a holiday," he asserted, "but a tragedy [written by] a great Russian and world tragedian."[13] Its universalizing "paschal" character notwithstanding, there is a lingering sense in which Bakhtin's celebratory carnival is not entirely at home within the Russian context. Not surprisingly, there are those (like Bakhtin's student Vadim Kozhinov), who regard Lotman's and Uspensky's comments about the impossibility of true laughter and Bakhtinian carnival in Russia as a calumny against its culture.[14]

CARNIVAL AND THE GROTESQUE BODY POLITIC

At this point it becomes clear that certain tensions lurk under and occasionally furrow the seemingly benign physiognomy of carnival. Surely the integration of the individual into the body politic is tantamount to the former's assimilation, loss of identity, or even destruction. It is this more disturbing ramification of Bakhtin's carnival that will now be examined. Far from contradicting

Bakhtin's positive statements about carnival, these more sinister aspects are of one piece with the same aesthetic of ambivalence and change that he describes elsewhere in the book. The tension-filled dynamics of the Stalin era provide an illuminating backdrop to some of these overtones of carnival, less perceptible when the institution is taken off the historical stage. Some of these tensions are evident from the following passage from the Rabelais book, where Bakhtin describes the "overcoming of cosmic fear and eschatology" that emerges as a leading theme in Rabelais's novel:

> In the development of this theme the grotesque body plays a most important part. It is the *people's* [*vsenarodnoe:* lit., the entire people's] growing and ever-victorious body that is "at home" in the cosmos. It is the cosmos' own flesh and blood [*plot' ot ploti i krov' ot krovi kosmosa*], possessing the *same elemental force* but better organized. *The body is the last and best word* [*slovo*] *of the cosmos, its leading force.* There is nothing it has to fear. Death holds no terror for it. *The death of the individual* [*smert' individa*] is only one moment in the triumphant life of the people and of mankind, a moment *indispensable* for their *renewal and improvement.* (340–41; 377)

The incarnational metaphor occasionally evident in "Discourse and the Novel" and "Forms of Time and the Chronotope in the Novel" extrudes from this passage as well. The reverberant Russian turn of phrase "plot' ot ploti i krov' ot krovi kosmosa" (which more closely corresponds to the liturgical formula "body of this body and blood of this blood") echoes eucharistic doctrine, particularly when taken together with the Johannine subtext suggested by Bakhtin's identification of the grotesque body with the cosmos's ultimate word. Most significant of all are the cosmic elements and powers whose diversity is implied by Bakhtin: for all their variety and differences among themselves, they become "organized" within the grotesque body. This nonhierarchical ordering of elements is strongly reminiscent of the diverse voices within the novelistic word meticulously described in the chronotope essay, "Discourse in the Novel," and elsewhere in Bakhtin's work.[15] The modulated harmony of polyphony, of the many parts grounded in the one discourse or logos, is abundantly evident in this passage.

The exact ontological significance of Bakhtin's transubstantiational metaphor, however, still remains unclear. The last three lines of the quotation above eerily echo Stalinist rhetoric, in particular the idea that the self-sacrifice of the individual is indispensable to the continued existence of the masses. This sacrifice can only be adequately expressed by one's physical demise: the gorging of the collective body on individual ones is death-dealing for the latter but life-giving for the former. Thus, the formation of a community is established by a kind of reverse communion, in which the many sacrifice themselves for the one instead of the One (Christ) sacrificing Himself for the many. The grotesque body of the cosmos takes on a truly macabre significance by demanding the "death of the individual." Bakhtin's discussion of the grotesque body in *Rabelais and His World* can be regarded as a gloss on the conception of polyphony that he espouses elsewhere. Here, the alignment of the many within the one—corresponding to the taming of heteroglossia (*raznorechie; raznogolositsa*) into polyphony—is celebratory yet also tragic and brutal. By underscoring the sanguinary aspect of the transubstantiational metaphor in his book on Rabelais, Bakhtin amplifies its christological aspect as well, which presumes that change can only be effected through death.

The murderous implications of Rabelaisian discourse—its constant undercurrent of violence—are obtrusive in Bakhtin's study. This potentially sinister aspect of Rabelais is vividly abstracted by Bakhtin in the sixth and penultimate chapter of his book, "The Images of the Material Bodily Lower Stratum." The "material bodily principle, earth and real time become the relative center" of the new view of the world advanced by Rabelais. From this new perspective, it is "[n]ot the ascent of the individual soul [*(n)e pod"em individual'noi dushi*] into the higher spheres but the movement forward of all mankind, along the horizontal of historic time, [that] becomes the basic criterion of all evaluations." The individual soul's importance lies precisely in its ability to sacrifice itself for a larger human aggregate: "[h]aving done its part upon the earth, [it] fades and dies together with the individual body." To an alarming extent, in what follows Bakhtin seems to rely heavily on some particularly unsavory and shopworn Soviet ideological clichés. Although the ephemeral nature of the individual in no way gainsays its importance, the self-sacrificial role it plays renders its victory bittersweet at best, for "the body of the people [*naroda:* or, nation] and mankind, fertilized [*oplodotvorennoe:* or, fecundated (cf. *oplodotvorenie*)] by the dead, is eternally renewed and moves forever forward along the historic path of progress [*sovershenstvovaniia:* lit., perfection]" (403–4; 447).[16] The earth becomes a merciless deity, almost a pagan fertility god, demanding periodic sacrifice in order to maintain its philoprogenitiveness. All of material reality, the bodily word of the cosmos, becomes an abattoir as the distinction between the flesh of humanity and the fruit of the earth collapses. The cosmos's swallowing up of the world and the flesh is therefore undeniably cannibalistic.

Recent scholarship on Bakhtin has gone a long way in exposing some of these darker shades of Bakhtin's carnival. *The Bakhtin Almanach* (*Bakhtinskii sbornik*), the first issue of an annual collection of articles on Bakhtin, was published in 1990 under the aegis of the Gorky Institute of Literature. One of the most interesting and controversial contributions to this volume is "Bodies of Terror: Theses Toward a Logic of Violence," Mikhail Ryklin's examination of *Rabelais and His World* in the context of Stalinism. According to Ryklin, for Bakhtin carnival is not necessarily an ideal or desirable state and, in fact, has a strongly negative component. In his reinterpretation of

Bakhtin's Rabelais study, carnival becomes an Aesopian metaphor for Stalin's purges. To be sure, this association was not entirely new even at the time of the appearance of Ryklin's article: the possible significance of purging (*chistka; ochishchenie*) within Bakhtin's conception of the grotesque body had already been commented on by Clark and Holquist, who perceptively note that there the political metaphor of physical purification and occlusion is diametrically opposed to the Bakhtinian ideal of the spontaneous and open body.[17] As Ryklin demonstrates in his analysis of the Rabelais book, however, the orientation of carnival toward the events of the Stalin era is highly problematic and compromised. The carnivalesque or grotesque body functions on a steady regime (in both senses) of ideological purification and prophylaxis in what Caryl Emerson insightfully calls "Bakhtin's ostensibly joyous book on Rabelaisian carnival."[18]

Ryklin's interpretation of Bakhtin is highly idiosyncratic and hardly exhausts the levels of meaning in *Rabelais and His World.* His reading does, however, represent a judicious counterbalance to the view that the book constitutes an extended and unambiguous dithyramb of carnival.[19] According to Ryklin, the grotesque body demands the periodic lustration and self-abnegation of the many for the sake of one; in *Rabelais and His World,* it becomes the ultimate totem of ideological monotheism. Ryklin partially succeeds in demonstrating the sinister aspect of Bakhtin's conception of Rabelaisian carnival, an important point unacknowledged by most commentators who unequivocally extol the celebration and liberation that carnival often brings.[20] For Ryklin, carnival does not liberate: it enslaves. In this assessment he goes against the grain of most interpretations of Bakhtin's carnival. He does not directly address either the transubstantiational metaphor or christology in his article. As will be subsequently shown, however, the intersection between this metaphor—with all its christological and Johannine underpinnings—and Stalinism is particularly crucial to Bakhtin's work. It is at this point that Bakhtin's literary theory and the life he was compelled by circumstances to lead lie in a virtually direct relation to each other.

Ryklin makes a few points in the article that are essentially unassailable; for all the seeming iconoclasm of his piece, in many ways he simply logically extends or amplifies the muted concerns of Bakhtin's analysis of Rabelais. Particularly crucial from his point of view is Bakhtin's statement in chapter 5 that the individual is motivated primarily by fear, prompted by the ancestral memory of natural and societal disasters that continues to underlie human thought, word, and image (*zalozheny v samom fundamente chelovecheskoi mysli, slova i obraza*).[21] Ryklin portrays this fear of the cosmos as the dominant impulse of the grotesque body; in his article the carnivalesque becomes the expression of something very much like *thanatos,* a desire for self-annihilation and assimilation of one's individual identity to an amorphously eldritch monstrosity. However, a closer look at the paragraph from which this passage is extracted reveals that Ryklin is quoting a bit out of context. Bakhtin goes on to say that this fear was encouraged by the institution of the church in order to suppress the particular desires of the individual as much as possible; in fact, he asserts that one must struggle against this primeval fear in order to become harmonized with the cosmos. "The struggle against cosmic terror in all its forms and manifestations," Bakhtin explains, "did not rely on abstract hope or the eternal spirit, but on *the material principle in man himself.*" Man overcame this primeval terror by "assimilat[ing] the cosmic elements: earth, water, air, and fire;" it is thus that he "*discovered them and became vividly conscious of them in his own body.*" In other words, "[h]e became aware of the cosmos within himself" (355–56; 371–72). One could conclude from this that Bakhtin actually emphasizes the absorption of the cosmos into the individual, rather than the suicidal merging of the latter into the former. Nonetheless, Ryklin is correct in pointing to fear as an overlooked but important part in the functioning of the grotesque body. It would be more accurate to say, however, that Bakhtin characterizes fear as something like the spleen in the human body, playing a vital role in early development but subsequently becoming superfluous.

Ryklin is also undoubtedly insightful in pointing out the religious or sacramental nature of carnival, a feature that has been obscured by the anticlericism of Bakhtin's book. According to Ryklin, an almost liturgical conception of language underlies *Rabelais and His World,* in spite of the fact that Bakhtin himself is critical of such a reification and fetishization of language and implicitly warns against it. The text of terror "has a liturgical sound that is constantly being borne up"; there, "the folk perpetually celebrates a mass of its own blessedness, righteousness, unerringness." Ryklin characterizes this operation as taking place in "a sacralized atmosphere, [where] words become ultimate values and cease to signify things that can be seen, things that have a smell, things that act on us independently of their liturgical meaning."[22] Although words in this milieu become self-sufficient things-in-themselves, they become finalized as inmates in a verbal prisonhouse rather than as actors functioning in day-to-day existence. Ryklin believes that some sort of transformation is at work here, although clearly it seems to be a transubstantiation in the opposite direction from that which Bakhtin describes in his essays of the thirties; here, it moves toward insubstantiability rather than the fleshing-out of experience. Such evanescence of substance is "liturgical" only in the sense that the site of its transpiring is ritualistic; in fact, this transformation represents a kind of antitransubstantiation, the liturgical format only highlighting the sense of spuriousness. Ryklin's analysis points up the centrality of the transubstantive metaphor in Bakhtin's work, even when it is expressed in the inverted terms of its negative counterpart.

Later in this essay, Ryklin describes in greater detail the purview within which this transformation of language unfolds. Ryklin points out that Bakhtin highlights the double meaning of the Russian term *narod* as both "people" or "nation," often enclosing it within parentheses and other kinds of verbal framing (*slovesnoe obramlivanie*) that create a certain daunting mystique.[23] But in Voloshinov's book it is precisely the abolition or effacement of such markers of linguistic property that is crucial to a recognition of the way language truly develops. This clear contradiction between Rabelaisian carnival and Voloshinov's conception of normative linguistic change—unnoted by Ryklin himself—points up the anomalous nature of the former. Ryklin insists on the insidious artificiality of Rabelaisian carnival: "[the folk (*narod*)] appears before [Bakhtin] at the end of alchemical incantations, within the magic crystal of the *parole* [*slovo*]."[24] In such a society language is reduced to an oppressively unitary and ideological discourse, a kind of general or all-purpose speech whose nuances and internal differences become virtually invisible to all but the eye of the intellectual.[25] Rabelaisian carnival emerges from Ryklin's analysis as a virtually monological literary phenomenon, veering off into the totalizing and unitary tendencies of the authoritarian and monological word. Significantly, in describing this simulacrum of substance Ryklin uses the same image that Bakhtin avails himself of in "Discourse in the Novel," that of the light-refracting glass. Here, however, the crystal produces the trick of the light that constitutes an illusion.

Later in his analysis of Bakhtin's first famous work, Ryklin links this negative transformation to an historical phenomenon, the widespread networks of informants that became so prevalent during the Stalin era. Although not stated as such by Ryklin, the chronotope morally and ontologically redeems the impulse toward destructiveness in Rabelaisian carnival. More specifically, the concretization of chronotopic experience that Bakhtin describes in his essays of the thirties is a function of individuation, of breaking away from the collective body rather than communing with it. Consequently, individuation becomes opposed to liturgy and ritualism as they are understood from the Rabelaisian perspective. In the following passage Ryklin takes the term "bodies of recognition" from Michel Foucault, who uses it in referring to those bodies that are conscious of themselves and insist on their uniqueness and individuality.[26] As Ryklin points out, such a consciousness of one's own identity is incompatible with the collective body of the people (*narod*). As a result, "[d]enunciation definitely takes the place of confession or—and this represents the ideal outcome—speech shuts itself up and returns to divine self-devourment." Cannibalism becomes the paradigm for the state as "[t]he reality of denunciation and convulsions of suffering bodies, confessing their guilt under torture, is replaced by the coming into being of speech body-giants, gazing as if from the sidelines at the sufferings of their chance individual incarnations."[27] According to Ryklin, the relation between the individual and society is fraught with anxiety and dread in Bakhtin's study of Rabelais. In the carnivalesque worldview, the individual body only has substance when it cleaves itself unto the corporate guilt of the collective body; therefore, informing becomes the communicative equivalent of bodily assimilation whereas individuation is tantamount to separation from the body. But which is the more real transformation? Ryklin suggests that individuation is, in fact, a genuine change but that its occurrence and precise nature are obstructed by the collective body, which regards it as incidental. The body that is not identical to others or does not consume or merge with them is subjected to torture for its exclusionariness; and yet, it nonetheless represents an incarnation (*inkarnatsiia*) from a larger whole. Sentience belongs to the breakaway bodies, not to the ones that inform on and cannibalize each other; the latter are virtually inert, even inanimate, in their inability to experience pain and discomfort.

Ryklin's interpretation makes the connections between the Rabelais book and the essays of the thirties much clearer. The full realization of the chronotope consists precisely of this individuation and concretization of personality, of what Gary Saul Morson calls the "prosaic" as opposed to the ideologically driven "poetic." The hidden references in Bakhtin's work to the contemporary political situation are tightly woven into this opposition between the true and false (or apparent) instantiations of consciousness. The ethical criticism of the 1909 *Landmarks* collection and Bakhtin's early works such as "Toward a Philosophy of the Act" and "Author and Hero in Aesthetic Activity" finds a continuation in *Rabelais and His World.* For Bakhtin, ethics represent above all the concretization and particularization of phenomena rather than their abstraction into an amorphous base. In this light, Bakhtin's repeated reference throughout his writings to the Chalcedonian principle of union leavened by respect for difference emerges as a pointed critique of the relentless assimilation Ryklin describes.

Caryl Emerson has commented on Ryklin's piece as a radical rereading of the Rabelais book and Bakhtin's entire conception of carnival. As she succinctly summarizes his argument, the body of Bakhtinian carnival is "the product of a complex trauma" devolving upon Stalin's terror:[28] "Your body, my body became incidental, replaceable, invisible, synthetic, mute—and in its place the collective body of the people was granted all the reproductive and rhetorical rights, *it* became the collective guardian of the word."[29] Later in the same article she writes that Ryklin's essay reveals some of the more deeply embedded references to Soviet reality in the Rabelais book. To be sure, the possible references to Stalinism in *Rabelais and His World* have been pointed out before.[30] No one, however, has ever suggested that Rabelaisian carnival *itself* had, for Bakhtin, ideologically Stalinist properties. The sacrifice of the self to the collective at carnival time (described by Bakhtin and underscored by Ryklin) resonates with the massive influx of the peasantry into the Russian cities after the Revolution. As Emerson puts it in her incisive paraphrase of Ryklin, "[t]he Russian folk pours into the cities and sacrifices itself."[31] As already demonstrated, the idea of the reconstituted body is very important for Bakhtin in other contexts as well, particularly in his discussion of the chronotope and the transubstantive and transformational event it brings about in the novel.

Recent scholarship such as Emerson's and Ryklin's has uncovered such lines of continuity stretching not only from the chronotope essay to the Rabelais book but also from "Epos and the Novel" (1941) and even as far back as "Discourse in the Novel" (1934–35). Nonetheless, in spite of their seminal efforts, these scholars have delved into the political and historical dimensions of Bakhtin's works in a still somewhat sketchy and schematic manner. Sensing a trove of new discoveries in Ryklin's piece yet implicitly acknowledging a certain hesitation before such a domain of speculation, Emerson asserts as self-evident that "[t]he people's invisibility and faith in utopia were essential for the 'ecstasy of [the Stalin] Terror' to work." She continues: "In this chilling piece of literary criticism—which may or may not have uncovered Bakhtin's real intentions on writing on Rabelais—we see a very different side of Bakhtin's carnival mystique.[32] The ambiguity that Emerson recognizes in *Rabelais and His World* is reflected in the ideological and political ramifications of the transubstantive metaphor of that book. In this light, a renewed look at *Rabelais and His World* goes a long way in explaining the tense equilibrium between the categories of polyphony and the chronotope in Bakhtin's work. For Ryklin carnival represents an extreme or climactic moment in which social diversity becomes temporarily obliterated and a certain convergence takes place. In the social and historical sphere, however—as opposed to the realm of literary form with its internal dynamics—this virtually epiphanic and possibly utopian convergence of various consciousnesses is hardly pacific and can be ethically problematic. Bakhtin ultimately makes a distinction between the dynamics of social change and the literary creative process. Of course, these two realms are not always so easily separated, and their difficult coexistence is advanced by Bakhtin in his study of Rabelais. An extension of Ryklin's argument would envision carnival as a demonic Otherworld, disdaining the substance of individual bodies while feeding and subsisting on them. Nevertheless, it could be plausibly argued that his conclusions do not sufficiently come to grips with the seemingly positive tone that Bakhtin takes toward the collective body at a number of points throughout the book. This is reflected with particular clarity in Bakhtin's assertion of the durability of ancestral memory of collective disasters, a statement upon which Ryklin's entire argument turns. Ryklin underscores the menacingly restitutive effect that the demise of the individual body has upon the collective one. Taken in its entirety, Bakhtin's characterization of this interaction is in fact somewhat more ambiguous. The primary weakness of Ryklin's reading is that it effectively banishes ambivalence or ambiguity from Bakhtin's world. There can be no mediated or qualified state of mass murder, no word that can be truly or durably double-voiced when one side of it clamors for the extermination of the other. By investing carnival with terror, Ryklin himself eliminates an important theoretical catgory from Bakhtin's work.

Ryklin's outré interpretation is more understandable as a reaction to an earlier Russian reaction to Bakhtin's work, one no less critical of Soviet ideological clichés yet highly nostalgic for an idealized and devotional image of carnival. This view of Bakhtin's carnival is very much a product of 1960s dissident culture, an oppositional movement in the Soviet Union that criticized, among other things, the triumph of materialism and petty opportunism in Soviet society. To many, these patterns of behavior made any real sense of community and social responsibility impossible and were in some way linked to the absence of the spiritual and sacred in people's lives. In 1968, the Soviet Sinologist and Hindologist Grigory Pomerants wrote an article (published in the journal *The Nations of Asia and Africa*) in which he describes the importance of holidays and their various celebrations in Buddhism and in certain African religions. Pomerants asserts that much in contemporary life is understandable as vestiges of carnival and acknowledges Bakhtin's work in particular for pointing this out.[33] Pomerants goes on to say, however, that many of these contemporary manifestations of carnival are nothing more than remnants, vestigial limbs inherited from an era when they played a more dynamic role in human culture. He argues that the attenuation of holiday traditions in the modern world and the virtual disappearance of carnival from western Europe in particular cut off the individual from the human and universal continuum, leading to a spiritual alienation that found its supreme expression in Fascism.[34] Pomerants's discussion of these issues is peppered with references to Bakhtin both in the journal article and in his samizdat writings that were published in West Germany in 1972.[35] According to Pomerants, Bakhtin's Rabelais study represents the first serious attempt to view carnival from the perspective of its roots—not just as an excuse for temporary free license, but also as a sacred act (*sviashchennyi akt*).[36]

Pomerants's reading of Bakhtin's carnival is bold if a bit presumptive in its political and philosophical conclusions, emerging as a genuine complement to and continuation of the literary critic's work; his arguments about the universal character of carnival are striking in being conceived at a time of xenophobia, isolationism, and the onerous official culture in the Soviet Union. By modifying Soviet liberationist clichés he ultimately goes against their grain; he attempted to adapt and make malleable that which was by its nature inflexible, thereby violating it. What the Soviet censor undoubtedly found objectionable about some of Pomerants's articles was his somewhat obscured suggestion that carnival represents an unofficial cultural tradition with enormous potential to alter certain patterns of thought and behavior in modern Russian society. Certainly the late thirties and the Khrushchev-Brezhnev transition of the early sixties—the two periods that Bakhtin spent writing and rewriting his study of Rabelais—were times of intensifying intolerance and political conformism with often tragic consequences.

Pomerants's work is significant in stressing the theological ramifications of Bakhtin's carnival, an association that has been seldom made because of the prominent criticism of institutional religion in the Rabelais book. The Aesopian implications of Pomerants's observations have not gone unnoted by Dimitry Pospielovsky, one of the foremost specialists on the Russian church during the Soviet period. In a 1974 article about the difficulties besetting Orthodox belief in Soviet life, Pospielovsky notes that Pomerants's conception of alienation has precious little to do with Marx's. Reading between the lines of the 1968 piece, Pospielovsky states that "Pomerants sees as the source of alienation of man the disappearance of the feast (holiday, fiesta, carnival—all these combined as different aspects of the same thing) from human life and its replacement by the priority of work and action." Playing against the notion of Trinitarian *perichoresis,* Pospielovsky highlights this alienation as the "sense of separation from the Universe, the loss of a sense of wholeness and integrity, the division and compartmentalization of separate and mutually alienated sequences of activities" in one's daily life. He hears in Pomerants's article a call for restoring the "fulness of reliving of a religious mystical holiday-feast," an event through which the communicant "lose(s) the limiting effect of time on his life and experiences a mystical oneness with Eternity, with the Creation, with the Universe." Speaking in a voice that is perhaps more his than Pomerants's, he goes on to say that "[o]nly in the fulness of the genuine religious holiday is there a timeless fusion of the tragic, the serious-mystical, the joyful happiness of festivity, and even the carnival, which in their fusion are the wholeness of being and existence."[37] Pospielovsky notes that Pomerants "overstepped the permissible limits of discussion," as a result of which only the one of his essays on carnival was published (another circulated in the samizdat underground). Pospielovsky teases out the philosophical, political, and theological implications of Pomerants. Nonetheless, Pomerants is obviously not religious and (Pospielovsky notwithstanding) his writings cannot by any stretch be said to be theological; within his encoded critique of present-day society he does, however, treat sympathetically the notion of traditional ritual as counterbalancing not just fascism but also the hypocrisy and ideological pharisaism of Soviet society. Dominant in Pospielovsky's extension of the salient points made by Pomerants is the notion of integrality of the individual to both the historical process and to the human community at any given point in time. Although Pospielovsky does not mention Bakhtin by name, his paraphrase of Pomerants suggests that he has a firsthand aquaintance with *Rabelais and His World.* Pospielovsky's cosmological disquisition is, in fact, far more reminiscent of Bakhtin himself than Pomerants's insightful but brief and circumspect articles.

Pomerants and Pospielovsky are undoubtedly bearing in mind the second half of *Rabelais and His World,* where Bakhtin vividly highlights the close association between the individual and the universe at large in Rabelais's carnivalistic world, the life of the cosmos and the human body converging to the point where the one ultimately enters into and becomes an integral part of the other. Commenting on the influence on Rabelais of the element- and humor-driven theories of early medical texts such as the "Hippocratic Anthology," Bakhtin states that in these notions of the body "[c]osmic life and the life of the human body are drawn intimately together. . . . They are offered in their obvious unity of imagery" (356; 394). Continuing his discussion of this bodily cosmology, Bakhtin explicates its later variant in Paracelsus as a view in which "[t]he starry sky is contained in man himself. . . . [T]he body of man has an extraordinary wealth, being rich with all that exists in the universe." The universe becomes "reassembled in all its diversity [*vo vsem svoem mnogoobrazii*] within the human body; all its elements are found and connected [*soprikasaiutsia:* lit., come into contact] in the sphere [*v edinoi ploskosti:* lit., on a single plane] of the individual body" (361–62; 400). Although Pospielovsky does not emphasize the physiological component of consciousness as Bakhtin does, the parallel between his category of "man" and Bakhtin's of "the human body" (*chelovecheskoe telo*) is patent and has no clear antecedent in Pomerants's sketchy comments. The Chalcedonian formula of conditional merging of the personal and the cosmic is audibly resonant in Bakhtin's statements about the interaction between the elements and the body. Pospielovsky's commentary on conceptions of carnival in Soviet scholarship of the sixties quite possibly represents the first (albeit oblique) interpretation of Bakhtin's views in an explicitly theological light.

It was this kind of disingenuously pantheistic and idealized view of the body of the cosmos that Ryklin opposes, adhering to the same paradigm of celebration as communion and community but underscoring its structural dynamics of placing the individual at the slavish service of the cosmos. One could argue, of course, that many of these correspondences between Stalinism and the absorptive and engulfing collective body in *Rabelais and His World* are too elusive to constitute proof of Bakhtin's hidden commentary on the events of the thirties, forties, and early fifties. In a certain sense, both Ryklin and the camp of Pospielovsky and Pomerants are right: by interdwelling or becoming contained in the individuals through the ritualized act of ingestion, the cosmos fundamentally changes them and, in a sense, destroys their *former* identities or selves. What is central here is the profoundly transformative nature of carnival, its ontologically transgredient power. Taken together, these two opposed yet curiously related perspectives are testimony to the profound ambivalence of Bakhtin's carnival. Needless to say, Bakhtin could not openly advert to carnival as a demonic Stalinist version (or, rather, inversion) of communion. But there is evidence of an even more profound level of political allegory in *Rabelais and His World,* one that is not noted by any of its commentators but that is consistent with many of their conclusions about the contemporary significance of carnival. It is a level astonishingly resonant with the tragic domestic events of the Stalin era.

PRAISE, BLAME, AND DEATH: THE MECHANICS OF THE MARKETPLACE WORD?

Living through the public trauma of Stalin's purges affected everybody in Soviet society, and Bakhtin was no exception. Holquist and Clark were the first to draw the shrewd parallel between the constricting influence that the "serious" culture of the church exerted on daily life in Rabelais's time and the self-abnegation extolled as a virtue during the Stalin period, with no direct or clear-cut references to Stalinism in *Rabelais and His World,* the two scholars ultimately draw the tentative and sensible if unsurprising conclusion that Bakhtin probably viewed Stalinist society as repressive and rigidly hierarchical.[38] An overt criticism of Stalinism can hardly be expected in a dissertation submitted for review during the political frost of the late forties preceding the Cold War and to a committee of such staunch Stalinists as the Pushkinist Nikolai Brodsky, quoted earlier; any references to contemporary political phenomena would be framed in terms of Aesopian speech and have to be teased out by an indirect interpretive strategy.

Before approaching Bakhtin's own work in its political ramifications, the ideological stage needs to be set. In the contemporary Russian context, the close rhetorical association of praise with blame—and, by the the late thirties and forties, the sense in which the shift from the one to the other had taken on the air of inevitability—was graphically demonstrated in the show trials and random arrests of citizens (numbering in the thousands) whose ideological loyalty seemed unassailable.[39] Under the influence of Articles 57 and 58 of the Soviet Criminal Code (first drafted in 1922), a denunciation need not have been substantiated to condemn a citizen to prison or the firing squad; needless to say, in such a legal milieu the speech-act took on enormous, even portentous, significance. Particularly incendiary in its vagueness and potentially applicability to random speech-acts was the code's statement deeming any act to be counterrevoltionary that "endangers the fundamental political or economic conquests of the proletarian revolution."[40] These articles rendered any sort of salient speech, whether it was highly public in its mode of address or merely idiosyncratic, immediately subject to relentless juridical interpretation: the more extravagant or stentorian the oral or written pronouncement, the more sharply would it be probed with the tools of politicized exegesis. Not surprisingly, under such circumstances the shift from praise to blame was often a very short one indeed, praise virtually becoming the necessary preface or preliminary for blame as the interval between them progressively shrank. In a dizzying series of arrests and libelous legal proceedings that spanned the late twenties to the beginning of the fifties, yesterday's revolutionary heroes such as Yezhov and Zinoviev became the turncoats of the day.

It was in this troubled setting that, on the late winter day of 13 March 1938 (when Bakhtin was already intensively at work on his study of Rabelais), the Soviet public witnessed in the Supreme Court of the USSR the end of a private and public ordeal that had begun ten days before. This event, the trial of the so-called Bloc of Rightists and Trotskyites, represents one of the most difficult periods in the Russian legal system within living memory. Although it turned out to be the last—and most famous—of the show trials, it effectively codified the precedent of ideological paranoia that continued to be observed at least through the death of Stalin in 1953. No less a personage than Andrey Yanuarevich Vyshinsky himself, the procurator of the USSR, was enlisted to head the prosecution against Nikolai Bukharin, former head of state security Yagoda, and nineteen others accused of treason. In his concluding statement at the trial, Vyshinsky concluded his speech for the prosecution on a stirring and unexpectedly optimistic note, expressing certainty in a brighter future for Soviet society while pungently giving vent to a striking conflation of rhetorical extremes:

> There exist no words with which one could depict the monstrousness of the crimes committed by the accused. But, I ask, do we need any more words for that? No, Comrade Judges, these words are not needed. All the words have already been spoken. Everything has been analyzed to the minutest details. The entire people now see what monsters these are. Our people and all honest people throughout the world are waiting for your just verdict. May this verdict of yours resound throughout the whole of our great country like a bell calling to new feats of heroism and to new victories! May your edict resound as the refreshing and purifying thunderstorm of just Soviet punishment! . . .
>
> Time will pass. The graves of the hateful traitors will grow over with weeds and thistle, they will be covered with the eternal contempt of honest Soviet citizens, of the entire Soviet people. But over us, over our happy country, our sun will shine with its luminous rays as bright and joyous as before. Over the road cleared of the last scum and filth of the past, we, our people, with our beloved leader and teacher, the great Stalin, at our head, will march as before onwards and onwards, towards Communism![41]

To say that treachery and fidelity are the only two moral forces recognized by Vyshinsky is to simplify the mechanics of his statement. He begins his peroration by asserting that language has reached its limits in describing the atrocities committed by the conspirators; all that remains is to simply reiterate the fact of their odiousness. Having driven that point home, it is then that he launches his panegyric to the future. Exhausting its expressive possibilities in the downward spiral of castigation, he suddenly ascends to a paean of an inchoate yet keenly perceived future. The topographics of Vyshinsky's ideological landscape vividly come to life: the enemies of the people represent dirt and vegetative infestation, trampled on by the true heroes of socialism who are guided by a luminous ideal from above. Throughout the cross-examination of Bukharin and his reputed fifth-columnists as well as in the speech excerpted above, Vyshinsky and his assistant prosecutors repeatedly characterize the defendants as "filth" and "muck." Justice and truth were portrayed in these proceedings along an uncompromising vertical axis, the bottom representing uncleanliness and insidious organic pullulation and the top a purifying beacon. Perhaps even more significant than this binary opposition is that, according to Vyshinsky, treachery not only offsets and helps to define loyalty more effectively, but also constitutes the actual engine of purification. In other words (although he does not explicitly acknowledge as much), the prosecutor is submitting the necessity of scapegoating for the continued health of the body politic. The dual transmogrification of the people into new and higher beings is brought about only through contumely and degradation. On a purely structural level, certain Marxist categories are central to Vyshinsky's screed: for him, the interaction between praise and blame is nothing if not one link in the historic dialectic tending toward progressive social change.

Of the possible correspondences between *Rabelais and His World* and the collective traumas experienced during its writing, none is more compelling in its specificity than Bakhtin's idea of the ambivalence of the marketplace word, treated in chapter 2 ("The Language of the Marketplace in Rabelais"). According to Bakhtin, the word of the marketplace is an amalgam of praise and verbal abuse, public humiliation and exaltation, and represents one of the hallmarks of Rabelais's rendering of the carnivalesque into novelistic form. The arbitrariness and swiftness of the shuttling from panegyric to excoriation in the specific form of a highly public denunciation is strongly reminiscent of the purges and the rhetoric that attended them. Although the following extract from chapter 2 is admittedly lengthy, it needs to be quoted thus in order to appreciate the resonance of the Rabelaisian word with the Soviet scene. Bakhtin carried this segment over from his 1940 thesis with virtually no changes:[42]

> The passing [or: transfer (*perekhod*)] from excessive praise [*ploshchadnoi khvaly:* marketplace praise] to excessive blame [*unichtozhaiushchim prokliati-*

> *iam:* annihilating curses] is characteristic, and the change from the one to the other is perfectly legitimate. [Marketplace] Praise [*khvala*] and abuse [*bran'*] are, so to speak, the two sides of the same coin. If the right side is praise, the wrong side is abuse, and vice versa. The billingsgate idiom [*Ploshchadnoe slovo:* lit., the marketplace word] is a two-faced Janus [*dvulikii Ianus*]. The praise, as we have said, is ironic and ambivalent. It is on the brink [*na granitse*] of abuse, praise is filled with [*chrevata*] blame and it is impossible to draw the line between them [lit., it is impossible to say where one begins and the other ends (*nel'zia ukazat', gde konchaetsia odno i gde nachinaetsia drogoe*)]. Though divided in form [*Khotia khvala i bran' i razdeleny v iazyke*] they belong to the same body, or to the two bodies in one, which abuses while praises and praises while abusing [*kotoroe khvalia braniat i brania khvaliat*]. This is why in familiar Billingsgate talk abusive words, especially indecent ones, are used in the affectionate and complimentary sense. (We shall further analyze many examples from Rabelais.) This grotesque language, particularly in its oldest form [*v ee drevneishikh plastakh:* lit., in its most ancient strata] was oriented toward the world and toward all the world's phenomena in their condition of unfinished metamorphosis: the passing from night to morning [*perekhoda ot nochi k utru*], from winter to spring, from old to new, from death to birth. Therefore, this talk showers both compliments and curses. Perhaps our example does not clearly typify this, but its ambivalence raises no doubt. This ambivalence determines the organic and spontaneous character of the change from praise to blame and back to praise again, as well as [a familiar] uncertainty [*neopredelennost'*] as to whom the talk is addressed [lit., the "unprepared" state of the addressee of praise and blame (*"negotovost'" adresata etoi khvaly i brani*)]. (164–65; 182–83)[43]

The planes of signification in this seemingly descriptive analysis of Rabelais's art almost unfold by themselves with the slightest prod. Bakhtin's insistence on the centrality of the public square (*ploshchad'*) brings to mind a number of associations. As outlined in the previous chapter of this study, *ploshchad'* is both phonemically and semantically suggestive. Derived from *ploskii* ('flat'), the term refers to the horizontality of existence affirmed during carnival against the verticality characteristic of the status quo at other times of the year; furthermore, it belongs to the alliterative chain of terms *plod/plot'/ploskii/ploshchad'* (lengthened here by *plasty* [strata]) that denotes for Bakhtin the reification of the individual effected by carnival. Here Bakhtin connects the phonemic cluster of [*plo/pla*] all the more firmly to the Stoicist and pre-Johannine dichotomy of the internal essence versus external word: it is the plangent surface that becomes the site of genuine transformation. This theological subtext is reinforced by Bakhtin's reference to Chaldedonian doctrine in the statement "[t]hough divided [*razdeleny*] in form, [praise and blame] belong to the same body, or to the two bodies in one." Interestingly, the statement that "praise is filled with [*chrevata*] blame and it is impossible to draw to where one [speech mode] begins and the other ends" echoes Bakhtin's assertion in chapter 1 of his dissertation about the positive and negative poles within *risus paschalis*, which, as already shown, has a distinct Chalcedonian dimension. The bookish short form adjective *chrevata* is derivationally linked, furthermore, to the noun *chrevo* which, as previously mentioned, has the double meaning of "womb" and "belly." In complete keeping with Bakhtin's conflation of ingestion and gestation discussed in the last chapter, praise both devours and is impregnated by blame. All this, first written during the late thirties, seems to reinforce Ryklin's claim about the frightening synthesis of anthropophagy and philoprogenitiveness in the grotesque body politic of the Stalin era.

Nonetheless, the association of marketplace or square (*ploshchad'*) and its cognates with the kind of highly public superlative speech that Bakhtin describes above inevitably strikes a certain note of authoritarian stricture in spite of its potentially liberating double-voicedness. Reading the passage above in light of Vyshinsky's famous speech and other contemporary events, one realizes that it is perhaps partly *because* of such rhetorical ambivalence that such a political regime can be maintained. As a Russian and Soviet topos for punishment and judgment, *ploshchad'* here retains a historical-juridical specificity, the verbal acts of praise and blame taking on greater and more binding significance than most circumstances would dictate. The significations of the term *ploshchad'* are by no means exhausted by the corporeo-vegetative metaphor of transformation, (*fruit/flesh/flat*); one also thinks not just of Red Square itself (*Krasnaia ploshchad'*) but also of the famous "Place of the Forehead" (*Lobnoe mesto*) located on it, the circular platform from which declarations were read and sentences of execution reputedly passed during the sixteenth and seventeenth centuries.[44] This structure was also referred to as *lobnaia ploshchadka*, or "platform" of the forehead, *ploshchadka* a diminutive of *ploshchad'*.

Other details of Bakhtin's praise/blame (*khvala/bran'*) dichotomy become more comprehensible in the context of the purges. Iswolsky's translation of *bran'* as "blame" does not fully convey the orality of the term: *bran'* is specifically verbal abuse or revilement. This Church Slavonic term does have, however, a secondary, more archaic meaning referring to actual violence, particularly at wartime (such as in the poetic phrase *pole brani*, "field of battle"), and in this respect is semantically as well as derivationally linked to other terms from the same morphophonemic family, such as the noun *oborona* ('[military] defense'). During the late thirties in the Soviet Union—a period of deferred involvement in the European tragedy temporarily guaranteed by the Stalin-Hitler pact, the purging of 80 percent of the officers' corps in the Soviet army, and mass arrests and executions carried out in the name of national defense and almost always based exclusively on hearsay and oral testimony—a member of the old Russian intelligentsia like Bakhtin must have vividly apprehended the often duplicitous and murderous possibilities of speech. From the perspective of the Stalinist body politic of the time, the concatenation of physical and verbal abuse was the only guarantor of security, affirmation and condemnation the double-barreled weapon indispensable for waging the war within. Felicitously, the image of Janus is doubly significant here, its intimation of perfidy or treachery fitting well in the topos of an arbitrary public judgment. According to its original legend, the Roman deity was often regarded as a sentinel god, a sculpture of which would be placed in front of Roman homes to watch over events both inside and outside one's property.[45] As a scholar steeped in the classical tradition, Bakhtin could not have been unaware of this component of the deity's legend. As the god of surveillance, Janus is the fittest dispenser of praise and blame, particularly in an age of Yagodas and Yezhovs.

This is not the only place in Bakhtin's work where the image appears. He notes in "Toward a Philosophy of the Act" that the ethical act gazes like the two-faced Janus in different directions of reality, one face turned toward the objective unity of the cultural sphere and the other toward the unrepeatable uniqueness of experienced life.[46] For Bakhtin in the earlier essay, Janus is an unequivocally pejorative image, representing the forced incommensurability of different aspects of existence; there, however, as already demonstrated in Chapters 2 and 3 of this study, the chasm between phenomenology and aestheticism *can* in fact be bridged. The reference in the extended quotation above to Janus's appearance on Roman currency fits in nicely with the whole dynamic of exchange and interchangeability between praise and blame. Bakhtin's attitude toward the marketplace is qualified by an awareness of its indifference to the individual's existence. The exaltation/denigration dynamic that Bakhtin is talking about in the passage above recalls Vyshinsky's incantation of metamorphosis: both of these processes compel subjects to undergo the metaphorical cycle of death/ingestion—gestation/digestion—regeneration/rebirth that occurs within the belly/womb of the earth. Other details of Bakhtin's praise/blame dichotomy make sense in the context of the purges. The mention of the shift of one of these modes of discourse to the other during the transition (*perekhod*) from night to morning brings to mind the practice of the NKVD in the thirties to make its arrests at night and eerily resonates with oral accounts from this period of detainees being taken away in nothing but their sleepwear.[47] No wonder Bakhtin underscores the familiar uncertainty and unpreparedness of the addressee beset by praise and blame. The fate of such people is anything but secure, and they can never prepare themselves for the sudden indictment.

This connection to the specifically Russian subtext lurking under the broader marketplace implications of Rabelais's "marketplace word" (*ploshchadnoe slovo*) is elsewhere deliberately magnified by Bakhtin. At the end of *Rabelais and His World* Bakhtin quotes from the Pretender's nightmare in Pushkin's *Boris Godunov,* where the aspirant to the Russian throne dreams of climbing up the winding staircase of a Kremlin tower, from which he sees an anthill of jeering Muscovites on the square (*na ploshchadi*) pointing and laughing at him. As Bakhtin explains in this final paragraph of the book, the topos of the public square and its irreverent crowd figures in all epochs of a culture's history (*Vsegda, vo vse epokhi proshlogo, sushchestvovala ploshchad' so smeiushchimsia na nei narodom*).[48] As Clark and Holquist judiciously note, the temptation to see the reference to Pushkin's Pretender as an Aesopian trope for Stalin's unworthiness as a political leader should be avoided insofar as it might encourage a politically reductive interpretation of the entire book.[49] The contemporary political implications of this allusion to Pushkin are thrown into sharper relief, however, when one bears in mind Bakhtin's earlier description of the public square as the site of carnivalesque praise and blame with its subtext of the reversals of political fortune during the thirties. Then the issue is no longer the tendentious one of Stalin's worthiness as a leader but that of the specific linguistic dynamics of the political order he controlled. It is surely significant that Bakhtin points up the Russian specificity of square (*ploshchad'*) at the end of his book on Rabelais: it is a reading of the term that stays with the reader and gives a more overtly political coloring to earlier uses of the term.

The Stalin subtext of Bakhtin's Pushkin reference is perhaps more patent in his use of it later in his career, in the 1963 *Problems of Dostoevsky's Poetics.* There, Bakhtin refers to the same lines from *Boris Godunov* as a subtext for Raskolnikov's dream. A comparison and contrast of these two citations is most revealing. In the later book Bakhtin quotes a fuller extract from Pushkin's play, including the Pretender's description of climbing up the winding staircase of a Kremlin tower, seeing the mocking anthill of Moscow and then falling headfirst into it from his perch.[50] With new information that has come to light of Bakhtin's attempts to publish his dissertation as early as 1944, the political subtext of the final paragraph of *Rabelais and His World* becomes more sharply defined. The fuller citation from the Pretender's dream would have been far too reminiscent of Stalin for readers of the mid-1940s but more permissible during the Khrushchev era, even during its stringent final years. The scholar A. A. Smirnov petitioned in 1944 for the publication of the dissertation, to no avail. He wrote to Bakhtin that one of the reasons for its nonpublication was that some editors were frightened off by a certain part of the work, although they themselves were loath to admit as much.[51] Although one can only speculate what that "certain part" might have been, the change Bakhtin made in his subsequent quotation of the Pretender's speech eloquently testifies to the political saturation of at least one literary reference in the Rabelais book. The marketplace or square (*ploshchad'*) emerges as the site of the word's manifestation in the world of social discourse, providing for both condemnation (*bran'*) and the rebirth and reinvigoration (*khvala*). At another point of *Problems of Dostoevsky's Poetics* Bakhtin states that in "creative, ambivalent carnival laughter . . . mockery and triumph, praise and blame [*khvala i bran'*] are inextricably fused [*nerazdel'no slity*]."[52] The Chalcedonian subtextualization of this passage has already been discussed in Chapter 4 of this study. Suffice it to say that Bakhtin emphasizes here the *simultaneity* of praise and blame and not their alternation.

Within the context of the dream-logic of the Pretender's and Raskolnikov's nightmares, such conflation makes perfect sense. What is far from clear, however, is the form that such ambiguity would take in waking reality. So far, in terms of language and speech, the correspondences between irreverent and abusive Rabelaisian discourse and Stalinist institutional practice seem far-reaching indeed. They attain something of an apogee in chapter 6, where Bakhtin links verbal abuse with the periodic purgation and renewal of the body politic. In this characterization of Rabelais's appreciation of historic and linear time, Bakhtin produces a series of images that appear incongruous, if not clashing:

> During the Renaissance all these images of the lower stratum, from cynical abuse to the image of the underworld, were filled [*proniknuty:* penetrated] with a deep awareness of historic time, of the change of epochs in world history. In Rabelais this element of time and of historic change deeply pervades [*pronikaet:* penetrate] all his images of the material bodily lower stratum and lends them historic coloring. In his work the dual body [*(d)v-u-telost'*] becomes [historical] dual world [*istoricheskoiu dvumirnost'iu*], the fusion [*slitost'iu*] of the past and future in the single act of the death of the one and the birth of another, in the image of the grotesque historic world of becoming and renewal. Time itself abuses and praises [*rugaet-khvalit*], beats and decorates [*b'et-ukrashaet*], kills and gives birth [*ubivaet-rozhdaet*]; this time is simultaneously ironic and gay, it is the "playing boy" of Heraclitus, who wields supreme power in the universe. (435; 480)

Bakhtin returns to the image of carnival as symbolized by Heraclitus's childish sovereign of the universe, but with some new twists. The terms relating to penetration, fusion (*slitost'*), and the dual bodies and worlds are clear allusions to the doctrine of the twin natures espoused at the ecumenical council at Chalcedon. The child becomes, in effect, the epitome of the Chalcedonian ideal. But now he is also ominous in his insouciance and death-dealing irresponsibility and seems out of place in this context. For one thing, the tenor of the metaphor goes against the substance of Bakhtin's argument: carnival and play represent *unofficial* discourse and culture whereas Heraclitus's image of time as a child clearly represents a sort of regnant power and is a tyrant, if an unknowing one. Bakhtin's yoking of the themes of violence and filiation is disturbing, if generally consistent with the Chalcedonian topos of the dual natures.

A closer look at the passage above reveals a conceptual pattern, at least by contrast: the verbal chain abuses/beats/kills (*rugaet/b'et/ubivaet*) signals a progression toward violent extinction that stands in a vaguely dialectical opposition to the power of life represented by childhood. Much of this passage is, of course, conceptually strikingly close to the praise/blame dichotomy delineated earlier in the book. Here the ever-juvenile figure of time takes the place of Janus; elsewhere in the conclusion of the book Bakhtin replaces him with the figure of the political leader: "*The ruler is the mother nursing her child, the gardener is the healing physician.* The bad ruler is given the grotesque nickname of 'people-eater,' the one 'swallowing and gorging himself on the people' [*'pozhiratel' naroda,' 'glotaiushchii i pozhiraiushchii narod'*]" (450; 498). The way in which Bakhtin here describes the just and unjust ruler is significant for the way in which the latter conforms to the ideal orality manifest by the grotesque body. Thus it would seem that Bakhtin identifies the grotesque body with the phenomenon of Stalinism and that Ryklin's reading is justified. But the actual situation in Bakhtin's famous study of Rabelais is considerably more complex than even Ryklin suspects.

Whether or not Bakhtin reference to Heraclitus's "playing boy" of the universe has the Aesopian subtext of referring to the Soviet leader is impossible to say with any certainty. The praise/blame dialectic does, however, resonate with the arbitrary nature of domestic political events under Stalin's rule in the late thirties, when Bakhtin wrote the first version of his study of Rabelais. Several years later, in an 1947 essay on dialectical and historical materialism, Stalin himself applauded Heraclitus as the first dialectician, singling out in particular the Greek philosopher's view that the world is forever locked in a cycle of being regularly consumed by fire and cooling from it (*"[mir] zakonomerno vosplameniaiush[ii]sia i zakonomerno ugasaiushch[ii]"*).[53] Both ideologically and in terms of his psychopathology, it is revealing that Stalin emphasized the cycle of purifying fire and cold in Heraclitus's philosophy. On the face of it, a Stalin-like figure becomes the anarch of a mercilessly cyclical social universe in Bakhtin's Rabelais book; he is an autocrat who combines the figures of mother and Paraclete, of carefree yet cruel child and intent cleric administering the sacrament. As Julien Benda points out, the transfer of political passions from the individual to the collective body amplifies rather than mitigates their power, in effect imparting to them a divinized validation: "To wish to possess material advantages *in one's own nation,* to want to feel distinct from other men *in one's own nation,* is still the desire to possess material advantages, still the desire to feel distinct from other men."[54] The joining with the collective body thus represents as much separation and alienation (in a larger and more universal sense) as it does the obliteration of the ego; in fact, ontologically speaking, the individual's death occurs precisely at the moment when the nation is subject to the temperamental whims of the autocrat. Since Stalin's declaration of the doctrine of "Socialism in One Country" shortly after the death of Lenin in 1924, the Soviet Union in many ways became a vivid example of such isolationist xenophobia. The christological schemata of interrelation (not discussed by Ryklin but consistent with many of his conclusions) and the topos of Stalinism thus intersect in a way that is most disconcerting: the political leader became the communicant in a debased version of the eucharistic act. In *Rabelais and His World* carnival is not, of course, defined by political authority in the way this conclusion suggests; clearly something must still remain after the figure of the tyrant (who is mostly peripheral to Bakhtin's discussion of carnival) is removed from the square. The question is how much is left standing and untainted.

SYNCHRONY VERSUS DIACHRONY IN PRAISE AND BLAME: THE REDEMPTION OF CARNIVAL

All of this seems to jeopardize the positive value that many commentators have assigned to carnival. To be sure, there have been some scholars who have criticized the tendency to unthinkingly valorize Bakhtin's carnival, albeit not in reference to the death-dealing ambivalence of speech-acts during the thirties. In his pathbreaking article Ryklin points out that Bakhtin consistently frames the gorging of the collective body in terms of violence to the individual identity that are resonant not only with collectivization but also with the purges; from a somewhat different perspective, Western leftist critics such as Stallybrass and White caution that carnival can have a legitimizing as well as subversive effect, the periodic and highly ritualized release of social tensions ultimately militating against any movement toward genuine revolutionary change. Tellingly, the praise/blame dichotomy is never treated extensively by Bakhtin again and is only parenthetically referred to in the 1963 edition of his Dostoevsky study. If Bakhtin implicitly compares Shrovetide's disorder and role-reversals to the randomness of political fortune in general and to the caprice of a Stalinist ruler in particular, surely he must be calling the ethics of carnival as a whole into question, notwithstanding the seemingly unequivocal paeans he addresses to it elsewhere in the book.

And yet we come closer to resolving this dilemma (or, as some might less charitably view it, conceptual inconsistency) if we return to the base issue of the relation between the individual and culture as a whole. Pausing for a moment on Bakhtin's distinction (quoted above) between the good and bad ruler, the ideal political ruler emerges as the one who maintains a separation between himself and his subjects; he does not assimilate them into his symbolic person, eucharistically devouring them to consolidate and centralize his position. The ideal ruler is the facilitator, a figure who is secondary to the nation and therefore utterly inconsistent with the monarchic and autocratic ideal. Nothing could be further from the "cult of personality" in politic leadership that swayed during the Stalin years. Now Bakhtin's statement about Rabelais as a figure anticipating modern statehood makes sense. Autocracy, defined broadly as the system where the ruler *is* the state, is anathema to the political progressivism of which carnival is a harbinger. A person is not a state, and a state cannot be conceived in any metaphorical sense as an individual. The cosmic ideal of carnival involves only individuals and the universe at large; the state is simply not a player in this operation. It is the transfer (*perekhod*) or homologous translation (*perevod*) of the functions of carnival from the body of the universe to the body politic that has murderous consequences. When a single society takes on the role of all of human reality and attempts to eclipse it, then true merging and joining with other individuals becomes impossible. The inconceivable merging that occurs is between subject and state. Carnival itself becomes impossible, its Chalcedonian mechanism of balanced interrelation shut off. In a certain sense, one can speak of a genuine and false form of carnival. This ambiguity—the tenuous and unstable nature of carnival—is what Ryklin perceptively saw in *Rabelais and His World.* However, he glosses over the balancing power of ambiguity (evident in the praise/blame opposition) and does not make the crucial distinctions between the different kinds of bodies arising out of carnival.

Bakhtin's piece "Additions and Changes for 'Rabelais' " (written in 1944) contain the most extensive and, politically speaking, suggestive elaboration of the praise/blame dichotomy in Bakhtin's work. In these sketchy notes Bakhtin stresses that praise and blame are simultaneously present in carnival laughter—a point asserted but not fully developed either in the 1939 dissertation or in the final published book. In these remarks he states that any sequential rather than unisonal voicing of praise and blame reinforces hierarchy rather than abrogating it; specifically, it is the alternation between encomium (*proslavlenie*) and calumny that represents a betrayal of carnival's evocative ambivalence.[55] At one point, Bakhtin laconically writes in one three sentence sequence "[t]he self-exaltation of Eastern despots and deities in the history of praise. The apologetics of gravesite prayers. Forms of coronation (of heroes, emperors)." He renders his views on such matters explicit in the next paragraph, noting the both "topographical aspect of praise (heights, summit, distance, face, forward)" and its "relation to size (large, exaggeration, in juxtaposition with the withering curse)." In such unalloyed praise we hear "hyperbole" in all its "dual significance." Bakhtin continues: "The role and meaning of the superlative degree, its types and manifestations. For it is here, in the realm of pure praise that the forms of finalized and hermetic individualism are made, gaining the upper hand over the dual body."[56] All of this is strikingly applicable to the dynamics of Stalin's personality cult with its excessive self-praise and massive aesthetic monumentalism designed to eclipse the figure of every individual besides that of its subject. In another, more private, meditation from the preceding year, Bakhtin writes that there is an "[e]lement of violence in cognition and the artistic form. Directly proportional to violence is the element of the lie. The word promises, engenders hope, glorifies *or* abuses [*branit*]. The merging [*sliianie*] of praise and blame neutralizes the lie."[57] Bakhtin's insistence on the necessary simultaneity of praise and blame exists in a highly complex and even tormented relation with the contemporary events of the Purges; it is surely significant that he developed this theory during those proceedings, referring to certain kinds of speech acts that dominated them. But, as we have seen, the dynamics and timing of carnival are significantly different from those events. What Bakhtin attempts in *Rabelais and His World* is nothing less than a redemption of the public square.

The idea of any actual ambiguity of speech acts is inconceivable from the Stalinist perspective; if fully understood, such double-voicedness would divest such them of their usability in a court of law. During the late thirties in the Soviet Union, innocence and guilt were perceived as overwhelming qualities inhering to particular bodies: the guilty were thoroughly animated by treacherous designs against the workers' state, and the only truly innocent were among the dead, memorialized into a fresco of martyrs for the cause. It was the rigid sequentiality of rhetorical modes that was endemic to the language of the purges and the show trials, strikingly articulated by Vyshinsky in his attempt to effect a shift from excoriation to glorification in his 1938 speech. In *Rabelais and His World* Bakhtin states that all carnival is essentially paschal laughter. Vyshinsky's vision of a new world built on the bones of traitors was articulated five days after the beginning of Orthodox Lent in 1938; like many revolutionary pronouncements, the eschatological and residual christological echoes of his statement would have been powerfully suggestive to his Russian audience, even uttered as it was five years before Stalin's loosening of restrictions over the Russian Orthodox Church during the war. For Bakhtin, however, carnival offers the possibility of liberation as something that is ever-present; it does not represent deferred enjoyment or fulfillment in the form of an anticipated Judgment Day or an unrealized-but-aspired-toward Utopia.

Clearly, this conclusion does not quite square with Ryklin's assertion of the hypertrophy of the grotesque collective body fed by the individual ones of all-too-willing victims, nor with Isupov's more recent statement that Bakhtin's conception of dialogue hinges on an "apophatic aesthetic of creative death," one in which the "I" requires the death of self and other in order to resurrect itself according to the uncompromising ethic of saintly self sacrifice that the Russian Orthodox tradition espouses.[58] Years before Ryklin and Isupov wrote their provocative articles, Houston Baker effectively used the same incarnational metaphor of mass victimization as the chief sustenance of the ravenous body politic, the American literary canon representing the celebration of a bloody mass in which the enslaved African body is devoured in order to ensure the convenant of American culture. According to Baker, the canon-formation of the white United States represents not only a ceremony in which "the idea of sacrifice" is central, but also one that foregrounds "the materialization and engorgement of the body as a promise" or covenant.[59] Like any body, the American body promptly forgets what it devours, the "unnatural" African body serving at best as a zone "where the natural [American] man's revolutionary imagination proposes dreams of order."[60] Bakhtin does not idealize the sanguinary image of collective communion, and in fact delineates an alternative to it that is unacknowledged by either Ryklin or Isupov. In a series of disjointed notes he wrote in 1946, the Russian critic states that there are two different experiences of memory: one small (*malyi*) that relates only to one free and cognicizing subject who regards everybody else as dead and to whom everybody is mute, and another, big (*bol'shoi*) one in which everything is alive and speaks, endowed with the memory of thousands of years of the human experience embodied (*voploshchennykh*) in the unofficial symbolic systems of culture.[61] Bakhtin is more interested in the idea of embodiment as a principle than as a ritual; he is drawn to its theological aspect and not its ceremonial or liturgical one, an important distinction that neither Ryklin or Isupov make. Significantly, in the article "Bodies of Terror" all of the images of carnival as a kind of demonically inverted divine mass are Ryklin's interpretive paraphrases and cannot be found anywhere in *Rabelais and His World.*

What Bakhtin calls the small kind of cultural experience is eerily resonant with the Stalinist cult of personality and arguably has conceptual antecedents in Solovyov's subjective sociology, which (as shown in Chapter 4 of this study) relies on the metaphor of society as the only fully viable creative consciousness. Vyshinsky glorifies precisely this narrowly conceived and pinched form of memory, one in which the corpses of excuted human failures are jettisoned and forgotten on the way to a promised land; he delineates a vertical gravitation to a rarefied ideal away from stifling corporeality that Bakhtin defines as the central dynamic of official discourse. What Ryklin does not see in *Rabelais and His World* is that Bakhtin posits the possibility that carnival can easily degenerate into authoritarianism. The book is as much about the redemptive potential of carnival as it is a contemplation of the collective traumas of the Stalin era. It is precisely this partaking of the ambiguous real that becomes, for Bakhtin, the ideal.

Chapter Seven

The Ethics of Authorship in Bakhtin's Last Writings

> I have tried to look in some of my own previous work at the complex relations between comedy and radical politics, in the context of a political left not exactly celebrated for its uproarious good humor. The names of Mikhail Bakhtin and Bertolt Brecht signify something of this conjunction in our time, but so also does that of Oscar Wilde. One of the many paradoxes of a transformative politics is that it is in the end all about pleasure, fulfilment, ease and serenity of being, but is forced, sometimes tragically, to forego some of these precious qualities in the essential rigor and seriousness of its practice.
> —Terry Eagleton

THE TURNING point in Bakhtin's life after his rediscovery by the then graduate students Vadim Kozhinov, Sergei Bocharov, and Grigorii Gachev is one of the most memorable moments in the Bakhtin legend. With references in the late fifties to the Russian critic by Roman Jakobson and Victor Shklovsky and the use of *Problems of Dostoevsky's Art* in classes at Moscow University and the Gorky Institute of Literature, Bakhtin's name gradually reentered scholarly circulation. In the late fifties, Kozhinov's discovery of the Dostoevsky book and his inquiries about its author, politically repressed and assumed dead, led to the startling discovery that he was in fact alive. "Please forgive the unfamiliar people who venture to disturb you," Kozhinov wrote in November 1960, "[b]ut we see in the creator of *Problems of Dostoevsky's Art* a good and close friend." On 6 June 1961 Kozhinov received an invitation from Bakhtin's wife to come for a visit to Saransk. As described in various accounts, the trip to the Mordovian capital was nothing less than a pilgrimage for Kozhinov, Bocharov, and Gachev.[1] The moment also proved to be something of a revivification of Bakhtin, who soon significantly reworked the Dosteovsky book and up to the early seventies wrote a series of notes in which he clarified and interrelated many of his earlier ideas, for the first time bringing Rabelaisian carnival into the world of Dostoevsky's novels. It is not too much to say that the encouragement and support of the three fledgling scholars from Moscow influenced Bakhtin's style of writing for the better, inaugurating a period of intense productivity and newfound clarity of approach in his work:

the forceful style of these essays and books differs significantly from anything else he had written before. Bakhtin's statement in his last miscellany of notes that nothing is absolutely dead and that every meaning has its own holiday (*svoi prazdnik*) of rebirth or resurrection (*vozrozhdeniia*)[2] takes on a certain autobiographical significance when viewed in the context of his own personal and professional renascence.

AUTHOR AS CHARACTER IN "TOWARD A REWORKING OF THE DOSTOEVSKY BOOK"

The first visible fruit of this new period in Bakhtin's life was his rewriting of the Dostoevsky book. But *Problems of Dostoevsky's Poetics* was not the very first piece Bakhtin wrote after his "rediscovery." In 1961 Bakhtin put together a fragmentary conspectus for the new version of his Dostoevsky book that was posthumously published in 1975 as "Toward a Reworking of the Dostoevsky Book." Before finishing these notes—which resemble more a series of *aperçus* than an actual summary of a project or a proposal—Bakhtin wrote in a letter to Kozhinov that he intended to treat in greater detail Dostoevsky's discovery of the individual personality (*lichnost'*) as a live and commensurate consciousness (*zhivoe polnopravnoe soznanie*), an entity representing a mutable truth (*chuzhaia pravda*) that resists the author's attempt to circumscribe it.[3] "Toward a Reworking of the Dostoevsky Book" is interesting for a number of reasons, but perhaps the most salient is that here Bakhtin returns to the conception of personality (*lichnost'*) that figured so prominently in "Art and Answerability" and his essays of the twenties. These notes are a particularly vivid example of the reformulation and thoroughgoing orchestration of terms and categories that characterized the final decade of Bakhtin's work.

Although in these preliminary remarks Bakhtin does follow up on points he raised in his letter to Kozhinov, there are some additional twists and turns in his subsequent development of ideas. What is genuinely new here in comparison with his earlier writings is his insistence on the personality of the author as existing fundamentally on the same plane as those of his characters. Here the scheme of "I" and "Other" that was so eloquently outlined in "Toward a Philosophy of the Act" is complicated by the deliberate entrance of the author himself onto the stage of his own creation. Bakhtin makes a particularly revealing distinction between personality and character (*kharakter*) as he discusses the new role of the author. As in many other parts of "Toward a Reworking," the remarks take the form of analytic imperatives toward the projected work:

> Examine in detail the distinction between *character* [*kharakterom*] and *personality* [*lichnost'iu*]. Even character is to some extent independent of the author

> (Tatyana's marriage, which Pushkin did not expect), but this independence (its own logic) has an objectified character. The independence of personality is of a qualitatively different nature: personality is not subordinate to (that is, it resists) objectified cognition and reveals itself only freely and dialogically (as *thou* for *I*). The author is a participant [*uchastnik*] in the dialogue (on essentially equal terms [*na ravnykh pravakh*] with the characters), but he also fulfills additional, very complex functions (he holds the reins [*privodnoi remen'*] between the ideal dialogue of the work and the actual dialogue of reality).[4]

The individual personality (*lichnost'*) of this passage is a stronger recasting of the one almost forty years before. In "Toward a Philosophy of the Act" the assumption that the personality is a viable category is instrumental to the creation and operation of real ethical obligation, the fulfillment of the Kantian "ought" (*dolzhenstvovanie*) possible only when there is an acknowledgment of the existence of the unitary personality (*edinstvennoi lichnosti*) within it.[5] In the passage above Bakhtin is apparently outlining the "new structure of the image (*obraza*) of the person" that he refers to at the beginning of "Toward a Reworking."[6] Particularly significant in the passage above is Bakhtin's attempt to link up personality to a poetics of dialogue, a connection only tentatively suggested in "Toward a Philosophy of the Act." Both the *Problems of Dostoevsky's Poetics* and the notes he wrote toward a reworking of it manifest an effort to develop more fully topics that had been partially put aside years ago. Dialogue now becomes the crucible for the formation of personality.

For reasons of space, only a few of the more conspicuous reminiscences of Bakhtin's previous work in "Toward a Reworking" can be pointed out here. At first glance, much of this piece seems to consist of a series of seemingly random comments. Bakhtin seems either not to have cared about defining the literary-critical genre of this piece or deliberately fudges the distinction between an aphoristic essay and a series of "Notes" or "Remarks." There is, in fact, much in the tone and sequence of presented ideas here that suggests a level of essayistic organization and recalls the homilistic "Art and Answerability." As in his first published piece, at the beginning of "Toward a Reworking," Bakhtin outlines a trichotomy; here it is of the three discoveries made by the writer of polyphonic fiction. According to Bakhtin, these discoveries are sequential. The first discovery is the initial autonomy of the author's own person (*lichnost'*), which is problematized by his interaction with characters in a work of literature. "The author, like Prometheus," he explains, "creates (or rather re-creates) living beings who are independent of himself and with whom he is on equal terms [*na ravnykh pravakh*]." The author is subject to the same quandaries of individual identity that beset the characters he has created; in a certain sense, he himself joins the fauna of his novelistic world. As a result of his loss of authorial privilege, he "cannot finalize [these characters], for he has discovered what distinguishes personality [*lichnost'*] from all that is not personality. Objective reality [*bytie:* (ontological) being] has no power over it."[7] Only the true novelist is able to distinguish the true consciousness from the spurious or half-formed. This act of mere cognition is profoundly creative, setting into motion the process whereby the characters become increasingly independent. These characters eventually enter onto the same plane of existence occupied by the author. Subsequently, the author as one consciousness among many others is inevitably drawn into or implicated by this world. The second discovery by the modern writer is the portrayal ("*izobrazhenie*" [emphasis in original]) or, more precisely, re-creation (*tochnee, vossozdanie*) of the self-developing idea ("*samorazvivaiushcheisia* idei") that is inseparable from personality (*neotdelimoi ot lichnosti*) of the author; the third discovery is that of dialogicity (*dialogichnost'*) as a special form of interaction (*vzaimodeistviia*) among equal and commensurate consciousnesses (*mezhdu ravnopravnymi i ravnoznachnymi soznaniiami*).[8] Although the emphasis on the unfinalizability of authorial discourse is as weighty here as ever before, the writer or artist is now a firebrand whose arrival on the structural scene of the novel is essential for the triumph of an ethical state among consciousnesses.

"All three discoveries," Bakhtin continues, "are essentially one [*ediny*]: they are three facets [*grani*] of one and the same phenomenon."[9] But what all three discoveries share is something much more significant than E. M. Forster's famous if commonplace imperative of "only connect." While the novelist's personality within the novel is not fundamentally more coherent or ascendent than those of the characters, it does figure as something of a special entity inasmuch as it represents the link or reins (*privodnoi remen'*), connecting dialogue in the literary work itself with the actual dialogue experienced in reality. What is curious here is not only that Bakhtin's author quickly recedes into the background after creating a particular novelistic world, but that the act of creation itself seems so minimal. One thinks of Bakhtin's description in *Problems of Dostoevsky's Art* of the role played by plot (*siuzhet*) in the novel, serving as something of a stage director bringing various voices in contact with each other but then departing, "having fulfilled its service function."[10] It is interesting to note that Bakhtin dropped this description of the plot's function in the 1963 edition of the book. In what is perhaps the most significant change over the *Problems of Dostoevsky's Art*, the figure of the author himself replaces plot in the act of novelistic creation. This shift is more telling than any critique of Formalism offered up by Medvedev in *The Formal Method of Literary Scholarship;* it is far more expressive and eloquent of Bakhtin's movement away from critical approaches operating under the assumption of a paradigmatic preexisting structure as prime mover. As already shown in Chapter 1 of this study, the concept of plot as intercessor in the 1929 edition has distinct christological overtones; in *Problems of Dostoevsky's Poetics,* Bakhtin brings the process of humanization of the novel full circle. The author very clearly becomes at this point of Bakhtin's writing a third presence that is indispensable to the full realization of dialogue, a mediator between the Dostoevskian hero and his interlocutor(s). Although it can be said of Bakhtin's new vision that the author increasingly becomes a deity in his created world, he nonetheless emerges as a highly changeable and susceptible demiurge, one who re-creates rather than makes and who mediates rather than creates ex nihilo. For Bakhtin, the novelist is preceded by his novel, and truly becomes an author only after his characters have taken shape.

Stressing their sequentiality, Bakhtin states that the three discoveries mentioned above "affect both form and content." As he puts it, "[t]heir contribution to questions of *form* is more profound, more condensed [*sgushchennee*], more general than is the concretely ideological, changeable content that fills [*napolniaet*] them in Dostoevsky."[11] Bakhtin's wording of this passage is significant because in it one can discern links not only to "Toward a Philosophy of the Act" but also to the essays of the thirties, and in particular to the essay "Forms of Time and of the Chronotope in the Novel." As already shown, the term "condensed" (*sgushchennyi*) in both of those earlier essays refers to the reification and fleshing-out of reality that occurs when time and place come together into the confluence that true dialogic meaning represents. The lexeme *napolniaet* (fills) is also significant in this regard because (as demonstrated in Chapter 1) it is used in the earlier works to describe metaphorically the quickening of linguistic and cultural meaning that occurs during dialogic interaction. For Bakhtin, form is not an abstract design, a schematic conceptual outline that one transfers onto the topography of experience like an architect's transparency: form *is* substance, a concretized product that forms from within the interstices of reality. Meaning should not fill the vessel of a particular literary work (as it monologically sometimes does even in Dostoevsky), separate from the process of self-definition that the form undergoes as the author truly interorients himself within the world of his novel. And yet, form is also antiteleological: what is important is not the concretized artifact itself or any ideological meaning grafted on to it later, but the act of becoming, the mutually ethical development of author, character, and reader that results from their collision with one another. Together with this incarnational aspect and the utter confounding of linear time, the intensive interorientation of these consciousnessess suggests a profound integration of the theological paradigms of integrative *perichoresis* and the Johannine logos.

Later in his remarks about the renewed Dostoevsky project, Bakhtin charts out the development of the idea born from the individual personality in a way that more distinctly echoes both the chronotope essay and "Discourse in the Novel." Bakhtin stresses the impossibility of the truly independent idea; as already shown, only personalities can be said to be independent, and even they are so only in the most conditional of ways. There is a "logic governing the development of the idea itself, taken independently of individual consciousness [*individual'nogo soznaniia*] (the idea in itself, or in consciousness generally, or in the spirit [*v dukhe*] generally)." The idea undergoes a "referentially logical and systemic development;" one can therefore speak of a "special logic governing the development of an idea embodied in the personality [*voploshchennoi v lichnosti*]." "Here the idea," Bakhtin continues, "insofar as it is embodied in the personality, is regulated by the coordinates *I* and *another*, refracted [*prelomliaetsia*] variously in different zones" (299; 344). The "idea itself" is ultimately a simulacrum, a useful if limited construct enabling us to parse the components of our experience; like the individual, it is concretized within the act of ethical becoming. All this brings us to the realization of what Bakhtin considers to be the true paradigm:

> The word, the living word, inseparably [*nerazryvno*] linked with dialogic communion [*s dialogichskim obshcheniem*], by its very nature wants to be heard and answered. By its very dialogic nature it presupposes an ultimate dialogic instancing. To receive the word, to be heard. The impermissibility of *second-hand* resolution. My word remains in the continuing dialogue, where it will be heard, answered and reinterpreted. (300; 344–45).

To be sure, the term *obshchenie* (translated above as "communion") by itself does not carry theological connotations; it has no ready or felicitous equivalent in English, referring in most instances to social existence or interaction with others in general. And yet, Caryl Emerson's rendering of this term seems completely appropriate within the present context. After all, Bakhtin does indeed emphasize the direct contact among people through the intercession of a logos-like word or discourse. The incarnational poetics so vividly manifest in the essays of Bakhtin's early and middle periods (discussed in Chapters 1 through 3 of this study) reappears in this seemingly modest and workmanlike prolegomenon to Bakhtin's next project. The word once again becomes for Bakhtin both the birthplace and vessel for the transubstantiation between I and Other. Also repeated here from essays of the thirties such as "Discourse in the Novel" is the image of the aspects of this embodiment, which refract meaning in various zones; given greater emphasis as well is the constellation of personality (*lichnost'*), I (*ia*) and the Other (*drugoi*), which in this essay, unlike the earlier "Toward a Philosophy of the Act," emerges as a well-defined triad. Although the personality of the author may be the idea's birth parent, the idea is taken in and raised by the adoptive parents of I and Other.

The correspondences and echoes between "Toward a Reworking" and earlier essays by Bakhtin are amplified by the remarkable consistency and dovetailing of certain terms. At one point in the later essay, Bakhtin writes in a way that reads like the lost final draft of the fragmentary "Toward a Philosophy of the Act," summoning up the categories of passivity (*passivnost'*) and self-activity or activeness (*aktivnost'*). Bakhtin underscores that the author is far from powerless and supine; in spite of the organic and mutual influence between himself and his creation. We should "in no way assum[e] a passivity on the part of the author, who would then merely assemble others' truths, completely denying his own point of view"; instead, what we have now is "a completely new and special interrelationship [*vzaimootnoshenii*] between the author's and the other's truth." The novelist is the paradigm of a new kind of agency:

> The author is profoundly *active* [*aktiven*], but his activity is of a special, *dialogic* sort. It is one thing to be active in relation to a dead thing, to voiceless material [*bezglasnogo materiala*] that can be molded and formed as one wishes, and another thing to be active *in relation to someone else's living, autonomous consciousness* [*soznaniia*]. This is a questioning, provoking, answering, agreeing, objecting activity; that is, it is dialogic activity [*dialogicheskaia aktivnost'*] no less active than the activity that finalizes, materializes, explains, and kills casually, that drowns out the other's voice with nonsemantic arguments. (285; 328)

Certain categories that Bakhtin discusses here leap out to any reader. For one thing, the dichotomy of passive versus active presented here is completely of a piece with Bakhtin's explanation of it in "Toward a Philosophy of the Act." It will be recalled from the earlier essay that the quality of being active (*aktivnost'*) is not a literal-minded pragmatic concept in which the zealotry of action is existentially prized over thought. Nor does passivity (*passivnost'*) constitute, as such, volitional lassitude or indifference to action. Such characterizations would for Bakhtin be rooted too deeply in an almost fetishistically individualist conception of behavior. Passiveness and activeness are not emotional states; they are modes of conduct and, more precisely, attitudes toward the world, ways of relating or (as is sometimes the case) not relating or engaging with others. As already noted, in the earlier essay Bakhtin does not give any concrete or specific illustrations of these categories. Nevertheless, although the reader is not standing on ground here that is much more substantial than before in terms of specific examples, Bakhtin does make preeminently clear in this later sketch that *aktivnost'* consists specifically of *perichoresis*-like dialogic interrelation (*vzaimootnoshenie*) and exchange between voices. As already shown, the giving up of oneself to others is fundamentally viewed as a gesture of Christian unselfishness. The precise nature and internal dynamics of that selflessness are not, however, necessarily what one would expect in terms of conventional morality.

A final meditation on the ramifications of the passage above as they branch out into the rest of "Toward a Reworking" compellingly exposes the deeper, well-wrought internal unity of his methodology. One of the primary differences in the literary theory of "Toward a Philosophy of the Act" and that of the later piece is the emergence of the triad in the latter over the valorized dyad of the former. Bakhtin's interpretation in "Toward a Philosophy of the Act" of Pushkin's lyric poem to Amalia Riznich already manifested a movement toward just such a trichotomy of author and two interlocutors, the critic drawing a link between the author and Christ's self-renunciation, that "great example of self-activity [*aktivnost'*]." One can argue that Bakhtin's characterization in "Toward a Reworking" of dialogical activity (*dialogicheskaia aktivnost'*) continues to have a christological subtext for three felicitously intertwining reasons: (1) the triad of the novel's discoveries is suggestive of a christological triunity, particularly with Bakhtin's emphasis on a *perichoresis*-like interrelation between the author's word and those of the participants in dialogue; (2) just as the Johannine word both precedes and yet is simultaneous with the created universe, so does the author's personality at first occupy a particular niche in time that is eroded as he or she dwells among the characters in its created work; and (3) the image of the idea as embodied (*voploshchennaia*) from the author entails the subtext of transubstantiation at a particular moment of the intersection between voices, a transformation also extensively described in *Rabelais and His World.* As noted by commentators from the turn of the century to those of the present day writing on Bakhtin, as a philosophical term *voploshchenie* (embodiment, enfleshment) is highly marked by a theological residue of the instantiation of the humanity of Christ.[12] The internal unity of Bakhtin's terminology is reinforced by the christological motifs outlined here, which, by the time of the early sixties, Bakhtin shapes into a clearly defined foundation for his conception of dialogue.

THE CONTINUED LIFE OF THE WORD

At this point, however, the ramifications of such a subtext within the particular textual universe of Bakhtin's work must give one pause. Clark and Holquist have commented on the prominence of the "theological trope" of Christ in both Dostoevsky's work and Bakhtin's book on him, particularly in describing the relations among author, characters, and literary work: "According to this metaphor, the authors' relation to their characters are akin to the relations of God to humans. This relation, after all, is one of creator to created, which is why it is so often described by terms taken over from religion."[13] It could be argued that the de facto likening of the author to a deity-like or demiurgical figure carries within it the seeds of its own destruction as a concept. A deity whose very being is implicated in the circumstances of the human universe is in fact at the mercy of contingency, and is therefore no deity at all. For someone who is supposed to represent the ideal of self-activity (*aktivnost'*), Bakhtin's author-intercessor is curiously passive while mingling with the persons of his or her creative universe. That this activity has shifted from being the self-actuated ones in "Toward a Philosophy of the Act" (which foregrounds Christ's self-renunciation and the metempsychosis of Pushkin's poetic persona to his lover) to being a dialogic one in *Problems of Dostoevsky's Poetics* only reinforces the sense of a radical decentering of the subject in Bakhtin's conceptual universe.

Much of this seeming incongruity between Bakhtin's christologically tinctured ideal of *aktivnost'* and the reality of the author's actual functioning as described in his criticism can be explained if we eschew a literal-minded framing of the concept of self-sacrifice. Significantly, the term does not appear in *Problems of Dostoevsky's Art*. Why did he resurrect it in rethinking his 1929 study? Returning to Bakhtin's statement about the nature of dialogic activity, it is useful to bear in mind his assertion that the "activeness" of the author does not consist of such palpable gestures as the transformation of any dead thing or shaping of voiceless (*bezglasnyi*) material. Bakhtin implies that *aktivnost'* is more profoundly transformative of reality than any other category of action. Although dialogic interaction with other *live* consciousnesses—the imbrication of the author in human reality—may not be regarded as action-oriented in a traditional or Nietzschean way, they are no less transformative and influential. Bakhtin hints at this qualification when he states that the author's activeness bears a special and dialogic character. This is clearly quite different from the idea of selflessness as voluntary self-immolation or acceptance of scapegoating as necessary for the body politic. As he put it in the early twenties, the self-renunciation in which "I actualize with utmost activeness [*maksimal'no aktivno*] and in full the uniqueness [*edinstvennost'*] of my place in Being" is not self-anninilation, for "[t]he world in which I, from my unique place, renounce myself does not become a world in which I do not exist, a world which is indifferent, in its meaning, to my existence: self-renunciation is a performance or accomplishment that encompasses Being-as-event."[14]

As demonstrated in the previous chapter, the subsequent period in Soviet history was abundant with examples of precisely the opposite and literal-minded view of self-sacrifice, and their impact upon Bakhtin was quite profound, particularly during his work on Rabelais. Although Bakhtin always remained aloof from political affiliations of any kind, in Duvakin's 1973 interviews he explicitly states that he was opposed to all forms of political extremism in the teens and the twenties, singling out all stripes of the socialist left as well as the monarchists. There he speaks positively only of Stolypin's reforms aimed at creating a strong and productive middle class among the peasantry, calling it "the only right way of saving Russia from the Revolution."[15] One need not look long among the famous political pronouncements of even the twenties to find openly expressed the belief on the necessity of human sacrifice. Even Trotsky (whom Bakhtin groups together with the political "extremists" in the Duvakin interview) voiced such a view in 1920, rebutting the notion of the sanctity of human life with the statement "[t]o make the individual sacred we must destroy the social order which crucifies him. And this problem can only be solved by blood and iron."[16] All this suggests that already in "Toward a Philosophy of the Act" Bakhtin was polemicizing with the agitational and often openly sanguinary views of contemporary politics; certainly his pointedly argumentative statements in that work suggest an urge to redefine the notion of self-sacrifice in response to then regnant attitudes. In defining the self's activity toward the Other as a *dynamic* of self-renunciation rather than a suicidal act and by highlighting it as a philosophical issue of prime importance, Bakhtin was prescient of future political realities. In his 1961 "Toward a Reworking" Bakhtin returns to the existential concerns of his work from the early twenties, infusing his earlier work on Dostoevsky with the conception of dialogue as a dynamic of mutual involvement and sacrifice. Notwithstanding Isupov's interesting argument in "Death of the Other," death can never be, in Bakhtin's view, a dialogic gesture.

The theological subtext in Bakhtin's late work becomes more comprehensible if the sacrificial aspect of the Christ-like or mediator figure of the author is thought of not in the literal terms of physical death (as, for example, in the medieval Russian legend of the knights Boris and Gleb) but of giving oneself over in ways that are multifacetedly communicative, simultaneously constituting both a transcendence of one's individual existence and an affirmation of life. Bakhtin makes this clear in the following series of semiparatactic segments from "Toward a Reworking," where dialogue is portrayed as life-giving and affirming (although not without upheavals) to conceptions of the self as a closed entity:

> Not an analysis of consciousness in the form of a sole and single *I* ["edinogo i edinstvennogo *ia*"], but precisely an analysis of the interactions [*vzaimodeistvii*] of many consciousnesses [*mnogikh soznaniii*]; not many people in the light of a single consciousness, but precisely an analysis of many equally and privileged and fully valid consciousnesses. Non-self-sufficiency, the impossibility of the existence of a single consciousness. (287; 329–30)

The relations among consciousness is once again framed in terms of interpenetrative aesthetics, and one inevitably thinks not just of the patristic *perichoresis*, but also of the category of "multiple-hypostaticness" (*mnogoipostasnost'*) that was so important for Russian philosophers such as Solovyov, Lossky, and Zenkovsky in their descriptions of what intersubjectivity should be. As Bakhtin asserts later in this essay, Dostoevsky was hostile to "those world-views which see the final goal in merging [*v sliianiii*], in a dissolution of consciousnesses in one consciousness [*v odnom soznanii*], in the removal of individuation. No nirvana is possible for a *single* consciousness. A single consciousness is *contradictio in adjecto.* Consciousness is in essence multiple [*mnozhestvenno*]. *Pluralia tantum*" (288; 331). Bakhtin's polemic against the valorization of the "single consciousness" must be read not only as an attack on personal selfishness and various forms of narcissism, but also on the idea of society as a single collective consciousness in the neo-Solovyovian sense. It is a pointed critique of the constitutional order of the Khrushchevite Soviet Union, still laboring under the remnants of the Stalinist legacy with its identification of leader with state. As many historians have noted, the attempts Khrushchev made from 1960 to his ouster in 1964 to reshape the Soviet legal system into a bastion against the cult of personality were at best unsuccessful and at worst tellingly halfhearted.[17] Reworking his Dostoevsky book during this tense period of looming statist restoration in the wake of Khrushchev's juridicial and economic failures and what one political memoirist calls the Soviet leader's patriarchal authoritarianism,[18] Bakhtin must have been constantly impressed by the inner contradictions of authorial discourse with its authoritarian grounding in the single isolated individual. Self-sacrifice in the form of self-destruction carries with it a distinct ideological marking; it is an act that requires no contact or *obshchenie* with particular others. In its utter self-sufficiency as a culmination of a dialogue of ideas, the collective body politic represents the consummate gesture of a culture of aggregate individuality masquerading as democracy. Asserting as it does the charisma of interactive multiplicity, the Chalcedonian formula "without separation or division" is the ideal vehicle for critiquing such ideological practices, positing (as Bakhtin puts it in "Towards a Reworking") a unity "not as an innate one-and-only [*odno-edinstvennoe*], but as a dialogic *concordance* [*soglasie*] of unmerged [*nesliianykh*] twos or multiples" (289; 332). By balancing interaction or merging with the preservation of individuation, Bakhtin adverts to the Chalcedonian paradigm in the most profound and fundamental of ways, extending its applicability to the nontheological while consistently grounding himself in its doctrinal content.

From this perspective, Soviet society from the thirties to the sixties represents the culture of individualism par excellence. This conclusion—following from Bakhtin's belief that merging with the state entails the impossibility of such transcendent contact among people themselves—is certainly not the first thing that leaps to mind when thinking about the Soviet legacy with its collectivist ideals. And yet, it is precisely these ideals in their form of paternalistic authoritarianism that rendered Soviet culture anything but collectivist. Although this contemporary relevance is somewhat muted as Bakhtin proceeds to describe the landscape of such an interactive space, it is nonetheless present in his portrayal of dialogue as contestation rather than consensus:

> Not that which takes place within, but that which takes place on the *boundary* ["na *granitse*"] between one's own and someone else's consciousness, on the *threshold* ["na *poroge*"]. And everything internal gravitates not toward itself but is turned to the outside and dialogized, every internal experience ends up on the boundary, encounters another, and in this tension-filled encounter [*v etoi napriazhennoi vstreche*] lies its entire essence. This is the highest degree of sociality (not external, not material, but internal). Thus does Dostoevsky confront all decadent and idealistic (individualistic culture), the cultural of essential and inescapable solitude, the illusory nature of solitude. The very being of man (both external and internal) is the *deepest communion* [*glubochaishee obshchenie*]. *To be* means *to communicate* ["*Byt'*—znachit *obshchat'sia*"]. Absolute death (nonbeing) is the state of being unheard, unrecognized, unremembered (*Ippolit*). (287; 330)

Change and real existence occurs in extremis or on the edge (*granitsa*) or at the threshold ("na *poroge*"), when one's individuality in a narrowly egotistical sense is at stake. The thematics of boundaries or demarcation are particularly highlighted here, a person's being defined as crossing borders in order to be (however confrontationally) with others. But what almost escapes one's notice in this excerpt is Bakhtin's unarticulated but essential premise that *both* speakers move toward the border: pictured visually, this encounter of full reciprocity would actually require the two to switch places. The participants in dialogue meet only when each take the place of the other, and contact is always contituted by an inner or psychological inversion that results as a subjective correlative of the concrete encounter between them. As Bakhtin explains in the 1962 entry of his sketchbook, in the unshakably hierarchical and one-sidedly serious official model of the world, the slave and the tsar can never change places.[19] His full integration of carnival—with its powerful reversals that always function in conflations, rather than mere inversions, of high and low—into his discussion of Dostoevskian dialogue was as inevitable as it was necessary. In a particularly Chalcedonian turn, Bakhtin states in *Problems of Dostoevsky's Poetics* that the carnivalistic rituals of crowning and decrowning are "inseparable [*nerazdelimy*], they are dualistic [*dvuediny*] and they pass one into the other; in any absolute dissociation [*razdelenii*] they would completely lose their carnivalistic sense." These moments from the 1963 edition and Bakhtin's preliminary work toward it are remarkable in encapsulating the history of his terms over the course of his career, from the patently theological vocabulary of the essays of the twenties to its more submerged presence in the Rabelais book's foregrounding of the boundaries and divisions within experience, and finally to the the reemergence of the Chalcedonian principle in closer connection with *perichoresis* and incarnational aesthetics.

Yet unlike before, there is a certain poignancy and even bitterness here. This sense may be colored by the reader's knowledge of Bakhtin's virtual oblivion for many years, possibly hinted at in the statement that absolute death and nonexistence is the state of being unheard, unrecognized, and unremembered. A vivid sense of this loneliness and isolation can be poignantly heard in one of Bakhtin's first replies to the Moscow student who contacted him, in which he wrote from Saransk "I am already acquainted with all of you who wrote the letter, through your published works; I was attracted to them *by their style,* which sharply stands out against the general run of our literary criticism. . . . I have the warmest desire to become acquainted with you."[20] An elusive sense of malaise pervades the meditation on solitude from "Toward a Reworking" that is not overtly present in the final published version of the Dostoevsky book. For one thing, in this essay dialogue requires intensive effort or work, which is why terminal gestures of absolute self-abnegation are deemed utterly inadequate. The statement that the essence of dialogue consists in the tension-filled encounter (*v etoi napriazhennoi vstreche—vsia ego sushchnost'*) suggests that at this point of his career Bakhtin sees more dissonance than harmony in novelistic polyphony. In the passage above, Bakhtin's crowning stroke testifying to this sense of contrariety is his alliteratively highly marked assertion that dialogue—that highest degree of sociality (*vysshaia stepen' sotsial'nsoti*)—is a fundamentally internal and not external or materially oriented phenomenon (*ne vneshnei, ne veschnei, a vnutrennei*). Bakhtin is, of course, describing the internalization of the dialogic word that always takes place in the consciousnesses of interlocutors after a verbal exchange. But here, unlike earlier essays such as "Discourse in the Novel," Bakhtin's juxtaposition of inner and outer word is taken to a new level of dilemma and paradox. From the way Bakhtin describes it, one wonders how such a word is even possible.

In *Problems of Dostoevsky's Poetics,* Bakhtin finally remedies the structural instability of novelistic discourse by fully linking it to carnival, a category completely missing from both the 1961 "Toward a Reworking" and the 1929 *Problems of Dostoevsky's Art.* One gets the distinct sense that Bakhtin hesitated in introducing this concept into his discussion of the novelist. In the recently published remainder of his 1961 notes for revising *Problems of Dostoevsky's Art,* Bakhtin briefly mentions Menippean satire but studiously avoids discussing its modern manifestation in carnival; in fact, his first substantive discussion of Dostoevskian carnival before the 1963 publication of *Problems of Dostoevsky's Poetics* occurs a year later in his sketchbook journal, where he schematically outines the centrality to Dostoevsky's world of the carnival customs of crowning and uncrowning (*uvenchanie-razvenchanie*).[21] The spatial orientation among voices that was so graphically described in *Problems of Dostoevsky's Art* is abundantly evident in the second edition, although in the latter it is subsumed into a larger picture of the ethical involvement of the author. The new portions of *Problems of Dostoevsky's Poetics* represent something of an expansion of the 1929 edition combined with a reinfusion of the ethical concerns of "Toward a Philosophy of the Act" because of the way in which Bakhtin combines the former's structural analysis of the authorial word with the latter's ethical evaluation of the interaction between self and other.

The revisions Bakhtin made in his Dostoevsky book for its second and expanded edition throw into sharper relief his growing emphasis on the ambivalence of discourse. *Problems of Dostoevsky's Art* bears some distinct marks inherited from "Toward a Philosophy of the Act," written a few years earlier. Foremost among these shared features is the patent (though nonetheless partial) indebtedness to Husserl and a certain preoccupation with the dilemma of subjectivity. Both of these traits would become subsequently more submerged and less clearly marked in Bakhtin's later work. In *Problems of Dostoevsky's Poetics* Bakhtin takes the contextualization of the individual consciousness and its interconnectedness with others as axiomatic and focuses his exposition on the specific dynamics of this ontological socialization. In a passage carried over from the 1929 edition with virtually no changes, Bakhtin explains that polyphony resides within the novel's protagonist from the very beginning; the permutations of his inner dialogue merely depend on the modulation of an already provided set of keys:

> That internal ideological struggle which the hero wages is a struggle for a choice among already available semantic possibilities, whose quantity remains almost unchanged throughout the entire novel. The motifs "I didn't know that," "I didn't see that," "that was revealed to me only later," are absent from Dostoevsky's world. His hero knows and sees everything from the very beginning [*s samogo nachala*]. This is why it is so common for heroes to (or for a narrator who is speaking about a hero) to announce, after a catastrophe, that they had known and foreseen everything in advance. . . .
>
> Almost no evolution of thought takes place under the influence of new material, new points of view. . . . [A]ll these discourses [*slova*] are usually given in their entirety at the very start [*s samogo nachala*]. . . . We could put it this way: from the very beginning a certain stable multiplicity exists, with unchanging content [*soderzhatel'no niezmennoe smyslovoe mnogoobrazie*], and all that occurs within it is a rearrangement of accents [*peremeshchenie aktsentov*]. Even before the murder Raskolnikov recognizes Sonya's voice from Marmeladov's stories, and immediately decides to go to her. From the very beginning [*s samogo nachala*] her voice and her world enter Raskolnikov's field of vision, and are attached in [lit., "join with" (*priobshchaiutsia*)] his inner dialogue.[22]

The reshuffling of content values—described here in terms suggestively spatial—is accompanied by a disruption of linearity of time. Judging from the passage above, the protagonist's belated awareness of his ventriloquizing of others' voices (the latter suggested by the terms "inner ideological struggle" and "rearrangement of accents") is as much an egoistic loss as it is an aesthetic boon. Both this excerpt and the one before it from "Toward a Reworking" stress the Dostoevskian hero's ultimate helplessness when confronted by the cacophony of voices within him. As Bakhtin points out in a segment of the *Problems of Dostoevsky's Art* that he omitted in the 1963 edition, this alienation of the protagonist is something of a dislocation of space as well as time, Dostoevsky's characters coming together outside of those dimensions "as two beings [*sushchestva*] in infinity [*v bespredel'nosti*]," their consciousnesses, worlds, and fields of visions intersecting.[23] The term "infinity" (*bespredel'nost'*), in its literal meaning of "without limit" once again highlights Bakhtin's insistence on the necessity of transcending the self, an imperative also voiced by Gumilev. In his already quoted poem "The Word," the Acmeist poet decries the barren limitations or boundaries (*skudnye predely*) of existence. Here, however, as in *Rabelais and His World*, Bakhtin does not assert that such boundaries are contrived, much less call for their wholesale destruction. In his highly synchronic and seminal conception of discourse Bakhtin adopts the stance of an interested observer of and believer in phenomenological border crossings, not a proponent of the usurpation or dissolution of identity.

But the term *predel* (limit) is significant not only in recalling the use of it by Russian poets early in the century but also in its appearances in traditional theological sources. Bakhtin's delineation of the synchronic yet almost infinitely varied and divisible phenomenon of polyphony bears a striking resemblance to certain ideas and terms that can be found in John Chrysostom's commentaries on John 1:1. The terms of the Russian translation of these texts, published in 1902 by the Saint Petersburg Theological Academy, are especially reverberant with those Bakhtin uses. Like Bakhtin, Chrysostom insists that any conception of "beginning" is highly problematic and should not—indeed cannot—be comprehended in a literal or direct way: " '[w]as in the beginning,' is nothing else than ever being and being infinitely (Russian, *bespredel'noe*)."[24] In a certain sense, in their treatments of the relation between time and space both Chrysostom and Bakhtin subvert the concept of "beginning": the latter stresses the importance of the synchronic and anticipatory nature of perception and the former asserts that the beginning is, in fact, ever-present.

Other parallels between Bakhtin's terminology and Chrysostom's Johannine christology become more clear-cut on the basis of the latter's fourth commentary or sermon on the verse from John. There he identifies the Son of God as the divine Word, casting Christ in the role of a mediator between time and space. He describes the interrelations between Christ, the Word, and the

Holy Spirit in a manner that for a reader of Bakhtin's criticism immediately recalls several motifs, among them the syncretic makeup of the chronotope, the mediating role of discourse in the novel, and the Dostoevskian hero's blurred, synchronic sense of time:

> Again, tell me, were not all ages, and every interval [Greek, *diastima*] created by Him? Any man not deprived of his senses must necessarily confess this. There is no interval [Greek, *medon* (lit., "middle" or "middle ground")] therefore between the Son and the Father, and if there be none, then he is not after, but Co-eternal with Him [Russian, *sovechen Emu*]. For "before" and "after" [Russian, *prezhde* and *posle*] are notions implying time, since, without age or time, no man could possibly imagine these words; but God is above time and ages.[25]

As in Bakhtin's "Forms of Time and of the Chronotope in the Novel" the undermining of time is expressed spatially. Similarly, just as Dostoevsky's characters as described by Bakhtin know everything from the very beginning and, in the final analysis, are not wholly cognizant of "earlier" and "later," so does Chrysostom's generational dyad call into question literal-minded apprehensions of the linearity of time and the substantiality of space. The issue here is not whether Chrysostom's homily is an actual subtext for Bakhtin, but rather that of the striking conceptual affinities in the critic's work to certain aspects of traditional biblical exegesis.

But why did Bakhtin leave out of the 1963 edition the interesting image of two beings provoked by the plot to collide and intersect in a way that ultimately transcends the bounds (*predely*) of plot-related conflict, a formulation that seems so resonant with the Johannine logology sketched out by Chrysostom? On the face of it, it is a highly effective and vivid trope for understanding the kind of intersubjectivity that animates Dostoevsky's novels. The answer lies partly in the segment he replaced it with, one that, in keeping with the "Reworking" notes, projects a more thorough and consummate interaction and equality between author and characters. Although his comments in *Problems of Dostoevsky's Art* about the service function of plot occur in the chapter devoted to Dostoevsky's treatment of the adventure plot, he seems to be speaking there about the general functioning of novelistic plot. In *Problems of Dostoevsky's Poetics,* Bakhtin is absolutely clear about the highly specific operation of the adventure plot in tandem with the monologic hero. As the critic explains there, although the eternal man of the adventure plot is a real, corporeal-spiritual being, the moment he steps outside that plot he is "quite empty," unable to establish any "extra-plot connections with other characters." By being wholly at the service of the idea, the adventure plot "places a person in extraordinary positions that expose and provoke him, . . . connect[ing] him and mak[ing] him collide with other people under unusual and unexpected circumstances precisely for the purpose of testing the idea" itself, "for testing the 'man within the man.' "[26] In other words, the principle that motivates the plot is also ultimately drawn into question and therefore involved in the confrontational world of the novel; no longer does it irresponsibly retreat after inciting the conflict among characters, as described in *Problems of Dostoevsky's Art*. In *Problems of Dostoevsky's Poetics* Bakhtin goes on to clarify the origins of the adventure plot in carnivalized folklore and literature, a discussion completely missing from the 1929 edition. By no longer portraying plot as a distant deity in the manner of an Aristotelian unmoved mover, Bakhtin moves away from a conception of discourse inspired by traditional logology to one that treats *every* element of a novel as susceptible to mutual influence and change. In effect, the Johannine model of the multifaceted word that served as an important subtext of "Discourse in the Novel" has been displaced or absorbed by a maximized form of Trinitarian interpenetration or *perichoresis* as the principle guiding the carnivalistic impulses of Dostoevsky's world.

Needless to say, the apparent conceptional and even terminological similarities between Chrysostom and Bakhtin cannot obscure the vast philosophical differences between a heterodox twentieth-century Russian critic and a doctrinally pugnacious and inflexible Byzantine theologian from the fourth century. In the same homily Chrysostom develops a metalinguistic reading of the verse that is similar in many respects to Augustine's but that is considerably more dualistic: "For many are the words of God [Russian, *slov bozhestvennykh*] which angels execute, but of those words none is God; they are all prophecies or commands."[27] Chrysostom dubs the human word "the simple word [Russian, *prostoe slovo*]" and, although he does assert that it is an agency of God, locates it in a somewhat confrontational position vis-à-vis the divine Word. In Bakhtin's view (which is closer to Augustine), the multivalent word impinges upon the Absolute whereas for Chrysostom the reverse is true. Clearly, there are highly suggestive structural similarities between the Trinitarian paradigm of "three in one" or later doctrinal innovation at Chalcedon of "not merged yet not separate" and Bakhtin's conception of polyphony within discourse. However, from the mid-nineteenth century up to the Revolution the doctrine expounded in various Russian Orthodox church handbooks and in commentaries on John 1:1 in the main emphasize the unitary and totalizing essence of the divine Word.[28] The influence of the incarnational paradigm on Bakhtin's conception of discourse (*slovo*) cannot be interpreted in a literally minded biographical manner as a direct expression of his personal piety: the model reached Bakhtin through a series of filters, some more directly concerned with theology (the "God-Seekers") and others primarily literary (Acmeism and Formalism). Bakhtin diverges from all of these sources in highlighting the primacy of the individual perception, while balancing it with the principle of social and cultural interaction, a belief that can be traced as far back as "Art and Answerability," his first published essay.

In *Problems of Dostoevsky's Poetics*, it is precisely those "prophecies and commands" that Chrysostom speaks of that are the sites of transformation and transcendence; it is the words that become corporealized, the form of the Word merely providing a frame for such concreticization.

This aestheticization of christology is abundantly evident in Bakhtin's other writings from that period. Like many of his essays, "Forms of Time and of the Chronotope in the Novel" was more or less abandoned by Bakhtin when he first wrote it. This essay is unique in Bakhtin's work, however, in being augmented but not revised by him many years later. As in the case of *Rabelais and His World* and his study of Dostoevsky, Bakhtin had been greatly encouraged to return to old projects by then graduate students such as Sergei Bocharov and Vadim Kozhinov. The so-called Concluding Remarks of "Forms of Time and of the Chronotope in the Novel" is one of the last things Bakhtin wrote. These belated synoptic comments represent one of Bakhtin's most incisive theoretical statements and provide an exemplary summing-up of both the chronotope essay and many of the concerns of "Discourse in the Novel." An examination of these remarks (written in 1973, two years before Bakhtin's death) reveals a distinct return to the life of novelistic discourse. The chronotope functions "as the primary means for materializing [*materializatsiia*] time and space; it "emerges as a center for concretizing representation [*izobrazitel'noi konkretizatsii*], as a force giving body to [*voploshcheniia:* lit., embodying] the entire novel." The chronotope functions very much like the ideological form in Dostoevsky's world, taking shape through a reificatory process that results from the interaction among various aspects of the novel's spiritual life. The chronotope's "representational significance" becomes evident when "[a]ll of the novel's abstract elements—philosophical and social generalizations, ideas, analyses of cause and effect—gravitate [*tiagoteiut*] toward [it] and through it take on flesh and blood [*napolniaiutsia plot'iu i krov'iu:* lit., fill up with flesh and blood] permitting the imaging power of art to do its work [*priobshchaiutsia khudozhestvennoi obraznosti:* lit., joining or communing with the imaging power of art]."[29] The "abstract elements" spoken of here are at least to some extent equivalent to the discordant voices in "Discourse in the Novel": they, too, are made concrete in the process of moving away from their point of origin toward a site of consolidation and reification. In the interval between the two essays, Bakhtin had moved away from totalizing and polemical statements originating in the Soviet linguistic disputes of the thirties toward a phenomenology of literary stylistics. But what is particularly significant in the passage above is the metaphor of embodiment, which is expressed here with a clarity and obviousness unprecedented in Bakhtin's work. In this last phase of his career, incarnational aesthetics represents the key to understanding one of his most renowned concepts.

CONCLUSION: BAKHTIN'S DISCOURSE WITH THEOLOGY

In his 1970–71 notes Bakhtin distinguishes between context (which for him means a dynamic, concretizational form) and code in the sense of a finished ideological worldview. "A context," he states, "is potentially unfinalized [*nezvershim*]." "A code" on the other hand, "must be finalized [*zavershimym*]" and "has only a technical means of transmitting information, it does not have a cognitive, creative significance"; it is "a deliberately established, killed [*umershchvlennyi*] context."[30] In the same text Bakhtin tersely mentions the ancient teachings about logos and the Gospel of John, begging the question whether he considers it to be, like semiotics, a dessicated and code-oriented approach that deals only in the "transmission of ready-made communication [*gotovogo soobshcheniia*]."[31] Bakhtin does not provide a clear-cut answer to this query. Certainly the heavy use he makes of the christological metaphor suggests a reliance on its form or structure at the expense of its substance. One only has to think of his dislocation of the Chalcedonian paradigm, which originally referred only to the blending of the two very different natures of the human and the divine. In Bakhtin's hand, the paradigm becomes a tool for characterizing the interaction between two or more ontologically equal participants in dialogue; he subverts not only its originally cosmological meaning as a bridge between the corporeal and the spiritual but also disrupts the dualism so central to the spirit of the doctrine, rendering it into a pullulating multiplicity. In this respect, his 1961 characterization of unity as "a dialogic concordance of unmerged twos or multiples" is particularly incriminating. Similarly, as filtered through Trinitarian conceptions such as Chrysostom's, the author becomes for Bakhtin a godhead and the hero his only-begotten son in a intensified vision of interaction or *perichoresis* between the two. It is, of course, a metaphor that is vividly illustrative yet problematic from the point of view of actual belief.

Bakhtin's flexible approach to the theological code (and the "abstract element" or "philosophical generalization" that it represents) is also graphically reflected in both *Rabelais and His World* and *Problems of Dostoevsky's Poetics*. Bakhtin's appropriation of theological schemata and his subsequent ideational transformation of them in fact represents one of the most prominent chronotopes in his own work. Bakhtin's christological chronotope is indeed an "organizing center for the fundamental narrative events" in his work; at the same time, it is also located in source material outside the text, the "ancient public square's spirit of carnival and mystery," which, according to Bakhtin, is the most vivid manifestation of those doctrinal precepts. Over the course of his career as a critic Bakhtin creates a narrative of theological discourse; he effectively novelizes christology over the fifty-year span of his work. Seen from this panoramic perspective, a great deal about the sinuous development of Bakhtin's terminology begins to make sense. Homologously following the main points of the theogonal narrative, Bakhtin's lifelong work can be read in the following manner. First, the ethics of interpenetrative communal life (treated in his essays of the twenties) are fraught with the tensions of different natures coming into contact, resulting in the clash of the demands of life and art, society, and personality. Their protracted intersection and interrelation ultimately cause them to be embodied in the incarnational aesthetics of discourse described so vividly in "Discourse in the Novel" and *Rabelais and His Word.* There remain, however, tensions within this unitary vision, and the embodiment of the word continues to be periodically threatened by the urge toward fragmentation and stratification, the grotesque body politic in its worst manifestation consuming breakaway bodies. Only carnival can restore the complex interrelation that guarantees the provisional unity of the embodied word. Then, in the final stage of his narrative and with his most significant departure from traditional christology, in *Problems of Dostoevsky's Poetics* and other works of the sixties and seventies Bakhtin describes how the frangibility of embodied discourse leads to its ramification into a network of embodied voices rather than a single hypostatic word. Now the words (rather than the single Johannine word) take on flesh when they come among people. The christological thematics of Bakhtin's work are represented by the chronotope of corporeal words, of the traditional Johannine word made and unmade as the critic reshapes it to serve the demands of his theory.

Given this unfolding conceptual intricacy of Bakhtin's thought, it is perhaps not surprising that there is little in it that could provide directions for a clear-cut political program. A summing-up of Bakhtin's ideas from such morally normative perspectives almost always leads to embarrassing statements of the banally obvious. The beliefs holding that unfettered individualism is pernicious but that a basic preservation of the individual personality is important—that one must know when to openly communicate with others and, if necessary, be prepared to sacrifice oneself for them—are truisms and platitudes that few people from any devotional creed or segment of the political spectrum would argue with. What does emerge as a constant from Bakhtin's criticism is its tightly knit terminology, a conceptual structure that changed somewhat over a period of years. The interrelatedness of Bakhtin's own lexicon is perhaps his most graphic and convincing demonstration of the interaction among categories that he espouses. His christological motifs themselves are a brilliantly wrought metacritical correlative to the internally consistent and dynamic textual universe of Dostoevsky's world. By stressing this conditional subjectivity Bakhtin adapts the christological metaphor of the Johannine word in a way that none of his literary and philosophical precursors in modern Russian letters had attempted. Bakhtin makes divinity utterly a part of the concrete reality of the individual consciousness or personality, undermining the assumption of the total separation between the two; he makes a Chalcedonian *perichoresis*—itself a doctrinal hybrid—the guiding principle of a human theology.

In this regard, Terry Eagleton's insightful comparison of Bakhtin to Oscar Wilde is significant in other ways that the British Marxist perhaps did not expect. Bakhtin's relation to Orthodoxy was in several respects similar to Oscar Wilde's toward Catholicism, both writers undergoing a period of apostasy from the faith in which they were baptized and ending their lives with a qualified return to it. In Wilde's case this apostasy was much more evident up until the time of his arrest and trial, as is the insinuation of religious imagery in late works such as "The Ballad of Reading Gaol."[32] The christological imagery in Bakhtin's early work made an overt comeback later on, and even his subversion of it in certain works such as *Rabelais and His World* bespeaks its deeper influence upon him. In the Rabelais book Bakhtin commits a double blasphemy, one against the political orthodoxy of Stalinism by linking to it the marketplace word's duality of praise/blame (*khvala/bran'*) and the other against the religious orthodoxy by comparing the internal contradictions of the Johannine word to those of the Stalinist one. At the same time, the paradigmatically Chalcedonian configuration of this dichotomy—Bakhtin's shrewd casting of it in the mold of the counter-balanced twin natures of Christ—also suggests ways in which such ambiguity can explode the monological and authoritarian text from within. In other words, Bakhtin redeems carnival by (almost obsessively) elaborating upon the structural dynamics of the theological trope he uses. The essentially salvific role played by theological images in Bakhtin's criticism is evidence of his circuitous return to their axiological content; it demonstrates that Bakhtin ultimately took them seriously in their philosophical and religious settings and did not regard them as strictly metaphorical conceits or examples of postmodernist *disjecta membra*. Significantly, the praise/blame dichotomy was never treated extensively by Bakhtin again and is referred to only very parenthetically in the 1963 Dostoevsky book and in some of the sketches for it. As already shown, the recently published notes that Bakhtin wrote for the Rabelais study during the forties contain an extensive and, in political terms, highly suggestive elaboration of this dichotomy.[33] Clark and Holquist report that during the sixties and seventies as he reworked his early essays Bakhtin excised a number of religious passages.[34] The two scholars also speculate about his reason for refusing the last rites at his deathbed, noting his wariness of ritual and the greater stock he placed on "inner spirituality and communion."[35] Given the emphasis in his late work on the *perichoresis*-like structure of the individual perception, this speculation is judicious.

There is much that suggests that Bakhtin was contemplating theological categories of language at this late stage of his career. Bakhtin's work is framed at the beginning and end of his career by telling references to the ancient teachings about the Johannine logos and its possible relation to metalinguistics and the philosophy of the word.[36] Similarly, the last decade of Bakhtin's work manifests a renewed interest in Chalcedonian and perichoresical terminology, one first seen in his first extant essay, "Art and Answerability." As already seen, the actual form that such doctrines took in his work stripped them of their theologically normative meanings, relegating them to the status of metaphors describing human society instead of the cosmos. In a certain sense, the theological paradigms of Bakhtin's writing become considerably transformed in their thorough humanization as features of dialogue and carnival. But these concepts serve a purpose that is powerfully heuristic in its suggestion of a reanimation of theological principles themselves, an effort to reengage those notions in the ethical dimensions of dialogue. Striking a resonantly Chalcedonian note in one of his last writings, the "Response to a Question from the *Novyi Mir* Staff," Bakhtin writes that "[i]n the realm of culture, outsideness [*vnenakhodimost'*] is a most powerful factor in understanding [and] it is only in the eyes of *another* culture that foreign [*chuzhaia*] culture reveals itself." "A meaning only reveals its depths," he continues, "once it has encountered and come into contact with another, foreign meaning." However, this engagement does not entail a sheepish self-abnegation. Far from it. For "[w]ithout one's own questions one cannot understand anything other or foreign," and "such a dialogic encounter of two cultures does not result in merging [*ne slivaiutsia*] or mixing. Each retains its own unity and *open* totality, but they are mutually enriched."[37] Bakhtin lived in a country in which religion and theology were largely anathematized. In his christological chronotope of corporeal words Bakhtin attempts to integrate ethical and political thought with theology, which had been marginalized into a peripheral culture, one foreign to a country declared by its political leaders to be the examplar of "Developed" socialism. Recently Grigorii Pomerants (one of Bakhtin's earliest Russian disciples) described the murder of the dissident priest Aleksandr Men' as motivated by the Orthodox fundamentalism that regards the razing of the barriers between Russia and the Christian world as a heresy. Pomerants ends his obituary with the expatriate Russian theologian G. P. Fedotov's warning at the end of the Stalin era that "[t]he hate for the other [*nenavist' k chuzhomu*]—the absence of love for the other—represents the chief pathos of nationalism, and not only in fascist countries."[38] Then and now—during the Cold War and in the pseudopeace of the so-called end of history—Bakhtin's effort to integrate yet preserve different cultural traditions in all their fundamental strangeness is more relevant than ever.

Notes

MIKHAIL BAKHTIN AND RUSSIAN ORTHODOXY

1. In an otherwise favorable examination of his theories Kristeva lists as Bakhtin's limitations "psychologism, the lack of any theory of the language user, [and] the unrecognized influence of a humanist terminology (there are continual references of the heroes' 'soul' and 'conscience')" ("The Ruins of a Poetics," 107). Also see Tzvetan Todorov's book *Mikhail Bakhtin: The Dialogical Principle*, 3–5; and his article "Human and Interhuman: Mikhail Bakhtin," in his *Literature and Its Theorists: A Personal View of Twentieth Century Criticism*, 70–88. The Bakhtin-Kagan correspondence offers an oblique view onto attitudes toward religion among Bakhtin's circle of friends; see K. Nevel'skaia, ed., "M. M. Bakhtin i M. I. Kagan (Materialy semeinogo arkhiva)."

For Clark and Holquist's comments on Bakhtin's relation to religion see their *Mikhail Bakhtin*, 120 and passim. See also Holquist, "Bad Faith Squared," 214–34.

Caryl Emerson's "Russian Orthodoxy and the Early Bakhtin" provides one of the best speculative overviews of the issue. For other remarks on possible theological reminiscences in Bakhtin's early work, see her "Problems with Bakhtin's Poetics" (520, 523). Oleg Il'insky offers a sketchy treatment of the topic in "Religioznye vzgliady rannego Bakhtina."

2. Graham Pechey, "On the Borders of Bakhtin: Dialogization, Decolonization," in *Bakhtin and Cultural Theory*, ed. K. Hirschkop and D. Shepherd, 39.

For a non-Marxist opposition to the possibility of a theological Bakhtin, see I. R. Titunik, "The Bakhtin Problem: Concerning Katerina Clark and Michael Holquist's *Mikhail Bakhtin*," 91–93. Titunik takes particular issue with what he sees as Clark and Holquist's tendency to see the christological metaphor as the guiding aesthetic and philosophical principle in Bakhtin's criticism. He states that since the critic's "(supposed) Russian Orthodox kenotic view of Christianity stresses the 'enfleshment' of Christ/The Word, anything to do with the human body and even anything *material* discussed in the later works is claimed as a development from the masterplan." As a result, he contends that "the connections made between the later works and that master plan often seem strained and far-fetched" (92–93).

3. Allon White, "The Struggle Over Bakhtin: Fraternal Reply to Robert Young"; Ken Hirschkop, "A Response to the Forum On Mikhail Bakhtin," in *Bakhtin: Essays and Dialogues on His Work,* ed. G. S. Morson, 73–79; Stanley Aronowitz, "Notes From Underground: Mikhail Bakhtin Changes the Face of Criticism."

4. A typical recent example of this conceit of Bakhtin's catacomb leftism: "Bakhtin may very well have been hostile to the monologism that Stalinism and the Zhdanovite apparatchiks used to organize post-revolutionary Russia under the name of 'marxism', but this cannot be used as evidence to dispute the sociological marxism that concerned him and was a part of his work from the beginning" (Michael Bernard-Donals, "Mikhail Bakhtin: Between Phenomenology and Marxism," 172). In his 1986 article "The Road to Vitebsk," Raymond Williams characteristically discusses the writings of Bakhtin together with those of his circle, suggesting that taken together they complement the work of the Frankfurt School (21–26).

5. An example of this kind of interpretation is the appreciation of Bakhtin offered by Anthony Ugolnik in his overview of contemporary Orthodoxy. Ugolnik, a deacon in a Greek Orthodox church in Lancaster, Pennsylvania, begins his suggestive examination of the Christian ramifications of Bakhtin's work with the remark that "[w]e can see an example of a Christian working through a secular idiom in the critical work of the Soviet literary scholar Mikhail Bakhtin" (*The Illuminated Icon,* 158–59).

6. "[E]mu prishlos' etu rol' ispolniat'—nekoei zhivoi tserkvi, byt' khramom" (G. Gachev, "Preface to Turbin's 'Golod i bol' Mikhaila Bakhtina,' " 6).

7. Russian State Archives of Literature and Art (Moscow), fund 2718, inventory 1, item 723.

8. Quoted from *Mikhail Mikhailovich Bakhtin v Saranske. Ocherki zhizni i deiatel'nosti,* a 1989 memoiristic miscellany edited by K. G. Karpunov and others (17).

9. "Vy znaete, konechno, chto Bakhtin vsedga byl rezko protiv marksizma." Ivanov made this statement to me during a March 1987 interview in Moscow.

10. S. G. Bocharov, "Ob odnom razgovore i vokrug nego," 76–77.

11. Ibid., 72, 80.

12. Nicholas Rzhevsky, "Kozhinov on Bakhtin," 434–35, 437–38, 440.

13. V. Kozhinov, "Bakhtin i ego chitateli. Razmyshleniia i otchasti vospominaniia," 145–48.

14. Hirschkop's interesting remarks about "Discourse in the Novel" appear in two articles, his "Dialogism as a Challenge to Literary Criticism," in *Discontinuous Discourses in Modern Russian Literature,* ed. Kelly and Shepard, 18–32, and "Bakhtin, Discourse and Democracy," 104–110. Representative of the disdainful attitude of some leftist scholars toward the work of Slavic specialists is the following revealing statement from one group of editors explaining their decision not to publish Russian submissions in their volume of proceedings from a Bakhtin-oriented conference: "[W]e felt that the very significant and radical Russian contribution to recent developments in literary-critical theory deserved more attention within the rather conservative world of Slavic studies, where theory has generally been adopted—if at all—with considerable caution as a means of reinforcing cherished concepts and practices" (introduction to *Discontinuous Discourses in Modern Russian Literature,* xi).

15. K. G. Isupov, "Smert 'drugogo.' "

16. Isupov couches this idea about the political continuum of Russian religious thought in his commentary on the writer Mikhail Prishvin's expression of approval of Stalinist policy: "The liquation of all 'I's' as a class [Likvidatsiia vsekh 'ya' kak klassa]"; ibid., 108–9.

17. For an interesting speculation on Bakhtin's conception of group identities, see Caryl Emerson, "Keeping the Self Intact During the Culture Wars: A Centennial Essay for Mikhail Bakhtin," 110–111.

18. M. M. Bakhtin, "K pererabotke knigi o Dostoevskom II," 75.

19. Vladimir Nabokov, "Translator's Foreword," in *A Hero of Our Time. A Novel by Mikhail Lermontov,* xix.

20. See Hirschkop and Shepherd, "Bakhtin and the Politics of Criticism," 117.

21. M. M. Bakhtin, "Iz chernovykh tetradei," 158.

22. Michael André Bernstein, "When the Carnival Turns Bitter: Preliminary Reflections Upon the Abject Hero" in *Bakhtin: Essays and Dialogues on His Work*, ed. Gary Saul Morson, 117–18. Bernstein insightfully notes that Bakhtin does not seem to recognize the violence that almost always inheres to the rite of the saturnalia. I agree with Bernstein's appraisal of carnival and differ only in arguing (particularly in Chapter 6 of this study) that Bakhtin was in fact aware of the tyranny of the public square.

23. M. M. Bakhtin and V. M. Duvakin. "Razgovory s Baktinym," 160.

24. Clark and Holquist point in particular to the corporeality of Christ emphasized in the so-called kenotic tradition of the Eastern church as a fertile prototype for the leitmotif of "the word made flesh" and the I/Other dichotomy that appear in the essays of the twenties. The two scholars provide a succinct outline of these possible connections (*Mikhail Bakhtin,* 86). According to Clark and Holquist, what interests Bakhtin is the cognitive change that

occurs as a result of the contact between self and Other; this transformative process is strongly reminiscent of the transubstantiation or embodiment (*voploshchenie*) that is one of the central theological tenets of early, non-Gnostic Christianity. Clark and Holquist go on to adduce the connection that Bakhtin himself makes between christology and the self/Other dichotomy in "The Author and Hero in Aesthetic Activity." They do not argue that the christological metaphor was central to his work, only that it was highly relevant to the early essays that they group under the heading of the "Architectonics of Answerability." The following statement from V. N. Voloshinov is especially supportive of their argument: "[C]onsciousness itself can arise and become a viable fact only in the material embodiment of signs [v materiale znakovogo voploshcheniia]" (Voloshinov, *Marxism and the Philosophy of Language,* 11).

25. "K filosofii postupka," 109; *Toward a Philosophy of the Act,* 37. Epiphanius [Premudryi], "Zhitie Stefana Permskogo," 193. For a detailed discussion of Bakhtin's punning of terms denoting oneness and unity, see Chapter 2.

26. Caryl Emerson, "Translating Bakhtin: Does His Theory of Discourse Contain a Theory of Translation?" 26.

27. Gary Saul Morson and Caryl Emerson, *Mikhail Bakhtin: The Creation of a Prosaics*, 414. In the same spirit Clark and Holquist point out that Bakhtin "emphasizes the philosophical dimension in religion, rather than religion itself, because such *concepts* as soul, and grace, and transcendence help him articulate his own model of creation and communication with terms such as the I-for-itself, gift of completedness, and transgredience" (Clark and Holquist, "A Continuing Dialogue," 100).

28. "Pepel i almaz. Iz rasskazov M. M. Bakhtina, zapisannykh V. D. Duvakinym," 6.

29. "The theologians of our time are the least of whom one can say that they speak as those *possessing power* [Bogoslovy nashego vremeni menee vesgo sut' te, o kom mozhno skazat' chto oni govoriat kak *vlast' imeiushchie*]" (Pavel Florensky, "Khristianstvo i kul'tura," 74; emphasis in original).

30. See Dimitry Pospielovsky, *The Russian Church Under the Soviet Regime, 1917–1982,* 1:196–200, and his *A History of Marxist-Leninist Atheism and Soviet Antireligious Policies,* 1:64–65, 67–68.

31. Holquist and Clark describe this moment without giving the name of the priest present. Their account and the priest's identity have been confirmed by other accounts. Holquist and Clark are correct in stating that "there is an established Orthodox tradition of refusing [last rites] and Bakhtin himself had always been skeptical about formal religious ritual, believing in the greater importance of inner spirituality and human communion" (*Mikhail Bakhtin,* 343). On Dudko's dissident status as a priest, see "Iz interv'iu ottsa Dmitriia

Dudko" in *Vokrug imeni ottsa Aleksandra*, ed. A. I. Zorin and V. I. Iliushenko, 44.

32. P. A. Florensky, "Zapiska o pravoslavii," 98.

33. Peter [*sic*] Yakovlevich Chaadaev, *Philosophical Letters and Apology of a Madman*, 37.

34. Holquist and Clark, *Mikhail Bakhtin*, 105–8; on Bakhtin and Yudina, also see A. M. Kuznetsov's introduction to his edition of their correspondence, "Iz perepiski M. V. Iudinoi i M. M. Bakhtina (1941–1966)," 38–40.

35. "Da sokhranitsia nad vami oboimi Bozhie blagoslovenie, ne vziraia na to, chto vy predaete starogo i [illegible] druga . . . Prostite menia" (Russian State Library Archives [Moscow], M. V. Yudina collection [fund 527], carton 8, item 10, p. 13).

36. Russian State Library Archives, M. V. Yudina collection (fund 527), carton 10, items 21, 23, 41.

37. Clark and Holquist, *Mikhail Bakhtin*, 124–29, 139–41. Also see the recently published criminal proceedings related to Bakhtin ("K biografii M. M. Bakhtina. Vstuplenie, publikatsiia i primechanie V. Laptuna. Posleslovie S. Bocharova," 128–41).

38. Vladimir Turbin, "Golod i bol' Mikhaila Bakhtina."

39. Russian State Library Archives, M. V. Yudina collection (fund 527), carton 7, item 8, p. 14. For an account of Yudina's eclectic religiosity, see M. M. Bakhtin and V. M. Duvakin, "Razgovory s Baktinym," *Chelovek* 1 (1995): 157–63.

40. "Discourse in the Novel," in *The Dialogic Imagination*, 300 (*Voprosy literatury i estetiki*, 113). See also Bakhtin's description of structuring as orchestration in the same essay (262–63; *Voprosy literatury i estetiki*, 76–77).

41. "Three fragments from *Problems of Dostoevsky's Art*," in *Problems of Dostoevsky's Poetics*, 277 (*Problemy tvorchestva Dostoevskogo*, 100).

BAKHTIN'S CONCEPTION OF DISCOURSE *(SLOVO)*

1. "Iz zapisei 1970–71 godov," *Estetika slovesnogo tvorchestva*, 377; "From Notes Made in 1970–71," *Speech Genres and Other Late Essays*, 152.

2. N. K. Bonetskaia, "M. Bakhtin v 1920-ye gody," 53–54 and passim.

3. Clark and Holquist, *Mikhail Bakhtin*, 86–87, 304, 306.

4. The scholarly literature on John is enormous, particularly with regard to its sources. For a general discussion of the evangelist's polemical relation with contemporary Gnosticism and its evidence in the Johannine prologue, see Wilbert F. Howard's "John: Introduction," 451–53.

5. A. A. Long, *Hellenistic Philosophers*, 144.

6. See ibid., 145–47, and G. T. W. Patrick's commentary on Heraclitus's use of this term (*Heraclitus of Ephesus*, 115).

7. S. Trubetskoi, "Logos," 900.

8. Patrick, *Heraclitus of Ephesus,* 103.

9. M. Bakhtin, *Tvorchestvo Fransua Rable i narodnaia kultura srednevekovia i renessansa,* 95, 163, 219, 480. The political implications of Bakhtin's repeated references to this passage from Heraclitus will be examined in Chapter 6.

10. Quoted from Jean Pépin, "Logos," 12.

11. M. M. Bakhtin and V. M. Duvakin, "Razgovory s Baktinym," *Chelovek* 4 (1993): 150, 152.

12. M. Bakhtin, Postcard (Nevel, 30 July 1919); Russian State Library Archives, M V. Yudina collection (fund 527), carton 10, item 41.

13. *Estetika slovesnogo tvorchestva,* 336.

14. Jaroslav Pelikan, *The Spirit of Eastern Christendom (600–1700),* 25–26.

15. See Pelikan, "Divinity Made Human," 78–80.

16. English translation by Pelikan, "Divinity Made Human," 73–74; Russian translation from "Khalkiedonskii sobor," 21.

17. "Khalkiedonskii sobor," 21.

18. This is not to say that Chalcedonian terminology in regard to the Trinity never occurs in the liturgy or the writings of the church fathers. It does, however, tend to be used to describe one hypostasis, such as in Saint Basil's statement that the Holy Spirit is "wholly present in each one everywhere, yet, so divided, he knows no division" (*On the Holy Spirit,* quoted in M. J. Le Guillou, *The Spirit of Eastern Orthodoxy,* 27) or in the services for Lent where the Lamb of God is described as divided (*razdeliatsia*) yet indivisible (*nerazdelenyi*) (*Sluzhebnik,* 270).

19. G. Fedotov, *Stikhi dukhovnye: Russkaia narodnaia vera po dukhovnym stikham,* 25–27.

20. See in particular the first two articles in Archimandrite Fiodor's series "About the Contemporary World in Relation to Orthodoxy," (A. M. Bukharev [Arkhimandrit Fedor], *O dukhovnykh potrebnostiakh zhizni,* 54–70).

21. Harry Austryn Wolfson, *The Philosophy of the Church Fathers,* vol. 1, *Faith, Trinity, Incarnation,* 418–21.

22. See ibid., 423–25, and Leporskii, "Troitsa," 872.

23. Kallistos Ware, *The Orthodox Way,* 33–34.

24. For a summary of these views as espoused by the church fathers, see John Dillon, "Logos and Trinity," 11–13.

25. Quoted in Pelikan, "Divinity Made Human," 77.

26. *The Dialogic Imagination,* 276; *Voprosy literatury i estetiki,* 89–90.

27. P. Leporskii, "Troitsa," 868–70.

28. Nils Åke Nilsson, "The Dead Bees: Notes on a Poem by Nikolaj Gumilev," 574–77.

29. Andrei Bely, *Lug zelenyi Kniga statei,* 25, 28.

30. Steven Cassedy, "Bely's Theory of Symbolism as a Formal Iconics of Meaning," 290–91.

31. Naftali Prat, "Orthodox Philosophy of Language in Russia," 18–19.

32. Maksimilian Voloshin, "Horomedon," 58.

33. For the relevant manifestoes by Kruchenykh, Khlebnikov, and Livshits, see *Manifesty i programmy russkikh futuristov,* ed. Vladimir Markov, 53–76.

34. Quoted from Markov, *Russian Futurism,* 126–28.

35. "Zapis' lektsii M. M. Bakhtina ob Andree Belom i F. Sologube. Publikatsiia S. Bocharova, kommentarii L. Silarda," 229.

36. Nilsson, "The Dead Bees," 573.

37. Nikolai Gumilev, *Sobranie sochinenii v chetyrekh tomakh,* 2:39.

38. Victor Shklovsky, "The Resurrection of the Word," 41, and "Voskreshenie slova," 2:16.

39. Osip Mandel'shtam, *Sobranie sochinenii v trekh tomakh,* 4:223.

40. Victor Terras, "Osip Mandel'shtam i ego filosofiia slova," 458–59

41. Mandel'shtam, *Sobranie sochinenii,* 4:245.

42. *The Dialogic Imagination,* 279; *Voprosy literatury i estetiki,* 92.

43. As Ewa Thompson has pointed out in her *Russian Formalism and Anglo-American New Criticism: A Comparative Study,* the Formalist approach to language has interesting parallels with Anglo-American New Criticism. A revealing example of a literary expression of the latter movement's theory can be found in the poem "Communion" by the New Critic Yvor Winters, a devout Catholic:

> The changing mind, like sun that stirs on stone,
> Deep in some wooded shade,
> Is the incarnate word, grown more alone,
> Made and unmade.
>
> Bridging the pure divide, in search of ways
> To reach through night and sleep
> And bind our fear into the strength of days
> So rooted deep.
> (Winters, *The Collected Poems,* 207)

Winters's poem is something of a mirror-image of Gumilev's "Slovo": both pieces attempting to describe the manifestation of the unbodied force of the divine in the corporeal word. For many of the New Critics—as for certain

Formalists, Acmeists, and other Russian theorists of language—theology, linguistic theory, and literature were natural links in the same chain.

44. Nevel'skaia., ed. "M. M. Bakhtin i M. I. Kagan (materialy semeinogo arkhiva)," 268.

45. *Voprosy literatury i estetiki,* 81.

46. Shpet, *vnutrenniaia forma slova,* 143.

47. Ibid., 67.

48. *The Dialogic Imagination,* 262–63; *Voprosy literatury i estetiki,* 76.

49. *Voprosy literatury i estetiki,* 76–77.

50. A. F. Losev's *The Philosophy of the Name* (*Filosofiia imeni*) is another, if more mitigated, exception to the theoretical approach to the logos doctrine in Russian philosophy.

51. *Voprosy literatury i estetiki,* 137–38; *The Dialogic Imagination,* 324.

52. Anne Shukman, "M. M. Bakhtin: Notes on His Philosophy of Man," 244–45.

53. *Voprosy literatury i estetiki,* 112; *The Dialogic Imagination,* 299–300.

54. *Voprosy literatury i estetiki,* 112.

55. *The Dialogic Imagination,* 342–43; *Voprosy literatury i estetiki,* 155–56.

56. *Voprosy literatury i estetiki,* 113; *The Dialogic Imagination,* 300.

57. Holquist, "Bakhtin, Mikhail Mikhailovich," 35.

58. *The Dialogic Imagination,* 292; *Voprosy literatury i estetiki,* 105.

59. Quoted in Wolfson, *The Philosophy of the Church Fathers,* vol. 1, *Faith, Trinity, Incarnation,* 366.

60. Ibid., 366–67.

61. Harry Austryn Wolfson, *Philo: Foundations of Religious Philosophy in Judaism, Christianity and Islam,* 1:332–35.

62. See Wolfson on Philo's dichotomy of an inner and irrational essence (Greek, *ousia*) and an outer one (*Philosophy of the Church Fathers,* 1:369). Although Wolfson does not mention Eastern Orthodox theology, his discussion of Philo's system swiftly brings one to the realization of how relevant this writer was to its development. For a Russian perception from the turn of the century, see S. N. Trubetskoi, "Filon Aleksandriiskii," 819–20.

63. Florensky, "Stroenie slova," 348–51.

64. Ibid., 357.

65. *Problemy tvorchestva Dostoevskogo,* 240. This passage was translated by Caryl Emerson, who excerpted parts of Bakhtin's first Dostoevsky study as an appendix to her translation of the 1963 edition (*Problems of Dostoevsky's Poetics,* 280).

66. In his brief essay "Kenotafiia" [Cenotaph] Shklovsky discusses the

potential of cinematic art in terms that are strikingly similar to his "Resurrection of the Word," describing the classics and silent film as a graveyard and cinema in general resurrecting itself with the introduction of sound. "The word [*slovo*] has deepened the meaning of film" (*Zhili-byli. Vospominaniia. Memuarnye zapisi,* 464–65).

67. *Problems of Dostoevsky's Poetics,* 183; *Problemy tvorchestva Dostoevskogo,* 245.

68. *Rabelais and His World,* 11; *Tvorchestvo Fransua Rable,* 17.

69. See J. Massyngberde Ford, "Commentary," 313, 321.

70. For a detailed discussion of this term and its subtexts, see Chapter 6.

71. Sergius Bulgakov, "Was ist das Wort?" 1:26–27.

72. *Voprosy literatury i estetiki,* 76–79.

73. Quoted in M. J. Le Guillou, *The Spirit of Eastern Orthodoxy,* 58.

74. "Shklovsky, "Voskereshenie slova," 12.

75. M. M. Bakhtin, *Toward a Philosophy of the Act,* 105.

76. Saint Augustine, *Tractates. On the Gospel of John 1–10,* 51.

77. *Literaturno-kriticheskie stat'i,* 21.

78. Vl. Dal', *Tolkovyi slovar' zhivogo velikorusskogo iazyka,* 2:776.

79. Wolfson, *Philosophy of the Church Fathers,* 1:417.

80. *Problems of Dostoevsky's Poetics,* 276–77; *Problemy tvorchestva Dostoevskogo,* 100.

81. Vasilii Zen'kovskii, "Printsipy pravoslavnoi antropologii (prodolzhenie)" 76.

82. V. N. Voloshinov, *Marxism and the Philosophy of Language,* 14; *Marksizm i filosofiia iazyka,* 19.

83. Prat, "Orthodox Philosophy," 16.

84. The most significant passage in this regard from the chronotope essay has already been quoted. Another typical example of the numerous passages in "Discourse in the Novel" that make use of this vocabulary is Bakhtin's statement from the third chapter that in the novel heteroglossia is always personified, embodied [*voploshcheno*] in the individual images of people in all their contradictions (*Voprosy literatury i estetiki,* 139).

85. *Voprosy literatury i estetiki,* 398–99; *The Dialogic Imagination,* 250.

86. *Toward a Philosophy of the Act,* 65; "K filosofii postupka," 131.

87. *The Dialogic Imagination,* 84–85; *Voprosy literatury i estetiki.,* 235.

88. *Literaturno-kriticheskie stat'i,* 57; *Art and Answerability. Early Philosophical Essays by M. M. Bakhtin,* 287.

89. *Literaturno-kriticheskie stat'i,* 378–79; *The Dialogic Imagination,* 69.

ANSWERABILITY AND ETHICS: TOWARD A PHILOSOPHY OF ACTIVISM

1. S. G. Bocharov, "Vstupitel'naia zametka," 80–81.

2. Ibid., 81.

3. "K filosofii postupka," 97. All subsequent page references this chapter are to this text; when two numbers appear, the second is the Liapunov translation, *Toward a Philosophy of the Art.*

4. Aristotle, *Aristotle's Metaphysics,* trans. Apostle, 103–4.

5. Edmund Husserl, *The Paris Lectures,* 12–13.

6. Dostoevsky's narrator makes this statement in part 1, chapter 10 (Dostoevsky, *Zapiski iz podpol'ia*, 26).

7. For Bakhtin's critique of Kant's categorical imperative, see "K filosofii postupka," 100–102.

8. Clark and Holquist first discussed the sense of *sobtyie* as "co-being" in their study *Mikhail Bakhtin.*

9. Caryl Emerson, "Soloviev, the Late Tolstoy, and the Early Bakhtin on the Problem of Shame and Love," 663–71.

10. Vl. Solovyov, "Kant," 332.

11. An excellent example of this view is Skobtsova's statement that Solovyov believed Russians to be the only "organically Christian" nation (Skobtsova, *Mirosozertsanie Vl. Solov'eva,* 33).

12. Vl. Solovyov, *Dukhovnye osnovy obshchestva,* 137.

13. Solovyov, "Kant," 331–33.

14. Ibid., 333.

15. Vl. Solovyov, "The Idea of the Superman" (*Ideia sverkhcheloveka*), reprinted in *Izbrannoe*, 223, 225.

16. See Gary Saul Morson's articles "Bakhtin, Genres, and Temporality" (esp. 1071–76) and his "Bakhtin and the Present Moment," 201–22.

17. The translation is Liapunov's (*Art and Answerability: Early Philosophical Essays of M. M. Bakhtin,* 2).

18. Cf. similar statements in "Art and Answerability" about the integration of art and life.

19. Husserl, *Paris Lectures*, 12.

20. Henri Bergson, *Introduction to Metaphyisics,* 6.

21. The textual situation of the fragment of the first chapter of "Author and Hero in Aesthetic Activity" is unfortunately somewhat complicated. Two published versions of this piece exist, both published in 1986 and clearly reflecting the work of different editors. One of these was printed as an appendix to the first edition of "K filosofii postupka" and the other appeared in the Bakhtin anthology *Literaturno-kriticheskie stat'i.* Due to the vagaries of Soviet publishing and the fact that in neither edition is the

other acknowledged, it is impossible to say which takes precedent. Both versions clearly originate from the same manuscript since the wording and highlighting are absolutely identical and the notations of illegible words and sentences occur in exactly the same spots of the text. With one significant exception, all the differences between the two texts can be traced to different editorial decisions. In the yearbook edition many of the contiguous paragraphs reflecting shifts in argument are in the anthology edition merged together into longer sections, a sure sign that the former bears a strong editorial signature whereas the latter probably reflects the paragraph division found in the manuscript. Unlike the anthology edition, the yearbook piece begins with a sentence taken in medias res and the remainder of a paragraph that apparently mark the beginning of the extant manuscript. Presumably the anthology editors decided that such an abrupt beginning with unknown antecedents would be confusing to the reader and add nothing to a better understanding of the piece. The only substantial textual difference between the two editions is that the anthology contains two sentences absent from the yearbook. This spot occurs about two-thirds through the text at the end of a paragraph in both editions. The paragraph in the yearbook edition ends with the sentence "One can say the following: before occupying a purely aesthetic position in relation to the hero and his world, the author must occupy one that is purely life-oriented towards life" (153); the anthology, however, follows up this sentence and ends the paragraph with two more: "Rhthym, the object's moment of meaning [*smyslovoi moment*]. This is not a moment of the work, but of its object, of the world context [*mirovogo konteksta*]" (21). The only explanation for the elision of these two sentences in the yearbook edition is that of editorial carelessness. Since on the whole the anthology edition seems more reliable, it will be used in subsequent discussions of the piece.

22. On Tolstoy's appreciation of the poem, see Tomashevsky, *Pushkin.*

23. O. S. Murav'eva, "Ob osobennostiakh pushkinskoi liriki," 29.

24. Liapunov trans., 66.

25. S. I. Ozhegov, *Slovar' russkogo iazyka,* 18th ed., (Moscow: Russkii iazyk, 1986), 725.

26. Dal' gives the definition of *plontyi* as "sbityi, szhatyi, gustoi, soderzhashchii mnogo veshchestva (ploti?) v malom ob"eme" (*Tolkovyi slovar' zhivogo velikorusskogo iazyka,* 3:128).

27. *Literaturno-kriticheskie stat'i,* 10.

28. Ibid., 9.

THE RUSSIAN INTELLIGENTSIA: BAKHTIN'S IDEOLOGICAL CRITIQUE

1. M. M. Bakhtin and V. M. Duvakin, "Razgovory s Baktinym,"

Chelovek 4 (1993): 152.

2. Ibid., 152–53.

3. *Estetika slovesnogo tvorchestva*, 370–71.

4. "Uchenie zhe o dominante mozhet byt' *shiroko razrabotano i primenenot ne tol'ko* fiziologii." Russian State Library Archives, M. V. Yudina collection (fund 527), carton 4, item 1, pp. 52–53.

5. "Nash tsentr klassichskoi filologii" (Russian State Library Archives, M. V. Yudina collection [fund 527], carton 4, item 1, p. 37). On Tadeusz Zielinski and his possible influence on Bakhtin, see James C. Curtis, "Mikhail Bakhtin, Nietzsche, and Russian Pre-Revolutionary Thought," 344–51.

6. S. Bernshtein, "Tragicheskaia stranitsa iz istorii slavianskoi filologii," 77–82.

7. M. M. Bakhtin and V. M. Duvakin, "Razgovory s Baktinym," *Chelovek* 5 (1993): 140.

8. Ibid., 139–40.

9. Russian State Library Archives, M. V. Yudina collection (fund 527), carton 4, item 1, p. 36.

10. Russian State Library Archives, M. V. Yudina collection (fund 527), carton 5, item 4, p. 7.

11. A. Bely, "Pravda o russkoi intelligentsii: Po povodu sbornika *Vekhi*," 66.

12. St. Petersburg National Library, fund 474, album 1 (Medvedev), p. 24.

13. M. M. Bakhtin and V. M. Duvakin, "Razgovory s Baktinym," *Chelovek* 5 (1993): 140.

14. M. Bakhtin, *Art and Answerability*, 1; *Estetika slovesnogo tvorchestva*, 7.

15. *Estetika slovesnogo tvorchestva*, 7; *Art and Answerability*, 1.

16. *Art and Answerability*, 1; *Estetika slovesnogo tvorchestva*, 7.

17. Particularly revealing in this regard is a passage in which Bakhtin describes how the voices of other characters find their way into Raskolnikov's consciousness, resonanting in one consciousness and becoming mutually penetrable (*vzaimopronitsamymi*) to each other, intersecting (*peresekaiut*) each other (*Problemy poetiki Dostoevskogo*, 178)

18. G. W. F. Hegel, *Encyclopedia of Philosophy*, paragraph 164, pp. 154–55.

19. *Estetika slovesnogo tvorchestva*, 7; *Art and Answerability*. 1.

20. A. Umanskii, "Marksistskoe izuchenie literatury," 9.

21. *Art and Answerability*, 2; *Estetika slovesnogo tvorchestva*, 7.

22. The Pushkinist Blagoi summarizes the nineteenth- and early twentieth-century partisan appreciations of this poem (D. D. Blagoi, "Zhizn' i tvorchestvo Aleksandra Pushkina," 33–34). Tomashevsky takes the compelling position contrary to Bakhtin's that the figure of the poet is in fact not

opposed to the public virtues voiced by the rabble. On an ideological level, the opposition between the two characters is therefore far from clear-cut (Tomashevsky, *Pushkin,* 389).

23. *Art and Answerability,* 2; *Estetika slovesnogo tvorchestva,* 7.

24. *Estetika slovesnogo tvorchestva,* 7; *Art and Answerability,* 1.

25. *Estetika slovesnogo tvorchestva,* 8; *Art and Answerability,* 2.

26. M. Holquist, "Introduction: The Architectonics of Answerability," in *Art and Answerability,* xlii–iii.

27. The entire text is printed in S. S. Konkin and L. S. Konkin's *Mikhail Bakhtin. Stranitsy zhizni i tvorchestva,* 346–48.

28. One contributor to the rebutting 1910 volume *"Vekhi" kak znamenie vremeni* goes so far as to assert that, as exemplified by Mikhailovsky, the legacy of the Russian radical intelligentsia dealt with *lichnost'* far more successfully than the contributors to *Landmarks* (I. Brusilovskii, "K voprosu o lichnosti i obshchestvennosti, in *"Vekhi" kak znamenie vremeni,* 166).

29. Quoted by Florovsky in his history of Russian theology (*Puti russkogo bogosloviia,* 442).

30. Florenksy, *Stolp i utverzhdenie istiny,* 597.

31. This argument in Florensky's work is summarized by Gustav A. Wetter in his insightful essay "Russkaia religioznaia filosofiia i marksizma" (103).

32. Clark and Holquist, *Mikhail Bakhtin,* 121.

33. Ibid., 136. Holquist also points this out elsewhere in his " 'Bad Faith' Squared: The Case of M. M. Bakhtin" (223).

34. Clark and Holquist, *Mikhail Bakhtin,* 136–37.

35. From a letter quoted by Sergei Averintsev, which is apparently from the Florensky family archive (S. S. Averintsev, " 'Stroenie slova' P. A. Florenskogo," 344).

36. *Art and Answerability,* 2; *Estetika slovesnogo tvorchestva,* 8.

37. Florensky, *Sobranie sochinenii I: stat'i po iskusstvu,* 209.

38. Ibid., 210.

39. In the same section from which the passage above was taken, Florensky characterizes *litso* as an icon-painter's medium or preparatory sketch (*podrisovka*) for a ideal portrait (210). Later in the same article, he holds up art of the Renaissance and Reformation as failures at embodying the ontology of a sitter (259–63).

40. Quoted in Wetter, "Russkaia religioznaia," 102.

41. Several collections appeared that same year that dissented strongly with the views expressed in *Landmarks.* One of the most forthright, if not strident, was *"Vekhi" kak znamenie vremeni.*

42. V. I. Lenin, "O 'Vekhakh,' " 106–14. Every Soviet encyclopedia entry for *Landmarks* follows the lead of Lenin's article; a few examples from the 1960s are reprinted in a facsimile edition of the collection ("Vmesto

predisloviia," *Vekhi* [facs. ed., n.d.], pp. iii–viii). For a fuller and more recent elaboration of this political reading of *Landmarks* in specific reference to the "God-Seekers," see Semenkin's *Filosofiia bogoiskatel'stva. Kritika religiozno-filosofskikh idei sofiologov*, esp. 23–26. Some Western scholars have adopted a similar if nonmilitant interpretation by emphazing the importance of nationalism and cultural idealism for the *Landmarks* contributors, somewhat more evident in their other writings: see Jeffrey Brooks, "*Vekhi* and the *Vekhi* Dispute," 33–35.

43. Richard Pipes, "False Alarm," *National Review* (9 August 1993), 59.

44. A. Bely, "Pravda o russkoi intelligentsii: Po povodu sbornika *Vekhi,*" 68.

45. Leonard Schapiro, "The *Vekhi* Group and the Mystique of Revolution," 78–79. This 1955 article contains the best summary of the view of *Landmarks* as reformist and politically independent.

46. A recent example of this view articulated with regard to Bakhtin is Gary Saul Morson's "Prosaic Bakhtin: *Landmarks,* Anti-Intelligensialism, and the Russian Counter-Tradition," 35–74.

47. *Vekhi*, 3, 8–9.

48. *Landmarks*, 14; *Vekhi*, 13.

49. *Estetika slovesnogo tvorchestva,* 7.

50. *Vekhi,* 20.

51. Ibid., 171.

52. Ibid., 22.

53. Ibid., 47; *Landmarks,* 44.

54. *Vekhi,* 91. For other illuminating comments about the category of *lichnost'* in Gershenzon's controversial article, also see pp. 89 and 91 of the Russian text.

55. Ibid., 187–89.

56. *Vekhi,* 74; *Landmarks,* 68.

57. See K. G. Isupov, "Slovo kak postupok (o filosofskom uchenii A. A. Meiera)," 94–95; D. S. Likhachev, "Ob Aleksandre Meiere"; S. Danilskii, introduction to A. A. Meier's *Filosofskie sochineniia*, 7–10.

58. National State Library, Polovtsev collection (fund 601), item 1605, pp. 10, 11.

59. Ibid., 8–9

60. A. A. Meier, "Religioznyi smysl messianizma," 102–7.

61. National State Library, Polovtsev collection (fund 601), item 1586, pp. 64–65.

62. Florensky, "Zapiska o pravoslavii," 97–98.

63. Julien Benda, *The Treason of the Intellectuals*, 28–29.

64. K. G. Isupov, "Mikhail Bakhtin i Aleksandr Meier," in *M. M. Bakhtin*

i filosofkaia kul'tura XX veka. Problemy bakhtinologii. Vypusk pervy. Chast' 2. Sbornik nauchnykh statei, 68.

65. *The Dialogic Imagination,* 343.

66. "K filosofii postupka," 97. All subsequent page references in this chapter are to this text; if two numbers are given, the second is to the Liapunov translation, *Toward a Philosophy of the Act.*

67. *Estetika slovesnogo tvorchestva* 380.

68. *Art and Answerability,* 2.

69. Quoted in A. Walicki, *A History of Russian Thought from the Enlightenment to Marxism,* 443.

70. *Vekhi,* 93.

71. Ibid., 64–65.

72. Ibid., 68.

73. S. Bulgakov, "Ot avtora," in his *Ot marksizma k idealizmu. Sbornik statei (1896–1903),* vi–vii.

74. *Vekhi,* 208; *Landmarks,* 182.

75. See esp. 182–83 in *Vekhi.*

"WITHOUT CONFUSION OR SEPARATION": BALHTIN AND THE CHALCEDONIAN IDEAL OF THE DIVIDED UNION

1. Susan Stewart, "Shouts from the Street: Bakhtin's Anti-Linguistics," 266.

2. A. V. Kartashev, *Vselenskie sobory,* 273.

3. Ibid., 247–48.

4. Steven Cassedy, *Flight from Eden,* 119–20.

5. Kartashev, *Vselenskie sobory,* 270–73.

6. N. M. Minsky, *Religiia budushchego,* 64–66.

7. Ibid., 65. About Minsky and the Chalcedonian formula, see S. N. Broitman, "Istochniki formuly 'nesliianost' i nedazdel'nost" u Bloka," 80.

8. Broitman, "Istochniki formuly 'nesliianost' i nedazdel'nost" u Bloka," 80–81, 83, 87.

9. Ibid., 81–83.

10. Vl. Solovyov, *Sobranie sochinenii.* 1:390–91.

11. N. O. Lossky, "Mir kak organicheskoe tseloe," 238–40.

12. N. O. Lossky, "O sovremennom vitalizme," 142–44.

13. *Problemy poetiki Dostoevskogo,* 278. The translation is Caryl Emerson's *Problems of Dostoevsky's Poetics,* 208.

14. *Problemy poetiki Dostoevskogo,* 155–56.

15. Ibid., 277.

16. The statement also appears in the 1929 edition (*Problemy tvorchestva Dostoevskogo,* 42).

17. See, for example, *Problemy tvorchestva Dostoevskogo,* 139–40.

18. I. F. Stone, "Papal Metaphysics," 293.

19. National State Library, Polovtsev collection (fund 601), item 1605, p. 2.

20. Ibid., 6.

21. Bocharov stated to me that this conversation took place in 1972 (interview, 17 June 1994).

22. See chapter 9 ("Razryvy i sviazi") from Florovsky's book *Puti russkogo bogosloviia*, esp. 513–15.

23. For some commentary on the confluence of "God-Seeking" (*bogoiskatel'stvo*) and "God-building" (*bogostroitel'stvo*) with Russian Marxism, see Gustav A. Wetter, *Dialectical Materialism,* 90–91.

24. "Preniia po referatu," in Vl. Solovyov, *Izbrannoe,* 427, 432.

25. "K filosofii postupka," 83; *Toward a Philosophy of the Act,* 2–3.

26. M. M. Bakhtin, "Iz chernovykh tetradei," 156.

27. Solovyov, *Sobranie sochinenii,* 1:391.

28. Ibid., 395.

29. "The human personality is the possibility for the realization of an unlimited reality; [it is] a special form of limitless meaning" (*Chelovecheskaia lichnost' est' vozmozhnost' dlia osushchestvleniia neogranichennoi deistvitel'nosti, ili osobaia forma beskonechnogo soderzhaniia*). Quoted in A. N. Golubev, "Poniatie lichnosti v etike Vladimira Soloviova," 129.

30. N. Lossky, *Intutivnaia filosofiia Bergsona,* 74.

31. "K filosofii postupka," 91; *Toward a Philosophy of the Act,* 13.

32. S. L. Frank, *Nepostizhimoe,* 164, 191, 193, 264–65.

33. Vl. Solovyov, "Materiia, material'noe nachalo, materaial'naia prichina," 802.

34. M. M. Bakhtin, "Iz zametok o komicheskom (publikatsiia V. Kozhinova)," 223.

35. *Problemy poetiki Dostoevskogo,* 221; *Problems of Dostoevsky's Poetics,* 164.

36. The following passages represent only a few of the instances where the concept of *perichoresis* (or one very much like it) occurs in the 1963 edition, usually derived from the root *pronik-*: 79, 83–84, 114, 161, 164, 181, 211, 217.

37. See Robert Conquest, ed., *Religion in the USSR,* 47–61; and Dimitry Pospielovsky, *The Russian Church Under the Soviet Regime, 1917–1982,* 2:328–58.

38. Bakhtin explicitly associates the negative (*otrittsatel'noe*) with se-

riousnessness (*ser'eznost'*) in his posthumous piece "Iz zametok o komicheskom," 222.

39. *Problemy poetiki Dostoevskogo,* 6, 36; *Problems of Dostoevsky's Poetics,* 7, 26–27. The statements also occur in the 1929 edition (*Problemy tvorchestva Dostoevskogo,* 8, 42).

CARNIVAL AND EMBODIMENT IN *RABELAIS AND HIS WORLD*

1. See Clark and Holquist for an account of the journey of Bakhtin's Rabelais study from dissertation to book (*Mikhail Bakhtin,* 263, 322–25). The original copy of Bakhtin's thesis (in two volumes, with corrections written in what is very recognizably his own hand) is housed in the archive of the Institute of World Literature in Moscow (fund 427, inventory 1, item 19). Some notes for the dissertation have been preserved in the Manuscript Division of the Russian State Library Archives in Moscow (fund 527, carton 24, item 27). These notes (written in pencil and badly faded) are arranged according to chapter and are in many instances remarkably close to the final, typed, and corrected version of the thesis. Although not complete, for all intents and purposes they represent a draft.

2. Clark and Holquist, *Mikhail Bakhtin* 335.

3. "Stenogramma zasedaniia Uchenogo soveta Instituta mirovoi literatury im. A. M. Gor'kogo. Zashchita M. M. Bakhtinym dissertatsii *Rable v istorii realizma,*" 72–73.

4. *Rabelais and His World,* 304; *Tvorchestvo Fransua Rable i narodnaia kul'tura srednevekov'ia i renessansa,* 338. All subsequent page references in text for this chapter are to these two works, with the translation cited first.

5. *Tvorchestvo Fransua Rable,* 344. The translation of the latter term is Iswolsky's (*Rabelais and His World,* 309).

6. *Tvorchestvo Fransua Rable,* 12.

7. Clark and Holquist, *Mikhail Bakhtin,* 296.

8. In her translation Iswolsky leaves out the bodily acts of "growth, old age, sickness, death, physical torment [*rost, starost', bolezni, smert', rasterzanie*]." I have restored them to her rendering of this passage.

9. Clark and Holquist, *Mikhail Bakhtin,* 311–12.

10. Iswolsky neglects to translate Bakhtin's statement about the makeshift and unfinalized state of the body.

11. *Rabelais and His World,* 320.

12. The English renderings are taken from the King James Version.

13. "Plod" in the sense of the newborn animal is listed in Dal's *Tolkovyi slovar' zhivogo velikorusskogo iazyka,* 3:127. See also his entry for "oplodotvoriat'" (3:680).

14. Iswolsky elides Bakhtin's reference to the forms of literature (*v slovesnykh [formakh]*). I have restored it and modified her translation for syntactical purposes.

15. Iswolsky leaves out or mistranslates a few terms from this passage. She has a singular for the plural "reincarnations" and leaves out the adjective "multivalent." I have made the according changes in her translations of this segment.

16. Although Iswolsky's rendering of this term as "reincarnation" is felicitous and wise, its literal meaning is "re-embodiment" (*Rabelais and His World,* 39).

17. Interestingly, about fifteen years before Bakhtin began writing his dissertation on Rabelais the critic and aesthetician I. I. Lapshin defined a closely related term, *perevoploshchaemost'*, as the ability to transform oneself into another being's consciousness. Discussing this in terms that are highly reminiscent of the concept of the Husserlian concept of *Einfühlung* that Bakhtin invokes in "K filosofii postupka," Lapshin asserts that this transformation can only come about through a process of empathy (*protsess vchuvstvovaniia*), an approach, he states, that is particularly important for the professional actor. This use of *perevoploshchaemost'* is, of course, strikingly similar to Bakhtin's assertion that the mask is associated with the joy of change and reincarnation (Lapshin, *Khodozhestvennoe tvorchestvo*, 10–11, 84, 105, 113–66).

18. In her loose translation Iswolsky omits the term "word" (*slovo*), the subordinate construction "all notions about contemporary life," and misleadingly renders *vytravit'* (to exterminate, root up/out) as "to break up." I have made the necessary changes to her translation.

19. M. Vasmer, *Russisches Etymologisches Wörterbuch* 2:376.

20. To this translation I have restored several words that Iswolsky omitted.

21. See, for example, G. Hüttle-Worth, "Diglossiia v drevnei Rusi."

22. Gary Saul Morson and Caryl Emerson, *Mikhail Bakhtin: The Creation of a Prosaics*, 42.

23. Iswolsky omits several phrases and terms in this passage that I have had to restore to her translation because of their importance to my argument. She reduces the long italicized sentence in the passage to "[t]he boundaries between periods of time and between philosophies were actually realized." She also leaves out the second occurrence of the phrase "within the confines."

24. Iswolsky does not translate the last two clauses of the Russian text. Their translation in the quoted excerpt is mine.

25. The Iswolsky translation here is frustratingly inadequate, leaving out numerous phrases and inaccurately rendering several key terms. I have restored these in my paraphrase and quotation.

26. In her translation Iswolsky copes with this clause by eliding it altogether. She dilutes "istoricheskaia *smena iazykov*" into "historic change of language" and leaves out the rest of the sentence in its entirety (*Rabelais and His World,* 471).

27. *Tvorchestvo Fransua Rable,* 501.

28. Vl. Dal', *Tolkovyi slovar' zhivogo velikorusskogo iazyka,* 2:314.

THE WORD MADE AND UNMADE: RABELAIS, BAKHTIN, AND STALIN

1. Hélène Iswolsky's English translation appeared in 1968.

2. See Peter Stallybrass and Allon White, *The Politics and Poetics of Transgression.*

3. *Rabelais and His World,* 144; *Tvorchestvo Fransua Rable,* 158. All subsequent page references in text this chapter will be to these two works, with the translation cited first.

4. "Stenogramma zasedaniia Uchenogo soveta Instituta mirovoi literatury im. A. M. Gorkogo. Zashchita M. M. Bakhtinym dissertatsii *Rable v istorii realizma,*" 98.

5. Iswolsky does not translate the last sentence of this passage, which I have provided.

6. "Chelovek kak by pererozhdalsia dlia novykh, chisto chelovecheskikh otnoshenii. Otchuzhdenie vremenno ischezlo" (*Tvorchestvo Fransua Rable,* 15).

7. Iswolsky translates *molodost'* as "youth" (*Rabelais and His World,* 147), a misleading rendering, with an ambiguity in English that does not exist in Russian.

8. "Fransua Rable v istorii realizma," 152–53. *Tvorchestvo Fransua Rable,* 162–63; *Rabelais and His World,* 146–47. In her translation Iswolsky shifts around some of Bakhtin's statements.

9. "Fransua Rable v istorii realizma," Dissertation 37.

10. D. S. Likhachev and A. M. Panchenko, *"Smekhovoi mir" Drevnei Rusi;* D. S. Likhachev, ed., *Istoriia russkoi literatury X-XVII vekov,* 417–25. See also Likhachev's "Drevnerusskii smekh."

11. Iu. Lotman and B. Uspenskii. "Novye aspecty izucheniia kul'tury drevnei Rusi," 153–54.

12. Ibid., 160.

13. " 'Stenogramma zasedaniia Uchenogo soveta Instituta mirovoi literatury im. A. M. Gor'kogo," 81.

14. Vadim Kozhinov, "Bakhtin i ego chitateli. Razmyshleniia i otchasti vospominaniia," 147–48.

15. One example of an earlier version of this conception of an ordered yet nonhierarchical diversity can be found as early as *Problems of Dostoevsky's Art,* where Bakhtin describes the varied interactions among Dostoevsky's heroes: "Their consciousnesses, each with its own world, intersect [*skreshchivaetsia*]; their integral fields of vision intersect. At the points where their fields of vision intersect [*v tochke peresecheniia*] lie the culminating points of the novel" ("Three Fragments from the 1929 Edition *Problems of Dostoevsky's Art,*" in *Problems of Dostoevsky's Poetics,* trans. Emerson, 277; *Problemy tvorchestva Dostoevskogo,* 100).

16. Iswolsky singularizes "spheres" (*sfery*). I have inserted my correction into her translation.

17. Clark and Holquist, *Mikhail Bakhtin,* 311–12.

18. Caryl Emerson, "Preface to Mikhail K. Ryklin's 'Bodies of Terror,' " 48.

19. This view is most articulately expressed by Renate Lachman in her article "Bakhtin and Carnival: Culture as Counter-Culture." Lachman asserts that carnival represents the ideal of a "permanent revolution" against the reified dogmatism of the socialist revolution (123).

20. Among many others, the work of Robert Stam, Peter Stallybrass, and Allon White represent the liberationist view of Bakhtin's carnival.

21. Mikhail K. Ryklin, "Bodies of Terror: Theses Toward a Logic of Violence," 52; Russian text, "Tela terrora (tesisy k logike nasiliia)," 371.

22. Ryklin, "Bodies of Terror," 52 "Tela terrora," 61.

23. "Tela terrora," 62.

24. Ryklin, "Bodies of Terror," 55; "Tela terrora," 62.

25. "Tela terrora," 64.

26. Ibid., 76.

27. Ryklin, "Bodies of Terror," 54; "Tela terrora," 63–64.

28. Emerson, "Preface to Mikhail K. Ryklin's 'Bodies of Terror,' " 48.

29. Ibid., 12.

30. Clark and Holquist, *Mikhail Bakhtin,* 305–14.

31. Emerson, "Bakhtin and Women," 13.

32. Ibid., 13.

33. Pomerants, "Karnaval'noe i ser'eznoe," 109.

34. Ibid., 108–9, 115–16.

35. G. S. Pomerants, *Neopublikovannoe. Bol'shie i malen'kie esse. Publitsistika,* 236–37.

36. Pomerants, *Neopublikovannoe,* 237; "Karnaval'noe i ser'eznoe," 109.

37. D. Pospielovsky, "The Search for the Meaning of Life in the Soviet Union," 78.

38. Clark and Holquist, *Mikhail Bakhtin,* 310–16.

39. For a description of the dynamics of denunciation under Stalin and a detailed account of the Bukharin trial (among others) see Robert Conquest, *The Great Terror: A Reassessment,* 252–56, 364–74.

40. Mervyn Matthews, ed., *Soviet Government: A Selection of Official Documents on Internal Policies,* 241.

41. *Report of Court Proceedings in the Case of Anti-Soviet "Bloc of Rights and Trotskyites." Heard Before the Military Collegium of the Supreme Court of the U.S.S.R. Moscow, March 2–13, 1938. Verbatim Report.* (Moscow: People's Commissariat of Justice of the U.S.S.R., 1938), 696–97. For a further exploration of the purges from the perspective of Vyshinsky, see Vaksberg's *Tsaritsa dokazatel'stv: Vyshinskii i ego zhertvy,* esp. 81–83, 106–8, and 120.

42. "Fransua Rable v istorii realizma," 180–82.

43. Once again, Iswolsky has given an incomplete translation. Her most significant omission is the statement that "praise is filled with blame," which I have restored to this passage.

44. " 'Lobnoe mesto." *Entsiklopedicheskii slovar',* 70:886–87.

45. James George Frazer, *The Golden Bough,* 192–93.

46. "K filosofii postupka," 83.

47. Conquest, *The Great Terror,* 261–62.

48. *Tvorchestvo Fransua Rable,* 525.

49. Clark and Holquist, *Mikhail Bakhtin,* 306–7.

50. *Problemy poetiki Dostoevskogo,* 228.

51. "[V]ozmozhno, chto oni vse zhe poboialis' spetcifiki nekotoroi chasti materiala, khotia i ne khotiat v etom priznat'sia." "Ot publikatora," *Voprosy filosofii* 1 (1992): 134.

52. *Problems of Dostoevsky's Poetics,* 164; *Problemy poetiki Dostoevskogo,* 221.

53. Quoted in "Geraklit efesskii," *Bol'shaia sovetskaia entsiklopediia 10,* 74.

54. Julien Benda, *The Treason of the Intellectuals,* 35–36.

55. M. M. Bakhtin, "Dopolneniia i izmeneniia k 'Rable'," 135–37.

56. Ibid., 137.

57. M. M. Bakhtin, "Iz chernovykh tetradei," 153.

58. K. G. Isupov, "Smert' 'drugogo,' " 110–11.

59. Houston Baker, "The Promised Body: Reflections on Canon in an Afro-American Context," 352–53.

60. Ibid., 342–43.

61. M. M. Bakhtin, "Iz chernovykh tetradei," 158–59.

THE ETHICS OF AUTHORSHIP IN BAKHTIN'S LAST WRITINGS

1. Quoted from the introduction to Bakhtin's recently published letter from the sixties; see V. Kozhinov, ed. "Iz pisem M. M. Bakhtina," 175. Other accounts can be found in Kozhinov, "Bakhtin i ego chitateli. Razmyshleniia i otchasti vospominaniia," 143–45; and Clark and Holquist, *Mikhail Bakhtin,* 330–33.

2. M. M. Bakhtin, "Zametki," *Literaturno-kriticheskie stat'i,* 531. According to Bocharov and Kozhinov (the editors of this anthology of Bakhtin's articles), "Zametki" represents notes Bakhtin had written from the 1920s to 1974. Certain segments of these remarks had been published in the almanac *Den' poezii* in 1981 and 1984. Regrettably, neither in the earlier printings nor in the later anthology are any of the notes glossed for the dates of their writing either speculatively or in reference to manuscript evidence. Bocharov and Kozhinov apparently did adapt some kind of chronological ordering, inasmuch as the first section clearly consitutes some sort of draft or series of notes for "Toward a Philosophy of the Act" and subsequent ones follow a rough sequence corresponding to later stages in Bakhtin's career (that is, the novelistic word, Dostoevsky's polyphony, and so forth). Judging from the fact that Bakhtin's remarks about rebirth occur at the end of "Zametki" and in a section where he explicitly refers to Structuralism, it seems likely that these are the remarks that Bocharov and Kozhinov refer to as being written in 1974.

3. Bakhtin, *Estetika slovesnogo tvorchestva*, 424. In their notes to "Toward a Reworking" the editors of this volume quote from Bakhtin's letter to Kozhinov, dated 30 July 1963, which otherwise remains unpublished.

4. *Problems of Dostoevsky's Poetics,* 298; *Estetika slovesnogo tvorchestva*, 342–43. Subsequent page references in text this chapter are to these two works, with *Problems* cited first.

5. "K filosofii postupka," 113.

6. *Estetika slovesnogo tvorchestva,* 327.

7. Ibid.

8. Ibid.

9. "Toward a Reworking of the Dostoevsky Book," in *Problems of Dostoevsky's Poetics,* 284; *Problemy poetiki Dostoevskogo,* 327.

10. "Three Fragments from the 1929 Edition *Problems of Dostoevsky's Art,*" in *Problems of Dostoevsky's Poetics,* 276–77; *Problemy tvorchestva Dostoevskogo,* 100.

11. M. M. Bakhtin, "Toward a Reworking of the Dostoevsky Book," in *Problems of Dostoevsky's Poetics,* 284–85. *Estetika slovesnogo tvorchestva,* 327.

12. P. V. "Voploshchenie," *Entsiklopedicheskii slovar'*, 188. Charles Lock, "Carnival and Incarnation: Bakhtin and Orthodox Theology," 70–72.

13. Clark and Holquist, *Mikhail Bakhtin*, 248.

14. *Toward a Philosophy of the Act*, 16; "K filosofii postupka," 94–95.

15. M. M. Bakhtin and V. M. Duvakin, "Razgovory s Baktinym," *Chelovek* 1 (1994): 158, 161.

16. Ibid., 159. Leon Trotsky, *Terrorism and Communism*, trans. Max Shachtman, 63.

17. F. Burlatskii, "Khrushchev (Shtrikhi k politicheskomu portretu)," in Afanas'ev's collection *Inogo ne dano*, 433–35.

18. Ibid., 434.

19. "Iz chernovykh tetradei," 165.

20. From a letter dated 26 November 1960 ("Iz pisem M. M. Bakhtina," 176).

21. "K pererabotke knigi o Dostoevskom II," 75; "Iz chernovykh tetradei," 165. From all indications, the "Reworking" notes were composed sometime in the first half of 1961. In a letter dated 11 November 1961 he indicates that he is at work on the new carnival chapter (V. Kozhinov, ed., "Iz pisem M. M. Bakhtina," 179). Bakhtin passingly refers to Dostoevskian carnival in two footnotes to the Rabelais book (*Tvorchestvo Fransua Rable*, 91, 261).

22. *Problems of Dostoevsky's Poetics*, 239–40; *Problemy poetiki Dostoevskogo*, 321–22.

23. "Three Fragments from the 1929 Edition *Problems of Dostoevsky's Art*," in *Problems of Dostoevsky's Poetics*, 276–77; *Problemy tvorchestva Dostoevskogo*, 100.

24. *The Homilies of St. John Chrysostom*, 8; Ioann Zlatoust, *Tvoreniia. Tom vos'moi*, 18.

25. *The Homilies of St. John Chrysostom*, 17; Ioann Zlatoust, *Tvoreniia. Tom vos'moi*, 36.

26. *Problems of Dostoevsky's Poetics*, 105; *Problemy poetiki Dostoevskogo*, 140.

27. *The Homilies of St. John Chrysostom*, 16; Ioann Zlatoust, *Tvoreniia. Tom vos'moi*, 34–35.

28. See Arkhipiskop Mogilevskii Evsevii, *O pravoslavnoi vere. Kniga pervaia*, 107; and I. Bukharev, *Tolkovanie na Evangelie ot Ionna*, 11.

29. *The Dialogic Imagination*, 250; *Voprosy literatury i estetiki*, 399.

30. *Speech Genres and Other Late Essays*, trans. Vern W. McGee, 147; *Literaturno-kriticheskie stat'i*, 372. McGee has perpetrated a glaring mistranslation in one segment of this quotation. He writes that a code "also has cognitive, creative significance" whereas Bakhtin says the exact opposite,

placing a negative particle before the verb ("*ne* imeet"). I have corrected his translation.

31. *Speech Genres and Other Late Essays,* 147; *Literaturno-kriticheskie stat'i,* 371.

32. The following is a representative stanza from "The Ballad of Reading Gaol," published in 1898 shortly after Wilde's release from prison:

A prison wall was round us both,
Two outcast men we were:
The world had thrust us from its heart,
And God from out His care:
And the iron gin that waits for Sin
Had caught us in its snare.

(lines 169–73; Trilling and Bloom, eds. *Victorian Prose and Poetry,* 712)

Reading this, one almost expects the intervention of Grace.

33. M. M. Bakhtin, "Dopolneniia i izmeneniia k 'Rable,' " 136–37, 156.

34. Clark and Holquist, *Mikhail Bakhtin,* 340.

35. Ibid., 343.

36. *Estetika slovesnogo tvorchestva,* 377.

37. *Speech Genres and Other Late Essays,* 7; *Literaturno-kriticheskie stat'i,* 354.

38. G. Pomerants, "Novoe vremia muchenikov," in *Vokrug imeni ottsa Aleksandr,* ed. A. I. Zorin, and V. I. Iliushenko, 86–87.

Works Cited

THE WRITINGS OF BAKHTIN AND HIS CIRCLE

Bakhtin, M. M. "Dopolneniia i izmeneniia k 'Rable.'" *Voprosy filosofii* 1 (1992): 134–64.

———. *Estetika slovesnogo tvorchestva.* Moscow: Iskusstvo, 1987.

———. "Fransua Rable v istorii realizma." Ph.D. diss., Institute of World Literature, 1940. Institute of World Literature Archives (Moscow), fund 427, inventory 1, item 19. 2 vols.

———. "Iz chernovykh tetradei." *Literaturnaia ucheba* 5–6 (1992): 153–66.

———. "Iz zametok o komicheskom (publikatsiia V. Kozhinova)." In *Den' poezii 1986,* 222–23. Moscow: Sovetskii Pisatel, 1986.

———. "K filosofii postupka." In *Filosofiia i sotsiologiia nauki i tekhniki. Ezhegodnik 1984–1985,* 82–160. Moscow: Nauka, 1986.

———. "K pererabotke knigi o Dostoevskom II." *Dialog karnaval khronotop* 1 (1994): 70–82.

———. *Literaturno-kriticheskie stat'i.* Moscow: Khudozhestvennaia literatura, 1986.

———. *Problemy poetiki Dostoevskogo.* Moscow: Sovetskii Pisatel, 1963.

———. *Problemy tvorchestva Dostoevskogo.* Leningrad: Priboi, 1929.

———. *Tvorchestvo Fransua Rable i narodnaia kul'tura srednevekov'ia i renessansa.* Moscow: Khudozhestvennaia literatura, 1990.

———. *Voprosy literatury i estetiki.* Moscow: Khudozhestvennaia literatura, 1975.

Voloshinov, V. N. *Marksizm i filosofiia iazyka.* Leningrad: Priboi, 1929.

"Zapis' lektsii M. M. Bakhtina ob Andree Belom i F. Sologube. Publikatsiia S. Bocharova, kommentarii L. Silarda." *Studia Slavica Hungarica* 29 (1983): 374–83.

ARCHIVES

Institute of World Literature, Moscow.
National State Library, Saint Petersburg.
Russian State Library Archives, Moscow.
Russian State Archives of Literature and Art, Moscow.

CORRESPONDENCE

Kozhinov, V., ed. "Iz pisem M. M. Bakhtina." *Moskva* (November–December 1992): 175–82.

Kuznetsov, A. M., ed. "Iz perepiski M. V. Iudinoi i M. M. Bakhtina (1941–1966)." *Dialog karnaval khronotop* 4 (1993): 38–86.

Nevel'skaia, K., ed. "M. M. Bakhtin i M. I. Kagan (materialy semeinogo arkhiva)." In *Pamiat': Istoricheskii sbornik 4.* New York: YMCA Press, 1981: 249–81.

TRANSLATIONS

Bakhtin, M. M. *Art and Answerability: Early Philosophical Essays.* Translated by Vadim Liapunov. Austin: University of Texas Press, 1990.

———. *The Dialogic Imagination: Four Essays.* Translated by Michael Holquist and Caryl Emerson. Austin: University of Texas Press, 1981.

———. *Problems of Dostoevsky's Poetics.* Edited and translated by Caryl Emerson. Minneapolis: University of Minnesota Press, 1979.

———. *Rabelais and His World.* Translated by Hélène Iswolsky. Bloomington: Indiana University Press, 1984.

———. *Speech Genres and Other Late Essays.* Translated by Vern W. McGee. Austin: University of Texas Press, 1986.

———. *Toward a Philosophy of the Act.* Edited by Vadim Liapunov and Michael Holquist. Translated by Vadim Liapunov. Austin: University of Texas Press, 1993.

Voloshinov, V. N. *Marxism and the Philosophy of Language.* Translated by L. Matejka and I. R. Titunik. Cambridge: Harvard University Press, 1986.

INTERVIEWS

Bakhtin, M. M., and V. M. Duvakin. "Razgovory s Baktinym." *Chelovek* 3 (1993): 131–43; 4 (1993): 141–53; 1 (1994): 158–72; 3 (1994): 169–82; 4 (1994): 178–89; 1 (1995): 156–76.

"Stenogramma zasedaniia Uchenogo soveta Instituta mirovoi literatury im. A. M. Gor'kogo. Zashchita M. M. Bakhtinym dissertatsii *Rable v istorii realizma.*" *Dialog karnaval khronotop* 2–3 (1993): 55–101.

SUPPLEMENTARY SOURCES

Afanas'ev, Iu. N., ed., *Inogo ne dano: Glasnost, demokratiia, sotsializm.* Moscow: Progress, 1988.

Aristotle. *Aristotle's Metaphysics.* Translated by H. G. Apostle. Bloomington: Indiana University Press, 1966.

Aronowitz, Stanley. "Notes From Underground: Mikhail Bakhtin Changes the Face of Criticism," *Village Voice Literary Supplement* (March 1989): 22–24.

Augustine, Saint. *Tractates: On the Gospel of John 1–10.* Translated by John W. Rettig. Washington, D.C.: Catholic University Press of America, 1988.

Averintsev, S. S. "Lichnost' i talant uchenogo." *Literaturnoe obozrenie* 10–11 (1977): 58–61.

———. "Mikhail Bakhtin: Retrospektiva i perspectiva." *Druzhba narodov* 3 (1988): 256–59.

———. " 'Stroenie slova' P. A. Florenskogo." In *Kontekst 1972,* 343–47. Moscow, 1972.

Baker, Houston. "The Promised Body: Reflections on Canon in an Afro-American Context." *Poetics Today* 9, no. 2 (1988): 339–55.

Bely, Andrei. *Lug zelenyi. Kniga statei.* New York: Johnson Reprint, 1967.

———. "Pravda o russkoi intelligentsii: Po povodu sbornika *Vekhi.*" *Vesy* 5 (May 1909): 65–68.

Benda, Julien. *The Treason of the Intellectuals.* Translated by Richard Aldington. New York: Norton, 1969.

Bergson, Henri. *Introduction to Metaphysics.* New York: Philosophical Library, 1961.

Bernard-Donals, Michael. "Mikhail Bakhtin: Between Phenomenology and Marxism." *College English* 56, no. 2 (February 1994): 170–88.

Bernshtein, S. "Tragicheskaia stranitsa iz istorii slavianskoi filologii." *Slavianskoe slavianovedenie* 1 (1989): 77–82.

Berrong, Richard M. *Rabelais and Bakhtin: Popular Culture in "Garganutua and Pantagruel."* Lincoln: University of Nebraska Press, 1986.

Blagoi, D. D. "Zhizn' i tvorchestvo Aleksandra Pushkina." In *Sobranie sochinenii v shesti tomakh,* 1:3–76. Moscow: Pravda, 1969.

Bocharov, S. G. "Ob odnom razgovore i vokrug nego." *Novoe literaturnoe obozrenie* 2 (1993): 70–89.

———. "Sobytie bytiia." *Chelovek* 4 (1993): 137–40.

———. "Vstupitel'naia zametka." In *Filosofiia i sotsiologiia nauki i tekhniki. Ezhegodnik 1984–1985,* 80–82. Moscow: Nauka, 1986.

Bonetskaia, N. K. "M. Bakhtin v 1920-ye gody." *Dialog karnaval khronotop,* no. 1 (1994): 16–62.

———. "M. M. Bakhtin i traditsii russkoi filosofii." *Voprosy filosofii* 1 (1993): 83–93.

Broitman, S. N. "Istochniki formuly 'nesliianost' i nedazdel'nost' u Bloka." In *Aleksandr Blok: Issledovaniia i materialy*, 79–88. Leningrad: Nauka, 1987.

Brooks, Jeffrey. "*Vekhi* and the *Vekhi* Dispute." *Survey* 19, no. 1 (1973): 21–50.

Bukharev, A. M. [Arkhimandrit Fedor]. *O dukhovnykh potrebnostiakh zhizni.* Moscow: Stolitsa, 1991.

Bukharev, I. *Tolkovanie na Evangelie ot Ionna.* Moscow, 1915.

Bulgakov, Sergei. *Ot marksizma k idealizmu. Sbornik statei (1896–1903).* Saint Petersburg, 1903.

———. "Was ist das Wort?" In *Festschrift T. J. Masaryk zum 80. Geburstag,* 1:25–46. Prague, 1930.

Cassedy, Steven. "Bely's Theory of Symbolism as a Formal Iconics of Meaning." In *Andrei Bely: Spirit of Symbolism,* edited by John E. Malmstad, 285–312. Ithaca, N.Y.: Cornell University Press, 1987.

———. *Flight from Eden: The Origins of Modern Literary Criticism and Theory.* Berkeley and Los Angeles: University of California Press, 1990.

Chaadaev, Peter [*sic*] Yakovlevich. *Philosophical Letters and Apology of a Madman.* Translated by Mary-Barbara Zeldin. Knoxville: University of Tennessee Press, 1969.

Clark, Katarina, and Michael Holquist. "A Continuing Dialogue." *Slavic and East European Journal* 30, no. 1 (Spring 1986): 96–102.

———. *Mikhail Bakhtin.* Cambridge, Mass.: Harvard University Press, 1984.

Conquest, Robert. *The Great Terror: A Reassessment.* Oxford: Oxford University Press, 1990.

———, ed. *Religion in the USSR.* London: Bodley Head, 1968.

Curtis, James E. "Mikhail Bakhtin, Nietzsche, and Russian Pre-Revolutionary Thought." In *Nietzsche in Russia,* edited by Bernice Glazer Rosenthal, 331–54. Princeton, N.J.: Princeton University Press, 1986.

Dal', Vladimir. *Tolkovyi slovar' zhivogo velikorusskogo iazyka.* Saint Petersburg, 1881.

Davydov, Iu. N. "U istokov sotsial'noi filosofii M. M. Bakhtina." *Sotsialogicheskie issledovaniia* 2 (1986): 170–81.

Davydov, Iu. N., and Aleksandr Arkhangel'skii. "Vse vzyvaet k postupku." *Literaturnoe obozrenie* 2 (1987): 102–7.

Dillon, John. "Logos and Trinity: Patterns of Platonist Influence on Early Christianity." In *The Philosophy in Christianity,* edited by Godfrey Vesey, Cambridge: Cambridge University Press, 1989.

Dostoevsky, F. M. *Zapiski iz podpol'ia.* Ann Arbor, Mich.: Ardis, 1982.

Eagleton, Terry. "Saint Oscar: A Forward." *New Left Review* 177 (September–October 1989): 125–28.

Emerson, Caryl. "Bakhtin and Women: A Non-Topic with Immense Implications." Paper presented at the conference "Glasnost in Two Cultures," New York Institute for the Humanities, 22 March 1991.

———. "Keeping the Self Intact During the Culture Wars: A Centennial Essay for Mikhail Bakhtin." *New Literary History* 27 (1996): 107–26.

———. "The Politics of Mikhail Bakhtin." Paper presented at the Williams College Seminar, Williamstown, Mass., 27 February 1990.

———. "Preface to Mikhail K. Ryklin's 'Bodies of Terror,'" *New Literary History* 24, no. 1 (Winter 1993): 45–49.

———. "Problems with Bakhtin's Poetics." *Slavic and East European Journal* 32, no. 4 (Winter 1988): 503–25.

———. "Russian Orthodoxy and the Early Bakhtin." *Religion and Literature* 22, nos. 2–3 (Summer–Autumn 1990): 109–30.

———. "Soloviev, the Late Tolstoy, and the Early Bakhtin on the Problem of Shame and Love." *Slavic Review* 50, no. 3 (Fall 1991): 663–71.

———. "Translating Bakhtin: Does His Theory of Discourse Contain a Theory of Translation?" *Revue de l'Université d'Ottawa* 53, no. 1 (1983): 23–31.

———. "Perevodimost'." *Slavic and East European Journal* 38, no. 1 (Spring 1994): 84–89.

Epiphanius the Wise [Premudryi]. "Zhitie Stefana Permskogo." In *Khroestomatiia po drevnei russkoi literature XX–XVII vekov,* edited by N. K. Gudzii, 101–09. 5th ed. Moscow: Uchpedgiz, 1952.

Evsevii, Arkhipiskop Mogilevskii. *O pravoslavnoi vere. Kniga pervaia.* Saint Petersburg, 1863.

Fedotov, G. "Otvet N. A. Berdiaevu." *Za svobodu: Izdanie N'iu-Iorkskoi partii sotsialistov-revoliutsionerov* 17 (September 1946): 57–69.

———. *Stikhi dukhovnye: Russkaia narodnaia vera po dukhovnym stikham.* Moscow: Gnosis, 1991.

Florensky, Pavel. "Khristianstvo i kul'tura." *Simvol* 21 (June 1989): 69–83.

———. *Sobranie sochinenii I: stat'i po iskusstvu.* Paris: YMCA-Press, 1985.

———. *Stolp i utverzhdenie istiny.* Moscow, 1914.

———. "Stroenie slova." In *Kontekst 1972,* 348–75. Moscow, 1973.

———. "Zapiska o pravoslavii." *Simvol* 21 (June 1989): 91–98.

Florovsky, George. *Puti russkogo bogosloviia.* Paris: YMCA-Press, 1983.

Ford, J. Massyngberde, "Commentary." *The Anchor Bible.* Vol. 38, *Revelation,* 313–25. Garden City, N.Y.: Doubleday, 1975.

Frank, S. L. *Nepostizhimoe. Ontologishekoe vvedenie v filosofiiu religii.* Paris, 1939.

Frazer, James George. *The Golden Bough. A Study in Magic and Religion.* Abridged ed. New York: Macmillan, 1951.

Gachev, Georgii. Preface to Turbin's "'Golod i bol' Mikhaila Bakhtina." *Literanaia gazeta* 24 (15 June 1994): 6.

"Geraklit efesskii." In *Bol'shaia sovetskaia entsiklopediia 10,* 74–75. Moscow: Sovetskaia entsiklopediia, 1952.

Godzich, Wlad. "Correcting Kant: Bakhtin and Cultural Interactions." *Boundary 2* 18, no. 1 (Spring 1991): 5–17.

———. Foreword to *The Formal Method in Literary Scholarship,* by M. M. Bakhtin and P. N. Medvedev. Translated by Albert J. Wehrle, vii–xiv. Cambridge, Mass.: Harvard University Press, 1985.

Golubev, A. N. "Poniatie lichnosti v etike Vladimira Soloviova." *Voprosy filosofii* 3 (1978): 125–36.

The Greek New Testament. Edited by R. V. G. Tasker. Oxford: Clarendon Press, 1964.

Gumilev, Nikolai. *Sobranie sochinenii v chetyrekh tomakh.* Vol. 2. Washington, D.C.: Victor Kamkin, 1964.

Hegel, G. W. F. *Encyclopedia of Philosophy.* Translated by Gustav Emil Mueller. New York: Philosophical Library, 1959.

Hirschkop, Ken. "Bakhtin, Discourse and Democracy." *New Left Review* 160 (December 1986): 92–113.

Hirschkop, Ken, and David Shepherd, "Bakhtin and the Politics of Criticism." *PMLA* 109, no. 1 (January 1994): 117.

Holquist, James M., and Katarina Clark. "The Influence of Kant in the Early Work of M. M. Bakhtin." In *Literary Theory and Criticism. Part I,* edited by Joseph P. Strelka, 299–313. Bern: Peter Lang, 1984.

———, eds. *Bakhtin and Cultural Theory.* Manchester: Manchester University Press, 1989.

Holquist, Michael. "'Bad Faith Squared': The Case of M. M. Bakhtin." In *Russian Literature and Criticism: Selected Papers from the Second World Congress for Soviet and East European Studies,* edited by Evelyn Bristol, 214–34. Berkeley, Calif.: Berkeley Slavic Specialties, 1982.

———. "Bakhtin, Mikhail Mikhailovich." In *Handbook of Russian Literature,* edited Victor Terras, 34–36. New Haven, Conn.: Yale University Press, 1985.

———. *Dialogism: Bakhtin and His World.* London: Routledge, 1990.

———. Introduction to *Speech Genres and Other Late Essays,* by M. M. Bakhtin. Translated by Vernon W. McGee, ix–xxiii. Austin: University of Texas Press, 1986.

———. "Politics of Representation." *Allegory and Representation,* edited by Stephen J. Greenblatt, 163–83. Baltimore: Johns Hopkins University Press, 1981.

Howard, Wilbert F. "John: Introduction." In *The Interpreter's Bible.* Vol. 8, *The Gospel According to Luke. The Gospel According to John,* 437–63. New York: Abingdon Press, 1952.

Husserl, Edmund. *The Paris Lectures.* Translated by Peter Koestenbaum. The Hague: Martinus Nijhoff, 1967.

Hüttle-Worth, Gretta. "Diglossiia v drevnei Rusi." *Wiener Slavisitisches Jahrbuch* 24 (1978): 108–23.

Inge, W. R. "Logos." In *Encyclopedia of Religion and Ethics,* edited by James Hustings, 8:133–38. Edinburgh: T. and T. Clark, 1915.

Ill'inskii, Oleg. "Religioznye vzgliady rannego Bakhtina." *Russkoe vozrozhdenie. Nezavisimtyi russkii pravoslavmyi zhurnal* 31 (1988): 59–70.

Isupov, K. G. "Slovo kak postupok (o filosofskom uchenii A. A. Meiera)." *Voprosy filosofii* 7 (1992): 93–102.

———. "Smert' 'drugogo.'" In *Bakhtinologiia: issledovaniia, perevody, publikatsii,* 103–16. Saint Petersburg: Atelei, 1995.

Ivanov, Viach. Vs. "O Bakhtine i semiotike." *Rossiia/Russia* 2, 284–97. Turin: Giulio Einaudi, 1975.

"K biografii M. M. Bakhtina. Vstuplenie, publikatsiia i primechanie V. Laptuna. Posleslovie S. Bocharova." *Voprosy literatury* 3 (March 1991): 128–41.

Karpunov, K. G., et al., eds. *Mikhail Mikhailovich Bakhtin v Saranske. Ocherki zhizni i deiatel'nosti.* Saransk: Izd. Saratovskogo universiteta, 1989.

Kartashev, A. V. *Vselenskie sobory.* Moscow: Respublika, 1994.

Kelly, C., M. Makin, and D. Shepard, eds. *Discontinuous Discourses in Modern Russian Literature.* New York: St. Martin's, 1989.

"Khalkiedonskii sobor." *Entsiklopedicheskii slovar'* 73:21–22. Saint Petersburg, 1903.

Khoruzhii, S. S. *Posle pereryva, puti russkoi filosofii.* Saint Petersburg: Ateleia, 1994.

Konkin, S. S., and L. S. Konkin. *Mikhail Bakhtin. Stranitsy zhizni i tvorchestva.* Saransk: Mordovskoe knizhnoe izdatal'stvo, 1993.

Kozhinov, Vadim. "Bakhtin i ego chitateli. Razmyshleniia i otchasti vospominaniia." *Moskva* (July 1992): 143–51.

———. "Bakhtinskaia kontsepsiia liricheskoi poezii." In *Den' poezii 1986,* 220–21. Moscow: Sovetskii Pisatel, 1986.

———. "Tak eto bylo . . ." *Don* 10 (1988): 156–60.

Kristeva, Julia. "The Ruins of a Poetics." In *Russian Formalism,* edited by S. Bann and J. E. Bowlt, 19–28. Edinburgh: Scottish Academic Press, 1973.

Lachmann, Renate. "Bakhtin and Carnival: Culture and Counter-Culture." *Cultural Critique* 11 (Winter 1988–89): 115–52.

Landmarks: A Collection of Essays on the Russian Intelligentsia, 1909. Edited by Boris Shragin and Albert Todd. Translated by Marian Schwartz. New York: Karz Howard, 1977.

Lapshin, I. I. *Khodozhestvennoe tvorchestvo.* Saint Petersburg, 1923.

Le Guillou, M. J. *The Spirit of Eastern Orthodoxy.* Translated by Donald Attwater. Glen Rock, N.J.: Paulist Press, 1964.

Lenin, V. I. "O 'Vekhakh.'" *Sochineniia,* 16:106–14. 4th ed. By Lenin. Moscow: Gos. izdat. politicheskoi literatury, 1941–67.

Leporskii, P. "Troitsa." In *Entsiklopedicheskii slovar',* 66:866–72. Saint Petersburg, 1901.

Likhachev, D. S. "Drevnerusskii smekh." In *Problemy poetiki i istorii literatury. Sbornik statei v chest' 75-letiia M. M. Bakhtina,* 73–90. Saransk, 1973.

———. "Ob Aleksandre Meiere." *Voprosy filosofii* 7 (1992): 92–93.

———, ed. *Istoriia russkoi literatury X–XVII vekov.* Moscow: Prosveshchenie, 1980.

Likhachev, D. S., and A. M. Panchenko. *"Smekhovoi mir" Drevnei Rusi.* Leningrad, 1976.

"Lobnoe mesto." *Entsiklopedicheskii slovar',* 70:886–87. Saint Petersburg, 1896.

Lock, Charles. "Carnival and Incarnation: Bakhtin and Orthodox Theology." *Journal of Literature and Theology* 5, no. 1 (March 1991): 68–82.

Long, A. A. *Hellenistic Philosophers: Stoics, Epicureans, Sceptics.* 2d ed. Berkeley and Los Angeles: University of California Press, 1986.

Losev, Lev. *Filosofiia imeni.* Moscow, 1927.

Lossky, N. O. *Dostoevskii i ego khristianskoe miroponimanie.* New York: Izdatel'stvo imeni Chekhova, 1953.

———. *Intuivnaia filosofiia Bergsona.* Saint Petersburg, 1922.

———. "Mir kak organicheskoe tseloe." *Voprosy filosofii i psikhologii* 1–4 (1915): 87–98, 99–152, 203–43.

———. "O sovremennom vitalizme." *Dialog Karnaval Khronotop* 4 (1993): 116–50.

Lotman, Iu., and B. Uspenskii. "Novye aspecty izucheniia kul'tury drevnei Rusi." *Voprosy literatury* 3 (1977): 148–66.

M. M. Bakhtin i filosofkaia kul'tura XX veka. Problemy bakhtinologii. Vypusk pervy. Chast' 2. Sbornik nauchnykh statei. Saint Petersburg: Obrazovanie, 1991

Mandelker, Amy. "Semiotizing the Sphere: Organicist Theory in Lotman, Bakhtin and Vernadsky." *PMLA* 38, no. 1 (May 1994): 385–96.

Mandel'shtam, Osip. *Sobranie sochinenii v trekh tomakh.* Vol. 4. New York: Inter-language Literary Associates, 1971.

Markov, Vladimir. *Russian Futurism: A History.* Berkeley and Los Angeles: University of California Press, 1968.

———, ed. *Manifesty i programmy russkikh futuristov.* Munich: Wilhelm Fink, 1967.

Mathiesen, Robert. "Bible, Church Slavonic." In *The Modern Encyclopedia of Russian and Soviet Literature,* 3:5–12. Gulf Breeze, Fla.: Academic Press International, 1979.

Matthews, Mervyn, ed. *Soviet Government: A Selection of Official Documents on Internal Policies.* New York: Taplinger, 1974.

Matthiessen, F. O., ed. *The James Family. Including Selections From the Writings of Henry James, Senior, William, Henry and Alice James.* New York: Knopf, 1961.

Meier, A. A. *Filosofskie sochineniia.* Paris: Presse Libre, 1982.

———. "Peterburgskoe Religioznoe-filosofskoe obshchestvo." *Voprosy filosofii* 7 (1992): 107–15.

———. "Religioznyi smysl messianizma." *Voprosy filosofii* 7 (1992): 102–7.

Minsky, N. M. *Religiia budushchego: Filosofskie razgovory.* Saint Petersburg, 1905.

Morson, Gary Saul. "Bakhtin and the Present Moment." *American Scholar* 60, no. 2 (Spring 1991): 201–22.

———. "Bakhtin, Genres, and Temporality." *New Literary History* 22 (1991): 1071–89.

———. "The Bakhtin Industry." *Slavic and East European Journal* 30, no. 1 (Spring 1986): 81–90.

———. "Prosaic Bakhtin: *Landmarks*, Anti-Intelligentsialism, and the Russian Counter-Tradition." *Common Knowledge* 21, no. 1 (Spring 1993): 35–74.

———, ed. *Bakhtin: Essays and Dialogues on His Work.* Chicago: University of Chicago Press, 1986.

Morson, Gary Saul, and Caryl Emerson. *Mikhail Bakhtin: The Creation of a Prosaics.* Stanford, Calif.: Stanford University Press, 1990.

———, eds. *Rethinking Bakhtin: Extensions and Challenges.* Evanston, Ill.: Northwestern University Press, 1989.

Murav'eva, O. S. "Ob osobennostiakh pushkinskoi liriki." In *Pushkin. Issledovaniia i materialy 13,* 21–32. Leningrad: Nauka, 1989.

Nabokov, Vladimir. "Translator's Foreword." In *A Hero of Our Time. A Novel by Mikhail Lermontov,* Vladimir Nabokov and Dmitri Nabokov, v–xix. Garden City, N.Y.: Doubleday Anchor Books, 1958.

Nilsson, Nils Åke. "The Dead Bees: Notes on a Poem by Nikolaj Gumilev." In *Orbis Scriptus: Dmitrij Tzchizevskij. Zum 70. Geburstag,* edited by D. Gerhardt et al., 573–80. Munich: Wilhelm Fink, 1966.

"Ot publikatora." *Voprosy filosofii* 1 (1992): 134.

Patrick, G. T. W., ed. and trans. *Heraclitus of Ephesus.* Chicago: Argonaut, 1969.

Pelikan, Jaroslav. "Divinity Made Human: Aesthetic Implications of the Incarnation." In his *Imago Dei: The Byzantine Apologia for Icons,* 67–98. Princeton, N.J.: Princeton University Press, 1990.

———. *The Emergence of the Catholic Tradition (100–600).* Chicago: University of Chicago Press, 1971.

———. *The Spirit of Eastern Christendom (600–1700).* Chicago: University of Chicago Press, 1974.

Pépin, Jean. "Logos." In *Encyclopedia of Religion,* edited by Mircea Eliade, 9:10–15. New York: Macmillan, 1987.

Picchio, Riccardo. "The Function of Biblical Thematic Clues in the Literary Code of 'Slavia Orthodoxa.'" *Slavia Hierosolymitana* 1 (1977): 1–31.

Pomerants G. S. "Karnaval'noe i ser'eznoe." *Narody Azii i Afriki* 2 (February 1968): 107–16.

———. *Neopublikovannoe. Bol'shie i malen'kie esse. Publitsistika.* Frankfurt am Main: Possev, 1972.

Pospielovsky, Dimitry. *A History of Marxist-Leninist Atheism and Soviet Antireligious Policies.* Vol. 1. New York: St. Martin's, 1987.

———. *The Russian Church Under the Soviet Regime, 1917–1982.* Vols. 1 and 2. Crestwood, N.Y.: Saint Vladimir's Seminary Press, 1984.

———. "The Search for the Meaning of Life in the Soviet Union." *St. Vladimir's Theological Quarterly* 18, nos. 3–4 (1974): 69–95.

Prat, Naftali. "Orthodox Philosophy of Language in Russia." *Studies in Soviet Thought* 20 (1979): 1–21.

Pushkin, A. S. *Sobranie sochinenii v shesti tomakh.* Moscow: Pravda, 1969.

Report of Court Proceedings in the Case of Anti-Soviet "Bloc of Rights and Trotskyites." Heard Before the Military Collegium of the Supreme Court of the U.S.S.R. Moscow, March 2–13, 1938. Verbatim Report. Moscow: People's Commissariat of Justice of the U.S.S.R., 1938.

Ryklin, Mikhail K. "Bodies of Terror: Theses Toward a Logic of Violence." *New Literary History* 24, no. 1 (Winter 1993): 51–74.

———. "Tela torrora (tesisy k logike nasiliia)." *Bakhtinskii sbornik,* 1:60–75. Moscow, 1990.

Rzhevsky, Nicholas. "Kozhinov on Bakhtin." *New Literary History* 25 (1994): 429–44.

Schapiro, Leonard. "The *Vekhi* Group and the Mystique of Revolution." In his *Russian Studies,* edited by Ellen Dahrendorff, 68–92. New York: Viking Penguin, 1988.

Semenkin, N. S. *Filosofiia bogoiskatel'stva. Kritika religiozno-filosofskikh idei sofiologov.* Moscow: Potitizdat, 1986.

Shklovsky, Victor. "The Resurrection of the Word." In *Russian Formalism,* edited by S. Bann and J. Bowlt, 41–47. New York: Barnes and Noble Books, 1973.

———. "Voskreshenie slova." In *Texte der Russiachen Formalisten,* edited by Jurij Striedter, 2:2–17. Munich: Wilhelm Fink, 1972.

———. *Zhili-byli. Vospominaniia. Memuarnye zapisi.* Moscow: Sovetskii pisatel, 1966.

Shpet, Gustav. *Vnutrenniaia forma slova.* Moscow, 1927.

Shukman, Anne. "M. M. Bakhtin: Notes on His Philosophy of Man." In *Poetry, Prose, and Public Opinion: Aspects of Russia, 1850–1970. Essays Presented In Memory of Dr. N. E. Andreyev,* edited by William Harrison and Avril Pyman, 241–50. Letchworth, United Kingdom: Avebury, 1984.

Skobtsova, E. *Mirosozertsanie Vl. Solov'eva.* Paris: YMCA Press, 1929.

Sluzhebnik. Belgrade: Sveti Arhijirejski Sinod, 1983.

Solovyov, Vladimir. *Dukhovnye osnovy obshchestva.* Brussels, 1958.

———. *Izbrannoe.* Moscow: Sovetskaia Rossiia, 1990.

———. "Kant." In *Entsiklopedicheskii slovar',* 27:321–39. Saint Petersburg, 1895.

———. "Krasota." In *Entsiklopedicheskii slovar',* 32:321. Saint Petersburg, 1895.

———. "Materiia, material'noe nachalo, materaial'naia prichina." In *Entsiklopedicheskii slovar',* 36:802–3. Saint Petersburg, 1896.

———. *Sobranie sochinenii.* Vol. 1. Moscow: Mysl', 1989.

———. *Sobranie sochinenii.* Vol. 10. 2d ed. Saint Petersburg: Prosveshchenie, 1911–14.

Stallybrass, Peter, and Allon White. *The Politics and Poetics of Transgression.* Ithaca, N.Y.: Cornell University Press, 1986.

Stam, Robert. "Mikhail Bakhtin and Left Cultural Critique." In *Post-modernism and Its Discontents: Theories, Practices,* edited by E. Ann Kaplan, 116–45. New York: Verso Books, 1988.

———. "On the Carnivalesque." *Wedge* 1 (1982): 47–55.

Stewart, Susan. "Shouts from the Street: Bakhtin's Anti-Linguistics." *Critical Inquiry* 10, no. 2 (December 1983): 265–81. Reprinted in *Bakhtin: Essays and Dialogues on His Work,* edited by Gary Saul Morson, 41–57. Chicago: University of Chicago Press, 1986.

Stone, I. F. "Papal Metaphysics." *The Nation* (26 September 1987): 292–93.

Stupart, G. T., trans. *The Homilies of St. John Chrysostom. On the Gospel of St. John.* Oxford: J. H. Parker, 1848–52.

Terras, Victor. "Osip Mandel'shtam i ego filosofiia slova." In *Slavic Poetics: Essays in Honor of Kiril Taranovsky,* edited by Roman Jakobson et al., 455–60. The Hague: Mouton, 1973.

Titunik, I. R. "The Bakhtin Problem: Concerning Katarina Clark's and Michael Holquist's *Mikhail Bakhtin." Slavic and East European Journal* 30, no. 1 (Spring 1986): 91–95.

Thompson, Ewa W. *Russian Formalism and Anglo-American New Criticism: A Comparative Study.* The Hague: Mouton, 1971.

Todorov, Tzvetan. "Human and Interhuman: Mikhail Bakhtin." In his *Literature and its Theorists. A Personal View of Twentieth-Century Criticism,* translated by Catherine Porter, 70–88. Ithaca, N.Y.: Cornell University Press, 1987.

———. *Mikhail Bakhtin: The Dialogical Principle.* Translated by Wlad Godzich. Minneapolis: University of Minnesota Press, 1984.

Tomashevsky, B. *Pushkin. Kniga vtoraia. Materialy k biografii (1824–1837).* Moscow and Leningrad: Akademiia nauk SSSR, 1961.

Trilling, Lionel, and Harold Bloom, eds. *Victorian Prose and Poetry.* New York: Oxford University Press, 1973.

Trotsky, Leon. *Literatura i revoliutsiia.* Leningrad, 1924.

———. *Terrorism and Communism.* Translated by Max Shachtman. Ann Arbor: University of Michigan Press, 1969.

Trubetskoi, S. "Filon Aleksandriiskii." *Entsiklopedicheskii slovar',* 70:819–20. Saint Petersburg, 1902.

———. "Logos." In *Entsiklopedicheskii slovar',* 900–901. Saint Petersburg, 1896.

Turbin, Vladimir. "Golod i bol' Mikhaila Bakhtina." *Literaturnaia gazeta* 24 (15 June 94): 6.

Ugolnik, Anthony. *The Illuminated Icon.* Grand Rapids, Mich.: Eerdmans, 1989.

Umanskii, A. "Marksistskoe izuchenie literatury." *Put' bor'by. Rabochaia kniga po literature dlai rabfakov, shkol vzroslykh i dlia samoobrazovaniia. Chast' pervaia,* edited by N. Kreminskii et al., 9–17. Moscow: Doloi negramatnost', 1927.

Vaksberg, Arkady. *Stalin's Prosecutor: The Life of Andrei Vyshinsky.* Translated by Jan Butler. New York: Grove Weidenfeld, 1991.

———. *Tsaritsa dokazatel'stv: Vyshinskii i ego zhertvy.* Moscow: Kniga i biznes, 1992.

Vasmer, Max. *Russisches Etymologisches Wörterbuch* 2. Heidelberg: Carl Winter, 1953.

"Vekhi" kak znameni vremeni. Sbornik statei. Moscow: Zveno, 1910.

Vekhi: Sbornik statei o russkoi intelligentsii N. A. Berdiaeva, S. N. Bulgakova, M. O. Gershenzona, A. S. Izgoeva, B. A. Kistiakovskogo, P. B. Struve, S. L. Franka. 2d ed. Moscow, 1909.

Voloshin, Maksimilian. "Horomedon." *Zolotoe runo* 11–12 (1909): 55–60.

"Voploshchenie" [P.V.] *Entsiklopedicheskii slovar',* 13 (1892): 188.

Vygotsky, L. S. *Myshlenie i rech'. Izbrannye issledovaniia.* Moscow, 1956.

Walicki, Andrzej. *A History of Russian Thought from the Enlightenment to Marxism.* Translated by Hilda Andrews-Rusiecka. Stanford, Calif.: Stanford University Press, 1979.

Ware, Kallistos. *The Orthodox Way.* Crestwood, N.Y.: St. Vladimir's Seminary Press, 1986.

Wetter, Gustav A. *Dialectical Materialism.* Translated by Peter Heath. New York: Praeger, 1958.

———. "Russkaia religioznaia filosofiia i marksizma." In *Russkaia religiozno-filosofskaia mysl' XX veka,* edited by Nikolai P. Poltoratzky, 104–20. Pittsburgh: University of Pittsburgh Press, 1966.

White, Allon. "The Struggle Over Bakhtin: Fraternal Reply to Robert Young." *Cultural Critique* 8 (Winter 1987–88): 221–24.

Williams, Raymond. "The Road to Vitebsk." *New Left Review* 158 (July–August 1986): 19–31.

Winters, Yvor. *The Collected Poems.* Manchester: Carcanet, 1978.

Wolfson, Harry Austryn. *Philo: Foundations of Religious Philosophy in Judaism, Christianity and Islam.* Vols. 1 and 2. 3d rev. ed. Cambridge, Mass.: Harvard University Press, 1962.

———. *The Philosophy of the Church Fathers.* Vol. 1, *Faith, Trinity, Incarnation.* Cambridge, Mass.: Harvard University Press, 1970.

Young, Robert. "Back to Bakhtin." *Cultural Critique* 2 (Winter 1985–86): 71–92.

Zen'kovskii, Vasilii. "Printsipy pravoslavnoi antropologii (prodolzhenie)." *Le Messager: Vestnik russkogo khristianskogo dvizheniia* 154 (1988): 67–91.

Zernov, Nicholas. *The Russian Religious Revival of the Twentieth Century.* New York: Harper and Row, 1963.

Zlatoust, Ioann. *Tvoreniia. Tom vos'moi.* Saint Petersburg, 1902.

Zorin, A. I., and V. I. Iliushenko, eds. *Vokrug imeni ottsa Aleksandra.* Moscow: Kul'turnoe vorozhdenie, 1993.

Index

absolution (final rites), Bakhtin's refusal of, 13, 233, 238n31
accountability. *See* responsibility, personal
Acmeists, 24, 26–27, 94, 229, 242n43. *See also* Gumilev, Nikolai
act, creative, for Meier, 132–34
act, performed *(postupok)*, 39–40, 45, 47, 52–65, 70, 138–39; relationship to self-activity, 65–66, 69; rift between content and product of, 111–12, 121–22; role in understanding ethics, 71–72, 74; theoretical and aesthetic perspectives, 135–36; the word preceded by, 85
activeness (*aktivnost';* self-activity), 62, 64–66, 69, 74–75, 78, 138; of the author, 219–20, 221
Adamism, 27
"Additions and Changes for 'Rabelais'" (Bakhtin), 209–10
Aesopian speech, 191, 199
aesthetic, the (aesthetics; *esteticheskoe)*, 52, 93, 111–14, 135–36, 156, 162; interaction with theory, 122–23; relationship to ethics, 46, 78–79, 84
aestheticism *(estetisizm)*, 51–52, 64, 120; Bergson as representative of, 78–79, 112; relationship to theoretism, 69, 79, 111–16, 120, 121–22, 139, 143
aestheticization, of classical theological notions, 24, 229–30
agency, 45, 126, 219; mediated, 21–33
Akhmatova, Anna, 27
alienation, 61–64, 73, 81, 207; Brechtian, 49; of the Russian intelligentsia, 117–18, 120; spiritual, Pomerants on, 196–97
"all-oneness" ("all-unity"; *vseedinstvo)*, 127, 142; Solovyov's philosophy of, 71, 100, 129, 134
anarchism, 108, 119
ancestral memory, 191–92, 195–96
Anderson, Benedict, 80
animal world, as metaphor, 158–60, 167, 251n13. *See also plot'*
answerability. *See* responsibility, personal
anticlericalism, 117, 183, 186, 192, 197
antirationalism, 128
architectonic motif, 40–41, 55, 56–57, 77
Arianism, 49
Aristotle, 55, 77
Arnold, Matthew, 173
Aronowitz, Stanley, 2, 6
art, relationship to life, 74, 92–100, 111–15, 122–23, 136–37
"Art and Answerability" (Bakhtin), 11, 52, 79, 91–98, 101, 229; Chalcedonian formula in, 127, 136–37, 234; christological metaphor in, 15–16, 41, 75; on domains of human culture, 99–100, 115; interplay between Church Slavonic and East Slavic word forms, 115; *Landmarks* views reflected in, 104–6, 119–20; parallels with "Toward a Reworking of the Dostoevsky Book," 214–15; on the relationship between art and life, 74, 92–97, 100–101, 111–13, 122–23
Art's Day (Den' iskusstva) (journal), 91

"as it were" (kak by), significance of use before "disembodiment," 63
atomism, of Bergson, 142–45
Augustine, St., 22, 40, 45, 110, 229
author, 214–20, 223; ethical involvement of, 226; relationship to character/hero, 220–21, 231
"Author and Hero in Aesthetic Activity" (Bakhtin), 11, 48, 52, 88, 91, 194; analysis of Pushkin's "For the Shores of a Distant Homeland," 51, 80, 84, 244n21; christological motif in, 40–41, 238n24
authoritarianism, 6, 8–9, 211, 237n16
authoritative word *(avtoritarnoe slovo)*, 32
autocracy, 209; of the Russian intelligentsia, 116
Averintsev, Sergei S., 55, 77, 120

Baker, Houston, 211
Bakhtin, Mikhail, 25, 52, 87–91, 108, 195; association with Meier, 108; dissertation defense, 149–50, 184, 188, 199; Eagleton on, 213, 233; fallow period involving arrest, exile, and illness, 14, 49, 225; last rites refused by, 13, 233, 238n31; 1958 guide to students, 97–98; purges' effects on, 199, 201; turning point in early 1960s, 213–14, 225. *See also individual concepts and works*
"Bakhtin, Discourse and Democracy" (Hirschkop), 237n14
Bakhtin Almanach, The (Bakhtinskii sbornik), 190
"Bakhtin and Carnival: Culture as Counter-Culture" (Lachman), 254n19
Bakuninites, 108, 169
"Ballad of Reading Gaol, The" (Wilde), 233, 258n32
baptism, Meier's use as metaphor, 108–9
Basil, St., 240n18
"Beauty in Nature" (Solovyov), 128–29
behavior: denoted by act *(postupok)*, 54; passive and active modes within a particular culture, 62, 64–65; volition and deliberateness in, 78
being *(bytie; litso)*, 66–67, 84, 100, 119; affirmation of self in, 139; co-being, 69, 84, 244n8; product of aesthetic activity as communion with, 112–13; relationship to *lik* and *lichnost'* for Florensky, 101–2, 247n39
Being-as-event *(bytie-sobytie)*, 39–40, 55–56, 58, 72, 75, 82–83; and aesthetic activity, 112–14; in discussion of Kantian categorical imperative, 65–66, 68–69; and Russian pretendership, 118–19, 120–21
Bely, Andrei, 24, 90, 103
Benda, Julien, 110–11, 207; quoted, 183
Berdiaev, Nikolai, 21, 102, 103–6, 134
Bergson, Henri, 26, 78–79, 112–13, 130–31, 142–45; Bakhtin's indebtedness to, 46, 66
Bernstein, Michael André, 9, 237n22
Bible, the, 48; James *5:7*, 158; Luke *1:42*, 158; Pauline epistles, 34–35; Revelation *19:13*, 36–37; as subtext in *Rabelais and His World*, 158–59. *See also John, Gospel of*
Billingsgate talk, in show trials, 201–2
birth. *See* childbirth
bisected unity. *See* Chalcedonian doctrine
Blagoi, D. D., 246n22
blame *(khula)*, as verbal abuse, 200. *See also* praise/blame dichotomy
Bloc of Rightists and Trotskyites, show trial of, 200–201
Blok, Aleksandr, 89, 109, 128
"Bobok" (Dostoevsky), 188
Bocharov, Sergei, 3, 52, 134, 250n21, 256n2; role in rediscovery of Bakhtin, 213, 230
"Bodies of Terror: Theses Toward a Logic of Violence" (Ryklin), 6, 12, 147, 190–96, 198, 208–9, 211; on grotesque body politic, 203, 207
body, as metaphor, 31–32, 156, 183–84, 198; lower stratum of, 151–56, 159, 161–62, 206. *See also* grotesque body
body politic, 183, 188–99, 201, 206, 210–11, 223; carnival's functions transferred to, 209; of the Stalin era, 203, 207, 210. *See also* collective body
Boethius, 170
Bonetskaia, Natalia, 17
border(s). *See* boundary/ies
Boris and Gleb, medieval Russian legend of, 222
Boris Godunov (Pushkin), 169, 205–6
boundary/ies (border[s]; *granitsa/y;* limit[s]; *mezhe/a; predel[y]; rubezh[i])*, 175, 179–80, 181

of existence for Gumilev and for Bakhtin, 227
of language, 172–74
as theme in "Toward a Reworking of the Dostoevsky Book," 224
use in *Rabelais and His World,* 150, 153, 154–55, 159–61, 164–65; political meanings, 156–58
bran': as Church Slavonic term, 203. *See also* praise/blame dichotomy
Brecht, Bertolt, 213
Brezhnev, Leonid, 197
Brodsky, Nikolai L., 188, 199
Bukharin, Nikolai, show trial, 200–201
Bulgakov, Sergei N., 6, 44, 134; contribution to *Landmarks,* 102–3, 107, 117–18, 119, 120–21; "Was ist das Wort?," 37–38, 117, 168, 170, 181
bytie. See being

cannibalism: as paradigm for the state, 100–01, in *Rabelais,* 150–60, 100
carnival, 6, 156–57, 196–97, 201–2; examples of in Russian tradition, 187–88; symbolized by image of Heraclitus's "playing boy," 206–7
carnival, for Bakhtin, 4, 8–9, 11, 144–47, 202, 232, 234
christological motifs in, 15
defined, 186
Dostoevskian: mentioned in footnotes to *Rabelais and His World,* 257n21; *Problems of Dostoevsky's Poetics* on, 140–42, 145–47, 214, 224, 225, 229, 256n2
in *Rabelais and His World,* 11, 146–47, 151–69, 177–82, 183–84, 254n19; sacral character of, 184–88, 192; sinister aspects of, 188–99
redemptive potential, 208–11
relationship to polyphonic discourse, 36–37
carnival square. *See* marketplace
Cassedy, Steven, 127
categorical imperative, Kantian, 53, 65–68, 70–71, 72
censorship, Soviet, 140, 196
Chaadaev, Piotr, 14, 103
Chalcedon, Council of (Fourth Ecumenical Council) (451), 21–22, 128–29, 131, 147. *See also* Chalcedonian doctrine
Chalcedonian doctrine, 21, 23, 125–27, 128–29, 139, 229; Lossky's use of, 130–31; political ramifications of allusions to, 131–35; Solovyov's use of, 128–29, 132, 135, 142–43
Chalcedonian doctrine, Bakhtin's use of, 11, 83, 84, 124, 126–27, 130–32, 170, 194
as christological topos, 7–8, 9, 15, 32, 51, 77
discussion of novelistic discourse framed in, 32–33, 35, 43
dislocation of, 231
in early work, 135–40; "Art and Answerability," 97, 127, 136–37, 234
laughter imbued with properties of, 187
as motif in "Toward a Reworking of the Dostoevsky Book," 223
in *Problems of Dostoevsky's Poetics,* 140–48, 224
renewed interest in during final years, 234
as subtext in *Rabelais and His World,* 150, 153, 156, 198, 202–3, 206–7, 233; on interaction among different language levels, 181–82
in theory of dialogue, 125–27, 128
in "Toward a Philosophy of the Act," 137–39
change *(smena),* of the language, 175–76
character, relationship to personality, 214–15
childbirth, metaphor of: use by Schneegans, 151–52; use in *Rabelais and His World,* 151–53, 155, 158, 159, 162, 179
Christ: body of, lexemes "fruit" and "flesh" used in reference to, 158; corporeality of, in kenotic tradition of Eastern Church, 237n24; descent into Hell, "Toward a Philosophy of the Act" on, 75, 78; divine and human natures of (*see* Chalcedonian doctrine); John Chrysostom on, 227–28; Nestorian and Monophysite doctrines on nature of, 126; as a paradigm for ethical being, 76
Christianity, 14, 19, 99, 108–9, 110, 134. *See also* Eastern Orthodoxy; Russian Orthodox Church
christology, 20–22, 109, 133–34; Solovyov's

use of, 70–71, 129. *See also* Chalcedonian doctrine
christology, Bakhtin's use of, 5, 7–10, 15–16, 40–44
as metaphor, 12–13, 44, 49, 127, 231–33, 235n2; in analyses of Pushkin's poem, 80–83; in *Problems of Dostoevsky's Poetics*, 141–48
as subtext, 37–39, 51, 122, 181, 220–23, 238n24; in later works, 12–13, 229–30; parallels with *Landmarks*, 117, 119–21, 122; in *Problems of Dostoevsky's Art*, 35; in *Rabelais and His World*, 150, 181, 210; in "Toward a Philosophy of the Act," 69, 73, 75–76, 80, 84–85, 181; in "Toward a Reworking of the Dostoevsky Book," 219–20
chronotope(s), 44–47, 88, 193, 195, 230; christological, 231–32; syncretic makeup of, 228
chronotope essay. *See* "Forms of Time and the Chronotope in the Novel"
Chrysostom, John, commentaries on Johannine divine word, 164, 227–29
church, the, 192; culture of, 183, 186, 188, 199; image of, 7, 131, 148. *See also* Eastern Orthodoxy; Russian Orthodox Church
Church Fathers, 22, 43, 48
Church Slavonic (language), 168–69, 203; Bakhtin's use of, 55, 73, 115, 137, 139
cinematic art, Shklovsky on, 242n66
circumincessio. *See perichoresis*
citizen, the, distinction between the ontological subject and, 131–32
Civil War, Russian (1918–20), 121
Clark, Katerina, 2, 235n2, 238n27. *See also Mikhail Bakhtin*
class(es), 117–18, 167, 169, 180, 221–22
class conflict, 104, 175
classless society, 132
clericalism, 89, 106, 122
co-being *(sobytie)*, 69, 84, 244n8
code, relationship to context, 231, 257n30
cognition, 48; Gershenzon on, 107; "Toward a Philosophy of the Act" on, 62, 65–66, 81, 111–12
Cohen, Hermann, 28, 53
Cold War, 149, 153, 234
collective body *(narod)*, 12, 189–90, 191, 193–96, 198, 207–8; Berdiaev's use of *narod* as pun, 105
collective consciousness, society as a single, 223
collective responsibility, as analogous to hypostases of the Trinity, 43
collective society, Meier on, 108–9
collectivism, 135, 139
collectivization (1930s), 12, 180
comic, the, 144–45, 188; art of southern Italy, 177–79. *See also* carnival
comic word, Bakhtin on, 151–52, 178–79
communality. *See* "all-oneness"; *sobornost*
communication, 7, 17–18, 29–30, 83, 112, 238n27. *See also* dialogue
communion, 12, 69, 73, 83, 198, 238n31
dialogic *(obshchenie)*, 218
with the earth, 25
eucharist, 11, 48, 75, 76, 78, 137; community established by, 189–90; vegetative metaphor as counterpart, 185
paradigm of in "Toward a Philosophy of the Act," 74–80, 120–21
prichashchenie as, 45, 76; and ritual nature of carnival, 185–86, 198
prichastnost' as, 11, 82–83, 119
prichastny as, 40, 67, 75, 185
priobshchenie as, 75, 76, 137, 147
priobshchitsia as, 112
"Communion" (Winters), 241n43
community, 148, 169, 189–90, 196, 198; sense of provided by carnival, 184–86; vision of in "Toward a Philosophy of the Act," 76–80, 84
concept, word as *(slovo-poniatie)*, 39–40
conception, metaphor of, use in speaking of language, 179–80
concretization *(uplotnenie)*, 45, 82–83, 125; of personality, 193–94
confession, potential for, 79
consciousness *(soznanie)*, 106–7
for Bakhtin, 172–77, 179, 216–19, 221–23; in analyses of "For the Shores of a Distant Homeland," 81, 82–83, 84; carnivalization of, 185; harmonization of with act, 40, 47; in "Toward a Philosophy of the Act," 58–60, 62, 65, 67, 72, 76
consciousness, individual (*lichnost'*; personality), 99–102, 104–10, 116–17,

119, 122, 135; Solovyov on, 128–29, 141, 250n29
consciousness, individual *(lichnost'*; personality), for Bakhtin, 8, 11, 20, 111, 122, 233; in "Art and Answerability," 91–92, 95–97, 98, 115, 123; comparisons with Florensky's treatment, 99–102; distinction between thing and, 31; individuation and concretization of, 193–94; *Landmarks* influence on, 102; in *Problems of Dostoevsky's Poetics,* 140, 141–42, 246n17; and Russian pretendership, 118–19; "Toward a Reworking of the Dostoevsky Book" on, 214–16, 218
conservatives, Russian, *Landmarks* contributors as, 103
Constituent Assembly, disbanded by Lenin, 109
consubstantiality *(edinosushchie; homoousia)*, 20–22, 43, 100, 130–31, 137, 154. *See also* Chalcedonian doctrine
context, relationship to code, 231
corporeal activity, for Florensky, 99–100
cosmology, 77, 142
cosmos (universe), individual's relationship to, 185–86, 189, 191–92, 198
counterrevolutionary acts, under Articles 57 and 58 of the Soviet Criminal Code, 199–200
Course in the History of Ancient Philosophy, A (Trubetskoi), 20
creation, Bakhtin's model of, 238n27
"Creative Self-Cognition" *(Tvorcheskoe samosoznanie)* (Gershenzon), 107
creativity, for Meier, 132–34
"Critical Self-Cognition" (Gershenzon), 116
culture(s), 16, 19, 114, 121–22, 173–75, 180; assumption of separate languages for, 168–70; of the church, 183, 186, 199; domains of, 99–100, 115; Meier on, 108; mixed *(smeshannaia kul'tura)*, 177–78; modes of behavior oriented within, 62, 64–65; relationship to individual, 58–59, 100, 208–9; repudiation and co-option of carnival, 183–84, 187–88

Dal', Vladimir, 40, 82, 158, 180
Dante, 56, 125
death, 188, 222; presence in carnivalistic images, 184, 189–90; realization of in "For the Shores of a Distant Homeland," 80–82
"Death of the Other, The" (Isupov), 5–7, 222
De Consolatione Philosophiae (Boethius), 170
deed *(ispolnenie)*: relationship to thought, 132–34, 139. *See also* act, performed
defecation/birth, yokings of as as distinctive of the grotesque body, 155, 159–60, 161–62
Den' poezii (almanac), 256n2
denunciation, under Articles 57 and 58 of the Soviet Criminal Code, 199–201
Descartes, René, 77
dialectical materialism, 9, 97, 207
dialects, 173–75
"Dialogism as a Challenge to Literary Criticism" (Hirschkop), 237n14
dialogue, 6, 125, 126
dialogue, for Bakhtin, 4–5, 9, 34–36, 40, 64, 125; between author and characters in "Toward a Reworking of the Dostoevsky Book," 215–20, 222, 224–25; as a moral category, 14–15; as relationship in double-voiced discourse, 30–31; theological paradigms in, 1–2, 4, 7–8, 11, 35–36, 125–27, 231, 234
Dieterich, study of Pulcinella, 177, 178–79
"Diglossia," posited by West German Slavists, 168–69, 170
Dionysianism, of Nietzsche, 118–19, 120
disconnectedness *(razobshchennost')*, role in true ethical understanding, 81, 84
discord, role in development of a language, 175–76
discourse, 23–24, 98, 100
discourse, for Bakhtin, 10–11, 15, 17–18, 23, 37, 39–44; ambivalence, 226–29; Chalcedonian terms linked with, 137–38, 146; and Dostoevskian language, 130–31; novelistic, 5, 6, 19, 27–39, 44, 166, 223, 229–30; use in *Rabelais and His World,* 150–51, 156–57, 181. *See also slovo*
"Discourse in the Novel" (Bakhtin), 10, 27–39, 49, 98, 151, 193, 195; christological subtext in, 40, 181, 232; importance for Hirschkop, 4, 237n14; incarnational

metaphor in, 188–89; on the novelistic word, 19, 166, 229; parallels with the chronotope essay, 44–46, 230, 243n84; ramifications of logos in, 23; "Toward a Reworking of the Dostoevsky Book" linked to, 217–18
disembodiment *(razvoploshchenie)*, 78; place in Bakhtin's ethics, 60–62, 63–65, 68–69
dissidents of the 1960s, *Rabelais and His World* critiqued by, 196–98
diversity, 37, 141, 254n15; within unity, 19, 127, 178–79; of voices, 29–30, 33, 189
doer, relationship to thinker for Meier, 132–34
dominant, the, in organic structure, Ukhtomsky's lectures on, 88
Dostoevsky, Fyodor, 20–21, 25, 125, 220; "Bobok," 188; Lossky's book on, 130–31, 140; polyphony in works, 17, 30–31; quoted, 64, 244n6. *See also* *Problems of Dostoevsky's Art; Problems of Dostoevsky's Poetics;* "Toward a Reworking of the Dostoevsky Book"
Dostoevsky's Christian Understanding of the World (Lossky), 130–31, 140
dualism, of Chalcedonian doctrine, 136, 142, 147, 206–7
Dudko, Dmitri, 13, 238n31
Dukhovnye osnovy zhizni (The Spiritual Foundation of Life) (Solovyov), 70–71
Duvakin, Viktor M., 9, 88–90, 221–22; interviews with Bakhtin, 4, 12, 20, 87, 131

Eagleton, Terry, 233; quoted, 213
earth: identification of with the grotesque, 158–59; as a merciless deity for Rabelais, 190
Easter, 187, 210
Eastern Orthodoxy, 26, 39, 99, 187, 210, 238n31; christology, 20–22; for the "God-Seekers," 70–72; Philo's relevance to, 35, 242n62. *See also* Russian Orthodox Church; theology
East Slavonic (language), 115, 168–69
economic materialism, 104, 121–22
Ecumenical Councils (325–787), 20–22, 26. *See also* Chalcedon, Council of
edin- (word stem), use in "Toward a Philosophy of the Act," 55, 72, 115
education, higher, 87–91
Einfühlung (sympathy; *vzhivanie)*, 77–78, 79, 252n17
élan vital (life force), 130, 143–44
elect, the, belief in, 13
Eliot, T. S., 80, 181
elite, revolutionary, 104, 122
embodiment (enfleshment; *oplotnenie; voploshchenie)*, 24–25, 27; for Florensky, 102, 247n39; in Rabelais's *Gargantua and Pantagruel,* 161. *See also* incarnation
embodiment (enfleshment; *oplotnenie; voploshchenie)*, for Bakhtin, 27, 125, 158, 211, 232, 238n24; in analyses of "For the Shores of a Distant Homeland," 81, 82–83; in conception of activeness and ethics, 65–69, 73, 77; distinction between incarnation and, 58, 68–69; as example of prominence of *plo* in terminology, 166; image of in "Toward a Reworking of the Dostoevsky Book," 218, 220; images of and relationship to carnival in *Rabelais and His World,* 11, 12, 158–60, 166–68, of individual consciousness, 102, 247n39; of language/utterance in novelistic discourse, 31–32; metaphor of in "Forms of Time and the Chronotope in the Novel," 217, 230; theological significance, 7–10, 220; transubstantiation connoted by, 45, 58; the word as, 17, 44–49, 69n84
Emerson, Caryl, 10, 52, 70, 169, 218, 235n1; on *Rabelais and His World,* 191, 194–95
emotion, for Florensky, 99–100
empathy, 75, 77–78, 79, 119
enanthropsis, Russian renderings of, 40–41
enfleshment. *See* embodiment
"Epic and the Novel" (Bakhtin), 4
Epiphanius the Wise, 9–10
epistemology, 55, 88, 100–101, 112, 113–14 of Bakhtin, 67–68, 74; in earliest extant works, 90–91, 92, 122–23; link with ethics, 56, 63–64, 112
"Epos and the Novel" (Bakhtin), 195
esm', in Church Slavonic, use in "Toward a Philosophy of the Act," 73, 139
essence, dichotomy of internal and external, 35, 202, 242n62
"Ethic of Nihilism, The" (Frank), 102, 106–7, 120, 122
ethics, 99, 112, 116–17; christological

vision of, 70–71, 132, 133–34. *See also* categorical imperative; morality
ethics, for Bakhtin, 9, 11, 51, 84, 95, 194
author's involvement with in *Problems of Dostoevsky's Poetics,* 225–26
and the categorical imperative, 65–69
in the chronotope essay, 46
link with epistemology, 112, 122
link with Solovyov, 70–74
place in analyses of Pushkin's poem, 80–84
in "Toward a Philosophy of the Act," 39–40, 43, 46–47, 52–65, 87, 123; and Russian pretendership, 118; and the transubstantive act, 74–80
treatment in early works, 52, 95, 232
eucharist. *See* communion, eucharist
event *(sobytie),* 69, 111–12. *See also* Being-as-event
existentialism, Bakhtin seen as anticipating, 73–74
experience, for Bakhtin, 51, 56–57, 66–67, 69, 77, 111–16

Fascism, Pomerants on, 196–97
fear, 191; carnival seen as overcoming, 184, 189
fecundation *(oplodotvorenie),* 158, 159, 166
Fedotov, G. P., 234
fetus, as secondary meaning of *plod,* 158
"filth," Bloc of Rightists and Trotskyites described as, 200–201
final rites (absolution), Bakhtin's refusal of, 13, 233, 238n31
Fiodor, Archmandrite, 21
first [primary] philosophy *(prima philosophia),* 55–56
Fish, Stanley, 80
Five-Year Plans, 129
flat *(ploskii),* relationship to *ploshchad',* 166, 202
flesh of the body. *See plot'*
Florensky, Pavel Aleksandrovich, 13–15, 35, 44, 110; on individual consciousness, 99–102, 107, 119
Florovsky, George, 134, 143
folk culture of laughter, 160, 166–67, 178–79, 183, 185
Formalism, 16, 25, 31, 49, 96, 229; approach to language, 241n43; Bakhtin's dissertation accused of, 149–50; polemics against, 92, 93, 216. *See also* Shklovsky, Victor
Formal Method in Literary Scholarship, The (Medvedev), 92, 216
"Forms of Time and the Chronotope in the Novel" (Bakhtin), 10, 44–48, 189, 195, 228, 230; christological subtext in, 40; links to in "Toward a Reworking of the Dostoevsky Book," 217–18
Forster, E. M., 216
"For the Shores of a Distant Homeland" (Pushkin), 51, 80–84, 138, 220, 244n21
Foucault, Michel, 6, 193
Four Quartets, The (Eliot), 181
Frank, Semyon L., 102, 106–7, 120, 122, 143
Frankfurt School, 96, 236n4
French language, clash between classical and medieval Latin and, 170–73
"From Notes Made 1970–71" (Bakhtin), 12, 231
"From the Prehistory of Novelistic Discourse" (Bakhtin), 40
fruit of the earth. *See plod*
fusion *(sliianost'),* 124, 136, 140
Futurists, 38, 43, 94; use of *slovo,* 24–25, 26–27
Fyodorov, Nikolai, 129

Gachev, Georgii, 2
Gachev, Grigorii, 213
Gargantua and Pantagruel (Rabelais), 183; body as metaphor in, 154–55, 161–62; Picrochole war, 163–65; Russian translations, 184. *See also Rabelais and His World*
garment, as metaphor, 34–37
gay word of the people, *Rabelais and His World* on, 167–68, 178–79
"General Meaning of Art, The" (Solovyov), 128–29, 140–41
Gershenzon, M., 74, 102, 106–7, 109, 111, 116–17
Geschichte der Grotesken Satyre (Schneegans), 151–52
"God-building," 134–35
God-manhood, 29, 108–9, 129, 134–35
"God-Seekers," 11, 12–13, 44, 70–72, 102, 229, 248n42. *See also* Florensky, Pavel Aleksandrovich; Solovyov, Vladimir

Godzich, Wlad, 2, 3
Goethe, Johann Wolfgang von, quoted, 51
Gorky, Maxim, 135
Gorky Institute of Literature, 149–50, 190, 213
Gorodetsky, Sergei, 27
granitsa/y. See boundary/ies
Gregory of Nazianzus (Gregory the Theologian), 22
grotesque, the, Schneegans's examples of, 151–52
grotesque body, 19, 170, 189, 191–92; Bakhtin's conception of, 12, 151–62, 164, 191; as body politic of the Stalin era, 203, 207, 210
grotesque language, use in show trials, 201–2
Grundlegen zur Metaphysik der Sitten (Kant), 70
guilt *(vina)*, 194, 210; relationship to responsibility, 75, 95–96, 105–6
Gumilev, Nikolai, 25–27, 33, 42, 181, 227, 241n13; on linguistics, 87–88; quoted, 17

Hamlet (Shakespeare), quoted, 183
Hegel, G. W. F., 93, 97
Hell, Christ's descent into, "Toward a Philosophy of the Act" on, 75, 78
Heraclitus, 19, 113, 207; "playing boy" image, 174, 186–87, 206–7
hermeticism, Bakhtin's view of, 136, 139
heroism, Russian tradition of, 106, 107–8, 117–18
"Heroism and Asceticism" (Bulgakov), 106, 117–18
heteroglossia *(raznorechie)*, 29–31, 33, 141–42, 190
"Hippocratic Anthology" (medical text), influence on Rabelais, 198
Hirschkop, Ken, 2, 3–4, 6, 237n14
historical materialism, Stalin's 1947 essay on, 207
holidays, 186–87, 196–97
Holquist, Michael, 2, 33, 96, 235n2, 238n27. *See also Mikhail Bakhtin*
Holy Spirit, John Chrysostom on, 227–28
homoousia. See consubstantiality
"Horomedon" (Voloshin), 24–25
humanism, 170, 235n1
humanities, connection with the social sciences, 87–88
humanity, 40–41, 68, 78; carnival as ultimate mediator of, 181; individual's relationship to, 59 63, 68, 71
humanization of existence, 40–41
humility, 120–21
Husserl, Edmund, 42, 45, 56, 77; concept of *Einfühlung*, 77–78, 79, 252n17; influence on Bakhtin, 66, 226
Hylaea (Futurist group), 25
hypostases of the Trinity, 20–22, 26, 43, 240n18
hypostasis, revolutionary, *lichnost'* as, 99–102
hypostasis of Christ. *See* Chalcedonian doctrine

"Iconostasis" (Florensky), 101–2, 247n39
identity, 6–7, 126, 147, 208; individual, link to nationhood for Meier, 108–9; preservation of, 73, 121
Il'insky, Oleg, 235n1
image *(obraz)*, 39, 160–61
impenetrability/nonpenetrability, mutual, 69, 142, 153
incarnation, 41, 107
  for Bakhtin, 11, 49, 58, 65, 78, 194; adaptation of Johannine model, 5, 12–13, 229; distinction between embodiment and, 58, 68–69; use as metaphor, 48, 189, 210–11
  See also embodiment
individual, the, 6–7, 71, 105, 106, 207–8; link to nationhood for Meier, 108–10; relationship to society for Ryklin, 193–94, 198. *See also* self; subject
individual, the, for Bakhtin, 7, 72–74
  in *Rabelais and His World*, 184–86, 188–89, 191–92, 198; relationship to culture, 208–9; self-sacrifice, 189–90, 194–95
  relationship to society, 131–32, 135, 139
individualism, 135, 139, 223–24, 232
individuality, 121, 147, 224; place in ethics, 68–69, 74, 75, 78
individuation, 193–94, 223
Ineffable, The (Frank), 143
ingestion/cannibalism, yokings of as as distinctive of the grotesque body, 159–60

inner language *(logos endiathetos)*, 20, 28–29, 39
inspiration, 75, 101
intelligentsia, Russian, 87–91, 121–23, 134, 247n28; *Landmarks* criticism of, 102–11, 116–18
intentionality, Husserl's concept of, 56
interaction *(vzaimodeistvie)*, as term related to interpenetration, 145, 147
interconnectedness, phenomenological, *Rabelais and His World* on, 155
interdisciplinary studies, in Russian higher education, 87–88
Internal Form of the Word, The (Shpet), 28–30
interpenetrability, 73, 76, 129, 130
interpenetration. *See perichoresis*
interrelation *(vzaimootnoshenie)*, as term related to interpenetration, 145, 153, 155
intersubjectivity, 77, 109, 130, 222; Bakhtin on, 42, 75–77, 142
intonation of the word, 39–40
intuiting *([illegible])*, role in aesthetic activity, 113
intuition, 79, 112
Intuitive Philosophy of Bergson, The (Lossky), 142–43
I/other dichotomy. *See* self/Other relationship
isolationism, 136, 208
Isupov, K. G., 5–7, 210–11, 222
Iswolsky, Hélène, translation of Bakhtin, 151–52, 155, 203, 251n8, 252nn14–16, 18, 23–25, 253n26, 253nn1, 5, 7, 8, 255n43
Italy, 82; southern, 177–79
Ivanov, Viacheslav, 3, 120
Ivan the Terrible, 188
Izgoev, A. S., 89
"Iz zametok o komicheskom" (Bakhtin), 250n38

Jakobson, Roman, 213
James *5:7*, 158
James, Henry, Sr., 2, 16; quoted, 1
Janus, image of, 202, 204
Jews, restricted university enrollment of in pre-Revolution Russian, 88
Johannine logology, 17–18, 20–21, 24–25, 125, 153
Bakhtin's adaptation of, 5, 7, 15, 39–41, 48–49, 234; connected to linguistics, 17–18; integration with *perichoresis,* 217; inversion of, 85, 188; in *Rabelais and His World,* 189
early 20th-century Russian adaptations of, 24–27
John Chrysostom's homilies on, 164, 227–29
See also logos; Word, the
John, Gospel of, 34–35, 38, 231; *Chapter 1,* 45, 48, 49, 158, 164, 227–29 (*see also* Johannine logology; Word, the); *Chapter 5:52–58,* 129, 158
John Chrysostom. *See* Chrysostom, John
John of Damascus, 22, 41
John the Evangelist (St. John), 25
Judaism, historical concept of logos, 19
judgment: place in Kant's categorical imperative, 65–66; *ploshchad'* as topos for, 203
justice, portrayed along a vertical axis, 201

Kagan, Matvey Isaevich, 27–28, 235n1
Kaliazin Petition, 188
Kant, Immanuel, Solovyov's article on, 70–71
Kantianism, 46–47, 52–53, 65–68, 70–72, 118, 215
kenosis (emptying of the self), 5–6, 38, 75, 78, 130, 237n24
"Kenotafiia" (Shklovsky), 242n66
Kerensky, Aleksandr, 9
"K filosofii postupka" (Bakhtin), 252n17
Khomiakov, Aleksei, 121
Khrushchev, Nikita, 197, 205, 223
knowledge. *See* epistemology
Kozhinov, Vadim, 3, 6, 188, 256n2; role in rediscovery of Bakhtin, 213–14, 230
Kristeva, Julia, 2, 235n1
Kruchonykh, 25, 27, 39
Kuznetsov, A. M., 14

labor, division of, Marxist abolition of, 133
Landmarks (Vekhi) (1909), 89, 102–11, 111, 134–35, 194; critiques of, 98, 103, 247nn41, 42, 248n45; influence on Bakhtin, 11, 102–3; on Russian pretendership, 116–18, 119–24
langage, as Saussurian category, 44

language(s), 26–27, 44, 49, 168–76, 180–81, 235n1
- for Bakhtin, 10–11, 16, 28–31, 38, 43, 48–49, 234; influence on notions of dialogue, 125; in *Rabelais and His World,* 167–81, 192–93, 206–8; in "Toward a Philosophy of the Act," 39–40; use of Church Slavonic and East Slavic, 55, 73, 115, 137, 139
- of Dostoevsky as bifurcated, 130–31
- East Slavonic, 115, 168–69
- heteroglossia, 29–31, 33, 141–42, 190
- Kruchonykh's concept of, 25
- for Lossky, 130–31
- for Shpet, 28–30
- Slavistics decimated during Stalin era, 88
- type used in show trials, 200–201
- *See also* Church Slavonic; linguistics

langue, la: as Saussurian category, 44; use of *slovo* in sense of, 34
Lapshin, I. I., 252n17
Latin, classical and medieval, 170–73
laughter, 144, 177–79, 186, 188
Bakhtin's conception of, 144–45, 153, 180–81, 187, 210; relationship to folk culture, 160, 166–67, 170
law, rule of, and the categorical imperative, 70–71
learning *(nauka)*, Bakhtin's category of, 100
Lenin, V. I., 74, 109, 116, 122, 208; review of *Landmarks,* 103, 247n42
Leninism, 4, 7, 107
Lent, Orthodox, in 1938, 210
Leo II (Pope), 126, 128
Lermontov, Mikhail, 8
Lettres philosophiques, Les (Chaadaev), 14
Liapunov, Vadim, 63, 112, 115, 137, 139
liberals, Russian, *Landmarks* contributors as, 103
lichnost'. See consciousness, individual
life *(zhizn')*, Bakhtin on, 99–100, 112, 115, 135–36
- relationship to art, 98, 136–37; in "Art and Answerability," 74, 92–97, 99–101, 111–13, 122–23; in "Toward a Philosophy of the Act," 111–15, 122–23

life activities, Florensky on, 99–100
life force *(élan vital)*, 130, 143–44
lik (visage), 101–2, 137
Likhachev, Dmitri, 188
limit(s). *See* boundary/ies
linguistics, 17, 37–38, 87–88, 125, 242n43. *See also* language
literary theory, 94, 242n43; in Bakhtin's writings, 87–90, 91, 195
Liubimov, translation of Rabelais, 174, 184
Livshits, 25
logos, 18–24, 28–30, 71, 231, 242n50; Philo's conception of, 34–35; Stoic concept of, 18, 19–20, 23–24, 35, 39. *See also* Johannine logology; Word, the
logos endiathetos (inner language), 20, 28–29, 39
logos prophorikos (uttered *[vyskazannoe]* word), 20, 28–29, 39
logos spermatikos (seminal logos), 19–20, 21, 25
Lopatin, L. M., 13
Lord's Prayer, Kaliazin Petition as blasphemous parody of, 188
Losev, A. F., 44, 242n50
Lossky, Nikolai, 6, 130–31, 140, 142–43, 222
Lotman, Iurii, 6, 188
Luke *1:42,* 158
Lunacharsky, Anatoly, 135
lustration, of the many for the sake of one, 191

"Magic of Words, The" (Bely), 24
"Man Before Mirror" (Bakhtin), 139–40
Mandelshtam, Osip, 26–27
mankind. *See* humanity
marketplace *(ploshchad';* square), 147, 201–6, 210; as carnival square, 142, 146; derivation of Russian word, 166, 202
marketplace word *(ploshchadnoe slovo)*, ambivalence of, 201–6; correspondence with traumas of Stalinism, 201, 203–6, 233
martyrdom, Orthodox conceptions of, 5–6
Marx, Karl, 197
Marxism, 3, 104, 118, 175, 201; of Bakhtin, question of, 2, 3–4, 92, 96–97, 236n4; confluence with "God-seeking" and "God-building," 134–35; critique of literary movements, 94, 96; ideas of "God-manhood" coexisting with, 129, 134
Marxism and the Philosophy of Language (Voloshinov), 4, 44, 48, 193, 238n24

Marxists: view of Bakhtin's work, 2, 3–4, 8, 235n1, 237n14; Western, on co-option of carnival by repudiating culture, 184
masks, use at carnival time, 160–61
mass victimization: incarnational metaphor for, 210–11; during Stalin era, 199–201, 203–4
matching up *(primeriaiutsia)*, of languages, 176
materialism, 97, 116, 196; dialectical, 9, 27, 207; economic, 104, 121–22; ethical, 79–80
matter, 144–45
McGee, Vern W., 257n30
medieval world: carnival spirit, 160–61, 186, 187–88; and language change, 169–73; mystery plays, 56; Russian legend of Boris and Gleb, 222
Medvedev, 4, 92, 216
Meier, Aleksandr Aleksandrovich, 108–10, 111, 122, 127, 135, 147; "On Class Struggle," 108–9, 110, 132–34; use of Chalcedonian formula, 132–34, 137–40, 141, 146
Men', Aleksandr, Pomerants's obituary for, 234
Menippean satire, 225
metalinguistics, 39–41, 229, 234
Metaphysics (Aristotle), 55
mezha/i. See boundary/ies
Middle Ages. *See* medieval world
middle class, attempt to incorporate the peasantry into, 221–22
Mikhail Bakhtin (Clark and Holquist), 2, 17, 100, 127, 153, 191; on Bakhtin's refusal of last rites, 238n31; on contribution of Eastern Orthodoxy to Bakhtin's work, 9, 237n24; on friendship between Bakhtin and Yudina, 14; on 1960s and 1970s revisions of early essays, 233; on Rabelais study, 199, 205, 251n1
Mikhail Bakhtin: The Creation of a Prosaics (Morson and Emerson), 169. *See also* Emerson; Morson
Mikhailovsky, Nikolai, 247n28
Minsky, Nikolai, 128, 138
Mirkina sisters, transcription of Bakhtin's Vitebsk lectures, 25
Monophysitism, 126, 128, 144, 147
morality, 14, 52, 54–55, 57, 104–6, 118. *See also* ethics
Morson, Gary Saul, 10, 52, 74, 87, 169, 194
Moscow University, *Problems of Dostoevsky's Art* used at, 213
multiple-hypostaticness *(mnogoipostasnost')*, 222–23
mysticism, 99, 101, 108, 128

Nabokov, Vladimir, 8
naïeveté *(naivnost')*, attribution to Rabelais disputed by Bakhtin, 174
narod. See collective body
naroditsia, use as pun by Berdiaev, 105
national government, Rabelais's support for principle of, 162–63, 166, 182, 209
nationalism, 3, 108–10, 234; for the *Landmarks* contributors, 107, 248n42; religious, 13–14
nationalist literature, reactionary, 1909 *Landmarks* viewed as, 103
nationalists, Russian, interpretation of Solovyov, 70, 244n11
national language, clash with classical and medieval Latin, 170–73
National State Library, in St. Petersburg, 108
natural sciences, 74, 146
nesliianno i nerazdel'no, 126–27, 132, 137–39, 156. *See also* Chalcedonian doctrine
Nestorianism, 126, 128
"new canon" *(novyi kanon)*, 156–57
New Criticism, Anglo-American, 241n43
New Economic Policy, 61
Newman, John Henry, 23
"New Ways of the Word, The" (Kruchonykh), 25
Nicea, First Council of (325), 20–21
Nietzsche, Friedrich, 73, 80, 108, 118–19, 120
Nietzscheanism, modified, 129
nihilism, 95, 117, 119, 122, 185
Nilsson, Åke, 24, 25
"non-alibi," and personal responsibility, 57–58, 62, 72–73
non-fusion. *See* Chalcedonian doctrine; *nesliianno i nerazdel'no*
non-Gnostic Christianity, early, 238n24

non-interpenetration, of culture and life, 136, 138–39
not merged yet undivided. *See* Chalcedonian doctrine; *nesliianno i nerazdel'no*
novelistic discourse, 5, 16, 19, 27–39, 166, 223, 229–30. *See also* "Discourse in the Novel"
novyi kanon ("new canon"), 156–57

object-in-itself, knowledge of, 62–63
obraz (image), 39, 160–61
ochelevechennyi, meaning of, 40–41
odin- (word stem), use in "Toward a Philosophy of the Act," 114–15
ogranichennost'/ogranichennyi, 164–65, 167, 168. *See also* boundary/ies
"On Class Struggle" *(O klassovoi bor'be)* (Meier), 108–9, 110, 132
oneness. *See* "all-oneness"; unity
one (single) unique unity *(odno-edinstvennoe edinstvo). See* unity
"On Nature" (Heraclitus), 19
"On the Nature of the Word" (Mandelshtam), 26–27
ontology, 61–62, 185, 189
open societies, preference for, 157
oplodotvorenie (fecundation), 158, 159, 166
oplotnenie. See embodiment
orality, 10, 156, 176, 207
Orthodoxy. *See* Eastern Orthodoxy; Russian Orthodox Church; theology
ostranenie (Verfremdung), 49, 61–62. *See also* alienation
Other, the, 5–6, 31, 237n16. *See also* self/Other relationship

Pantagruel (Rabelais). *See Gargantua and Pantagruel*
pantheism, 198
Paracelsus, 198
Paris Lectures (Husserl), 56
parole, la, as Saussurian category, 44
passion, in politics and religion, Benda on, 110–11
passivity *(passivnost'),* 54, 62, 64–65, 74; of the author, 219, 221
paternalistic authoritarianism, in Soviet society, 223–24
Pauline epistles, image of the soul, 34–35
peasantry, the, 117–18, 194; Stolypin reforms aimed at, 221–22
penetrability, 129; mutual, 136
penetration, mutual, 129
perception, primacy of, 104
perichoresis (circumincessio; interpenetration; *vzaimoproniknovenie),* 22, 26–27, 132, 197, 217; Hegel on, 93, 97
perichoresis (circumincessio; interpenetration; *vzaimoproniknovenie),* Bakhtin's use of, 15, 36, 51, 119, 164–65, 168, 222; as christological topos, 7, 9, 10, 69, 93, 97, 125; in conjunction with Chalcedonian doctrine, 126–27, 136, 138, 140, 141–43; ethical equivalent of stressed, 73, 76; during final years, 234; for interaction among different language levels, 181; as metaphor for interaction between author and hero, 231; non-appearance in analysis of Pushkin's "Author and Hero," 83–84; in *Problems of Dostoevsky's Poetics,* 145–46, 229, 250n36; with reference to art and life in the individual, 92, 93, 95, 96, 97; with reference to medieval Latin across boundaries, 171–73; theological dimensions in *Rabelais and His World,* 153, 156, 160; in "Toward a Philosophy of the Act," 119
personality *(lichnost'). See* consciousness, individual
personality cult, Stalin's, 209–10, 211, 223
phenomenology, 57, 100, 126; Bakhtin on, 51, 77, 80, 143
Philo, 34–35, 36, 242n62
"Philosophical Verity and the Truth of the Intelligentsia" (Berdiaev), 103–6
philosophy, 55; ancient Greek, 20, 55, 77 (*see also* Stoicism); Bakhtin on, 54, 74, 91, 111–12, 122; as Bakhtin's self-characterized profession, 87
Philosophy of the Name, The (Losev), 242n50
Picrochole war, described in *Gargantua,* 163–65
piety, 13–14, 15
Pillar and Foundation of Truth, The (Florensky), 99–100, 102
"Pillar of Fire" (Gumilev), 25
"Place of the Forehead" *(lobnaia ploshchadka),* on Red Square, 203

plant world: as metaphor, 158–60, 167, 185. *See also plod*
play, principle of, embodied in use of the mask, 161
"playing boy" image, 174, 186–87, 206–7
Plekhanov, Georgy, 97
plo, as a phonemic triad, prominence in Bakhtin's terminology, 166, 202
plod (fruit of the earth): derivatives of used in *Rabelais and His World,* 158–60; as example of prominence of *plo* in Bakhtin's terminology, 166; relationship to the flesh of the body, 158–60, 181, 190, 203
ploshchad'. See marketplace
ploskii (flat), relationship to *ploshchad',* 166, 202
plot' (flesh): Bakhtin's use of derivatives, 45, 58, 67, 83, 158–60, 162, 166; of the grotesque body as immortal, 155; possible derivation of *plotnyi* from, 82; relationship to the fruit of the earth *(plod),* 158–60, 181, 190, 203; as root for derivation of *oplotnenie* and *uplotnenie,* 125; use in *plot' ot ploti,* 189
plot *(siuzhet),* in Dostoevsky's works, 42–43, 216–17, 228–29
"Poet and the Rabble, The" ("Poet i tolpa") (Pushkin), 94–95, 246n22
poetry, 24, 28; of Pushkin, 51, 80–84, 94–95, 138, 220, 244n21, 246n22
political leader (ruler), description in *Rabelais and His World,* 207, 208–9
politics, 88–90, 108, 110–11, 116–17, 139, 213; ramifications of allusions to Chalcedonian doctrine, 131–35, 147; role in views on *Landmarks,* 103–4, 247n42, 248n45; in 16th-century France, 168. *See also* Stalinism
politics, for Bakhtin, 32, 91, 111–12, 181–82; as context for *Rabelais and His World,* 150, 156–58, 162–65, 166–67, 194, 201–8; in "Toward a Philosophy of the Act," 56, 122
Polovtseva, Ksenia Anatolievna, 108
polyphony, 6, 215–16
 Bakhtin's concept of, 1–2, 5, 10, 23, 49, 189–90, 195; christological motifs in, 15, 41; in late work, 12, 225; in *Problems of Dostoevsky's Art,* 226–27; in *Problems of Dostoevsky's Poetics,* 141–43, 145, 147–48, 226–27, 229; related to *slovo,* 17, 19; relationship to carnival, 36–37; relationship to heteroglossia, 30–31
 See also voices
Pomerants, Grigorii, 196–98, 234
"Poor Folk" (Dostoevsky), 131
popovichi (sons of priests), 19th-century Russian intelligentsia as, 89
positivism, 74, 116
Pospielovsky, Dimitry, 197–98
possession *(oderzhanie),* 75, 101, 119, 120
postmodernism, 8
postupok. See act, performed
pragmatism, 52, 55
praise *(kvala)*/blame *(bran')* dichotomy, 8, 201–6, 208–10, 233; in Stalin era, 199–201, 233
Prat, Naftali, 44
predel[y]. See boundary/ies
pregnancy, used by Bakhtin to describe the grotesque body, 158, 159
pretendership, Russian: Bakhtin on, 116–17, 118–24; *Landmarks* on, 116–18, 119–24
prichashchenie (joining). *See* communion
prichastit'sia (to take communion), relationship to *prichashchenie,* 185
prichastnost'. See communion
prima philosophia (first [primary] philosophy), 55–56
primeriaiutsia (matching up), of languages, 176
priobshchat'-priobshchit', 136–37
priobshchenie, 75, 76, 83, 136, 147. *See also* communion; embodiment
Prishvin, Mikhail, 6, 237n16
"Problem of Content, Material and Form in Verbal Art, The" (Bakhtin), 41, 48, 49
Problems of Dostoevsky's Art (Bakhtin), 4, 8, 10, 31, 93, 98, 254n15; compared with *Problems of Dostoevsky's Poetics,* 225–29; concepts in late works compared with, 221; garment metaphor used in, 35–36; on novelistic discourse, 16, 152; on plot, 42–43, 216–17; reworking into *Problems of Dostoevsky's Poetics,* 213 (*see also* "Toward a Reworking of the Dostoevsky Book"); theological subtext, 10, 41–43, 49, 131; use in classes at Moscow University and the Gorky Institute of Literature, 213

Problems of Dostoevsky's Poetics (Bakhtin), 4, 7, 10, 125, 215–16, 221, 225–30
Boris Godunov passage used in, 205–6
carnival brought into world of Dostoevsky's novels, 214, 224, 225, 227, 256n2
garment metaphor used in, 36
on interpenetration of the aesthetic and the real, 93, 246n17
parallels with Lossky's work on Dostoevsky, 130–31
polyphony described in, 17, 30
pretender motif in, 118
reference to praise/blame dichotomy, 208, 233
theological subtext, 5, 126, 231–32; Chalcedonian doctrine, 127, 140–48; christological metaphor, 10, 12, 41–42
See also "Toward a Reworking of the Dostoevsky Book"
"Problems of Speech Genres" (Bakhtin; 1952–53), 49
progressivism, 90; attributed to Rabelais by Bakhtin, 162–63, 165, 167; in 16th-century France, 168
propaganda, manipulative, 98
prosaics approach to Bakhtin, 52. *See also* Emerson; Morson
public performance, motif of in *Rabelais and His World,* 142, 152–53
public square. *See* marketplace
Pulcinella, Dieterich's 1897 study of, 177, 178–79
punishment, *ploshchad'* as topos for in *Rabelais and His World,* 203
purges, Stalinist, 12, 191, 199–201, 203–4, 208, 210; and annihilation of the Other, 6; effect on Bakhtin's work, 149, 199, 203–4; effect on the Russian people, 13, 153
Pushkin, Aleksandr, 215; "Boris Godunov," 169, 205–6; poem to Amalia Riznich ("For the Shores of a Distant Homeland"), 51, 80–84, 138, 220, 244n21; quoted, 149; "The Poet and the Rabble," 94–95, 246n22

Rabelais, François, 153, 172–75, 198–99; Bakhtin's study of *(see Rabelais and His World);* political beliefs, 162–65, 168
Rabelais and His World (Bakhtin), 1, 7–9, 11–12, 146–47, 169–82, 230, 238n27; Bakhtin's interest in historical era, 88; correspondence with collective traumas under Stalinism, 201–8; direct references to Stalinism not made, 199; garment metaphor used in, 36; on the grotesque body and carnival, 151–66; logological subtext, 19, 20; 1960s dissident culture view of, 196–98; pretender motif in, 118; publication and translations, 149–50, 174, 183–84; Ryklin's essay on, 6, 147, 190–96, 198; theological metaphors in, 5, 231–32, 233
"Rabelais in the History of Realism" (dissertation, Bakhtin), 149–50, 184, 205, 251n1; Bakhtin's academic defense of, 149–50, 184, 188, 199
radical intelligentsia, Russian, 89–90, 247n28; *Landmarks* directed against, 103–11, 116–18
random arrests of citizens, during Stalin era, 199–201, 203–4
rationalism, 65–66, 71, 128
reality, 19, 56, 93, 161; concrete, 159; social, 102
rebirth, Bakhtin on in "Zametki," 214, 256n2
redemption, 8, 38–39
Red Square *(Krasnaia ploshchad'),* 203
reductionism, 78, 122, 150
reembodiment *(perevoploshcheniia),* 161, 252n17
religion, 3, 17, 71, 107, 110–11, 146; Bakhtin on, 56, 57, 78, 146–47, 238n27; institutional, 103, 197; intelligentsia's attitude toward, 116–17. *See also* Eastern Orthodoxy; Russian Orthodox Church; theology
Religion of the Future, The (Minsky), 128
religiosity, 13–15, 15, 89, 108
religious idealism, 139
"Religious Meaning of Messianism, The" (Meier), 109
Religious-Philosophical Society, Saint Petersburg, 108, 109–10, 132
religious philosophy, Russian, 28–29, 41, 43, 134. *See also* "God-Seekers"; theology
Renaissance, the, 173–74, 186, 206
"Response to a Question from the *Novyi Mir* Staff" (Bakhtin), 234
responsibility, personal (answerability;

otvetstvennost'), 99, 101, 119–20, 136, 169
Bakhtin's approach to in "Toward a Philosophy of the Act," 52–53, 56–59, 62, 64, 69, 72–73, 77–78, 116; parallels with "Art and Answerability," 136–37, 138–39
interpenetration of the individual's life, 75, 95–96
radical intelligentsia's denial of attacked in *Landmarks*, 105–6, 116–17
resurrection, imagery of, 38–39
"Resurrection of the Word, The" (Shklovsky), 26, 35–36, 38, 242n66
Revelation *19:13*, 36–37
Revolution, Russian, of 1905, 103, 122
Rickert, Heinrich, 53
Rightists, show trial of, 200–201
ritual, 108–9, 120–21, 186, 196–97; last rites refused by Bakhtin, 13, 233, 238n31. *See also* communion, eucharist
Riznich, Amelia, Pushkin's poem dedicated to, 51, 80–84, 138, 220, 244n21
rubezh[i]. *See* boundary/ies
ruler (political leader), description in *Rabelais and His World*, 207, 208–9
Russian and the Universal Church (Solovyov), 128
Russian Formalism and Anglo-American New Criticism (Thompson), 241n43
Russian language, 26–27, 168–69. *See also* Church Slavonic
Russian Orthodox Church, 103, 110, 146, 234; Bakhtin's relationship to, 1–2, 5–9, 23, 43, 233, 235n2, 237n24; Stalin's actions toward, 13, 210. *See also* Eastern Orthodoxy
Ryklin, Mikhail, 5, 12, 211
"Bodies of Terror," 6, 12, 147, 190–96, 198, 208–9; on grotesque body politic of Stalin era, 203, 207

salvation, 6, 76. *See also* soteriology
samizdat writings, of Pomerants, 196–97
Saussure, Ferdinand de, 33–34, 38, 44
savagery, denotement in *Rabelais and His World*, 12
scapegoating, Vyshinksy's justification for, 201
Schapiro, Leonard, 248n45
Schneegans, G., 151–52, 178, 180
scholarship, Bakhtin on in 1958 guide to students, 97–98
science, 74, 92, 99–101, 115, 146
"scum," Bloc of Rightists and Trotskyites described as, 200–201
self
Bakhtin on: in *Rabelais and His World*, 156, 167, 186; in "Toward a Philosophy of the Act," 59–63, 68–69, 75–78, 118–19, 120
Russian intelligentsia's preoccupation with, 119
for Western Marxist critics of Bakhtin, 6–7
See also individual; subject
self-abnegation, 191, 199, 207–8, 225, 234
self-activity. *See* activeness
self-creation of the grotesque body, 155
self-definition, undergone by the form, 217
self-developing idea, as inseparable from personality, 216, 218
selflessness, 8, 219, 221
self/Other relationship, 16, 71, 100, 130–31
self/Other relationship, in Bakhtin's work, 35, 75–76, 155, 218, 237n24, 238n24; in "Man Before Mirror," 139–40; place in ethics, 81–82, 138; in "Toward a Philosophy of the Act," 59–60, 69, 71, 73, 78
self-renunciation, 75, 221–22
self-sacrifice, 60–61, 221–23; of the individual, 189–90, 194–95, 232
self-transcendence, 109, 227
seminal logos *(logos spermatikos)*, 19–20, 21, 24–25
semiotics, 231
separated *(razdelennyi)*, 133–34, 147
separateness *(razdelennost')*, 55, 133–34, 141–42
seriousness, the negative associated with by Bakhtin, 147, 250n38
Shakespeare, William: *Hamlet* quote, 183
Shepherd, David, 3, 6
Shklovsky, Victor, 26, 27, 35–36, 38, 213, 242n66
show trials, during Stalin era, 199–201, 210
Shpet, Gustav, 28–30, 37
Shukman, Anne, 31
sight, faculty of, as metaphor, 45, 84, 165
signified and signifier, the word as, 33–34

single (one) unique unity *(odno-edinstvennoe edinstvo)*. *See* unity
situational concept of ethics, 56, 66, 112, 118
sketchbook journal, of Bakhtin, 224, 225
"Sketches on Philosophical Anthropology" (Bakhtin), 88
Skobtsova, E., 244n11
slovo, 24–27, 44, 241n43
  Bakhtin's use of term, 11, 39–44; as elusive in "Discourse in the Novel," 30–31, 38; as embodiment, 44–49
  translations of term, 17–18
  See also discourse; logos; utterance(s); word(s)
smekhovoi and *smeshannyi*, Bakhtin's wordplays on, 177–79, 181
Smirnov, A. A., 205
sobornost' (communality), 70, 100, 121
sobytie (co-being), 69, 84, 244n8
social accountability, 104, 196
social change, dynamics of, 195, 201
socialism, fused with God-manhood and Christianity by Meier, 108–9, 134
"Socialism in One Country" doctrine, Stalin's declaration of, 208
social sciences, 87–88
social structure, language as, 30
society, 157, 169, 174, 193–94, 223; relationship to the individual, 131–32, 135, 139
solipsism, 74, 92, 104, 110, 114, 135
Solovyov, Vladimir, 6, 7, 10, 41, 134–35, 222; Archimandrite Fiodor's influence on, 21; article on Kant, 70–71; Bakhtin's similarities and affinities with, 127, 140–42; Chalcedonian formula used by, 36, 128–29, 132, 139, 140–42, 146–47; criticism of Bergsonianism, 143–45; on egoism and personality, 141, 250n29; Gumilev's "The Word" as synthesis of Bergson and, 26; influence, 11, 12, 29, 70–72, 100, 103, 128; influence on Meier, 108–9, 134; philosophy seen as version of Monophysitism, 126; Russian nationalists' view of, 70, 244n11; subjective sociology, 211; view of Nietzsche, 73
soteriology, 8, 14, 43, 71, 84
soul, 190, 238n27; metaphors for, 34–36
Soviet Criminal Code, Articles 57 and 58, 199–201
Soviet Union, 1, 87; culture of society from 1930s to 1960s, 223–24; Khrushchev-Brezhnev era, 197, 205, 237n24; space industry, 129; Stalin-Hitler pact and German invasion, 149, 203. *See also* Stalinism
space, 41–43, 46–47, 57, 59, 186; relationship to ethics, 53, 65–67, 72–73, 81–82; relationship to time, 227–28
speech, official, Bakhtin on, 156–57
speech acts: ambivalence of during the 1930s, 208, 210; significance under Articles 57 and 58 of the Soviet Criminal Code, 199–201
speech types, 29–30; in pre-Risorgimento southern Italy, 177–79
Spiritual Foundation of Life, The (Dukhovnye osnovy zhizni) (Solovyov), 70–71
spirituality, 4, 99–100, 153, 162, 196, 238n31
spontaneity *(neprinuzhdennost')*, of Rabelais's language, 174
springtime, as carnivalesque, 186–87
square. *See* marketplace
Stalin, Joseph, 13, 200, 207–8, 210. *See also* Stalinism
Stalin-Hitler pact, 149, 203
Stalinism, 6, 199, 221–22, 223, 237n16; Bakhtin's attitude toward, 5, 13, 199, 236n4; effect on Bakhtin's life and publication, 146, 147, 201; show trials and random arrests, 199–201; as topos in *Rabelais and His World*, 12, 189, 190–96, 198, 199, 203–11, 233. *See also* purges, Stalinist
Stallybrass, Peter, 208, 254n19
state, the, 209; culture of, 183, 186
Stefan of Perm, St., 10
Stoicism, 22, 40, 49, 202; concept of logos, 18, 19–20, 23–24, 34, 35, 39
Stolypin, Pyotr, 221–22
Stone, I. F., 131–32
structuralism, 11–12, 16, 256n2
"Structure of the Word, The" (Florensky), 35
struggle, seen as indispensable for development of a language, 175–76
Struve, P. B., 102, 105

stylistics, Bakhtin's critical remarks on, 30, 37–38
subject, the, 5–9, 131–34. *See also* self
subject, the, for Bakhtin, 56, 73–74, 76, 78; interaction with the world, 57, 59, 95; merging between the state and, 209; place in epistemology, 67–68, 69
subjectivism, 134–35, 141–42, 211
subjectivity, 104, 226
substantiation. *See* consubstantiality; embodiment; transubstantiation
symbiosis, conflated with doctrine of *perichoresis,* 168
Symbolists, 24, 94; Bely, 24, 90, 103; Blok, 89, 109, 128; Ivanov, 3, 120
sympathy, 77–78, 79
syncreticism, 25–26

Tareev, M. M., 99
tautologies, in "Toward a Philosophy of the Act," 114–15
teleology, in Bakhtin's approach to language change, 177
Teriaeva, Maria, 150
Terras, Victor, 26
texts, religious canonical, 79–80
theology, 11, 55, 99–102, 242n43. *See also* Eastern Orthodoxy; Russian Orthodox Church; religion; *individual topics*
theology, for Bakhtin, 1–2, 4–5, 9–11, 14–16, 91, 231–34; eventual convergence with ethics, 71–72; in "From the Prehistory of Novelistic Discourse," 48; metaphors of coexisting with nontheological tropes, 146–47; ramifications of carnival stressed by Pomerants, 197; relationship to phenomenology, 51; as subtext in late work, 12–13, 101, 220–23; as subtext in *Rabelais and His World,* 202–3
theoretical, the *(teoreticheskoe)*, 114, 135–36
theoretical subject, 67–68
theoretism *(teoretizm)*, 51, 63, 64, 74, 137; in ethics, 53, 55, 62–66, 67–69; relationship to aestheticism, 79, 111–16, 120, 121–23, 139, 143
thinker, relationship to doer for Meier, 132–34
Thompson, Ewa, 241n43
thought, 53, 57–58; boundary separating experience from, 66–67; relationship to deed, 132–34, 139
time, 9, 19, 41–43, 206–7, 228
time, for Bakhtin, 9, 46–47, 113; carnival's way of measuring, 186, 190; dislocation of, 226–27; flow of within language systems, 172–73; relationship to ethics, 53, 72–73, 81
Titunik, J. R., 235n2
Tobit, Apocryphal Book of, 126
Todorov, Tzvetan, 2
Tolstoy, Leo, 80
Tolstoyism, 122
Tomashevsky, B., 246n22
totality, highlighted by Bakhtin's use of the stem *edin-*, 55, 72
"Toward a Philosophy of the Act" (Bakhtin), 9–11, 45, 48–49, 52, 91, 100, 185
 analysis of Pushkin's "For the Shores of a Distant Homeland," 51, 80–84
 on Bergson, 143
 christology as subtext in, 69, 73, 80, 84–85, 181; Chalcedonian formula use, 135–39; parallels with *Landmarks*, 117, 119–21, 122; in use of the term *aktivnost'*, 75–76
 civil and political conditions at time of writing, 60–61, 64
 concepts in late works related to, 91, 221–22, 226; in "Toward a Reworking of the Dostoevsky Book," 217–18, 220
 on ethics and responsibility, 39–40, 43, 46–47, 52–65, 72–74, 215; attitude toward Kant's categorical imperative, 65–69, 71–72; followed up on in *Rabelais and His World,* 194; Morson on, 87
 existentialism seen as anticipated in, 73–74
 interplay between Church Slavonic and East Slavic word forms, 114–15
 parallels with *Landmarks* on Russian pretendership, 116–17, 118–24
 on the redemption of individual experience, 111–16
 slovo used in metalinguistic and Johannine sense, 39–41, 43, 48
 on the transubstantive act, 74–80
"Toward a Reworking of the Dostoevsky Book" (Bakhtin; 1961), 12, 145, 214–20, 222–25, 227–28, 257n21

tragedy: carnival as, 184; Dostoevsky's "Bobok" seen as by Brodsky, 188
Trahison des Clercs, La (Benda), 110–11
transcendence, 25, 113, 139, 222, 238n27; dynamic of in Bakhtin's concept of carnival, 11, 156, 167, 186; for Kant, 65–66, 66
transfer *(perevod)*, 151–52
transgredience, 11, 238n27
transubstantiation, 25; Johannine, 45, 48, 126, 129 (*see also* Johannine logology)
transubstantiation, for Bakhtin, 9, 46, 58, 73, 238n24
  as metaphor, 82–83, 84; in *Rabelais and His World*, 185, 189–90, 191–92, 194
  relationship to ethics in "Toward a Philosophy of the Act," 74–80
  as subtext in "Toward a Reworking of the Dostoevsky Book," 218, 220
Trinitarian paradigm, 27, 40, 130, 229
  used by Bakhtin, 5, 12–13, 15, 51, 75–76, 83, 84, 170; in "Art and Answerability," 97, 101; in *Problems of Dostoevsky's Poetics*, 141–42; in "Toward a Philosophy of the Act," 136
  See also perichoresis
Trinity, the, 20–24, 26, 43, 99, 130, 240n18
Trotsky, Leo, 25, 222; quoted, 51
Trotskyites, show trial of, 200–201
Trubetskoi, Sergei, 19, 20, 23, 35
truth: portrayed along a vertical axis, 201; radical intelligentsia's attitude toward, 104
Turbin, Vladimir, 14
"Twelve, The" (Blok), 109

Ugolnik, Anthony, 236n5
Ukhtomsky, Aleksei Alekseevich, 88
Umanskii, A., 94
unincarnated *(neinkarnirovanyi)*, for Bakhtin, 57–58, 61–62
unitary full word *(edinoe polnoe slovo)*, 39
unity *(edinstvo)*, 5, 9–10, 76, 114–15, 135–36; diversity within, 19, 127, 178–79; of guilt and answerability, 95–96, 135–36; integration of science, art, and life into a, 92–97, 100, 137. *See also* "all-oneness"
universe (cosmos), individual's relationship to, 185–86, 189, 191–92, 198
Uspensky, Boris, 6, 188

utilitarianism, 107
utterance(s), for Bakhtin, 17–18, 23, 32–34, 36, 38, 46; connection to the written word, 98
uttered *(vyskazannoe)* word *(logos prophorikos)*, 20, 28–29, 39

Vaginov, Konstantin, 90
values *(tsennosti)*, Bakhtin on, 96; in "Toward a Philosophy of the Act," 59–60, 62, 64–65, 67–68
vegetative metaphors, 158–60, 167, 185. *See also plod*
Vekhi (1909). *See Landmarks*
"Vekhi" kak znamenie vremeni (1910), 247nn28, 41
verbal abuse (revilement): as translation of *bran'*, 203. *See also* praise/blame dichotomy
Verfremdung (ostranenie), 49, 61–62. *See also* alienation
Veselovsky, A. N., 174, 186–87
violence, 98, 190, 208, 210, 237n22; *bran'* as Church Slavonic term for, 200, progression toward, 206–7
visage *(lik)*, 101–2, 137
visual arts, Florensky's use of examples from, 102, 247n39
vitalism, 130
Vitebsk lectures, of Bakhtin, 25
voices, 127, 219–20, 226–27; diversity of *(raznogolositsa)*, relationship to heteroglossia, 29–30, 33; novelistic, 30–33, 44, 189. *See also* polyphony
Voloshin, Maksimilian, 24–25, 39
Voloshinov, V. N., 4, 44, 49, 193, 238n24
voploshchenie. *See* embodiment
Voskresenie (religious organization), 14
vseedinstvo. *See* "all-oneness"
Vyshinsky, Andrey Vanuarevich, 200–201, 203, 204, 210, 211
vzaimoproniknovenie. *See perichoresis*
vzhivanie (Einfühlung), 77–78, 79, 252n17

war, as topos in Rabelais's work, 163–64
Ware, Kallistos, 22
"Was ist das Wort?" (Bulgakov), 37–38, 117, 168, 170
weaving, as metaphor for mixing of cultures and languages, 9–10, 177–79

Weltanschauung. See worldview
West German Slavists, "diglossia" posited by, 168–69, 170
Wheel of Fortune, as metaphor, 170
White, Allon, 2, 208, 254n19
Wilde, Oscar, 213, 233; "The Ballad of Reading Gaol," 233, 258n32
will *(volia)*, for Gershenzon, 106–7
Williams, Raymond, 2, 236n4
Winters, Yvor, 241n43
"without division or separation." *See nesliianno i nerazdel'no*
Wolfson, Harry A., 242n62
women, restricted university enrollment of in pre-Revolution Russian, 88
word(s), 12, 35; for Bakhtin, 85, 151–53, 165–69, 218, 225; Dostoevskian, parallels with the Chalcedonian word, 130–31; marketplace word, 201–6, 233. *See also* logos; Word, the
Word, the, 12, 42, 44, 227–29; hypostatic, as a meaning for *slovo* in "Discourse in the Novel," 33–38; Trinitarian conceptions of, reliance on Stoicist dichotomy, 40. *See also* Johannine logology; logos
"Word, The" (Gumilev), 25–26, 227
"Word and Culture, The" (Mandelshtam), 26–27
"word-weaving" *(pletenie sloves)*, aesthetic of, 9–10
working class, intelligentsia's relationship to, Bulgakov on, 117–18
"World as an Organic Whole, The" (Lossky), 130
world at large: relationship to of the self, 57, 58–62; relationship to of the self and the Other, 75–76
worldview *(Weltanschauung)*, 77, 181; carnivalesque, 194; of Dostoevsky, 125; of Florensky, 101; medieval, 169; of the radical intelligentsia, 104, 117
World War II, 149, 153, 203

Yudina, Maria Veniaminovna, 14, 15, 88, 89–90, 108; quoted, 87

"Zametki" (Bakhtin), 214, 256n2
Zavadski, Yuri, 3
Zen'kovsky, Vasily, 43, 222
Zhdanovite apparatchiks, Bakhtin's hostility toward, 236n4
Zielinksi, Tadeusz, 88